Deconstructing Apartheid Discourse

ALETTA J. NORVAL

VERSO
London • New York

First published by Verso 1996

Verso
UK: 6 Meard Street, London W1F 0EG
USA: 388 Atlantic Ave, Brooklyn NY 11217

Verso is the imprint of New Left Books

ISBN 1-85984-989-X
ISBN 1-85984-125-2 (pbk)

British Library Cataloguing in Publication Data
A catalogue record for this book is available from the British Library

Library of Congress Cataloguing-in-Publication Data
Norval, Aletta J.
Deconstructing apartheid discourse / Aletta J. Norval.
p. cm.
Includes bibliographical references and index.
ISBN 1-85984-989-X (cloth). — ISBN 1-85984-125-2 (pbk.)
1. Apartheid. 2. South Africa—Politics and government—20th century—Philosophy. 3. Apartheid—South Africa. I. Title.
DT1757.N67 1996
968'.05—dc20 95-47511
CIP

Typeset by Keystroke, Jacaranda Lodge, Wolverhampton
Printed in the United States

With confidence we lay our case before the whole world. Whether we win or die, freedom will rise in Africa, like the sun from the morning clouds.

President Paul Kruger, February 1881

It is my genuine desire that when freedom day comes it should not find reconciliation too far to attain. . . . This immediately raises the question of the methods of struggle. The more jarring and shattering the methods, the deeper the alienation of our people and, consequently, the more difficult the process of healing the wounds and reconciling the people. Non-racialism as a method embodies the process of pulling black and white together so that they jointly dismantle apartheid. In the process they already have a chance of learning to know each other. And artificial suspicions, nurtured by years of apartheid myths and propaganda, are demolished. And when freedom comes it will not be the victory of blacks over whites but that of the people of South Africa over an evil system that has for so long set them up against one another.

Terror Lekota, April 1988, Delmas Trial
(Karis-Gerhart Collection)

Contents

Acknowledgements

The preparation of this book was eased by the assistance, advice and friendship of a number of people. My main intellectual debt lies with the group of scholars around the Doctoral Programme in Ideology and Discourse Analysis at the University of Essex. I have learned a great deal over the years from extended discussions with them. I am particularly indebted to Ernesto Laclau for his innovative theoretical work in the field of post-structuralist political theory which first inspired this study. I have also drawn heavily on the works of scholars in the field of Southern African studies, and my debt to them is clear in the text.

Much of the archival work for this book has been done in the National Party archives at the Institute for Contemporary History at the University of the Orange Free State. I would like to express my appreciation to the staff at the Institute, whose friendly assistance made the work there a pleasure, as well as to Lynette Naude and her family, who acted as gracious hosts during my visits to Bloemfontein, and provided me with friendship and support.

For their detailed comments on drafts of some or all of the chapters, I would like to thank David Howarth, Bernhard Windischer, Andries du Toit, Jelica Šumič-Riha and Ernesto Laclau.

I extend my special gratitude to my husband, David Howarth, with whom I have spent many hours over the past years developing theoretical arguments about South African politics, for giving generously of his time and knowledge.

I dedicate this book to my parents, Charles and Nanda Norval. They encouraged and fostered the development of critical thought in me, and supported me with their unstinting love throughout the years in which this book has been in the making.

Abbreviations

AB	*Afrikaner Broederbond* (Afrikaner Brotherhood)
ACVV	*Afrikaanse Christelike Vrouevereniging* (Afrikaans Christian Women's Association)
AHI	*Afrikaanse Handelsinstituut* (Afrikaans Commercial Institute)
ANC	African National Congress
ANS	*Afrikaanse Nasionale Studentebond* (Afrikaans National Students' League)
AP	Afrikaner Party
Assocom	Associated Chambers of Commerce
AVF	*Afrikaner Volksfront* (Afrikaner People's Front)
AWB	*Afrikaner Weerstandsbeweging* (Afrikaner Resistance Movement)
BC	Black Consciousness
BLA	Black Local Authority
BOSS	Bureau of State Security
BPC	Black People's Convention
BWP	*Blanke Werkersparty* (White Workers' Party)
CLPP	Coloured Labour Preference Policy
COD	(South African) Congress of Democrats
CODESA	Convention for a Democratic South Africa
COIN	counter-insurgency
CONTRALESA	Congress of Traditional Leaders of South Africa
COSAG	Concerned South Africans Group
COSATU	Congress of South African Trade Unions
COSG	Conscientious Objector Support Group
CPRC	Coloured Person's Representative Council
CPSA	Communist Party of South Africa
DPSC	Detainees' Parents' Support Committee
DRC	Dutch Reformed Churches

EAC	Economic Advisory Council
ECC	End Conscription Campaign
EDESA	Economic Development Bank for Equatorial and Southern Africa
FAK	*Federasie van Afrikaanse Kultuurverenigings* (Federation of Afrikaans Cultural Associations)
FCI	Federated Chambers of Industry
FFF	Five Freedoms Forum
FVR	*Federale Vroueraad* (Federal Women's Council)
GNP	*Gesuiwerde Nasionale Party* (Purified National Party)
HNP	*Herenigde Nasionale Party* (Reunited National Party) (formed 1940)
HNP	*Herstigte Nasionale Party* (Reformed National Party) (formed 1969)
ICU	Industrial and Commercial Workers' Union
IDASA	Institute for a Democratic Alternative for South Africa
IFP	Inkatha Freedom Party
JMC	Joint Management Centre
JODAC	Johannesburg Democratic Action Committee
KP	*Konservatiewe Party* (Conservative Party)
KWU	*Klerewerkersunie* (Garment Workers' Union)
MDM	Mass Democratic Movement
MK	*Umkhonto we Sizwe* (ANC military wing)
NCVV	*Natal Christelike Vrouevereniging* (Natal Christian Women's Association)
NEC	Native Economic Commission
NEUM	Non-European Unity Movement
NO	*Nuwe Orde Studie Kring* (New Order Study Circle)
NP	*Nasionale Party* (National Party)
NRT	*Nasionale Raad van Trustees* (National Council of Trustees)
NSMS	National Security Management System
NUSAS	National Union of South African Students
OB	*Ossewabrandwag* (Oxwagon Sentinel)
OFS	Orange Free State
OVV	*Oranje Vrouevereniging* (Orange Women's Association)
PAC	Pan-Africanist Congress
PFP	Progressive Federal Party

RDB	*Reddingsdaadbond* (League for the Act of Rescue)
RDP	Reconstruction and Development Programme
RENAMO	*Resistencia Naçional Mozambicana*
RSC	Regional Service Council
SAAU	South African Agricultural Union
SABC	South African Broadcasting Corporation
SABRA	*Suid-Afrikaanse Buro vir Rasse-Aangeleenthede* (South African Bureau for Racial Affairs)
SACC	South African Council of Churches
SACP	South African Communist Party
SACPO	South African Coloured People's Organization
SADCC	Southern African Development and Co-ordination Conference
SADF	South African Defence Force
SAIC	South African Indian Congress
SANAC	South African Native Affairs Commission
SAP	South African Party
SAP	South African Police
SASO	South African Students' Organization
SAVV	*Suid-Afrikaanse Vroueverenigin*g (South African Women's Association)
SBDC	Small Business Development Corporation
SSC	State Security Council
SWAPO	South West Africa People's Organization
UDF	United Democratic Front
UF	Urban Foundation
UNITA	*União Naçional para a Independência Total de Angola* (National Union for the Total Independence of Angola)
UP	United Party
USANP	United South African National Party
UWUSA	United Workers' Union of South Africa
VF	*Vryheidsfront* (Freedom Front)
WHAM	win over hearts and minds
YSKOR	*Yster en Staal Korporasie* (Iron and Steel Corporation)

Introduction
Accounting for Apartheid Hegemony: An Investigation into Its Political Grammar

The April 1994 elections formally brought the apartheid era to an end. However, the legacy of apartheid is bound to continue to influence, shape and limit the trajectory of development of a post-apartheid order for the foreseeable future. This is evident not only in the atavistic forms of identification informing the politics of Inkatha and elements of the far right, but also in the gross inequalities present in the distribution of material wealth across society. For this reason it is crucial that this most painful era in South African politics is subjected anew to analysis.

'Apartheid' has always been a notoriously difficult phenomenon to characterize. This is evident in the widely divergent adumbrations it has received in academic literature on South African history and politics. The term 'apartheid', for example, has been used to refer both to practices which came into being more than three hundred years ago, making the history of apartheid coincide with that of South Africa, and to the more narrowly defined set of certain legislative measures that came into being with the victory of the National Party (NP) in 1948.[1] Similarly, no consensus exists on the characterization of the specificity of the practices associated with apartheid, however periodized. The old race/class controversy, which framed theoretical debates between liberals and neo-Marxists on the nature and character of apartheid, continues unabated, though not as intensely, today.[2] My analysis of the apartheid era aims not to resolve those questions, but to address them from a different vantage-point, such that the presuppositions informing them are, in some sense, dissolved, or at least displaced.[3]

This book starts from the problem as to how apartheid – declared to be a crime against humanity – was possible, and durable. Framed in this manner, the inquiry into the nature of apartheid brings about a lateral shift in the types of questions posed and in the possible answers which may be provided. This study seeks to investigate how it was that apartheid came into being; how it succeeded in constructing and interpellating subjects; how it operated; and how its hegemony was put into question. In attempting to provide an account of these matters, it is my contention that it is necessary to take issue with approaches which hold that, in order to understand political phenomena, we need to probe beneath or below their surface to grasp their real, underlying meaning. In short, I take as problematic attempts to account for apartheid by searching for an essence hidden from view, for such attempts tend to be bewitched by a metaphysical illusion of depth.[4] As a result, they tend to disregard what lies open to view: the conditions to which apartheid was a response and the mechanisms through which it operated and became hegemonic. Rather than trying to penetrate below the surface of apartheid, this study takes as its object of investigation the discourse of apartheid: the multifarious practices and rituals, verbal and non-verbal, through which a certain sense of reality and understanding of the nature of society were constituted and maintained.[5] This analysis of the political grammar shaping and informing the construction of apartheid hegemony does not seek to uncover some dimension of activity covered over by ordinary language and practices. It is my contention that the view of the world constructed and disseminated by apartheid ideologues is already present and open to view in its ordinary, everyday language and material practices. This is not to say, however, that since these practices are already in plain view, no investigation of them is needed. Quite the contrary. Any attempt to come to an understanding of the political grammar of a particular discourse presupposes that there is a context to be explicated, and logics to be made visible.[6] In so doing, it is important that the account provided adheres to two central principles, namely that the discourse analysed be taken seriously, and that the theoretical tools utilized in such an analysis do not prejudge, in an a priori fashion, what is to be found. It may seem unnecessary to point out that a theoretical framework should not predetermine what is to be the result of the investigation, for if that occurs, the inquiry itself becomes largely redundant; it would merely serve to prove what has been asserted before the investigation started. It is, sadly, the case that this has happened all too often with accounts of apartheid. The race/class debate is a case in point, for the theoretical frameworks informing that debate predetermined how the essence of the apartheid project would be characterized. On these readings, apartheid was held to be concerned, for example, with furthering the aims and interests of either an atavistic group of white, Afrikaner racists, or of the Afrikaner petty bourgeoisie.[7] As a result of the substantive presuppositions of the theoretical frameworks deployed, in both cases, there has been a failure to come to grips with the specificity of the apartheid project.[8] In the former, because it has been assumed that an essential continuity informed racist practices since the seventeenth century; and in the latter, because the operation of apartheid has been reduced to its putative class basis.

In order to avoid these pitfalls, it is necessary to engage with the discourse of apartheid itself. Approaching the analysis of apartheid through an examination of its discursive construction may immediately raise the objection that one would only be able to produce an 'internalist' account. That is, one may remain at the level of a 'pure description'.[9] To argue thus, however, is to miss the point, for an investigation of the discursive production of a certain reality does not also presuppose that everyday language and discursive practices are innocent or neutral. Discourse is not a passive medium which merely reflects 'pre-discursive experiences' or 'objective interests'.[10] While political discourse as a general rule tries to present itself as a transparent medium through which reality is portrayed in an unmediated fashion, no discourse succeeds entirely in concealing its socially constructed and, therefore, ultimately contingent nature.[11] A careful reading of a particular political discourse will reveal the mechanisms through which that naturalization occurred and the discourse was dissimulated. There is, therefore, no need to introduce substantive, external categories into the analysis. Neither is it necessary, or possible, to 'measure' a given discourse against a presumed 'extra-discursive' reality. If all of reality is symbolically constructed, mediated and contested, then it is not possible to recover an extra-discursive realm, or an 'objective' set of criteria against which its adequacy could be measured and evaluated. This does not, however, rule out the possibility of making visible the manner in which the construction of reality in apartheid discourse has been contested by a series of other, opposing symbolizations of reality. This dimension, indeed, is crucial to any investigation of the operation of political discourse, for, as Foucault argues, the processes through which reality is constructed and dissimulated are always acts of power and will always be resisted and contested.[12]

The analysis of the grammar of apartheid discourse offered here proceeds through an investigation of the manner in which it brought about and institutionalized a certain vision of the world, of social and political reality. Therefore, it focuses on the mechanisms facilitating those processes. In what follows, I will briefly outline the main themes of investigation and relate them to the processes through which apartheid became hegemonic, and entered into crisis. Foremost amongst these is the question concerning the horizon of intelligibility – a framework delineating what is possible, what can be said and done, what positions may legitimately be taken, what actions may be engaged in, and so forth – instituted by apartheid discourse. A discourse can be said to be hegemonic insofar as it succeeds in instituting and maintaining such a horizon.[13] As I have argued, this delineation of the possible is always a matter of relations of force and of power. A hegemonic discourse typically rests on a combination of processes through which consent is forged or, failing that, domination is exercised.[14] Moreover, it is crucial that even domination must be justified; reasons must be provided for it, and these reasons form part and parcel of the process of forging consent. While the forging of consent and the exercise of domination may differ in degree, they do not differ in kind. That is to say, even where subjects are interpellated into a discourse and where they may be argued to have 'consented' in some sense, force is not entirely absent.[15] Keeping this proviso in mind, it is clear that in the construction of apartheid hegemony the organization of consent has tended to be aimed at and limited to those who were considered to be 'insiders', while the production of acquiescence, if not consent, with regard to 'outsiders' proceeded largely, although not wholly, through brute domination. This forging of consent and the exercise of domination did not take place along clear-cut and unchanging lines of division. For this reason, amongst others, it is important to investigate the manner in which the construction of reality within apartheid discourse proceeded, from the very start, by creating a representation of the nature of society and thus, of its unity, that had as its precondition the exclusion of a series of 'others'. As Lefort argues, any society, in order to relate to itself, and to exist as a human society, has to forge a representation of its unity.[16] And the creation of such representations of unity occurs through the drawing of boundaries, political frontiers articulated in discourse.[17] Hence, the question of social division is, from the outset, a question of its limits, or its 'outside'.[18] Political frontiers are those mechanisms through which social division is instituted, and 'insiders' distinguished from 'outsiders'; it defines opposition; it dissimulates social division; it makes it seem that the institution of social division is not itself a social fact. In apartheid, this drawing of frontiers operated in a very complex manner that can only be understood once it is clear to what the discourse of apartheid was a response.

Apartheid discourse was a response to a series of upheavals – associated *inter alia* with the increasing capitalization of agriculture, the concomitant rapid rise in rates of urbanization, and events such as the Second World War – which characterized the South African political landscape during the 1930s and 1940s. However, apartheid was in no sense the only possible response to these dislocatory events. It had to compete with a series of other discourses attempting to suture the dislocated structure of segregationism, and the fact that the discourse of apartheid won that battle has to be accounted for. It is my contention that this was facilitated by the specific reading it gave to those events. What is therefore crucial to analyse is the articulation of those dislocations, the meanings given to them, for, as Laclau argues, there is no necessary relation between the dislocation as such and the discursive space that is to constitute its form of representation.[19] The reading given to these dislocations was intimately related to the perceived failures of segregationist discourse: its inability to resolve the 'Native question', and its failure to construct 'white' unity. In accounting for apartheid it is, therefore, necessary to take cognizance of the specificity of the conditions in which it emerged and to which it was a response, and the reasons why apartheid, rather than any of the other available discourses, succeeded in constructing a horizon within which sense could be made of the events of the 1930s and 1940s. This is the subject-matter of chapter 1, where I provide both an initial contextualization of those conditions, an account of the relation between apartheid and other competing discourses, and a discussion of the precise sense in which 'dislocation' is used in this study.

The fact that apartheid was a particular response to a set of precise conditions also makes it necessary to take issue with analyses which subsume apartheid under segregation, as if a single and continuous form of racial domination informed both. This study locates the specificity of apartheid in the fact that it instituted a new form of social division. Hence, it is necessary to investigate the precise nature of this form of social division, and its relation to segregationism, the discourse dominating the construction of social division for the best part of the first half of the twentieth century in South Africa. This focus on the specificity and novelty of apartheid, however, does not seek to deny that there were continuities between apartheid and segregation. Apartheid displayed elements of both continuity and discontinuity with segregationist discourse. It was clearly continuous with segregation insofar as it maintained a 'colour' frontier as a crucial element of social division. But with apartheid, a new focus on the idea of the *volkseie*[20] came into being. This complexified social division considerably and introduced an element of discontinuity *vis-à-vis* segregationism that would have far-reaching consequences for the later development of social division. This disruption of the 'colour' frontier as a result of the focus on the *volkseie* can be elucidated through the Derridean category of 'iteration', which allows one to theorize a more complex relation between continuity and discontinuity, such that both can be accounted for without, however, reducing one to the other. Chapter 2 deals with the context in and processes through which the idea of the *volkseie* was brought into being. It investigates the construction of a new principle of reading – a myth articulated around the idea of the *volkseie* – by a set of organic intellectuals of the Afrikaner *volksbeweging* (movement of the *volk*) who sought to give meaning to the dislocations experienced by a particular group: 'the Afrikaner'.[21] This is crucial, for it is through the prism of that construction that the later recasting of the white/black or, to be more precise, the European/Native frontier would take place.

Moreover, from an investigation of the emergence of apartheid as a discourse attempting to make sense of a series of dislocations faced by the Afrikaner community, it is abundantly clear that it is impossible to reduce the concerns of the *volksbeweging* to the furthering of some putative 'objective economic interests'. Insofar as it addressed the economic position of 'Afrikanerdom', this made sense only within the wider concerns of the Afrikaner *volksbeweging*, which sought to recast the position of 'Afrikanerdom' *vis-à-vis* white English-speaking South Africans, on the one hand, and coloureds, Indians and Africans, on the other. For that reason, apartheid cannot be regarded as a mere superstructural reflection of deeper, underlying logics associated with the development of capitalism. It does not, however, follow from this that the nature of capitalist development can be reduced to the logic of the apartheid project; only that capitalist development did not take place in a historical vacuum and that the form it took cannot be viewed in separation from the apartheid project. This study does not set out to provide an account of capitalist development as such, even if that was possible. Rather, it aims to show, where relevant, how the precise form taken by capitalist development in the South African context was shaped by the wider horizon of intelligibility instituted by apartheid, and how the very nature of what constituted the interests of 'Afrikanerdom' was produced within the wider context of a concern with the *volkseie*. In this manner, the vexed question of the relation between apartheid and capitalism is displaced in favour of a focus on the manner in which apartheid, as a general horizon, set limits to the development of capitalist practices in a precise historical context.[22]

If one is to grasp apartheid's political grammar – the horizon of meanings, conventions and practices, and the modes of subjectivization instituted by it – it is necessary to engage with questions of naming and identity formation, for these acts brought into being new modes of identification.[23] In order to account for these processes, it is necessary to interrogate the terms in which identities were constituted in apartheid discourse. I, therefore, engage with what are usually treated as mere 'surface' features of apartheid discourse. Standard interpretations of apartheid tend to regard these features as nothing but sophistical efforts designed to cover over the 'real' nature of the project. By contrast, as I have argued, without an investigation of these features, it is not possible to come to terms with the mechanisms through which it dissimulated and naturalized the form of social division it instituted. Part of this process consisted in the production of novel images for identification through which new subject positions were constructed. The analysis of apartheid discourse offered here investigates the constitution and functioning of those images and the manner in which they sought to produce a reading of 'social reality' through which Afrikaners could make sense of their everyday existence. It is important to note, in this respect, that the initial deployment of those techniques of construction of subjectivity was aimed at the Afrikaner community, and not at other, subjected groups.[24] The concern of the Afrikaner *volksbeweging*, in the first place, was with the construction and purification of the Afrikaner community; it is only later that the same logic was extended to others. Just as it aimed to interpellate Afrikaner women, the Afrikaner youth and Afrikaner workers, it later sought to reconstruct the subject positions of coloureds, Indians and Africans. In so doing, it opened a space for the rearticulation of existing 'tribal' identities, and attempted to construct others where they were absent. These spaces for identification were taken up and utilized, most markedly by the so-called 'homeland leaders' and participants in the tri-cameral project. This constitutes one of the most important dimensions of the legacy of forms of social division and identificatory images fostered by apartheid. While it is not the case that apartheid created these forms of identification *ex nihilo*, it did foster and encourage them as part of an extension of the logic of the *volkseie* to other 'groups' in society.

The logic of apartheid discourse is at its clearest in the effects of the transposition of the idea of the *volkseie* to other 'groups' in society, for it is as a result of that process that the recasting of political frontiers – ordering relations between Afrikaners and English-speaking whites, and between 'whites' and 'blacks' – took place. These processes, and their sedimentation in institutional form, are the subject-matter of chapter 3. There I take issue with arguments that proceed from the thesis that a sharp distinction existed between the earlier negative and the later 'positive' phase of apartheid, between a discourse premissed on 'white supremacy' and on 'separate development'. I argue that what is usually considered to be the distinctive feature of the later phase, namely a concern with 'ethnic identity', already informed the institutionalization of practices of social division in the early 1950s. The fact that identity of the *volkseie* was constructed in the discourse of the intellectuals of the Afrikaner *volksbeweging* in opposition to a series of 'others' – ranging, for example, from English- and Afrikaans-speaking liberals, to imperialists and communists – shows that the processes through which identities are discursively constituted always take a relational form.[25] This study seeks to highlight that dimension of identity constitution by investigating the constitutive role that the 'other' played in the apartheid project. In this respect, it is necessary to emphasize an important caveat: what holds for the production of the identity of 'Afrikanerdom' also holds for the construction of its 'others'. It is not the case that the production of 'others' in apartheid discourse proceeded from natural and given, 'pre-discursive' identities. What is politically pertinent is precisely the construction and filling of the category of the 'other' within precise historical circumstances. It is therefore crucial not to turn the fact of the constitutive role of the other into an argument for continuist history. Those moments of discursive breaks in representation where the terms in which others are constructed change are of the greatest importance. What are usually regarded as vagaries and superficial changes in the terminology of apartheid – such as the change from 'Native' to 'Bantu' – assume in this analysis a new centrality, for it is precisely in those changes that it is possible to detect the impact of contestatory discourses upon apartheid. Apartheid was not a fully fledged blueprint for the ordering of society, and even in the attempt to become so, it constantly had to take cognizance of the forces opposing it. This is nowhere more evident than in the changes in the dominant discourse during the organic crisis of the 1980s. That crisis made visible what was already apparent much earlier, namely the fact that all processes of identity formation presuppose a moment of exclusion. And if such exclusion is a necessary feature of identity formation, then what is excluded as 'other' has the capacity to challenge and subvert the manner in which social division is constituted.[26] While my account concentrates on the formation and dissimulation of apartheid discourse, and does not examine in detail the nature and character of resistance discourses, the traces of resistance discourses within the apartheid project nevertheless constitute an important part of the analysis. It should therefore not be assumed that I take resistance discourses to be irrelevant or unimportant. Quite the contrary. Insofar as any identity is relationally constituted, and such constitution is an act of power, there will always be resistance to the imposition and formation of forms of social division. It is, however, impossible to offer any detailed account of both the dominant and resistance discourses within the confines of a single text. In terms of an analysis of the discursive horizon instituted by the apartheid imaginary, it will have to suffice to treat resistance discourses via an examination of the manner in which they impacted upon and thus necessitated the reformulation of the apartheid project.

It is a central contention of this study that apartheid hegemony was premissed upon the working of two sets of political frontiers which stood in a relation of tension to one another. This tension, discussed in chapter 3, was produced at the point in which apartheid changed from being a myth associated with the experiences of a particular group, to an imaginary horizon acting as a surface of inscription for the ordering of all social relations.[27] This movement from myth to imaginary involves, as Laclau argues, the metaphorization of the literal contents of particular social demands; that is, a retreat of the concrete demands informing the myth such that it starts to function as a general surface of inscription of any social demand.[28] This is what occurred once the logic of the *volkseie* – initially associated with the experience of the Afrikaner *volk* – began to act as a general principle for the organization of all social relations. The fact that political frontiers, as a result, were forged around both a 'colour frontier' and an ethnicist axis – neither of which can be separated from or reduced to the other – introduced a core area of 'undecidability' into apartheid discourse.[29] I argue that this undecidability was not simply the result of ambiguities in the language of apartheid evident, for example, in the fact that the signifier 'race' was used to refer both to differences between Afrikaners and the white English-speaking population and to 'colour' differences.[30] Rather, it was produced as a result of the political grammar of apartheid discourse; as a result of its formal and syntactical composition and articulation, which were embedded in material practices. As Derrida has shown with regard to the operation of 'undecidables' in philosophical texts, it is precisely in the suspension of 'decidability', in the simultaneous maintenance of both sets of frontiers and, thus, in its refusal to be decided in either direction, that its force is to be found.[31] Apartheid, thus, did not operate either through logics of exclusion, nor simply through differential forms of inclusion, but through the simultaneous retention of both those logics. Attempts to reduce apartheid to either of those dimensions will, thus, fail to grasp what constituted one of the strongest mechanisms of its hegemonization.

While the logic of the *volkseie* led to a recasting of the European/Native frontier, and seemed to provide a general answer to the position of Africans within the political order, it failed to address the position of coloureds, and of urban Africans. As a result of a complex set of overdetermined circumstances, discussed in chapters 4 and 5, a transformist project, aiming to effect a limited and differential inclusion of coloured and Indian South Africans, on the one hand, and urban Africans, on the other, was inaugurated by the NP. In chapter 4, I concentrate on an analysis of the role and position of the coloured population, usually given only passing reference in accounts of apartheid. I argue that the problem of placing coloureds into a framework of separate development made visible the internal limits of a project claiming to be based on 'difference' and, thus, can be taken as exemplary of what would become more and more evident during the 1980s: the impossiblity of incorporating sections of the population not easily representable within the political grammar of apartheid. With the development of the transformist project, the political frontiers delineating 'insiders' from 'outsiders' were considerably complicated and came to rely less and less on a 'racial' and/or an ethnicist mode of division. In this process, the position of 'internal migrants', squatters and so forth, increasingly began to disarticulate the logic of a coincidence between 'nationhood' and territorial, spatial separation. This is the subject-matter of chapter 5, in which I also analyse the manner in which resistance to the transformist project emerged, and impacted upon it. The development of resistance to that project forced the regime to construct ever more complicated lines of inclusion and exclusion until it, finally, was no longer capable of maintaining and controlling the terms of social division. It is at this point that apartheid discourse entered into an organic crisis, and could no longer fulfil its function of providing a principle of reading according to which sense could be made of existing forms of social division. As I argue in chapter 5, the movement from a conjunctural to an organic crisis cannot be ascribed to, or derived from, the economic conditions of the 1980s. While the reponses to those conditions by the

Afrikaner business community and organized capital at large, and several commissions of inquiry concerned with labour-related issues, made a crucial contribution to the form that the transformist project took, and while a crucial realignment of forces associated with the dominant bloc occurred, the project ultimately failed as a result of the resistance it engendered.

During this period of crisis, several new myths emerged that attempted to resuture the dislocated structure of society. These myths are discussed and analysed with a view to their longer term implications for the future of a post-apartheid society in chapter 6. While all of them were rooted in the various traditions which shaped twentieth-century South African politics, only one decisively contained the possibility of instituting a fundamentally new form of social division, one at odds with the most central feature of the political grammar of apartheid. The discourse of non-racialism, in the process of becoming a new imaginary, succeeded in challenging the apartheid project, not only because it managed to weld together a united front out of the inchoate forms of resistance of the early 1980s, but also because it articulated a vision of society which provided the possibility of constructing a form of unity across existing divisions. In so doing, it managed to disarticulate the set of forces around which the transformist project was based, and to rearticulate a new project, a new image around which the unity of society could be represented. In the concluding chapter, so as to address the question of the ordering of a post-apartheid society, I briefly examine the relation between the identitary logic informing apartheid and the logic of identification structuring the discourse of non-racialism.

1

Dislocated Identities: The Failure of Segregationism

In the life of our people, walls are torn apart and are in ruins; they call out to be rebuilt. Thousands live in poverty, in misery, in pitiful conditions, and there is degeneration in all areas of life, social, moral and spiritual.[1]

Much of the strength and specificity of Afrikaner nationalism as it re-emerged in the 1930s and 1940s can be accounted for by the precise articulation the *volksbeweging* gave to a series of painful and conflict-ridden experiences: the great drought, the Depression, the accompanying large-scale urbanization and social disruption, and the Second World War. While generally recognized, these factors are often relegated to a subordinate status, mentioned only to be disregarded as epiphenomenal. It is a central contention of this chapter that without a thorough-going analysis of the discursive articulation of these events the nature and character of Afrikaner nationalism, its relation to segregation and its expression in the doctrine of apartheid, will remain an enigma. Contrary to conventional wisdom, the political significance of the attempts to make sense of the dislocation of identity associated with these events cannot be read off from the events themselves. There is nothing, for example, inherent in rapid urbanization which determines the form and contents of responses to it. In this chapter, I provide an analysis which takes as its starting-point the need to come to a deeper understanding of the exact discursive construction of these experiences, as well as to a more adequate conceptualization of what is understood by the category of dislocation, used here not in sociological terms, but as connoting an 'experience' which makes visible the ultimate contingency of all forms of identification. To grasp the sense of dislocation as articulated in the emerging exclusivist Afrikaner nationalist discourse, it is necessary to contextualize the terrain in which they occurred to place the emerging discourse of the *volksbeweging* in relation to other responses to these events. Inevitably, such an analysis can only furnish us with the merest sense of the political and social alternatives that competed for hegemony during and in the immediate aftermath of the Second World War. Nevertheless, this is a task which cannot be discarded, for without that it will be impossible to grasp not only the ultimate openness of the terrain of options available, but also the hegemonization of that terrain by a precise political act. That is to say, in order to show the non-necessity of the later apartheid hegemony, as well as to grasp its specificity and novelty *vis-à-vis* its segregationist precursor, it is absolutely crucial to explore the nature of the dislocations of identity and the attempts to re-suture social space during the pre-1948 era. It is only once this has been done that the radically new form of social division instituted with apartheid becomes visible, and that the plurality and essential openness behind its apparent unity is revealed. This site of contestation is, therefore, the locus which is the condition for the institution of new myths and the constitution of new hegemonies.

While a number of excellent historical studies on this period of South African history exist, I contend that these studies are hampered by their failure to link together the various elements of the discourse and the terrains of contestation in which the struggle for the reconstruction of 'Afrikanerdom' was fought. The separation between, and inevitable prioritization of, singular elements of Afrikaner nationalism, such as its presumed class or ethnic basis, its roots in petty bourgeois interests or fascist ideology, make it difficult, if not impossible, simultaneously to grapple with the horizon instituted in the aftermath of the 1948 election. This failure to grasp the sense in which the apartheid slogan, lacking a precise content yet paradoxically full to overflowing, came to act as a powerful signifier promising the reconstruction of a lost unity is at the root of endless debates about the precise nature of Afrikaner nationalism and apartheid hegemony. It is important to emphasize that the point is not that Afrikaner nationalists found a community in place, a community that it could simply mould as it wished, but precisely that no such community ever existed, at least not in the sense in which it came to be understood after 1948, and that the task at hand was to construct the elements as if they were elements of a lost community.

It was thus not a question here of simply recovering an organic but lost community. As I will show, what presented itself as an 'organic community' was the result of articulatory practices, bearing a contingent relation to the dislocations of the 1930s and 1940s. One has to be careful here, however, for it is not a matter of uncovering some hidden dimension behind what was said and done. In redirecting attention to what lay ready to hand, on the 'surface' of things, it is possible to make visible the artificiality of the community without recourse to some 'pre-existing' objectivity.[2] Since ideology cannot operate without disclosing itself, without revealing itself as a discourse, it is possible to search for those traces which cannot be eliminated within the discourse itself.[3]

To explore the events of the 1930s and 1940s, one needs to start from the primary terrains of struggle on which the battle for the heart of the 'lost community' was fought: those of the 'Native question' and the 'poor white problem'.[4] What quickly becomes clear in the course of such an investigation is that their meaning was not given in advance. Indeed, during the two decades leading up to the victory of the *Herenigde Nasionale Party* (HNP, Reunited National Party) in 1948, both of those 'problems' would be given a novel interpretation, would be recast and re-formed in such a way as to alter decisively the contours of the South African political landscape.

The decades spanning the 1930s and 1940s wrought great change in South Africa. This was visible in the rapid expansion of secondary industry during and after the war years, in a massive growth in rates of urbanization of both Africans and white Afrikaners, and in the burgeoning resistance to changes in all spheres of life. The rapid process of secondary industrialization and the concomitant changes in labour processes have been well documented.[5] The effects of these changes on the occupational status and categorizations of African and white workers were far-reaching.[6] In a context in which industry showed the beginnings of a greater openness to employing Africans in semi-skilled positions, a context coupled by a rapid increase in the numbers of newly urbanized, unskilled white workers, the labour process increasingly became a site of severe antagonisms, echoing the struggles of the early 1920s between white and African workers. In addition, a series of disputes between craft and industrial unions complicated the situation, fostering intra-white labour struggles. During this period membership of unions rocketed, reaching a high of well over three hundred and thirty thousand by 1948.[7] Significantly, an independent African trade union movement also emerged and mushroomed during the 1930s, and by 1945 almost 40 per cent of all

African workers were unionized. The degree of militancy reached by these unions was particularly evident in the 1946 African mine workers' strike, and the breaking of the strike, leaving twelve dead and thousands injured, also brought to an end the Native Representative Council, the only form of political representation for Africans left at the end of the segregationist era.[8]

Together with the pull of mining and manufacturing industries in the 1930s and 1940s, changes in the rural economy increased the pressure for urbanization and proletarianization. The reduction in land available to Africans, as a consequence of the increasing capitalization of white agriculture, changes in relations between labour tenants, squatters and farmers,[9] and the deteriorating situation in the reserves, all contributed to the increase in the urban African male population during the 1930s and 1940s. These changes led to calls for the lifting of regulations limiting the free movement of Africans by 1943,[10] and by 1947 the Native Laws Commission was prepared to accept the 'inevitability' of the movement from the countryside to the cities.[11] With the process of urbanization came the development of a more coherent and comprehensive response to the policies of segregation by African, coloured and Indian political organizations. In the wake of resistance to the ten-year battle to introduce the Hertzog Bills which removed the Cape African franchise in return for an extension of the reserves – the latter thwarted by the war effort – African resistance moved from moderate and piecemeal campaigns towards challenges to the fundamental legitimacy of the state.[12] This was evident in the ANC's acceptance of the 'Atlantic Charter from the Standpoint of Africans in the Union of South Africa' and the 'Bill of Rights', which demanded the repeal of all laws and practices discriminating against Africans. The same period witnessed a rise in rural resistance,[13] as well as mounting defiance from coloured and Indian communities and increasing co-operation across the 'racial' boundaries.[14]

In the context of this broad mapping of events, it is important to keep in mind the unevenness and specificity of reactions to the processes of urbanization and proletarianization. As Bonner, Delius and Posel show with regard to Africans, distinctions have to be made between first- and second-generation urban migrants; between those forced off white farms, who saw their stay in the city as a relatively permanent phenomenon, and those coming from the reserves, who had a more ambivalent relation to urban life.[15] Patterns of identification and politicization differed between these groups. While it may be correct to assume widespread social disruption as a result of rapid urbanization, these different patterns show that much depended on the precise context and on the discursive articulation given to those experiences of disruption and upheaval. It is this point which has not been adequately stressed with regard to the similar processes underway in the Afrikaner community. As with Africans, pressure on land and the breakdown of the share-cropping system as a result of the capitalization of agriculture led to a large-scale movement of unskilled white workers to the cities.[16] In the sixty years preceding 1945, the Afrikaner urban population grew from 10,000 to 400,000, to form 33.6 per cent of the white urban population by 1946[17] and 65 per cent of the total Afrikaner population.[18] The effects of these changes on the Afrikaans-speaking population, who traditionally regarded themselves as a *Boerevolk*, were far-reaching and, some would say, potentially devastating. However, whereas the dislocations experienced by black South Africans led them to assert a non-racialist discourse that challenged discrimination based on race or creed, in the case of Afrikaners resistance tended in the opposite direction. The increasing exclusiveness of Afrikaner nationalism clearly did not inevitably follow from those conditions. It was the result of a battle fought over three decades in all walks of life, a battle that took its initial inspiration from the 'poor white problem' that deeply marked the decade of the 1930s. As the Carnegie Commission made clear, the poor white problem was in essence an Afrikaner problem: it conservatively estimated that more than three hundred thousand whites (one sixth of the white population) were 'very poor', and the bulk of them were Afrikaans-speakers. Conditions such as these gave a massive impetus to urbanization by unskilled Afrikaner workers. By 1939, Afrikaner workers formed a majority of urbanized unskilled workers. In contrast to this, Afrikaners contributed only between 3 and 15 per cent to the engineering, accounting, trading, legal and medical professions.[19]

It is generally accepted that the poor white problem had been solved by 1940 as a result of the industrial expansion during the war years.[20] However, Stals argues that the improvement of working and living conditions of whites, as a result of the prosperity which followed the Depression, had been short-lived. By 1938 there were growing signs of unemployment and appalling poverty.[21] Moreover, arguments that the poor white problem had been solved are generally accompanied by the assumption that once the problem of unemployment was solved, the poor white question had been resolved. However, if one investigates the systematic discursive construction of and engagement with the problem within the Afrikaner *volksbeweging*, it very quickly becomes clear that, however important unemployment was, much more was at stake here.[22] The urbanization and proletarianization of Afrikaner workers called forth a series of wide-ranging interventions, and in order to grasp their significance, one has to turn to the manner in which the meaning of these events, as well as the idea of unemployment itself, were constructed by the organic intellectuals of the nationalist movement during the 1930s and 1940s.[23]

During this tumultuous period of South African history several *Volkskongresse* (Congresses of the *volk*) took place and commisions of inquiry were appointed, giving voice to the issues which most concerned the various sections of the Afrikaner *volksbeweging* and influencing thinking within the National Party in opposition.[24] A conference on the poor white problem was held in Kimberley in 1934; the first *Ekonomiese Volkskongres* (Economic Congress) took place in 1939; another took place in Johannesburg in 1947 on the urbanization of the Afrikaner people. Church commissions inquired into communism (1939), mixed marriages (1937), the question of single-language medium schools (1942), the condition of the church in the cities (1947), and South African trade unions (1939).[25] These activities were complemented by the growth of a plethora of organizations addressing themselves to one or another aspect of the Afrikaner *volkslewe* (literally, the life of the people), including the *Afrikaanse Nasionale Studentebond* (1933) (ANS, Afrikaans National Students' League), the *Armsorgraad* (1937) (Poor Welfare Council), the *Nasionale Jeugbond* (1938) (National Youth League) and the *Reddingsdaadbond* (1938) (RDB, League for the Act of Rescue). Existing organizations such as the *Afrikaner Broederbond* (AB, Afrikaner Brotherhood) and the *Federasie van Afrikaanse Kultuurverenigings* (1929) (FAK, Federation of Afrikaans Cultural Associations) under its auspices became more active and influential, leading to the formation of the *Instituut vir Christelik Nasionale Onderwys* (1939) (Institute for Christian National Education) and the *Ekonomiese Instituut* (1939) (Economic Institute). In addition, a number of radical rightist political and labour organizations arose during the 1930s: the fascist Greyshirts and Brownshirts, the *Ossewabrandwag* (OB, Oxwagon Sentinel) and the *Nuwe Orde Studie Kring* (NO, New Order). The exact role and status of each of these movements and their precise influence on the formation of Afrikaner nationalist thought and the National Party is a matter of dispute, and I return to it shortly.[26] Nevertheless, it is clear that the battle for white Afrikaans-speaking South Africa was waged on all fronts: economic, social, cultural, religious and political. While much of this terrain is well documented, relatively little attention is given to the precise discursive elaboration of the dislocations of the 1930s and 1940s in nationalist thought, and where they are discussed at all, their treatment has tended to be overly reductionist.[27] In order to avoid these difficulties, it is important to have a sense of the nature and scope of concerns addressed by intellectuals within the nationalist movement at large.

Poor Whiteism, the Native Question and Urban Dislocation

From the start, the terrain in which the poor white question was formulated and solutions were sought was coupled with that of the 'Native question'.[28] The 1934 *Volkskongres* on the poor white problem consistently linked the co-existence of these two areas of concern. A.J.P. Fourie, Minister of Labour and participant in the congress, argued that 'white civilization' was completely encircled by 'self-developing' Natives, and that in that situation there could be no stasis: one had to go either forward or backward.[29] In this context, the congress did not hesitate to argue that discrimination against Natives and coloureds, resulting from policies designed to uplift poor whites, was acceptable since it was in the interest of the country as a whole.[30] In keeping with this general sentiment, several of its final resolutions stressed the need to keep 'a balance' between the number of 'civilized and uncivilized' labourers employed in industry.[31] However, even given their concern with issues of unemployment and economic policy, it is equally clear that the 'poor white problem' was considered in ways that went well beyond the narrow confines of economic reason. While, as he was later to do in the debate with the *Suid-Afrikaanse Buro vir Rasse-Aangeleenthede* (SABRA, South African Bureau for Racial Affairs),[32] Verwoerd emphasized the need for 'practical' rather than 'ideological' solutions, he also held that the whole problem of poverty could not be considered purely as a question of unemployment. Provision of work without welfare services would have been completely ineffective and the range of resolutions and solutions proffered in the report of the congress bears witness to this judgement.[33] The congress resolved, *inter alia*, to ask for the reorganization of welfare work,[34] the setting up of a permanent Housing Board, an expansion of health services in the rural areas and attention to recreation and amusement 'with a view to combating neglect and degeneration and the abuse of leisure time by the poor white in slums'. It offered suggestions for the employment and care of female employees, encouraged the employment of 'European domestic servants', asked for regulation of tenant-farm owner agreements, argued for the 'rehabilitation' of 'the workshy, vagrants and beggars' through compulsory labour colonies, and made a number of recommendations of a 'psycho-educational' nature. These recommendations, designed to improve and stabilize the social conditions of the poor white population, were coupled with suggestions on 'safeguarding' their position *vis-à-vis* the urbanized Native population. In addition to the proposed regulation of ratios of 'civilized' and 'uncivilized' labour, the congress resolved to make sure that no European would work under the supervision of Natives or Asiatics; that female European employees be separated from non-European employees; and that mixed housing of Europeans and non-Europeans would be combated.[35] Resolution of the Native question was thus central to the rectification of the poor white problem, both socially and economically.

These concerns were echoed in the reports of the *Federale Armsorgraad* (Federal Welfare Council) and the conference on the urbanization of the Afrikaner more than a decade later.[36] However, whereas the earlier *Volkskongres* showed relatively little concern with the Afrikaner as such – the problem was phrased as a *white* one affecting the Afrikaner community particularly strongly – the 1947 congress exhibited a much more marked concern with the specificity of the Afrikaner in the city. A number of additional themes, linked to the position of the *volk* as such, emerged at the congress. While the precise political context and struggles of the war years could account for much of this shift, it is my contention that a fuller understanding of it requires an investigation into what urbanization came to mean for the Afrikaner.

Tempora mutantur et nos in illis[37]

Contrary to those who assert that the generation of organic intellectuals who presided over the articulation of the emerging exclusivist Afrikaner nationalism was inspired by a romantic longing for a lost rural life, one of the most striking themes of the period is the complete acceptance of the permanence of the move towards the cities.[38] Indeed, the recognition of the importance of the city is one that goes back at least to D.F. Malan's clarion call to the *volk* on the occasion of the 1938 Great Trek Centenary celebrations:

> I would like to speak about the largescale movement of our white rural population to the cities: about the struggle which especially the Afrikaners,

> ... have to wage in order to safeguard their bread, their souls, their Afrikanerhood, as well as ... the white character of the country. It is out of that struggle, which continues mercilessly, and which will decide the future of our white Afrikanerdom, that a cry of distress is heard.[39]

Malan linked the destiny of white civilization as it was played out at Blood River to a new challenge: the struggle the Afrikaner faced in the city. Marshalling the symbols of Afrikaner history, Malan rearticulated them to a new urban context: the urban situation and labour market were to become the Afrikaner's new Blood River, and the battles to be waged there would be no less deadly than those of a hundred years before.[40] In this context there could be no space for nostalgia. Indeed, as Pauw argued at the 1947 *Volkskongres*, the task at hand was to outline an Afrikaner conception of the city (*stadsbegrip*), which would involve a banishing of the nostalgic longing for a lost past. Urbanization, on this reading, came to mean much more than a simple population movement to the city. It was characterized as a process which marked both the urban and rural populations and which could lead to a loss of the *volkseie*, a loss of one's own religion, spiritual, moral and social values, and even one's own language.[41] A set of equivalences were drawn between the city, Englishness, amorality, relativism, artificiality and atheism, while the *platteland* (countryside) was associated with a close communion with nature, God, a rounded humanity, simplicity and resoluteness characteristic of Afrikaner life. However, this contrasting of the foreign (*volksvreemde*) with the own (*volkseie*) did not lead to a rejection of modernity.[42] Quite the contrary: in order to conquer the city and to counter the perceived negative effects of modernity, Afrikanerdom would have to work hard to develop its own positive conception of the city.[43]

> There is a battle to wage,
> There is a nation to lead,
> There is work![44]

A constant refrain of almost every contribution to the *Volkskongres* on the Afrikaner in the city was the central need to address the position of the Afrikaner *arbeiderstand* (working 'class'). In his opening address, Ds J.R. Albertyn argued that the change from a rural to an urban setting caused untold dislocation in all spheres of life – in the domestic, intellectual, economic as well as the religious domains – and affected all 'elements' of the *volk*. None the less, it was necessary to focus more specifically on one of these elements: the Afrikaans-speaking working class. For Albertyn, Diederichs and

Albert Hertzog, all of whom addressed the conference on the issue of the Afrikaner working class and labour, this necessity arose from a previous neglect of the problem, as well as from the need to challenge fundamentally existing Afrikaner attitudes to Afrikaans-speaking workers. That a gap between segments of the community had already existed is clear from the incitement not to turn away in shame from the 'weaknesses' and 'lack of backbone' of the Afrikaans working class, an incitement already present in D.F. Malan's 1938 Blood River speech.[45] *Die Offerhande* (*The Sacrifice*), a play written by Hester Cornelius of the *Klerewerkersunie* (KWU, Garment Workers' Union), offers a further insight into existing Afrikaner attitudes towards labour in the cities,[46] which was not just based on a simple rejection of manual labour.[47] On the contrary: labour in the cities was intimately related to the loss of family farms, prevalent during the drought, a more general decline of the *boerestand* (farming 'class') and a strong sense of a loss of autonomy which was associated with working for a boss (*werk vir 'n baas*) in the cities.[48] Offering their own analyses of the rise of the Afrikaner working class, both Albertyn and Diederichs drew a sharp contrast between the *boerestand* and the working class. Recognizing a decline in the numbers of the former, both emphasized the rapid growth of the latter and its *lack* of roots in Afrikaner tradition:

> The urbanization process . . . not only extracted people from the only occupation in which they were at home. It also was accompanied by an inadequate adaptation to the occupational life of the city. Arriving in the cities, the Afrikaner came to the realization that . . . he was not adequately equipped for that struggle.[49]

Afrikaner workers had no background, no preparation and no education for the working life in the cities. They lacked experience, had no craft traditions running in families and, in addition, were faced by many exclusionary practices in trade unions when attempting to find work.[50] Moreover, it was argued that they did not know who 'the enemy' was, and that they had no knowledge of the century-long struggle between labour and capital.[51] These issues were raised again, this time much more systematically, in the report of the Dutch Reformed Churches' Commission the following year. In addition to an emphasis on the need to reinstitute racial divisions between whites and coloureds, the report emphasized the English nature of the cities, English control of trades via closed shop agreements, their dominance in trade union leadership, and the dangers of liberal capitalism and communism to the *volk*. In their place, the commission advocated the development of more Christian Afrikaner trade unions on the lines of the *Spoorbond* (Railway League), public control of key industries and a share by the workers of the fruits of their labour. It set itself unequivocally against both capitalism and communism, echoing similar concerns within the NP and the OB:[52]

> Both these evils end in dictatorship; in the case of the former, one finds a tyranny of private interests, a few ruling over the destiny of millions, while in the case of the latter, there is a tyranny of the state . . . limiting all individual freedom.[53]

Liberal capitalism failed the Afrikaner, and communism exploited unskilled, unemployed Afrikaner workers, thus weakening their sense of colour and instigating black hatred against whites.[54] It was therefore an urgent task to address the community of Afrikaans-speaking workers who faced 'denationalization'. The organic intellectuals of the Afrikaner nationalist movement were deeply aware of the differential impact of urbanization on 'segments' of the *volk* and they made it their task and calling to combat its divisive nature and the social evils arising from it. They concerned themselves not only with the newly urbanized, mainly male Afrikaner workers, but also with the changing position of the youth and women.[55]

The impact of urbanization on Afrikaner youth was discussed mainly in terms of juvenile delinquency. In their report, Albertyn, Du Toit and Theron single out for consideration juvenile crime during the 1940s, offering a breakdown of serious crime perpetrated by white youths, emphasizing that 55 per cent of these crimes were committed by Afrikaners and warning that most of these children came from poor families. This report reinforced the existing concerns already expressed in 1934 in the *armblankevraagstuk* (poor white question) conference, where it was recommended that separate 'homes' should be created for 'the backward and physically handicapped children, the problem children, the feebleminded, those with delinquent tendencies, the young unmarried mother, and others'.[56] The link between poverty and youth crime also featured strongly in the work of two influential Afrikaner criminologists, both of whom played an important part in the activities of the nationalist movement in the 1940s: Geoffrey Cronje and W.A. Willemse.[57] Cronje, who also played a key role in the *Volkskongresse* of 1934 and 1947, and whose contribution to the latter on racial policy, as a result of popular demand, was later published separately in book form, argued that crime and deviance were attributable to capitalist exploitation and the cultural decline of the Afrikaner. Capitalism created economic and social distances within Afrikanerdom between 'prosperous and impoverished' Afrikaners and, for Cronje, the only solution to these 'distances' was a restoration of the *volksverband* (bonds of the *volk*): Afrikaners should stand together economically and socially.[58]

The link established between poverty and crime had another dimension to it, once again showing the intimate connection between the general field of the poor white problem and the 'Native question'.[59] For Cronje, the impoverished conditions in the cities associated with the expansion of capitalism led not only to a general increase in crime, but to a very specific sort of deviancy: *rasvermenging* (miscegenation). It is here that Cronje's thought resonates with the much more general concern in the *volksbeweging* with the purity of women and the impact on them of urbanization. Two areas of concern were singled out for comment: the living and working conditions of newly urbanized women. Many stressed the need to find proper living conditions for these young *Boeredogters* (Boer daughters), although in 1938 Hester Cornelius reported that the government reneged on promises to provide hostels for young women.[60] Similarly, their working conditions were subject to great scrutiny. In both cases, however, concern was not so much with poverty as such, or with poor working conditions and wages. Rather, the fear of miscegenation permeated discussions of conditions of poor whites, and more particularly young, poor, white Afrikaner women, whose living conditions were described by Solly Sachs as 'hardly equalled by the worst slums in the world'.[61] Several strands of discourse combined in this site: those of degeneration; of a loss of moral values in the cities; of fears of 'blood mixing'; of crime and of social class. As Cronje made abundantly clear in his writings: 'mixed living areas' were considered to be one of the main causes of miscegenation, and the section of the population most exposed in this regard was the poor.[62] C.W. Prinsloo took the argument one step further, stating that only the 'weakest elements' of population groups would stoop to the level of miscegenation. For these intellectuals, miscegenation and poverty were linked further to other 'crimes'. Prinsloo, for example, quoted a certain Mjoen approvingly: 'Prostitutes and the "unwilling to work" are found more frequently among types showing strong race mixture than among relatively pure types.'[63] This reflected the wider equivalences established between urbanization, poverty, the loss of moral values and crime. These equivalences, when combined with the anti-communism of the Afrikaner *volksbeweging*, tended also to lead to a particularly strong investment in the 'protection' of working women. However, as with their housing and living conditions, concern did not seem to be with their economic well-being in the first place. Rather, they had to be 'safeguarded' from working too closely with African males. In the broader context of the racist fascination with miscegenation and racial purity, the reasons for this did not have to be spelt out. It was sufficient to state that Afrikaner women should not have to work alongside Natives.[64]

The poor white problem, its relation to the Native question and to the dislocations accompanying urbanization, was clearly given a precise articulation by the leaders of the *volksbeweging*, an articulation which was closely connected to the emergence of a discourse on the exclusivity and specificity of Afrikaner values and way of life. In this process, new modes of subjectivization were brought into being: the worker, the youth and the young woman became objects of discourse, invested with new meaning, bringing into being novel means of control and observation. This much is clear from the recommendations of the *armblankevraagstuk* conference to separate out, thus bringing into being, different categories of youths who were not properly 'integrated' into society, who in some way or another escaped the normalizing discourses of their age, isolating them in order to establish better control over them, and to increase the manipulability of each of the groups. A similar process was in operation with their discourse on women. The discourse of the *volksbeweging* is saturated with references to women who have 'fallen out of the national mould' (*uit volksverband geraak*).[65] It followed that these women had to be brought back into the mould of 'good morality', and to this end the Dutch Reformed Churches recommended, for example, that urban churches appoint 'Christian workers' to 'make contact' with the 'threatened daughters' in factories, shops, cafés, offices and slums. No doubt, the proliferation of discourses on women – fallen women, prostitutes, threatened daughters of the *volk* – was a double-edged one, sometimes involving genuine efforts to improve their lot, and sometimes ignoring socio-economic conditions, concentrating instead on their supposed moral degeneration, inciting the community to work on these women, to win them back from their 'sinful' and 'miserable' lives.[66] These modes of subjectivization, however, did not go unchallenged, and will be explored later in the rest of this chapter.

Rethinking 'Objective Conditions'

What is abundantly clear from the general set of concerns emerging with the attempt to give an 'Afrikaner' interpretation of the processes of urbanization and proletarianization is that they resist reduction to purely economic motivations. At stake here was not simply a petty bourgeoisie seeking to further its own material interests by creating a popular movement. Even if such Machiavellian motives could be attributed to segments of the nationalist movement, it is quite clear that the discursive horizon created during these years escapes such reduction and control. Consequently, it is quite untenable to separate out the 'economic' dimension from the wider horizon of meaning in the process of being instituted during the 1930s and 1940s. The production of that horizon was a complicated operation, exceeding the intentionality of any of its 'authors', and shaped by wider changes and battles being waged in South African society. To capture and understand the nature and specificity of the new emerging discourse, it is necessary to contextualize it and set it in relation to competing attempts – such as segregationism and the class-based discourses of organized labour – to provide 'answers' to the dislocations of identity experienced at the time. As I have argued, there is nothing in the nature of such dislocation which predetermines the responses to it. While attempts to make sense of the condition of black South Africans tended to be based upon arguments against discrimination, Afrikaans-speaking South Africans were interpellated into a racially exclusivist, identitary discourse. This needs further explanation. If such an explanation is to avoid the reductionism of neo-Marxist accounts, it will have to shift attention from seeking to delve deeper and deeper into supposed 'hidden' strata of interests, and focus on the everyday production of such modes of identification.

The production of new modes of identification in Afrikaner nationalist discourse, and its success in interpellating subjects, can therefore only be understood in terms of its context of emergence in the 1930s and 1940s, as it brought into being new subject positions which had to vie with those other discourses with which it competed for hegemony. The political landscape during these decades was dominated by a complex set of articulations of racial difference and superiority, on the one hand, and, on the other, discourses on class that sometimes intersected with and sometimes opposed those on race. Each of these proposed their own, distinct solutions to the crisis of the 1930s and the dislocations that accompanied it. Segregationism, which I will analyse presently, itself entered into a crisis by the middle of the 1940s and was finally unable to continue to hegemonize the political and social terrain. It was increasingly supplanted by discourses on class, addressing the dire living and working conditions of both white and black workers. However, discourses of class, institutionalized in such diverging sites as the Labour Party, the Communist Party and trade unions, ultimately also failed to capture the terrain of moral and intellectual leadership they needed to occupy if they were to become hegemonic themselves. Any account of the potency of the newly emerging nationalist discourses, which provided a seemingly successful principle of reading through which people could make sense of the changing conditions around them, has, therefore, to explore the reasons for the failure of segregationist and class-based alternatives.

The emergence of discourses informing apartheid cannot be accounted for by starting from the apparently 'objective' conditions of the 1930s, for, as I have shown, these conditions were subject to interpretation. It is precisely the *failure* of 'structural conditions' to continue to interpellate subjects which stands in need of explanation. To come to terms with the full implications of this proposition, it must be made clear that, first, on this reading, structures or structural conditions refer not simply to economic conditions, as is usually assumed, but to *all* sedimented social practices.[67] That is to say, they include modes of identification, social institutions and legal and economic practices all of which, in principle, are open to dislocation and resedimentation. Second, the emergence of a new set of discursive practices during the 1930s and 1940s in South Africa cannot in any way be read off from changing structural conditions. Changes in economic conditions, for instance, do not automatically give rise to new modes of identification. Orthodox Marxist accounts of both the emergence of segregationism and apartheid assert exactly what needs to be put into question here: namely that segregation and/or apartheid merely reflected the deeper, hidden changes in the domain of the economy. On this reading, the change from segregation to apartheid can be demystified by uncovering their 'real' class bases. O'Meara's account of the emergence of apartheid is a case in point. He argues that the question

> . . . why specific but differentiated collectivities of social agents . . . came to be collectively mobilized in . . . terms of an ethnic ideology of Afrikaner nationalism, rather than in one of the competing ideologies of the period ('South Africanism', socialism, etc.), can be explained in terms of the organization of class forces within the wider Afrikaner nationalist movement.[68]

Explanations of this type have been questioned increasingly by new revisionists.[69] This is the case especially with reference to the conditions of emergence of segregationism.[70] Not only has the *strong version* of the relation of determination between the 'objective' economic conditions of the 1920s and 1930s and the nature of segregationist ideology been questioned by writers such as Dubow, but characterizations of it as merely justifying and maintaining conditions under which cheap labour could be obtained have also been criticized decisively.[71] The new revisionists, such as Dubow, Marks and Cell, all contributed to the fashioning of accounts of segregationism which show the complexity and ambiguity of its racial ideology, thus problematizing earlier interpretations which treated segregation as a crude set of mechanisms masking capitalist domination.[72]

Notwithstanding their seminal individual contributions on the intellectual origins and functioning of segregation in different domains, these accounts fall short of providing us with a narrative which problematizes the *topographical* distinction between ideology and its presumed objective conditions of emergence. As a result, these accounts fail to grasp what I consider to be one of the essential conditions necessary to any understanding of the formation of both segregation and apartheid, namely the fact that these discourses instituted imaginary horizons which structured *all* social relations.[73] These imaginary horizons, far from being merely superstructural phenomena, served to delimit the sphere of the thinkable, setting the boundaries within which all social practices, including capitalist production, had to find their place. To reiterate, structural conditions themselves, then, are to be understood as relatively sedimented social practices, not as determinants of 'ideologies', not even in the weak sense favoured by the new revisionists. What is therefore important, if one is to account for changes from one imaginary horizon to another, is not simply to enumerate changes in structural or, more narrowly, economic conditions, but to show how it is that a certain imaginary, at a specific point in time, enters into crisis and consequently no longer can fulfil its function of interpellating subjects into stable, 'normalized' forms of identification.

With the benefit of hindsight, it is quite straight-forward to locate those areas of concern which segregationism failed to address during the crucial decades of the 1930s and 1940s. Two dimensions of the discourse of segregation are of crucial importance in this respect: first, South Africanism, or its treatment of relations within the dominant white community; and, second, its handling of the 'Native question'.

While segregation changed from an attempt to steer a middle course between scientific racism and Victorian assimilationist liberalism to an increasingly repressive and overtly racist discourse, there was an essential continuity in its articulation of both intra-white and white/black relations. It is precisely in this that one can find the seeds of its failure to continue providing adequate modes of identification around which a hegemonic set of forces could be welded together. Of course, it has to be stressed that there was nothing intrinsic in segregationism which led to its failure. Rather, it lost a contest, a battle for giving meaning to the dislocations of identity experienced during the two decades leading up to the Nationalist victory in 1948. Similarly, nothing in the discourse of the Afrikaner nationalist movement predetermined its victory. It simply succeeded in providing a plausible alternative reading of those events, and, through enormous effort and at high cost, won the battle for civil society, thus opening the possibility of restructuring the entire political landscape of South Africa.[74]

Segregation: The Production of a Native Identity

> Ambiguity has been the price of survival in a contradictory world.[75]

In order fully to account for the failure of segregationist hegemony in white politics, it is necessary first to specify precisely its delimitation of the possible forms of identification in terms of which whites made sense of their world. This requires an analysis of the character and unity of segregationist discourse, resulting from a complex set of articulations and overdeterminations of discursive elements. Different strands of thinking dominated the construction of segregation at different points. During the 1920s, liberals such as Evans, Pim, Brookes and Loram propagated segregation as a moderate policy of differentiation.[76] In their discourse, as a result of the influence of anthropological 'insights', 'civilization' was replaced by 'culture', 'progress' by 'differentiation', and 'individualism' by a 'collectivism of racial groups'.[77] Segregation could thus be presented as a just policy that could preserve white supremacy whilst at the same time facilitating the development of the Africans along their 'own lines'.[78] A movement away from this 'liberal' conception of segregation resulted in the introduction of much more extensive and repressive legislation during the later 1920s and the 1930s, culminating in the introduction of the Hertzog Bills. This period was dominated by the struggle between two conceptions of segregation; that held by Hertzog – who wanted to abolish the Cape Native franchise, to implement a 'civilized labour policy', and who was in favour of the industrial colour bar – and that propounded by Smuts.[79] While Hertzog held an exclusivist conception of segregation, Smuts favoured the more inclusivist and protective elements of liberal segregationism. The exclusivist conception won the day and far-reaching legislation deepening the existing racial divisions was introduced.

Much work done in this domain by new revisionists locates the force of segregationism in its ambiguity.[80] Most of these commentators remark on the fact that segregation was 'all things to all people', and in their analyses of its multi-faceted character point to the multiplicity of the discourses informing it. Dubow's account of the intellectual and theoretical sources of segregationist thought is a case in point. He argues that by 1910 a complex social vision of racial separation was in place and social theorists in South Africa began to draw increasingly on contemporary social theory, adapting these sources to the South African situation, and articulating a vision of segregation as a coherent principle of social division.[81] While noting the multiplicity of discourses informing segregation, Dubow, nevertheless, fails to locate the principle which can account for its coherence in the face of the *contradictory* nature of each of its constituent elements. To understand segregation, as a principle of reading which articulates elements in an ideological unity, one has to take account not only of the particularity and diversity of strands of discourses informing that unity, but also of the *unity* that is produced as a result of the condensation of those diverse and separated strands. It is precisely this element which is lacking in traditional intellectual histories.

To locate this source of unity, it is important to recognize that all the constituent discourses of segregation, however different in the minutiae of their analyses, were in agreement on the fundamental need to exclude the black South African population from the centres of political power, and thus depended upon the establishment of a relatively clear-cut political frontier between white and black. The articulated unity thus did not arise from a natural, common subject-matter, either in the form of a given 'white' subjectivity or in the form of an existing black identity. Rather, as Dubow remarks in a different context, segregation initially emerged as a defensive strategy developed by English-speaking liberals in order to consolidate white supremacy. This could only be done by excluding 'the Native' as other.

Let us confine ourselves for the moment to the various strands of thinking informing segregationism, and, more specifically, informing its analysis of the 'Native question'. I will shortly return to its rendering of intra-white relations. In a context where different forms of resistance to white supremacist discourses became more and more prevalent,[82] attention was turned to the areas where change was most devastating and most threatening: the urban areas. Concern with the 'results' of urbanization in one form or another was present in most of the discourses feeding into segregation, and it most often took the form of an articulation between elements such as a loss of rural life, proletarianization, loss of moral values and degeneration of racial stocks, and the need to segregate population groups from one another.[83] In contrast to the later apartheid discourse, segregationism, in both its articulation of South Africanism and the Native question, developed a homogenizing racism: a tendency to produce population categories by evening out differences and delimiting manageable subjectivities.[84] Making subjects alike had the effect of simplifying administrative procedures and thereby facilitating the development of a series of relatively uncomplicated disciplinary techniques, techniques which would become ever more intricate, and thus more difficult to manage, during the apartheid years.

A case in point is the proliferation of discourses on the Native question during the first half of this century. These discourses had a double-edged effect. On the one hand, they reflected the increasing significance of the black South African population in the political terrain by bringing Africans under racial forms of categorization, something which did not generally occur until the 1920s.[85] On the other hand, the production of knowledges about 'racial difference' subjected and marked Africans in new ways, not as merely different others, but as inferior others. In this sense Ashforth's work,[86] which is concerned with the *production* of the 'Native question', stands as an important corrective to other studies on segregation which tend to assume the existence of a 'problem' to which segregationists merely had to find an answer. The elaboration of a segregationist discourse on the Native question took place, *inter alia*, via a series of official inquiries. These inquiries, which forged new practices of subjection, provide us with an important record of the construction of the 'Native problem'. One of the most significant in this respect was the South African Native Affairs Commission (SANAC) (1903–5), which was charged with the task of finding organizational principles capable of unifying the structure of administration dealing with the African population in order to bring an end to the differential treatment of Africans in the different territories.[87] In order to accomplish this task,

SANAC literally had to *invent* the category of 'the Native'. The Commission recommended that the word 'Native' 'shall be taken to mean an aboriginal inhabitant of Africa, south of the Equator, and to include half-castes and their descendants by Natives'.[88] This process of naming not only brought into being a new subjectivity, but also provided a highly contestable reconstruction of African history which redefined the nature of 'tribalism'. A selective recognition of the tribal system as well as of Native law – except where such laws were 'repugnant to general principles of humanity and civilization' – led the Commission to conclude that though there were variations on the laws, 'a *great similarity* in their tribal systems' existed.[89] By focusing almost exclusively on these so-called 'similarities' in the tribal systems it was possible to portray 'the Native' as a *socially homogeneous* category. This enabled the Commission to recommend the establishment of land reservation and a division of territory, with a corresponding division in spheres of representation and administration, for Europeans and Natives.[90]

A number of commissions of inquiry followed in the wake of SANAC. The discourse of the Native Economic Commission (NEC) (1930–32), convened around the time that the Carnegie Commission was investigating the poor white problem, is indicative of the nature of segregationism during its repressive phase. The appointment of the Commission coincided with attempts by the Hertzog government to remove key privileges from certain categories of Natives and to establish them as a *politically homogeneous* category. Ashforth stresses the rationale behind this need for homogenization:

> Without the assumption of homogeneity in the 'Native' population, thereby allowing uniform political status, the logic and the divided state founded on territorial division breaks down. Without homogeneity, the anomalies in 'tribal' society, such as those unfortunate categories of 'detribalized Natives' or 'advanced Natives', or 'civilized Natives', or 'urban Natives' . . . would start to take on a manifestation as classes distinct from the 'mass of Natives'. These could then maintain special treatment.[91]

In contrast to SANAC, and as a result of the relative sedimentation of the segregationist discourse, the NEC was in a position to take the existing categories of population division for granted. In the process of clarifying terminology, it was argued that the term 'Native' was in common use throughout the Union, and that it referred to 'Bantu-speaking peoples'. In that sense, it had 'acquired the status of a proper noun'.[92] The NEC regarded the development of the reserves as a panacea for all the ills associated with the Native question: it would solve the problem of the uncontrolled movement of labour away from the reserves and the European farms; it would facilitate the process by which an adequate amount of labour could be ensured for industry and commerce; and, finally, it would solve the problem of the 'undercutting' of white labour.[93] As part of the means of developing the reserves, the NEC proposed that Africans should shoulder the cost of their own 'advancement'. 'Advanced Natives', it was argued, should return to the reserves and contribute to their development. By the return of advanced Natives to the reserves, they proposed to eliminate two problems at once: the development of the reserves as well as the threat of poor whites 'degenerating' to the level of urbanized Africans. This proposed course of action was premissed upon a discourse which assumed a 'civilization gap' between urban blacks and poor whites.[94] As I have already shown, poor whiteism was regarded a problem exactly insofar as such degeneration was considered a possibility. White workers themselves did not hesitate to appeal to this logic, arguing that while they might do similar work as Natives, it was expected of them to keep a European standard of living. Consequently, they needed higher wages than Natives. This sentiment is reflected in the report, which holds that it is 'obviously undesirable in the extreme to allow the standard of living of the European to fall' to the level of the 'great bulk of Natives'.[95] Light is thrown on this assumption of 'obviousness' when it is read together with the NEC's earlier rejection of miscegenation as 'ruled out by the ideals of both races in South Africa'.[96] Paradoxically, a strategy of retribalization was needed to bring about what people 'naturally desired' themselves, so as to solve the problems 'caused' by the disintegration of traditional African lifestyles brought about by urbanization and proletarianization.[97]

The presence of discourses on tribalism and the argument that one needed to be aware of the 'dangers' of detribalization do not mean that the discursive homogenization of the African subject was effective, or was even meant to be effective in all areas of social life. As I argued earlier, the incorporation of Africans into the cities, to take but one example, was characterized by extremely varied forms of identification. Differences existed between newly urbanized labourers, more established communities and marginalized men and women without a base in either the countryside or formal wage employment who may or may not have identified with some presumed 'tribal' origins.[98] Moreover, we know that hegemonic visions rarely attain the intended meaning in the minds of those at whom they are aimed.[99] What mattered, from the point of view of segregationists, was the establishment of a general, broad basis of exclusion, and this was only achieved with the final introduction of the Hertzog Bills in 1936–37 under the Fusion government.

Pivotal in this connection was the work of a joint select committee, greatly influenced by the cultural idealism of Heaton Nicholls. Nicholls had argued that two principles should underlie any discussion of the Native question: the need to ensure European supremacy and the need to recognize the Natives' right to their own development in such a way as to win their approval. Any form of African representation within the white state was rejected in principle by Nicholls, and, subsequently, also by the committee. Instead, it emphasized the need to recognize and protect the distinctiveness of a 'Bantu ethos'. From this point onwards the idea of trusteeship, based on the British notion of indirect rule and comprising the establishment of separate areas where Native interests could be paramount and exercised through Native institutions, was developed. This reflected an important change with respect to the question of political representation of the African population. While earlier forms of arguments for exclusion were based on the fear of 'swamping', by the 1930s the notion of an African vote was rejected simply as a 'useless institution'. A new form of representation was needed, and trusteeship, which retained the idea that the development of African agriculture and traditional political institutions were of far greater practical value for Africans than the dubious advantage of common citizenship, provided the horizon within which such a new form of representation could be thought.[100] By 1937, Hertzog's legislative programme, cast in the form of an increasingly repressive discourse of segregation, was complete. The status of the category of the Native was redefined: it no longer designated a temporary status of political subordination prior to full membership of a common society;[101] rather, it was transformed into specifying of a trajectory of advance 'along [the Natives'] own lines'. Nevertheless, it is important to note that the category of the Native still signified a homogeneous mass. For Hertzog, the issues were straight-forward: there were the 'Europeans' and there were the 'Natives'. While there was already some vague talk of 'the national aspirations of the Native', which were to be met in 'his own area', this meant nothing like what it came to mean under apartheid. 'Own areas' were *not* defined on ethnic grounds. The important lines of division were drawn on the grounds of the *similarity* of different 'tribal' systems and, thus, on differences between white and black.

Social conditions after the Second World War changed rapidly and had far-reaching consequences for the further development of policy around the Native question. In the reserves, the adverse effects of forcing too many people to live on too little land began to show. In addition, the 1940s were marked by a massive housing problem, labour unrest, the 1946 African miners' strike, the breakdown of the Native Representative Council, and the dissatisfaction of white farmers with the erosion of their labour supply, coupled with rising black expectations. Influx control measures were not yet systematically applied and shanty towns and squatter areas grew. Moreover, there was a more coherent response by African political organizations to the increasingly repressive nature of segregation, an increase in trade union organization and industrial militancy, and renewed struggles in response to the failure of ten years of resistance against Hertzog's Native Bills. In this social context, the United Party (UP) under the leadership of Smuts appointed the Native Laws Commission (1946–48) chaired by Fagan. This commission had practically no policy impact on South Africa. The NP, which won the next election, appointed its own commissions. It did, however, represent an important phase in official discourse on the Native question, reflecting signs of a generalized weakening of systems of control over Africans, especially in the sphere of labour where the job colour bar, pass laws and the system of migrant labour were criticized as unjust and inefficient. In addition, between 1939 and 1948, the job colour bar was eased, training facilities for Africans were expanded, Africans were included in the Unemployment Insurance Fund, and in 1942 the Native Affairs Department recommended the abolition of pass laws.

It was in this context that the National Party could argue that the United Party failed to solve the Native question, and that a much more radical approach was needed. However, the weak liberalization of restraints on the African community could not in itself have led to the failure of segregationism. In order to account for its inability to continue to hegemonize this domain, it is necessary to take cognizance of the second dimension of articulation of segregationism: that of its reading of intra-white relations. This is not merely an empirical requirement, but a necessity which arises out of the very nature of processes of identity formation: identities are not forged merely in positive terms, but are also relational in character, and thus gain their specificity in their difference from other identities.[102] On this reading, even Ashforth's attempt to show the contingency and non-naturalness of 'Native' identity does not go quite far enough, for his reading, however important, still focuses on the positivity of the production of a Native identity, and does not focus on the relational and therefore negative character of all processes of identity formation. It is crucial in this respect that the homogeneity of 'the other', the Native, could only be produced by assuming an equally unified white identity opposing it. Ashforth never emphasizes this, but assumes that the homogeneity produced, first socially and then politically, was exclusively the product of a positive discourse on the Native question. However, I contend that the systems of exclusion forged to separate the Native from the rest of society not only had as its mirror-image the production of an equally uniform notion of European identity, but could not have come into existence without that mirror-image. It is in this sense that the precise form in which the Native question has been discursively constructed is of decisive importance in accounting for the development of a European identity. While up to the 1940s, Natives were dealt with as a homogeneous category, the terms in which their continued exclusion was construed in apartheid discourse mark a radical rupture in official discourse. The roots of this rupture must be related to the resistance of certain members of the Afrikaans-speaking population to the constitution of a uniform European identity. And it is to the failure of segregation to constitute this uniform identity that I now turn.

South Africanism and the Fragmentation of White Unity

> 'A white South Africa!' That is the burden of our speeches at the present, and a sentiment which can always count upon receiving 'prolonged applause'.[103]

The decades of the 1930s and 1940s were marked not only by attempts to 'solve' the 'Native question', but also by severe rifts and divisions within the dominant white South African community. Segregationists attempted to address intra-white relations by way of a discourse fostering white unity. South Africanism became the ill-fated signifier of that attempt, doomed to be replaced by an organicist conception of identity, simultaneously supplementing and subverting segregationist efforts to foster an overriding sense of white identity. The new modes of identification brought into being by the Afrikaner nationalist movement during these decades supplemented South Africanism with a novel, narrower conception of Afrikanerdom, and so subverted its tendency to obliterate distinctions between Afrikaners and English-speaking white South Africans. As a result, a fundamentally new set of political frontiers was articulated around an ethnicist conception of identity, which would decisively alter the imaginary horizon instituted with segregation. The precise articulation between the new frontiers and the older segregationist horizon is what gave apartheid its identity and efficacy. In order to trace out the historical conditions for the emergence of this ethnicist discourse, it is necessary to take a closer look at the two decades spanning the period immediately prior to the Nationalist victory in 1948 from the point of view of intra-white political and social struggles. A series of events are of particular importance in this respect: the fusion of the South African Party (SAP) and the National Party (NP) into the United South African National Party (USANP) in 1933, leading to the split and formation of the *Gesuiwerde Nasionale Party* (GNP, Purified National Party) in 1934; the Great Trek Centenary celebrations in 1938; the contestation around the formulation of the Aliens Bill; and the decision to participate in the Second World War on the side of Britain. It is clearly not possible to represent fully all the dimensions and nuances of these intra-white struggles. Rather, the focus here falls on the manner in which the meanings given to these events by the actors involved in them undermined the segregationist attempt to establish white unity as the overriding form of identification for white South Africans.

Fusion

> The period during which this fusion took place (1933 to 1939) was one of prosperity and a lessening of tension between British and Afrikaners.[104]

The year 1933 was a milestone in South African history. Fusion between the South African Party under the leadership of General Smuts and the National Party led by General Hertzog sparked off a number of important changes within white politics. One of these took the form of a struggle for leadership of the Afrikaner community between the Boer War generals – Botha, Smuts and Hertzog – who represented the old landed notables prepared to compromise with mining capital, and the new intelligentsia mobilized since the 1920s around the language issue, who wanted to purge Afrikaner identity of its poor and 'coloured' elements, and attempted to reconstitute Afrikaner fiction, language and cultural institutions along exclusionist lines.[105] This struggle reflected the division between the secular leadership of the first three decades of the Union and the new organic intellectuals who forged the symbols of Afrikaner 'civil religion' and populist mobilization in the 1930s and 1940s.[106] From this point onwards, the *Afrikaner Broederbond*, Potchefstroom academics and intellectuals such as Verwoerd, Meyer, Diederichs and Cronje returning from overseas study played an increasingly important role in the reconstitution of an Afrikaner *volk*. Thus the re-emergence, in the 1930s and 1940s, of exclusive Afrikaner nationalism narrowly defined was not a spontaneous, natural development. It must be related to the perceptions of these intellectuals, who differed from the generation of generals, and saw in a variety of developments, ranging from capitalism to communism, a threat to the continued existence of the Afrikaner *volk*.[107] I discuss their interventions in chapter 2 in depth.

It is important to give a more detailed account of these changes during the Fusion period.[108] The Fusion government had established an articulation between nationalism and a two-stream policy – based on an absolute equality between Afrikaners and English-speaking whites – resulting in an emphasis on white unity and the protection of white civilization in the face of a 'black peril'. The United Party pledged to develop a 'predominant sense of South African national unity, based on the equality of the Afrikaans-speaking and English-speaking sections of the community',[109] thus establishing the flip-side of their construction of a homogeneous 'Native' identity. However, given the large income differentials between Afrikaners and English-speaking whites, the discrimination and exclusionary practices the newly urbanized Arikaners faced, the precise articulation of the 'poor white problem' as an Afrikaner phenomenon and the growing mobilization of the Afrikaans-speaking community on narrow ethnicist lines, a discourse on white unity which started from the premiss of 'equality' between language groups was bound to run into difficulties. And if, in addition, those endeavouring to foster white unity were regarded as collaborating with imperial/foreign capital, rather than being on the side of the worker, its chances for success were diminished even further. This is not to say that such a discourse could not succeed in principle, especially given the strength of the black/white frontier in segregationist discourse. However, coupled with the neutrality issue during the war, as well as the perceived weakening of the exclusionary practices surrounding African urbanization, segregationists increasingly found it difficult to present themselves as the party offering a solution to the dislocations of identity experienced during these two decades. Moreover, the intensification of the activities of the younger generation of Afrikaner organic intellectuals contributed to the perception that segregationism no longer presented the necessary answers to the new problems facing the Afrikaner *volk* in the cities.

The *Gesuiwerde Nasionale Party*, the most extremist nationalist group under Malan's leadership, broke away from the Fusion government on a bitterly anti-British platform.[110] The GNP enjoyed the support of the cultural and intellectual circle previously standing behind Hertzog, and now faced the difficult task of convincing Afrikanerdom that Hertzog had abandoned the cause of nationalism. While Hertzog saw no reason why the Afrikaans- and English-speaking sectors of the population could not work together in all respects, for Malan, Fusion put the 'soul of Afrikanerdom' at stake. Fusion between the SAP and the NP was regarded as an illegitimate merger of the Afrikaans- and English-speaking communities, with the former still being subordinate to the latter. For the GNP, it also represented a strengthening of bonds between South Africa and imperialist Britain. Moreover, by incorporating the financial interests on the Rand, it was felt that Fusion would lead to a process of party division along *class* lines which would destroy Afrikanerdom. Hertzog simply compromised too much with the 'Hoggenheimer' element of the SAP.[111]

It is important to reflect for a moment on the significance of the perceived coalescence between the segregationists' emphasis on white unity and their attitude to organized capital. This coalescence was crystallized in the popular imagination in the cartoon figure known as 'Hoggenheimer', who was portrayed as obese, with 'greedy eyes', a massive hook nose, protruding lips, and smoking large cigars,[112] thus condensing all the elements associated with the rising new large-scale capitalist class, divorced from the poverty and miserable conditions of the bulk of newly urbanized workers. Moreover, the Hoggenheimer stereotype had clearly Jewish overtones, and thus established a further set of overdeterminations between the anti-capitalism of the new organic intellectuals and the rising anti-Jewish feelings in mid-1930s South Africa.[113] The precise role and impact of fascist ideas in the nationalist movement will be discussed in the next chapter. Suffice it to say here that the condensation of these associations in the Hoggenheimer figure succeeded in indelibly marking the SAP with 'foreign', 'imperialist' and 'capitalist' characteristics, all of which were spurned by the GNP.

In order to vindicate the GNP's exclusivist position, Malan drew a distinction between *hereniging* (reunion) and *samesmelting* (fusion), as signifying different forms of unity.[114] The series of equivalences giving these terms their respective identities act as useful indicators of the nature of the divisions which were to become increasingly central in the years to follow Fusion. While *samesmelting* connoted a mixture of imperialists, capitalists and true Afrikaners, *hereniging* signified the bringing together of what 'belonged together out of inner conviction', and thus served as the basis upon which Malan could incite efforts to create the unity patently absent in Afrikaans-speaking circles at the time. *Hereniging* rested upon the view that the National Party had an inner unity which the South African Party lacked.[115] Fusion with the SAP was illegitimate precisely insofar as it was perceived to lead to the introduction of divisions within that which ought to be organically linked: the political, social and cultural dimensions of Afrikanerhood. A party, for Malan, could not be separated from the cultural and social spheres in which it operated. Against these divisionary logics, the GNP presented itself as the only party truly representative of Afrikaner unity (*volkseenheid*) in all its dimensions, a unity which of necessity had to exclude the imperialist and capitalist elements of the SAP held to be foreign to the character of the Afrikaner community. Genuine South African 'civic sentiment' was thus equated with the Afrikaans-speaking stream whose loyalty could not fluctuate between England and South Africa. The issue of 'Afrikaner unity', increasingly becoming incompatible with the segregationist conception of white unity, loomed large on the horizon throughout the 1930s and the divisions resulting from Fusion would set off bitter recriminations and struggles within the Afrikaans-speaking community, schisms that would become ever more central and solidified in the 1940s. It was still possible, however, with the 1938 Great Trek Centenary celebrations, to hope that a sense of unity, not only within Afrikanerdom, but between the two 'white races', could be re-established.

The *Voortrekker Eeufees*

> It is now a hundred years since our *volk* won a victory for freedom in the north. For our forebears, that was a day which should be remembered . . .[116]

The Centenary festivities started out as a government initiative to celebrate *Voortrekker* (pioneer) ideals, their history as pioneers, and their struggles and sacrifices to establish a state independent from the British colonial authorities. It was intended that the symbolic Oxwagon Trek and the country-wide celebrations accompanying it would culminate in the laying of the foundation stones of the *Voortrekkermuseum*, to be funded by the state. More significantly, it was envisaged as an occasion on which to foster a greater sense of unity between Afrikaans- and English-speaking South Africans: 'God save the Queen' would be played since it was the national anthem, and the British Governor General as representative of the Crown would be invited. However, the course of events and the emotions inspired by the symbolic trek made this well nigh impossible. The symbolic *Ossewatrek* (Oxwagon Trek), starting in Cape Town on 8 August 1938 and set to reach its destination at the site of the *Voortrekkermonument* in Pretoria on 16 December, inspired a surge of Afrikaner nationalist sentiment, resurrecting historical forms of identification. Traditional Afrikaner forms of address, *oom* (uncle), *tante* (aunt), *neef* (nephew) and *niggie* (niece), became prevalent; mounted commandos everywhere welcomed the arrival of oxwagons; men started to grow *Voortrekker* beards and women sported *Voortrekker* dresses; children were baptized at camping-sites and couples dressed in *Voortrekker* gear were married where the wagons congregated.[117] The symbolic *Ossewatrek* gradually took on the form of an extended re-enactment of the greatness of Afrikaner history, and was used to counter the Afrikaner sense of inadequacy, inferiority and loss experienced as a result of urbanization and proletarianization. Repeatedly Afrikaners were admonished to stop apologizing for being Afrikaans, to believe in their God, their *volk* and themselves.[118] The occasion also provided an opportunity to incite the *volk* to reach out and to engage themselves in an 'Act of Rescue': to collect hundreds of thousands of pounds to save themselves from poverty and ruin. 'The *volk* must save itself.'[119] Thus the beginnings of the 'economic movement'.

The exclusivist articulations which the events received from within the Afrikaner community, and it was quite clear that a plethora of Afrikaner organizations such as the AB and the *Nasionale Kultuurraad* (National Cultural Council) played a crucial role in steering events in this direction,[120] soon led to a growing sense of indignation at the thought of 'God save the Queen' being played at the highest point of the celebrations. It was felt that the British anthem symbolized the very force from which the *Voortrekkers* wanted to distance themselves; playing it would desecrate the memory of their forebears' struggle against imperialism. The government under leadership of Hertzog declared, as a result of the strong feelings aroused by the issue, that the event would no longer be regarded as a state affair, thus obviating the need to play the anthem. With this, another attempt to foster white unity foundered on the altar of Afrikaner exclusivism. Hertzog, once torch-bearer of Afrikaner nationalism, now declared to be an outcast and a traitor to the Afrikaner cause as a result of his insistence on equality between the two language groups, did not even attend. The laying of the museum cornerstones was carried out by female descendants of the *Voortrekkers*, and signified the opening of a new phase in the Afrikaner struggle for independence from the perceived continuing colonial domination.[121]

This struggle, increasingly articulated in calls for a republic, began to make inroads into the UP and Labour Party constituencies alike. Ten prominent Labour Party members, for instance, joined the Witwatersrand GNP, declaring it to be the only party in which the Afrikaner worker could find a home.[122] Afrikaner workers themselves were attracted by the resurrection of the historic symbols by the new nationalists. The clearest example of this was perhaps that of the Afrikaans-speaking women who were members of the *Klerewerkersunie* (KWU, Garment Workers' Union), led by Solly Sachs.[123] Captured by the fervour of the celebrations, these women decided to attend the cornerstone laying in *Voortrekker* dresses. Much time and effort was put into preparing the appropriate clothing for the *Kappiekommandos* ('Bonnet' commandos) by the Germiston branch of the KWU, and the *Klerewerker* – journal of the KWU – reported extensively on these preparations, encouraging the *niggies* to participate, and to learn the old folk songs so that they could all sing together on the great day.[124] The *Klerewerker* also carried articles on the importance of the history behind the Centenary celebrations to *Afrikaner dogters* (young Afrikaner women). Hester Cornelius, for instance, admonished Afrikaners not to take the events lightly and not to grow beards and wear the *Voortrekker* clothing for fun. Rather, they had to realize that without a Piet Retief, Piet Uys, Andries and Pieter Maritz, who led the *volk* and who suffered and struggled to be free from the yoke of imperialism, Afrikaners would not be where they were at the time. These forebears represented the true grit of Afrikaner character and, Cornelius continued, had to be distinguished from the 'handful of rich parasites and Nazi agents who are using Afrikaner national sentiment to bring Hitler into the country'.[125] Linking the *Voortrekker* struggle to the present, she argued that the new danger which faced the world was that of fascism. Together with fighting fascism, Afrikaner workers were encouraged to fulfil their duty towards the thousands of Afrikaner families who every day sank deeper and deeper into poverty and misery.[126] Like their forebears, they had to continue to struggle against all forms of oppression and domination. This remarkable articulation between Afrikaner history and the anti-colonial struggle, on the one hand, and the activities of the Union and Afrikaner women workers, on the other hand, was fostered by their leader, Solly Sachs, who thought it important to take cognizance of the specificity of their positions both as workers and as newly urbanized Afrikaner women. This, I would argue, formed the basis of the strength of their interpellation into a class-based discourse, and provided them with a solid basis from which to develop an ongoing critique of the increasingly narrow, exclusivist, racist and anti-semitic basis of the nationalist movement, and to resist the nationalist onslaught on the unions.[127]

As a result of the garment workers' vocal critique, their attendance at the Centenary celebrations was soon turned into another site of battle with the exclusivist nationalists who set up a committee to discourage the women from participation. In keeping with the more general attack by sections of the nationalist movement on 'liberal' and 'communist' trade unions, the *meisies* (young Afrikaner women) of the garment workers were portrayed as pawns in the hands of their 'communist' leader, Solly Sachs.[128] All possible measures were undertaken to discredit them. Central to this strategy was the portrayal of the women as passive, innocent victims of conspiratorial communists. Their mouthpiece, the *Klerewerker*, was scrutinized for articles which attempted to subvert the racist and anti-union propaganda of the GNP on the basis of a critique of exploitation of one class by another; articles written in Afrikaans were argued to be falling 'beneath the pail', providing evidence of a lack of respect and an *ontwortelde menslike natuur*, an uprooted human nature. The authenticity of the articles was also questioned, since they were held to be written in 'broken' Afrikaans.[129] All of these attempts to discredit the garment workers had one aim in particular: to contest their claims to be true members of Afrikanerdom. No holds were barred in this struggle, and Sachs's Jewish background soon became an issue. A letter from D.H.B. Grobbelaar to Sachs, arguing that the participation of the women in the celebrations would make a 'mockery of our national traditions', captures the vitriol of some of the attacks:

> The Afrikaner nation is busy uniting – to mobilize its forces against you and your sort. The thousands of Afrikaner daughters whom you have in your clutches will settle with you and with them the whole Boer nation who are finding themselves in this *Voortrekker* year. Our people do not want anything to do with Communism and the Jews. . . . The day when we Afrikaners begin to settle with you Jews, you will find out that Germany is a Jewish paradise compared with what South Africa will be!

> ... We Afrikaners recognize no 'classes' as you and your satellites are trying to introduce – therefore, we do not want the garment workers as a 'class' to participate in the celebrations, but together with us as Boers – the factory girl together with the professor's wife. You and Johanna Cornelius who all day organize and address *kaffirs* – will you dare to bring them also to the celebrations? They are your fellow workers and 'comrades'.[130]

The Afrikaner women of the KWU were thus excluded from the folds of the *volk* as foreign to the Afrikaner cause. The close links established between their class position and Afrikanership was rejected; instead they were argued to be the innocent victims of Jewish communism, bent on destroying the Afrikaner *volk*. Many of the themes prevalent in nationalist circles on the newly urbanized Afrikaner women, discussed earlier, were mobilized here: the women were portrayed as passive, poor victims, unable to speak for themselves, and standing in need of protection; the 'danger' of miscegenation associated with the communist egalitarian discourse was never far from the centre of the debates; and the figure of the Jew as enemy, so central to the discourses of the shirt movements of the 1930s, was pivotal in the attack on the KWU. Thus, not only did the *Voortrekker Eeufees* not succeed in bringing together the 'two white races' into a greater white unity, but it became dominated by the fervour of extreme right-wing nationalists, increasingly successful in capturing the credentials of 'true Afrikanerdom' for themselves.

Aliens and Other Unassimilables

> ... the Party in general welcomes the immigration of suitable assimilable white elements. ...[131]

As is clear from the foregoing, the exclusivist discourse becoming more and more central to the identity of the GNP was in no sense of the term a discourse based simply upon 'racial' exclusivity. The GNP and the wider nationalist movement's understanding in this respect differed quite strongly from the homogenizing articulations so prevalent in segregationism; they never hesitated to draw distinctions within the white community on the grounds of race. The origins of the vicissitudes in their understanding of difference, and, more specifically, of racial difference, will be analysed in more depth in the following chapter. It is, however, important to note here that relations to 'others', and therefore conceptions of difference and otherness[132] were never simply drawn on the basis of visible and empirically observable 'differences' as, for example, found in skin colour. Their racism was thus not simply of a 'biological' kind.[133] Increasingly intricate distinctions were in the process of being drawn between what was properly 'Afrikaans' and what was not, and the exclusion of the 'Native' constituted only one amongst these to be excluded from the inner domains of acceptability.

Other groups were coming under intensifying scrutiny. One of these was the 'Cape Coloured' community. While Hertzog insisted on treating them, in terms of political rights and privileges, on the same terms as whites, agitation from the GNP to remove coloureds from the common voters' roll started in 1936.[134] This agitation was not unconnected to the preoccupation with the 'poor white question' and the possibility of miscegenation in 'mixed' neighbourhoods in nationalist circles. In this the GNP drew support from Afrikaans churches as well as from a number of other Afrikaner organizations, including the *Afrikaanse Christelike Vrouevereniging* (ACVV, Afrikaans Christian Women's Association), the RDB and the *Christelike Jongliedevergenigings* (Christian Youth Associations). This widespread 'concern' signified the beginnings of an extended struggle by the NP not only to remove coloureds from the voters' roll, but also to introduce a series of social measures – ranging from the establishment of separate residential areas to the prohibition of 'mixed marriages' – to separate whites from coloureds.[135] However, no agreement existed within Afrikaner nationalist circles on the position of coloureds with respect to the 'white' community, and the desirability and possibility of implementing a vision of 'total segregation', socially, economically and politically, had to await the articulation of a comprehensive project which increasingly would go under the name of apartheid. It is nevertheless at this stage necessary to point out that the position of both the coloured and Indian communities played a crucial role in the intra-white battles being fought out during the two decades leading up to the victory of the HNP in 1948.

The dominant white groups were deeply divided on the position of the coloured population. A government commission on the 'Coloured question' reporting in 1937, for instance, took a position similar to the one the Fagan Commission would take a decade later on the 'Native question'. In spite of the climate of agitation fostered by the new nationalists, the commission argued for an extension of the Cape coloured vote to all coloureds in South Africa, as well as against the regulation of miscegenation by legal means.[136] This set what was to become a trend in white politics once the UP occupied the position of official opposition: rather than fundamentally rejecting explictly racist and exclusionary measures, it opted for a 'liberal' stance, opposing legal measures but agreeing in principle with the need to keep 'races' apart. The position of South African Indians caused less friction between the dominant parties, quite simply because both considered them to be a 'foreign' and 'unassimilable' population group. Their total exclusion, however, did not make them less vulnerable to legal exclusions, oppression and racist portrayal. Indeed, much of the literature produced by the new nationalists during the 1930s and 1940s was permeated by vituperative tales depicting Indians as occupying a 'middle position' between whites and Africans, living like the latter, but sharing the rights and privileges of the former.[137] The position of the Indian shopkeeper was singled out for comment, since this put the Indian in a 'superior' position to poor whites, and also gave him undue 'access' to white women.[138]

The constitution of the identity of the *volk* by the exclusion of 'foreign elements', as I argued earlier, was not reserved for those who could be discerned as different on the basis of their skin colour. White English-speaking South Africans also often found themselves at the receiving end of an exclusionary discourse which emphasized their 'foreignness' through their presumed links with England, and during the 1930s the South African Jewish community came under similar pressure. This was at its most evident in the discussions surrounding the introduction of the Aliens Bill. During the 1930s, strong anti-Jewish sentiment was evident in white politics. Already in 1930 a Quota Act was introduced in Parliament by D.F. Malan, limiting the number of immigrants allowed into the country. German immigration, however, was not affected by this law, and by 1933 German Jewish immigration to South Africa was steadily increasing.[139] A wave of Jewish immigration in 1937 resulted in the repeal of the Quota Act and the passing of a new Aliens Bill by Parliament. Although Jews were not specifically referred to in the Act, the intention clearly was to exclude as many of them as possible. Agitation against Jews increased throughout the 1930s, leading the 1937 Transvaal and Orange Free State NP Congresses to declare them ineligible for membership of the Party.

The prohibition of 'unassimilable' and 'foreign' population groups from immigration to South Africa formed the basis of the Aliens Bill, and it explicitly declared Yiddish a 'non-European' language, making it possible to prohibit immigration of Jews not in command of a 'European' language. During the 1937 Parliamentary debate, Malan argued that the South African 'Jewish problem' arose from the fact that commerce was exclusively in the hands of Jews. As long as Afrikaners were excluded from it, the poor white problem would remain unresolved. This argument was to be repeated in later discussions of the proposed amendments to the Bill by the NP. Malan argued, in addition, that the Jewish population was an 'unassimilable' group, evidence of which was to be found in the closedness of their communities, which could be likened to a 'state within a state'.[140] In contrast to the 'respectable anti-semitism' of the UP,[141] who argued that the immigration regulations were not directly aimed at Jews, but at 'foreign' elements in general, the NP was explicit about the 'need' to prevent further Jewish immigration, while attempting to fend off the accusation of stirring up racial hatred by arguing that the *volk* had a right to self-preservation, and that part of that right was to take account of its future 'composition'.

There can be no doubt about the fact that the NP's position on immigration was strongly affected and influenced by what it saw as 'economic' factors, cast in the wider mould of the fear of foreignness. Malan, in one of his most explicit speeches on the subject, argued the following:

> Coalition and Fusion were to a great extent the result of Jewish organization. The Jews did everything in their power to keep the Afrikaners from uniting, as they feared that South Africans would rise from their lowly and insignificant position to save South Africa for the South Africans.[142]

The figure of the Jew, however, was further overdetermined. In it were condensed the fear not only of continued economic servitude, but also of 'racial mixing' and 'communism'. Both Malan and Eric Louw on occasion argued that there were close links between communism and the Jewish community, and Solly Sachs was cited as a clear example of this. Moreover, the equivalences, here as elsewhere, were extended to the fear of miscegenation and the communist tendency to foster it by a discourse of equality:

> There is yet another aspect of Jewish Communism in South Africa. The Jews oppose discrimination because they fear discrimination against themselves. In South Africa this means miscegenation.[143]

Nevertheless, there is also no doubt that the opposition to Jewish immigration was riddled with anti-semitic generalizations, quite prevalent during the 1930s in South Africa. As Shain points out, imagery portrayed Jews as alien, disloyal, bent on exploitation, communist and inclined towards conspiratorial behaviour.[144]

In interpreting the portrayal of the 'Jew' in nationalist politics, it is important to stress the fact that there were multiple similarities between the treatment of Jewish and, for example, Asian immigrants. The anti-alienism of the NP dovetailed quite comfortably with the growing anti-semitic outbursts in the 1930s, and both fulfilled a crucial function in the constitution of an exclusivist Afrikanerdom against a generalized conception of 'white unity'. As Shain points out, the quintessential alien Jew helped to consolidate an all-embracing Afrikaner identity, understood in terms of cultural unity and opposition to foreigners.[145] And in that sense, it was no different from the vitriolic exclusions of other population groups considered to be 'unassimilable' at the time. In the same way that the general anti-semitic climate of the 1930s prepared the ground for the scapegoating of the Jew, the racist horizon instituted in colonialist and segregationist discourses facilitated the demonization of, for example, the Asian and even the white English-speaking population.

The War: Hardening Divisions within Afrikanerdom

These differences within the dominant white community were consolidated and solidified during the war years. The neutrality question not only brought the deep divisions between Afrikaans- and English-speaking South Africans on South Africa's relation to Britain to the fore, but acted also as the immediate catalyst in driving a wedge within the Fusion government between the Prime Minister Hertzog, who favoured neutrality, and Smuts, who wanted the Union to enter the war on the side of Britain. During the neutrality debate on Monday, 4 September 1939, Hertzog and Smuts put their respective positions to Parliament. Malan supported the neutrality motion, pointing out that, should South Africa agree to participate in the war, it could no longer be considered a free nation, but would be led into slavery by sentimental ties. Malan lost the vote, and South Africa entered the war on 6 September 1939. Oswald Pirow, commenting on the neutrality issue, argued that its consequences were far-reaching:

> Overnight the country was back to the *racial* division of the Anglo-Boer War. . . . The supporters of General Smuts were jubilant that the Imperial idea had triumphed. The Afrikaners were equally elated by the realization that, although General Smuts had a majority in Parliament, they were united as never before in their history.[146]

It did, however, take many more years for Afrikanerdom to become united in any sense of the term. As a result of strenuous efforts by the AB to unite all Afrikaners against the war, Hertzog and the thirty-seven MPs who withdrew from the UP rejoined Malan in January 1940 to form the *Herenigde Nasionale Party*.[147] Reunification, however, did not carry the support of the whole of the GNP. Strijdom and Verwoerd in the Transvaal especially were opposed to a compromise with Hertzog, and they mistrusted his late conversion to republicanism. In the Orange Free State (OFS), Swart was also opposed to letting former *smelters* (fusionists) into the ranks of the GNP, and when the OFS NP Congress rejected Hertzog's arguments for equal rights between Afrikaans and English speakers in a republic, Hertzog resigned from the HNP. With his followers he formed the Afrikaner Party (AP), which, in coalition with the NP, would win the 1948 election. Much water, however, still had to run into the sea before this was possible.

Not only did the war issue open up new rifts within the UP, but it also strengthened the position of far right movements both within the HNP and within the wider *volksbeweging*. Consequently, much of the 1940s bore witness to fierce struggles between different nationalist and other rightist groupings for hegemony within the *volksbeweging*, and attempts to rekindle a sense of unitary Afrikanerdom had to allow for the existence of 'cultural' movements along with, or as it turned out, under the umbrella of, the HNP. Within the HNP, the most significant grouping was the pro-fascist *Nuwe Orde Studie Kring*, led by Oswald Pirow. Pirow, who followed Hertzog in preaching equality between Afrikaans and English speakers, argued that

> . . . the coming 'New Order' would sweep away democracy and substitute a Christian, white National Socialist Republic, severed from the British Crown and founded upon the principle of 'state authority' and national discipline. In this vision, the paraphernalia of effete liberal capitalism, such as political parties, Parliament, elections, etc., would follow its demise.[148]

Pirow's NO drew its support from former fusionists in the Transvaal HNP and threatened the line followed by Strijdom and Verwoerd, who attacked the national socialism of the NO as a 'foreign importation'.[149] Strijdom and Verwoerd, however, had the support of the AB behind them, and after the HNP banned factions from operating within the party in January 1942, the NO was effectively silenced.

Outside of the party, one of the most significant of these 'splinter' groupings was the OB, an organization in the mainstream tradition of fascist movements, formed in November 1938 to cement the

Ossewagees (Oxwagon spirit) in South Africa.[150] Its programme of principles stated that it would fight for

> ... the maintenance, extension and consummation of the traditions and principles of the *Dietse Afrikaner*, the protection and promotion of the religious, cultural and material interests of the Afrikaner, the fostering of patriotism and national pride, and the ... unification of all Afrikaners ....[151]

The OB followed in the footsteps of a variety of ultra-rightist shirt movements – including the Greyshirts, Blackshirts and the South African Fascists – which had arisen in South Africa in the early 1930s.[152] Rather than focusing on anti-black feeling, their programmes were built around anti-semitic sentiments. In the case of the Greyshirts, under the leadership of Louis Weichardt, mobilization did not take place along language lines either. It was a bilingual organization, convinced of the need to foster and protect white racial unity, and it aimed at mobilizing poor whites and working-class people, both Afrikaans- and English-speaking. Weichardt, commenting in 1948 on their struggle for a white South Africa, restated his position in the following terms:

> We hear so often today that the struggle for a racial ideal, a *herrenvolk* is wrong. ... unfortunately it is the case that the Asian-Jewish race has succeeded in rousing the one white race against the other white *volk*, in order to dominate the one by the other in imperialist fashion. ... the struggle of White against White has to come to an end, white unity has to be established.[153]

Manie Wessels's Blackshirts or South African National Democratic Party, by contrast, focused almost exclusively on poor Afrikaners. The constituencies of these and other radical right splinter groupings[154] – the disadvantaged, the poor, the working class, as well as the youth – thus almost entirely coincided with that of the NP.[155] Their virulent anti-semitism was coupled with anti-capitalist rhetoric, as well as a strong sense of white superiority, combining many of the articulations present in the wider *volksbeweging*. Indeed, the context in which these movements arose, took root and came to influence the GNP is of the greatest importance, for it provides further evidence of the extent to which Fusionism could not provide solutions to the perceived dislocations of identity in the early 1930s.

At this time, in the wake of the Depression, the drought and the rapid urbanization following from it, the formation of the Fusion government, with its emphasis on white unity and its assumption of equality between Afrikaans- and English-speakers, created a political vacuum which was occupied by rightist groupings. Hertzog, once uncompromising in his championing of the cause of Afrikaner nationalism, had vacated that terrain, and the GNP had not yet succeeded in wholly monopolizing it. Indeed, many of the rightist leaders felt that the GNP could not be trusted to carry forward the ideals of the *volk*.[156] Weichardt himself argued that he left the NP in 1933 not because he did not share its 'national convictions', but because he had a 'deeper conviction': the *Boerevolk* had to be anchored in *race*; an Afrikaner is not someone who merely joins the NP, for then Jews could be Afrikaners as well. Afrikanerhood had to be purified of its illegitimate elements, and Weichardt did not trust the NP to do so.[157] The battle for the heart of the exclusivist articulation of 'Afrikanerdom' was thus on. The GNP and the Greyshirts, as well as the more influential OB, had to find a *modus operandi* which would allow them all space to work within the sphere of 'Afrikaner' politics.[158]

By October 1940, Malan had managed to pursuade the OB that its role was to work, on the 'cultural' terrain, for a Christian national republic, and to 'develop the religious, moral and economic life of the volk on the lines of the old *Voortrekker* principles, while pledging not to tolerate violence or "underground revolutionary activities" and not to undermine or prejudice the work of friendly political parties or bodies'.[159] Relations between the OB and the NP, however, did not develop smoothly, for Malan, far from being a radical, felt great dissatisfaction with the OB's attempt to establish a national socialist republic, which he considered to be too tainted with 'foreign' elements.[160] Malan succeeded, by 1943, in isolating his far rightist opponents and to consolidate his claim to the title of *volksleier* (leader of the *volk*) which was first attributed to him in June 1941.[161] This victory, however, did not occur without considerable shifts and rearticulations of matters of doctrine and principle within the NP, and the legacy of the extreme rightist, national socialist movements of the 1930s and 1940s marked the NP in several significant ways: it emerged a more authoritarian party in spite of its championing of 'democracy' against sections of the OB who favoured its destruction; it was tainted with anti-semitism; it incorporated many of the leaders and activists of the hard right movements into the NP; and, finally, the influence of the exclusivist AB grew rapidly within the party.[162] As a result of the agitation during the war, the NP began to move much more clearly in the direction of republicanism.[163] It would, however, take more than a decade for that ideal to be fulfilled. Nevertheless, by the mid-1940s, it seemed that the HNP had re-established its central position as guarantor of Afrikaner nationalism, and had effectively challenged the segregationist discourse of white unity.

Conclusion: Dislocation, Identity and the Failure of Segregationism

In this chapter I have argued that the conditions for the resurgence of an exclusivist Afrikaner nationalism in the 1930s and 1940s are not to be found in 'objective' conditions understood in the Marxist sense.[164] Contrary to what analysts such as O'Meara have argued, the 'class basis' of the re-emerging National Party in these decades had no pre-given and automatic identity. Nothing can be read off from the capitalist relations of production which for neo-Marxists such as O'Meara are the underlying conditions for the formation of nationalist ideology. Rather, as I have argued, the key to understanding the processes of division and struggle in these decades is to be found in the dislocation of identities experienced as a result of a series of contingent historical processes: the Depression, the great drought and the war. The consequences of the rapidly changing economic conditions during these decades, in addition, played a crucial role in bringing about these dislocations. However, as I have shown in the analysis of the 'experience' of urbanization in the Afrikaans-speaking community, that experience itself did not contain a necessary meaning. Rather, the meaning of urbanization itself had to be produced: it received, in the discourse of the *volksbeweging*, a particular articulation that was closely linked to their resistance to the dominant segregationist emphasis on white unity and the presumed equality between Afrikaners and English-speaking whites. The events of the 1930s, the Centenary celebrations, the war and the immigration issue, to name but the most important, received their meaning from the struggles within the dominant white group, as well as from divisions within 'Afrikanerdom'. None of them were other than brute facts, awaiting interpretation. And the interpretation they received, as we have argued, militated against the unicity and homogeneity of the segregationist conception of identity.

Incapable of thinking in terms other than that of Native and European, segregationists failed to recognize and articulate the deep sense of dislocation experienced by the newly urbanized Afrikaans-speaking community. Forging ahead with a homogenizing discourse on white unity in the face of those dislocations was a serious miscalculation. It is not accidental that Hertzog was continually accused of being 'out of touch' with the Afrikaner community of whom he once was considered to be the torch-bearer. Much more in contact with the experiences of the newly urbanized Afrikaner community were the new organic intellectuals – academics, clergy, teachers, civil servants, lawyers, and so on – those depicted within the neo-Marxist orthodoxy as the 'petty bourgeoisie' in search of a mass base. Instead of simply reducing an account of their activities to their presumed class position, I have argued that these intellectuals articulated a discourse allowing other Afrikaners to make sense of what was happening around them, a discourse which provided new forms of identification, attributing ills as well as offering positive solutions to their condition. In understanding the emergence and efficacy of the strands of discourse to be constitutive of apartheid it is, on my reading, more important to focus on the production of those new subject positions than to reduce politics to 'underlying class interests'. To do the latter would not only be to presume the existence of a priori interests, but also to miss what is crucial to any account of politics: the production of discursive horizons which allow people to make sense of their history. Without an understanding of the fashioning of these imaginary horizons, we will remain incapable of accounting for the reasons as to why the activities of these intellectuals succeeded in the manner they did.

My account also stressed that the process of producing a new imaginary was fraught with differences and divisions. The proliferation of fractions and struggles within the Afrikaner community in the 1930s and 1940s attests to the extent to which identities were dislocated. The spawning of what O'Meara calls an 'array of weird and wonderful lunatic fringe Afrikaner political groupings'[165] is evidence of the depth of the political vacuum which existed at the time, a vacuum which primarily consisted in the absence of discourses which could give coherence and sense to people's experiences. The condition of possibility for the 'weird and the wonderful' to exercise such a strong influence on the direction of the *volksbeweging* was a dislocation of previous modes of identification, modes which no longer seemed to provide the answers they once had. In their place, the production of a multiplication of 'others' abounded: to the Native and poor white questions the *volksbeweging* added the coloured, Asian and Jewish questions, overlayed with an incitement against the communist and British-imperialist dangers.

The question never addressed in the orthodox literature on Afrikaner nationalism concerns the precise role and function these 'others' had in the constitution of an imaginary articulated around an exclusivist Afrikaner nationalist identity. Central to the argument here is, as I have argued earlier, an understanding of the fact that a society can relate to itself only on condition that it forges a representation of its unity. This need for the representation of forms of unity, under normal circumstances, goes undetected. It is only once a society enters into a period of crisis, that is to say, a period in which the self-evident nature of its forms of representation is put into question, that it appears as a problem. It is my contention that the two decades spanning the period before the victory of the HNP at the polls constituted such a period of crisis. The dislocations of identity experienced at the time, discussed in the bulk of this chapter, called forth the need to reflect on and reconstitute a form of representation which would be able, once again, to suture the dislocated identities and reinstitute a 'normalized' or sedimented sense of order. However, for this to happen, a novel understanding of social division, of the limits of the social order, had to be put into place. And this is precisely what was in the process of being developed with the production of a proliferation of 'others'.

The discursive production of 'others' takes place through the construction of political frontiers, and, I have argued, these decades witnessed both a breakdown of the stark and homogenizing Native/European frontier characteristic of segregationism and the construction of new frontiers. The frontiers which were to become characteristic of apartheid were by no means consolidated by the late 1940s. It would take well into the next decade, and, one could even argue, into the early 1960s, for that to happen. To account for that process, it is necessary that the precise genealogy of the various strands of thinking informing apartheid discourse be analysed. That is the subject-matter of the next chapter. Suffice it to say here that the elements of those frontiers were already in place by the 1940s, even though they had not yet received their precise articulation. Nevertheless, it is important to note that the production of 'others' around which frontiers are constituted has precious little to do with 'concrete' or empirically given groups or boundaries. A discourse on frontiers can emerge precisely only once the thought of social division is no longer determined by that of a presumed pre-existing, objective space. A number of possibilities are, therefore, logically ruled out, ranging from the attempt to relate social division to the distribution of individuals in the process of production, to efforts to think it as somehow corresponding to existing political units such as the nation-state. Both class and national forms of social division are imaginary. That is to say, they arise from precise symbolic operations, instituting and constructing forms of community. The radicality of the moment of production of a new imaginary should thus not be ignored. 'Others' are produced in and through discursive, symbolic processes, which present that production as if it is natural, and it succeeds to the extent that it provokes the subject to respond to those productions in the form of a mis-recognition: we always knew they were imperialists, that their real home was 'England'; we already thought that they were barbaric, and their actions now only confirm this to us; etc. Moreover, the production of new modes of identification for the subject involves a determinate relation to the other: I can be myself only to the extent that the other no longer prevents me from being so. *The identity of the self is thus given, constituted, by the 'other'*. That is why the production of 'others' in the discourse of the new organic intellectuals has a significance which cannot ever be reduced to their presumed class basis. Their significance is to be found exactly in the fact that it is through their production and externalization that the very thought of an exclusivist Afrikaner identity became possible. Thus, 'Afrikanerdom' did *not* gain its identity merely from the positive contents of the discourse of the organic intellectuals – the discourse to be examined in the next chapter – but it did so from the exteriorization of a series of 'others'. An exclusive Afrikanerdom was what was left once communists, English-speakers, imperialists, Natives, Asians, coloureds, Jews, traitors, are all shown to be foreign, alien. Of course, as is clear from the extreme, 'wonderful and weird', proliferation of 'others' throughout the 1930s and beyond, the moment in which 'Afrikaner identity' in all its bareness, stripped of all its exclusions, is visible, never arrives. Hence the continual production of 'others'.

The drawing of frontiers through which 'others' are excluded from the domain of the legitimate, the self, the inside, is thus the political moment *par excellence*, and is what must be grasped if we are to come to terms with the full complexity of apartheid discourse and the modes of social division instituted with it. These frontiers, as I have shown, did not arise out of some 'objective' conditions, but were entirely imaginary productions. Having said that, it is of course important to note that even such radical institution takes place within a given context and an already instituted horizon of meaning from which it must distance itself, or, at the very least, in relation to which it must situate itself. But it can never be aduced from such conditions. The reason for this is simple: if a social imaginary is disrupted or in crisis, it can no longer play the role of providing naturalized forms of identification; it cannot, therefore, act as a source or origin, in the strong sense of the word, of a new imaginary. This can be seen only too clearly from the discourse of the new organic intellectuals. While the precise relation of their discursive interventions to that of segregationist discourse will be discussed in the next chapter, it is already evident that their discourse emerged precisely in the gaps left by segregationism: its inability to solve the 'Native question' and to address the position of the newly urbanized Afrikaners and other constituencies disrupted by the processes in operation during those decades.[166]

Finally, it is important to emphasize that to focus on the activities of these organic intellectuals, and to refuse a reduction of their activities to a class basis, is not simply to reinvent the discredited liberal argument on the 'Afrikaner complexion' of both segregation and apartheid discourses. Something much more radical is at stake here, namely a reinterpretation of the relation between capitalism, on the one hand, and segregation and apartheid, on the other. Contrary to conventional wisdom, which tends either to subsume the latter under the former, or to pose a strict separation between them, my position is that the orders instituted by segregationism, as well as by apartheid, provided horizons *within* which capitalist relations of production had to be ordered. This is not to say that there were no tensions between them. Rather, it is to emphasize that even questions of production, the economic ordering of society, and so forth, are, in the last instance, meaningful practices, and that they are fundamentally shaped by the horizons of intelligibility instituted with segregationism and apartheid. The precise differences in these horizons, and also of their relations to capitalist practices, will be explored in the rest of this book. It is already clear, however, from the discussion of the contestation around discourses of class, such as evidenced in the encounter between the *volksbeweging* and the KWU, that the extent to which subjects were interpellated by discourses of class was a matter of hegemonic struggle, and success depended upon which discursive horizon could make better sense of a series of dislocations of identity. The fact, for instance, that the KWU was successful in its resistance to the *volksbeweging's* anti-class offensive can be accounted for in large part by the fact that the Union did not shrink from addressing the specificity of the position of its workers: the Afrikaner women interpellated into the KWU were constructed not simply as homogenized class subjects, but as Afrikaner women from a rural background, newly urbanized and proletarianized.

The battle for the heart of 'Afrikanerdom' was thus a battle for hegemony, for the occupation of the terrain of moral and intellectual leadership from which sense could be made of economic changes and other contingent events which disrupted sedimented and naturalized forms of identification. It is in that context that dislocation, as a theoretical category, has to be understood. To talk of the dislocation of forms of identification is to make visible the sense in which all social and political identities, ultimately, are the results of contingent historical, symbolic practices, and not of underlying, a priori interests. This means that history also cannot be understood in terms of a Hegelian linear, teleological unfolding, or in terms of a Marxist conception of necessary stages, both of which presume the existence of an essential reality to be uncovered. Far from providing a picture of the way things 'really were', a historical articulation of the past, based upon a recognition of the contingency of identity, reveals the processes of production and construction of the representations through which history is given its sense. For me, this necessitates a focus on the moments of dislocation of established and given orders, those moments when things are still at stake. Accounting for historical events, on this reading, does not take the form of a reference back to a space of representation which is supposed to explain them in full. Rather, the analysis has attempted to show the contingent character of all forms of representation, as well as their ultimate failure to master history. This also means that our task is not to play the role of an omniscient observer of history whose gaze can detect the 'objective' sense of events which escape the historical agents themselves. The analysis aims at exactly the opposite: to dissolve the apparent fixity and naturalness of social and political structures, and to show the openness of the terrain in which they were constituted. I have already addressed the extent to which the 1930s and 1940s were decades in which such dislocation of identity took place, and have begun to analyse the precise meaning given to contingent historical events, shown in their contingency precisely as a result of the need to give them meaning. It is now necessary to turn to a more detailed analysis of the precise genealogy of the various movements which informed these meaning-giving practices.

2

Apartheid as Myth: A Genealogy of the *Volkseie*

> Ideologies ... are the 'true' philosophy, because they are those philosophical 'vulgarizations' that bring the masses to concrete action and to the transformation of reality.[1]

> ... if the genealogist refuses to extend his faith in metaphysics, if he listens to history, he finds that there is 'something altogether different' behind things: not a timeless and essential secret, but the secret that they have no essence or that their essence was fabricated in a piecemeal fashion from alien forms.[2]

In 'Nietzsche, Genealogy, History' Foucault draws out the operation of the different figures of the 'origin' in Nietzsche's writings, and proceeds to delimit his understanding of genealogy as an analysis which is not in pursuit of the pure essence of things, of what was already there in its full glory as primordial truth, but which seeks to locate this search in the context of invasions, plunderings, disguises and ploys.[3] In short, Foucault proposes, in opposition to the assumptions informing the field of 'history of ideas', to explore the ignoble beginnings of things, and their implicatedness in struggles, and their occurrence in sometimes unpromising places.[4] Genealogy is an irreverent, essentially political practice, disturbing what was previously considered immobile, fragmenting what was thought unified, showing the heterogeneity of what was imagined to be consistent with itself.[5] In order to grasp the full implications of this Foucauldian insight for the analysis of the beginnings of apartheid, it is necessary to tease out in greater detail what exactly is entailed in this practice of reading which aims to dissolve the apparent unity of forms of discourse such that the multiplicity and undecidability of discursive figures may become visible.[6] I have argued in chapter 1 that the ostensible unity of the Afrikaner *volksbeweging* belies the extent to which different conceptions of identity and a variety of 'readings' of the condition of dislocation of identity experienced during the two decades running up the electoral victory of the HNP in 1948 marked and informed the myth which was in the process of being articulated. This chapter explores these different, sometimes contradictory conceptions, as well as their articulation into a mythical form, in more detail.[7] This will furnish the basis for the argument concerning the specificity of apartheid *vis-à-vis* its segregationist precursor, and will foreshadow the analysis of the logic of apartheid in chapter 3.

If one of the aims of a genealogical analysis is to make visible the fragmentary basis of what is considered to be unitary, it is necessary to start our discussion with the characterization of 'Afrikanerdom' and the nature of apartheid. Studies on Afrikaner nationalism have recently begun to emphasize both the non-unitary nature of 'Afrikanerdom' and the only partially formulated character of 'apartheid' at the moment of its institution.[8] In the previous chapter I referred to O'Meara's work, which has been seminal in the initial discernment of the non-unitary nature of the nationalist project. Arguing against liberal conceptions of a self-generating, a priori, monolithic conception of 'Afrikanerdom', O'Meara holds that Afrikaner nationalism was a highly differentiated phenomenon, consisting of changing, yet identifiable class forces.[9] However, O'Meara's account contains several problematic assumptions. The most fundamental of these is the tendency to treat 'ethnic' forms of identification as if they could be reduced to a presumed class basis. Working from a neo-Marxist perspective, the liberal concern with a unitary *volk* is consequently replaced by a disaggregation of it in terms of its constituent class elements. A similar tendency can be discerned in the analysis of the 'content' of the apartheid project in Posel's work *The Making of Apartheid*. Posel starts by putting into question the idea that a single 'master plan' for the implementation of apartheid was in place by 1948, and shows the impact of resistance on its implementation. However, in the process apartheid is reduced to a concern with influx control policies.[10] Both the analysis of the constituent elements of 'Afrikanerdom' by O'Meara and the interpretation of the content of the apartheid project by Posel thus effected a disaggregation of the presumed homogeneity of Afrikaner nationalism. From the point of view of a genealogical analysis these accounts remain problematic for they simply substitute one form of unity for another. The disaggregation acted merely as a prologue to the reinscription of a unitary and necessary emphasis on class division.[11]

The race–class debate between liberals and neo-Marxists – from which O'Meara and Posel's work springs – seems antiquated from the point of view of theoretical developments in the 1980s and 1990s associated with the rubrics of post-structuralism, deconstruction and post-coloniality. However, many of the assumptions informing this debate are still in place and they have to be questioned on a theoretical level if the 'logic of addition', evident in many neo-Marxist responses to post-structuralist critiques of class reductionist accounts of social division, is to be problematized. Many neo-Marxists as well as social historians, in the name of a broadening of substantive interests, have taken on board issues concerning gender and, more recently, ethnicity.[12] The manner in which this has occurred is, nevertheless, highly questionable. A case in point is the work of Bonner, Delius and Posel, who argue that ethnicity and gender decisively shaped the history of black proletarianization in South Africa, without, simultaneously, inquiring into the reasons why an examination of these factors had previously been excluded from neo-Marxist analyses.[13] This empiricist tendency omnivorously to absorb the new – concerns with race, gender and ethnicity – without rethinking the old class-based paradigm raises a series of questions which cannot be resolved by remaining on the level of substantive analysis. It is my contention that the old framework of analysis cannot remain secure against the subversive effects of supplementarity introduced by the new categories of analysis. It is impossible to affirm both the purity and originary nature of class analysis, and therefore its fullness, and the need for supplementing the origin with additional categories of analysis. As Derrida argues, if a supplement supplements, if it fills, it fills a void. The supplement is not simply added on to the 'positivity of a presence', but is indicative of a certain lack in the original.[14] In term of the analysis the nature of South African politics, it means that the process of 'addition' cannot simply continue without a simultaneous recasting of theoretical paradigms.

While some attempts have been made to address these questions on a theoretical level, these attempts continue to be hampered by an inability to move away from a priori, substantive categories towards a non-substantial, non-aprioristic conception of identity formation which emphasizes the constitutive role of negativity in its production. Such a shift would problematize attempts to account for subject formation by drawing on positive knowledge, for the latter precisely negates the moment of the constitution of reality by placing itself in an illusory position of 'claiming to have an overview of Being'.[15] Put differently, this illusion involves the claim to having access to a viewpoint from which a total representation of history is possible. This tendency is at its clearest in liberal and neo-Marxist accounts of how racial or class-based forms of social division could have been superseded: in the case of the former, apartheid has been conceived of as a pre-capitalist remnant which would disappear as a result of economic modernization; in the case of the latter, apartheid was reduced to a class project which would be overcome with a social revolution. In both cases, there has been an attempt to offer a complete representation of a logic underlying the movement of history. Society has a being, it is argued, that exists independently of theory, and that constitutes its ultimate reality. The task of the theoretician is simply to reveal the movement of being. As I have argued in the conclusion to chapter 1, in the use of 'positive' categories of analysis, the problem of the political is entirely elided here. With the ascendancy of the logic of necessity – a necessary movement of history – the very problem of the institution of the social and the precise and historically specific, contingent forms that it may take is negated. Any attempt to take these considerations into account must, therefore, focus on the complex processes of simultaneous generation of social division and forms of identification, processes which cannot be accounted for by assuming in an a priori fashion what form such modes of identification will take.

Once the aprioristic nature of identity is put into question in favour of an analysis of the production of forms of identification, the problems discussed earlier are remedied. We no longer find ourselves in the terrain of a logic of addition, quite simply, for we no longer set out from the assumption of a pure, orginary form of social division which must, of necessity, mark all social formations, and in terms of which all other forms of identification are to be considered as secondary and supplementary. Rather, the problem of the political, that is, 'the problem of the institution of the social, . . . of the definition and articulation of social relations in a field crisscrossed with antagonism',[16] becomes the primary concern. In contrast to the objectivism of the neo-Marxist models of analysis, the investigation of the discursive production of images for identification thus emphasizes the essentially political character of these processes. It is only once this is realized that the relation between the political character of all forms of identification and the genealogical strategy of analysis becomes clear. As Foucault argues:

> . . . if interpretation is the violent or surreptitious appropriation of a system of rules, which in itself has no essential meaning, in order to impose a direction, to bend it to a new will, to force a participation in a different game, and to subject it to secondary rules, then the development of humanity is a series of interpretations. The role of genealogy is to record its history. . . . [17]

What my account of the formation of apartheid as myth aims at is to record the ignoble history of the contingent processes and struggles through which a new rule was imposed, through which it became hegemonic, and thus, through which the myth could be turned into an imaginary surface of inscription, imposing a direction and forcing participation in a different game. The analysis of this process consists, in the first place, of an investigation of the contradictory elements which entered into its formation. This chapter investigates the discourses produced at the Potchefstroom University for Christian Higher Education, the culturalist discourses of Meyer and Diederichs, the discursive reproduction of figures of race in the works of Eloff and Cronje, situating these interventions in the political terrain. In the second place, it offers an analysis of the construction of a new form of unity out of these contradictory discourses without a reduction of their differences. It is at this point that the theoretical and substantive pertinence of the category of myth for the analysis of symbolic formations will be shown. Finally, this reading of apartheid is situated by offering a distinct analysis of its relation to segregation in terms of the category of iterability, which allows one to rethink the elements of continuity and discontinuity between the two imaginaries. In all these cases, I start out from the premisses outlined above, resisting the temptation of assuming a priori forms of social division to be in existence, as well as avoiding the temptation to impute unity onto the discourse by reducing it to one of its constituent elements.

Organic Intellectuals and the Production of New Mythical Spaces

> The active man of politics is a creator, an innovator [*suscitatoro*]. But he neither creates from nothing nor does he move in the turbid void of his own particular dreams. He bases himself on the effective reality. . . . To apply one's will to the creation of a new equilibrium among the forces that really exist and are operative . . . one moves within the terrain of effective reality . . . in order to dominate and transcend it.[18]

The struggle over the meaning and implications of the notion of *volkseenheid* (unity of the *volk*) was fought out on a number of distinct fronts during the 1930s and 1940s. Of these, the struggle on the religious, cultural and political terrains, insofar as they could be separated, were of crucial importance.[19] In providing a genealogy of the formation of apartheid as myth, I analyse a number of important interventions in these fields, concentrating on the extent to which they provided distinct accounts of the condition of the Afrikaner *volk* in the 1930s and 1940s. This focus is one which emerges from the discourses themselves, and the account offered thus sets out to provide a reading of the internal logics of each of the interventions. In doing so, I also show how these primary concerns influenced and shaped other areas of analysis, such as their readings of the competing ideologies of fascism, national socialism, liberalism and communism, and of democracy. It is important that the limits of the discussion offered here are clearly specified: in this chapter, the emphasis falls on the production of the impossible object of the *volkseie*.[20] The effects which the production of this object had for the relation between whites and blacks is the subject of chapter 3.

Some peremptory theoretical remarks on the role of organic intellectuals in the production of new discursive formations are necessary here. It is customary in discussions of Afrikaner nationalism to concentrate on a number of intellectuals who are generally recognized to have played a crucial role in the production of Afrikaner nationalist discourse. More often than not, however, the activities of these intellectuals, and the question of their subjectivity, are not discussed.[21] It is to this that I now turn. I have argued that a genealogical analysis, emphasizing the political nature of all forms of identification, has to start from a non-substantive analysis of those very forms. This process, nevertheless, does not proceed without categories orienting the analysis. In this respect, the category of political frontiers and their constitutive role in the institution of forms of social division, as discussed earlier, is absolutely central. The process of production of new frontiers is intimately linked to the activities of the intellectuals for which a space is opened up in situations of severe dislocation. Hence, dislocation is the condition for the institution of a new myth. That is, it consists in the opening up of a terrain in which a 'decision' has to be instituted.

For this reason, the relation between the moment of the 'decision', that is, the establishment of a new common sense, rule or mythical space, and the nature of subjectivity appropriate to this operation has to be addressed. Laclau argues that the subject in a radical sense, the subject in terms of which the decision has to be theorized, is nothing but the distance between the dislocated structure and the decision.[22] The subject in this sense has to be distinguished from the subject positions agents may occupy in a given structure, which may be put into question as a result of the dislocation of the structure. Several dimensions open up here which need to be investigated systematically: the general and abstract argument concerning the opening of a space for subjectivity which acts as the condition of possibility for the institution of a new rule; the relation between the subject and the context of articulation; and, finally, the conditions of success pertaining to the dissemination of the thought of these organic intellectuals.

Let us start with an elaboration of the difference between the 'radical' conception of the subject – as subject of lack – and the idea of subject positions. The latter is theorized expressly against the notion of the subject as substantial, essential entity, given in advance and dominating the social process. In terms of the analysis of discursive formations, the emphasis in this case falls on the study of subject positions in social networks, disciplinary techniques, hierarchies, and so on; that is, the relative subject positions that empower, denigrate, subordinate, exclude.[23] In short, it takes us towards a Foucauldian analysis of the production of such subjectivities and the constitution and creation of positions of enunciation. It has, however, been argued that this sort of analysis misrecognizes the extent to which the subject is always constitutively marked by the impossibility of its own full constitution. Žižek articulates this position most fully, and it is worth quoting him at length:

> To explain this distinction between the subject and subject-positions, let us take again the case of class antagonism. The relationship between the classes is antagonistic in the Laclau/Mouffe sense of the term, i.e. it is . . . the 'impossible' relationship between the two terms: each of them is preventing the other from achieving its identity with itself, to become what it really is. As soon as I recognize myself, in an ideological interpellation, as a 'proletarian', I am engaged in the social reality, fighting against the 'capitalist' who is preventing me from realizing fully my human potential, blocking my full development. Where here is the ideological illusion proper to the subject-position? It lies precisely in the fact that it is the 'capitalist', this external enemy, who is preventing me from achieving an identity with myself: the illusion is that after the eventual annihilation of the antagonistic enemy, I will finally abolish the antagonism and arrive at an identity with myself. . . . However, to grasp the notion of antagonism in its most radical dimension, we should invert the relationship between the two terms: it is not the external enemy who is preventing me from achieving identity with

> myself, but every identity is already in itself blocked, marked by an impossibility, and the external enemy is simply the small piece, the rest of reality upon which we 'project' or 'externalize' this intrinsic, immanent impossibility.[24]

It is clear that the movement towards the subject of lack has some advantages for the analysis of the functioning of discursive formations and the production of myths: it allows one to make visible the ultimate impossibility of ever attaining a full identity, and thus points to the ever present need for identification of the subject. No one identification can succeed, in principle, in fully suturing the identity of the subject. However, as is abundantly clear in the above quoted passage, this shift also has further consequences for the precise form which an analysis of discursive formations is to take. The movement towards the subject of lack potentially entails a movement away from the analysis of the relation to the 'external enemy'. It is this dimension of the shift that could be damaging for political analysis, for once an anti-humanistic turn is taken, the important point *is* to focus on the study of disciplinary techniques, the production of subjectivities, and on those discursive mechanisms which offer images for identification. In short, the point is not simply to make visible the final impossibility of all identity, but also to analyse the manner in which subjects have historically been produced in and through micro-networks of power relations.[25] Only a combination of both these conceptions of subjectivity will produce the tools necessary to account for the articulation of a new common sense and the production of an alternative mythical space. Accounting for its production necessitates both the theorization of the bringing into being of something new, and the paradoxical effacement of the subject in this moment of the decision. As Žižek argues, the subject's act of decision succeeds by becoming invisible, by 'positivizing' itself in a new symbolic network wherein it locates and explains itself as a result of a historical process.

The 'subjects' articulating the new common sense of apartheid were neither radical creators, nor simply the occupiers of subject positions. As argued earlier, the articulation of a sense of dislocation in the case of the institution of the apartheid project drew upon available – alternative – elements, only to rearticulate them into a new horizon in terms of which they could construct their distinctive account of the predicament of the Afrikaner *volk*. In this sense, they acted as *bricoleurs* who encoded and recoded images and ideas, giving them new and uncharacteristic twists.[26] As Lévi-Strauss argues, the *bricoleur* 'interrogates all the heterogeneous objects of which his treasury is composed to discover what each of them could "signify" and so to contribute to the definition of a set which has yet to materialize . . .'. In a way, *bricolage* is society thinking itself. The *bricoleur*'s task is to provoke a confrontation which is so forceful that a new form of thought, of classification is released into the world.[27] This is precisely what occurred as a result of the activities of these intellectuals. *In the very process of the constitution of a new common sense, a new community and a new political grammar were brought into being*. They thus played the dual role of producers and representatives of the *volk*. In terms of their role of producing articulations constituting a new common sense, these *bricoleurs* can be considered to be founders of discursivity in the Foucauldian sense.[28] They are both the authors of texts in the traditional sense, and the constructors of a new discursive horizon. Rather than regarding them as 'free-floating' constructors, their interventions are to be analysed for the new elements which they brought into the discursive horizon, and, following from that, for the new possibilities opened up in them.[29] What is important, therefore, is not only what was literally said and written in their texts, but the manner in which these texts participated beyond, apart from their authors, in the production of a new discursive horizon. Their interventions fixed new limits to the sayable, established new meaning-giving horizons in terms of which events and history could be made sense of, created new spaces and positions of enunciation, and brought new discursive objects into being. In short, they participated in a process which created and sustained a horizon from which a novel discourse could be spoken and heard, and accepted as authoritative. This process went well beyond the activities of any one of these intellectuals. That is why, in addition to an investigation of the content and structure of their individual interventions, it is necessary to make visible the logic which informed the articulation which was to constitute the new common sense.

At this point the issue of the diffusion of new ideas and the condition of possibility for their success arises. Not just any discourse put forward will be successful. Certain conceptions take hold, while other do not. In chapter 1, I contextualized the reasons why the specific articulation of the sense of dislocation – associated with the process of rapid urbanization – provided by the new organic intellectuals succeeded. This involved two closely related processes: the meaning given to these experiences and the simultaneous disarticulation of the previous discourse of segregation. It is therefore clear that something more than the mere availability of discourses is at stake. They have to have a certain credibility. That is, they have to be related to the historical conditions and experiences of the group to which they are addressed. The thought of the organic intellectuals, to be discussed shortly, is remarkable precisely in the great care they took to relate their new readings to the 'historical experience' of the Afrikaner *volk*. What I have also shown was the extent to which this 'historical experience' came into being precisely as a result of their activities. In consideration of the conditions of success of the activities of these organic intellectuals, it is therefore important to investigate more closely the precise content of their articulations, although, as Gramsci points out, the rational and logically coherent form of new conceptions, while of significance, is far from decisive:

> It can be decisive, but in a secondary way, when the person in question is already in a state of intellectual crisis, wavering between the old and the new, when he has lost his faith in the old and has not yet come down in favour of the new. . . . [30]

The elements of logical coherence, authority of the speaker and organization are thus important insofar as a 'general orientation' of a crisis has been reached. To put it in our terminology, these factors come into their own only once a dislocation is experienced which makes possible the space for a rearticulation of old or an introduction of new conceptions. It is here that the repetition of arguments, the education of the populace and the production of new intellectual elites is of prime importance, for, as Gramsci points out, it is this which really modifies the 'ideological panorama' of an age.[31] Nevertheless, the precise content of the arguments are important insofar as they participate in the construction and reconstruction of political frontiers which give mythical spaces their identity.

To capture more precisely the nature of these new spaces and articulations, I use the term 'myth' in the sense in which Laclau has theorized it.[32] The processes through which the sedimentation of a new common sense is instituted can be formally disaggregated into two distinct moments: the formation of a mythical space and the transformation of this space into an imaginary. Here I concentrate only on the former.[33] A mythical space is a space of representation through which an attempt is made to provide a principle of reading of a given situation which is experienced as a dislocation. As Laclau formulates it: the work of myth is to suture that dislocated space by the constitution of a new space of representation. A myth, as a new principle of reading, thus attempts to reconstruct the social as objectively given; its operation is nothing other than an endeavour to reconstitute the absent, impossible unity of a society via the naturalization of its political frontiers arising from the demands of a particular group. Insofar as it succeeds, that is, insofar as it manages to become institutionalized, it can be said to have been hegemonic in its efforts to reconstruct a 'lost unity' through the absorption of dislocated elements. Under such circumstances, the myth becomes an imaginary surface of inscription capable of accounting not only for the 'experiences' and demands of a particular group, but for all possible demands which may arise. The thought of the organic intellectuals which we are about to discuss – the Scripturalists at the Potchefstroom University for Christian Higher Education, the cultural nationalists and the racial determinists – facilitated the production of such a new myth and put into place the conditions for the later expansion of that myth into an imaginary. The construction of this myth was closely linked to their reading of the condition of the Afrikaner *volk*, and, in that sense, aimed to produce that which was specific and particular to the 'experience' of the *volk*: the *volkseie*.

Scripturalists: The Articulation of Calvinist Christian Nationalism

Much has been written on the relation between apartheid and the group of Dutch Reformed Churches.[34] These churches played a crucial role not only in contributing to the formulation of apartheid discourse, but also in disseminating the discourse to the wider Afrikaner community.[35] Indeed, the beginnings of a sense of unease with the situation of the Afrikaner in the city was first articulated by the churches, which also played a seminal role in the formation of a number of commissions of inquiry investigating topics as wide-ranging as the question of 'mixed marriages' and the dangers of 'communism'. The point here is not to investigate in detail the range of interventions by these churches in the formation of the political and social order in South Africa prior to and during the decades of the 1930s and 1940s.[36] Rather, the aim is to make clear in what sense the formulation of a Christian national perspective,[37] particularly by the intellectuals associated with the Potchefstroom University for Christian Higher Education, contributed to the formation of the new common sense which was later to be named 'apartheid'. These intellectuals played a central role in its production, thus providing the politicians of the period with a new 'moral' language in which to couch their policies. From 1933, a small group at Potchefstroom began to explore questions concerning race, ethnicity and nationality in *Koers* (*Direction*), the mouthpiece of the Federation of Calvinist Student Associations.[38] In chapter 3, I will discuss the manner in which the groundwork layed in this journal was to be extended to wider and wider areas of concern. Here, however, I will concentrate on the work of H.G. Stoker and the precise manner in which he articulated a series of links between Calvinist theology and the emerging radical Afrikaner nationalist movement.

Shortly before his internment for his activities in the *Ossewabrandwag*, Stoker published *Die Stryd om die Ordes* (*The Struggle of the Orders*), in which he set out not only to develop a comparative understanding of communism (Bolshevism), fascism, national socialism, liberalism and Calvinism, but also to investigate the applicability of these different ordering principles to the South African context. Traditionally, Stoker's work specifically, and that of the Calvinist intellectuals[39] at Potchefstroom University more generally, have been treated simply in terms of their popularization of the Kuyperian concept of *soewereiniteit in eie kring* (sovereignty in own sphere).[40] However, the manner in which Stoker recast the notion of sovereignty of spheres is crucial, for while Kuyper had worked out the details of the principle of sovereignty in own sphere, he did not address the question of the *vervlegdheid* (intertwinedness) and mutual dependency of spheres.[41] This, Stoker saw as one of his main contributions and it is this which allowed him to offer his distinct political philosophy in opposition to both liberalism and national socialism.

Before discussing the specificity of Stoker's contribution, it is necessary briefly to reiterate what was at stake in Kuyper's principle of the sovereignty of spheres. Abraham Kuyper, as leader of the Dutch neo-Calvinist movement, was staunchly opposed to both the French Revolution and the spread of liberal secular ideals. In opposition to liberal uniformism, he proposed the notion of sovereignty of spheres according to which different domains of existence were to be regarded as separate from each other, while nevertheless subject to the ultimate authority of God. This allowed him to develop an argument for the separation of church and state, as well as the separation of peoples into different nations:[42]

> The division of humanity into states and peoples . . . did not come about as a result of human wisdom, but was brought about through the Grace of God. Humanity would much rather defend itself against division and fragmentation. Hence Babel and hence the recurring efforts to dissolve states into one world empire. And this is the real meaning of the confusion

> of tongues, that God thereby called into being the division of humanity into peoples, nations and states.[43]

The whole debate on 'Babel' and the specific articulation of it to the South African context only really came into full force in the context of the 1950s, and will be discussed in depth in chapter 3. It is crucial to note, in this respect, that Kuyper's work consisted in a delicate 'balance of paradoxes' from which no clear political position could be read off.[44] Much depended, therefore, precisely on how his thought was to be grafted onto the new context. It is quite clear from Stoker's work that the Kuyperian principle served as much more than 'a useful repository of evocative slogans'.[45] Indeed, Stoker's recasting of it in the context of South Africa in the 1940s led to the articulation of a distinct set of political doctrines developed specifically to address the situation of the Afrikaner *volk* in the context of the *broedertwis* (arguments between brothers) of the 1940s. In order to come to terms with the use to which Stoker put his development of Kuyperian Calvinism, it is useful to specify the precise context in which he articulated his thought.[46] Stoker's aim in *Die Stryd om die Ordes* was to develop a typology of competing principles of order: fascism, national socialism, communism, liberalism and Calvinism. The core of this text deals with the struggle between the different orders at a time in which calls for a 'new order' were prevalent, not only in South Africa, but also in Europe.[47] Stoker explicitly addressed the question as to whether South Africa needed such a new order. Echoing the statement of principle which introduced the series, *Koers in die Krisis* (*Direction in the Crisis*), namely that Afrikanerdom was being overwhelmed by alien cultural products, and was in a profound spiritual crisis, Stoker argued that the ignorance of the *volk* had to be banished. The *volk* had to know its enemies if it were to struggle against them, and against the imposition of foreign orders on it.

How did Stoker understand the nature of 'the *volk*' to which his remarks were addressed? In line with the emerging consensus of the time, Stoker held *volkere* and nations to be organic creations of God. It is here that the theological account of the language confusion at Babel took on its full significance in the thought of the Calvinist intellectuals. A conception of God as Hammabdil, the Great Divider, was the nodal point around which J.D. du Toit's (Totius) intervention at the 1944 *Volkskongres* on the 'Religious Basis of our Race Policy' was organized: just as God separated light and dark, heaven and earth, so did He ordain the separation of one nation from another.[48] Du Toit drew two conclusions from this, namely that what

God has joined together, no man should separate, and that which God has separated, no man should join together. From this it followed that the unity of the *volk* had to be protected. Against what was argued to be a 'deadly uniformity' inherent in liberal thought, Du Toit and other Calvinist intellectuals asserted that there could be no *gelykstelling* (equalization) and no *verbastering* (bastardization) of *volkere*. Stoker concurred in this general view, but emphasized that a *volk* was characterized by 'blood, language and culture': '[J]ust as body and soul formed a unity . . . so, too, the *volk*'s blood-tie and cultural bond formed a unity, in which the deeper organic nature of the *volk* was realized.'[49] For Stoker, the Afrikaner *volk* could only be characterized in terms of its history and, therefore, in terms of the struggles through which it was produced. The identity of Afrikanerdom was thus given insofar as it could be distinguished from and against a series of 'others'. This is the crucial context for the understanding of Stoker's intervention, for while 'British-Jewish capitalism' and Afrikaner liberalism are equally vilified, it is clear that the prime enemy of Afrikanerdom was British liberalism, both in its imperialist and South African forms.[50] Stoker emphasized the fact that the curse of *broedertwis* as well as of *volksverskeuring* (diremption of the *volk*) which characterized the internal history of Afrikanerdom had to be combated for they arose from attempts to unite with English-speaking compatriots.[51]

Die Stryd om die Ordes, moreover, set out to delineate the nature and character of the *true* Afrikaner *volk*. This occurred through a double articulation. On the one hand, the specificity of a truly Afrikaans principle of ordering, contained in a precise *Weltanschauung*, had to be specified. On the other, divisions within Afrikanerdom had to be addressed in order to come to an understanding of what it meant to be truly Afrikaans. These two dimensions were, of course, intimately related. Stoker argued that it was necessary to distinguish three distinct conceptions of Christian nationalism internal to Afrikanerdom – Christian national Afrikaans liberalism, Christian Afrikaans national socialism and Calvinism – all of which gave pride of place to God and religion while recognizing the autonomy of human bonds (the church, culture, and so forth); all of which emphasized the importance of the Afrikaans language, a republican state form and the need to liberate the *volk* from British-Jewish capitalist oppression; all of which were Christian, distanced themselves from national socialism and set out to fight foreign liberalism. While Christian Afrikaans liberalists distanced themselves from foreign British liberalism by emphasizing Afrikaner Christian nationalism, they, nevertheless, remained liberal in that they held onto the principle of the rational–moral individual. The root cause of division within Afrikanerdom was to be found in the activities of this grouping, for they propagated unity with English-speaking South Africans, and relegated 'being an Afrikaner' to something less than organic and less than determined by blood.[52] Christian Afrikaans national socialism, while distinguishing itself from its German form, nevertheless suffered from similar problems: it recognized only one (and therefore no) political party; government and the state were elevated above the *volk*; and it disregarded the autonomy of spheres of human life. Calvinism, then, emerged as the only ordering principle which, while countering both the evils of liberalism (the anarchy of competing and clashing philosophies of life) and those of national socialism (oppression and uniformity of philosophy of life), was also capable of taking into consideration what was 'true' in each of them. In particular, it could accommodate the autonomy both of the individual and of the *volk*, while adding to that the autonomy of other human bonds, uniting all of those under the principle of the absolute sovereignty of God. Just as segregationism earlier presented itself as steering a middle road between scientific racism (associated with repression) and Victorian liberalism (associated with assimilation), Calvinism now emerged as the middle course between two extremes, and had the additional advantage of being historically grounded in the experiences of the *volk*.

Politically, Calvinism recognized both the sovereignty of spheres and their interdependence (*vervlegtheid*). It is here that the import of Stoker's rearticulation of the Kuyperian principle is shown in full, for not only is each of the spheres of life (the church, the state, culture, science) autonomous, but they are mutually dependent. While each was sovereign in its own sphere, and had its own function and calling, they were characterized by their universal interaction and their harmonious supplementation of each other. Stoker distinguished three principles of interaction between spheres: that of free interaction, of *leenfronte* ('borrowing' fronts) and of *aksie fronte* (action fronts). Politically, the last had the most important consequences. For Stoker, the essence of human life consisted not in contemplation, but in action and struggle: the church, the *volk* and the state, each was called to action.[53] In conditions where any of the spheres did not fulfil their functions, a related sphere had to step in and act. So, for example, while the state was not normally concerned with industry, it had to step in where economic institutions did not fulfil their duties. As an example of such an intervention, the *Yster en Staal Korporasie* (YSKOR, Iron and Steel Corporation), one of the many parastatals created by the state, was cited by Stoker, and the whole conception of *volkskapitalisme* could be understood in these terms. It is important that wherever a specific sphere fell short of fulfilling its duties, criticism and change had to be brought about by constitutional means. Goal-oriented reform thus had to be distinguished from revolutionary and evolutionary conceptions of change. Reform connected the old and the new, the continuous and the discontinuous. This did not mean, however, that no radical schisms could occur. Indeed, as a result of the sinful nature of man, one often found oneself in a situation where the creation of new bonds was the only solution. For Stoker, the RDB on the economic terrain and the FAK on the cultural terrain were examples of organizations which came into being as a result of such necessary fractioning in order to struggle against that which undermined the *volk*.

While the detail of Stoker's account of the different ordering principles cannot be recounted here, it is necessary to focus on the political results of his problematization of both liberalism and national socialism, and on the conceptions of freedom and equality which arose therefrom. Communism, fascism, national socialism as well as liberalism and Calvinism all were universalistic principles of ordering. With the exception of Calvinism, they all were humanistic and anthropocentric. Calvinism was theocentric in contrast to the absolutization of the rational individual in liberalism, the worker in communism, the state in fascism and *blut und boden* nationalism in national socialism. Stoker, moreover, argued that, apart from Calvinism, none of them understood the problem of authority. Authority unequivocally came from God, and could not be based upon individual rights or economic laws. Similarly, none of them adequately grasped the relation between the different spheres of human life: they tended to a loose conglomeration (liberalism), a dissolution (communism) or complete integration (fascism) of the different terrains. Only Calvinism took full account of the autonomy and interdependency of spheres. This gave rise to the doctrine of 'diversity in unity'.

The Scriptural theory of 'diversity in unity' enabled church leaders to bring about an inversion of the Christian ethos of the uniqueness and importance of the individual, for the sake of some ultimate good to the group. The position put forward by these theologians did much to provide the later development of apartheid-cum-separate development with its 'moral' basis. The Calvinist emphasis on the respect for the principle of diversity led to the argument that different societal spheres were not to be divorced from one another. Unlike in liberal thought, there was no attempt to establish a simple division between church and nation (*volk*) and church and state. Rather, coherence and co-ordination between the different terrains and spheres was sought. Yet, this did not imply a movement towards a nullifying of differences and an eradication of the boundaries between church and state. National socialism was not acceptable. Each sphere had its own character, its own destiny and its own sovereignty. Thus, the Calvinist principle of diversity supported the separate identity of the Afrikaner people: the Afrikaner could not accept either 'dictatorial absolutism' or 'licentious liberalism'. This principle of difference was considered to be universal, while manifesting itself variedly in different historical circumstances.[54] Contrary to what liberals thought, the unity found in Christ was universal and cut across national boundaries, but it did not eliminate those boundaries.[55] The abolishment of diversity, the elimination of national and racial frontiers, proposed by liberals and the advocates of 'multi-racialism' alike, could only end in disaster. Integration would 'wipe out Afrikanerdom'.

A similar argumentative strategy was followed in discussions of freedom and equality. Human beings, it was argued, were free as such or before God. The distinctness of freedom was supplemented by a principle of 'developmental differentiation'. It did not 'deny' freedom but facilitated its development in different spheres. Equality existed only 'in the eyes of God' and was consistently held to be in opposition to the freedom inherent in difference. In terms of the political implications of these principles, differences did exist between Potchefstroom intellectuals. L.J. du Plessis, for example, held that Christian unity was compatible with the 'sharpest differences and inequalities (such as, for example, between master and slave) because it represented an invisible union of faith in Christ and did not demand the abolition of practical differences.' On the other hand, H. du Plessis held that since African cultural and racial characteristics had a divine origin, whites did not dare tamper with God's work; races had to be kept separate, but equal, and this demanded total segregation.[56] While the full implications of these differences of interpretation were only to become clear in the 1950s in the context of debates on the nature of apartheid, it is important that these articulations of notions of freedom and equality – which were inextricably bound up with divisions between 'groups' – arose from within the context of theological discussions during the 1930s and 1940s.

The creation of a new order thus had to avoid the anthropocentrism of foreign ideas, and had to be firmly grounded in the *volk*'s own tradition of Calvinism. It had to recognize the absolute sovereignty of

God, the dependent sovereignty of the individual, the autonomy of human bonds (sovereignty in own sphere), the free and interdependent interaction between the individual, human bonds and the sphere of culture. Above all, it had to recognize that the needs of the *volk* were greater than those of the individual or of any of the other human bonds.[57] This exaltation of the needs of the *volk*, and of the divine division of nations, was later more systematically to be articulated to the wider anthropological discourses which moved away from a Native/European division to that of ethnic divisions between peoples. The theological justification for the existence of separate *volkere* was also echoed in other domains of struggle, most notably that of the terrain of culture. Before we give attention to it, it is important to point out that this vision was utilized to interpellate not only the *volk* generally, but also the women of the *volk*, who were regarded as the bearers of tradition.

In *Uit Vroue-Harte* (*From Women's Hearts*), a text only published in 1950 but written during 1945–46 under the editorship of J.D. Vorster and H.G. Stoker, this is abundantly clear. The preface to this text, written by the well-known Afrikaans poet J.D. du Toit (Totius), stated that the call to 'save the children' had to be supplemented by the call to 'save the mothers'. The aim of the book was to address 'women's problems' as women saw them from a religious vantage-point, in order to give hope and encouragement to women on the road of Christian nationalism. While much has been made of the manner in which women were interpellated as subjects of Afrikaner nationalism, very little exists by way of dealing with their own contribution to its construction during the 1940s. Many Christian organizations, both social and church-based, existed which aimed specifically to foster and propagate the 'moral, cultural and social interests of the Afrikaner *volk* and its youth in accordance with national and Christian principles'.[58] These included the *Afrikaanse Calvinistiese Vrouevereniging* (ACVV, Afrikaans Christian Women's Association), the *Oranje Vrouevereniging* (OVV, Orange Women's Association), the *Suid-Afrikaanse Vrouevereniging* (SAVV, South African Women's Association) and the *Natal Christelike Vrouevereniging* (NCVV, National Christian Women's Association), all of which were affiliated to the *Federale Vroueraad* (FVR, Federal Women's Council) and which had a combined membership of 15,000 women by 1946. These organizations had representation on a variety of government councils, including the National Housing Council, the Labour Advice Bureau, the Propaganda Committee of the Nutrition Council and the National Welfare Council. Their activities concentrated on health campaigns, on adult education, care for the elderly, as well as on the creation of institutions for working 'boys and girls' who needed to be sheltered in an Afrikaans and Christian atmosphere from the 'damaging, sinful and foreign influences' of life in the cities.[59] While it is not possible here to go into the details of these activities, it is important briefly to survey the manner in which they saw the relevance of the Afrikaner nationalist project to them.

The topics dealt with by the women writers were wide-ranging. For example, Tini Vorster's contribution to *Uit Vroue-harte* entitled 'Ontworteldheid' ('Uprootedness')[60] echoed many of the concerns of the other contributors: the position of young *Boeredogters* who had to leave home to make use of the city's many labour possibilities, and who, in the process, lost (*losgeraak*) their bonds with the *volk*. The tone of the contributions was clearly set by a sense of the radical change to which the Afrikaner community had been exposed for over four decades. H.S. Brink described it in the following terms:

> Humanity is confused and bewildered in a maelstrom of hate and enmity. . . . This stream also flows over our *volk*, a stream of worldliness, immorality, sensual enjoyment and loss of religious bonds [*kerkloosheid*], and we pick the wry fruits of this in our divorce courts, in the moral degeneration of our people.[61]

Brink castigated other women for neglecting hearth and home, but ended her contribution with a call to Afrikaner women to serve their God, *volk* and country faithfully. This is a persistent theme in all of the writings of *Uit Vroue-harte.* Emmie Steyn du Toit and Gertruida Groenewald both focused their attention on the role of the Christian women in care for the *volk*. Groenewald argued that the *volk* had to be formed into a strong unity, and that the role of women in this process consisted in care for her family, neighbours, as well as in actively participating in its associational life. Steyn du Toit, calling on the examples of Eleanor Roosevelt, E. Wilkenson of the United Kingdom and E. Uralowa of the Soviet Union, asserted that women throughout history had been builders of nations, and that their activities were all the more important when nations were under threat.[62]

Before turning to the articulation of that threat in the thought of cultural nationalists, it is important to note that there were dissenting voices within the Afrikaner theological community on the interpretation given to the status of the *volk* in Calvinist theology. Serious criticism of the use of the Scriptures to underpin the emerging apartheid doctrine was first voiced by B.J. Marais in 1947, and these criticisms were subsequently published in his book, *Die Kleurkrisis in die Weste* (*The Colour Crisis in the West*).[63] Marais argued that the principle of diversity led to the false impression that peoples were static entities. Consequently, to regard 'mixing' as against the will of God would be to elevate the original division to the level of a permanent static division. While practical, pragmatic arguments for segregation of residential areas and government institutions could be made, these could not be justified on the basis of the Scriptures. Similar criticisms were raised by P.V. Pistorius and B.B. Keet. Keet specifically took issue with the transposition of the idea of diversity into division, and argued that emphasis on the latter ran the risk of distorting the central message of the Scriptures:

> I acknowledge that the demolition of walls of division is an ideal difficult to realise in our circumstances, but I do not want to appropriate to myself the right to relinquish the ideal because it is so difficult to attain. If I relinquish the ideal then I relinquish the gospel, demoting it to the reality in which I find myself; but should the ideal be maintained, as it has to be maintained for every Christian, then I do not determine the practice for ever, but still cherish the hope that it will one day be different.[64]

As a counter to the powerful views of those who were fuelled by Calvinist principles, and believed them to be supported by the historical experiences of the Afrikaner over centuries, the arguments of these theologians made little headway.[65]

Culturalist Afrikaner Nationalism

Piet Meyer and Nico Diederichs were of the generation of new Afrikaner intellectuals for whom the struggle on the 'cultural' terrain was of decisive influence.[66] Both Diederichs and Meyer occupied important organizational positions in the nascent *volksbeweging*. Both were members of the influential AB, and Diederichs acted as its chair from 1938 to 1942 and again from 1951 to 1952. Diederichs also headed the RDB, and became National Party MP in 1948, ending his career as state president (1975–78). During the 1930s Meyer simultaneously occupied the position of secretary of the Christian National Education Institute, the Economic Institute and the National Council of Trustees. After his return from a period of study in Europe in 1936, Meyer became assistant secretary of the AB and the FAK. In

1943 he resigned both posts to take up the position of the head of the *Ossewabrandwag*'s *arbeidslaers* (labour circles), which worked with urban Afrikaner workers, and, together with L.J. du Plessis, Meyer organized *studielaers* (study circles) to advise the Great Council of the OB on matters of finance, state and economics.[67] These organizational positions allowed them to disseminate their ideas to the wider *volksbeweging*, the control of which was virtually in their hands.[68]

Both Meyer and Diederichs were founding members of the ANS, which broke away from the National Union of South African Students (NUSAS), the liberal English-dominated national students' union, in April 1933.[69] The character of this organization and the manner of its inception can be seen as a microcosm for the wider culturalist movement. Its break-away from the NUSAS paralleled the growing split between the nationalist hard-liners and the fusionists in politics, and together with the fact that the organization was set up with the help of Hans Gerlach, a Nazi Youth Movement expert, it pointed to the emerging articulation between the nationalist rejection of liberalism and the assertion of cultural specificity which had a series of more or less tenuous links with Nazi Germany. The leading figures in the ANS – J.C. van Rooy, L.J. du Plessis, Geoffrey Cronje, J.D. du Toit, D.F. Malherbe and P.J. Meyer – articulated the founding principles of this movement expressly in terms of a rejection of liberal thought and an assertion of the Protestant-Christian and cultural nationalist basis of Afrikaner nationalism, which recognized 'the leadership of God in the sphere of culture as in every other sphere of life concerning the Afrikaans peoples' traditions as embodied in history'.[70]

In accounting for the thought of culturalists such as Piet Meyer and Nico Diederichs, it is customary to emphasize the fact that they were influenced both by a Fichtean conception of nationalism and by fascist thought.[71] This view was first popularized in the seminal study of Afrikaner civil religion by Moodie, and has most recently been reconfirmed by Furlong in his work on the fascist influence on Afrikaner nationalism during the 1930s and 1940s.[72] This view is, however, no longer generally accepted. Du Toit, for instance, has problematized the labelling of the thought of Diederichs, Meyer, Cronje and Verwoerd as neo-Fichtean, arguing that the 'the notion of a special linkage between German and Afrikaner nationalism, . . . would appear highly tenuous at best. Unless, that is, the "neo-Fichtean" terminology is taken as a euphemism for the reception of national-socialist ideas in Afrikaner politics.'[73] The problems of interpretation at stake here are clearly beyond the scope of the present study. Nevertheless, several points concerning the treatment of this question need to be elaborated upon. Literature on Afrikaner nationalism tends to fall into three distinct groups in this respect: those who completely discard any reference to national socialist thought and its influence; those who see Afrikaner nationalism as fascist *tout court*; and those, like Furlong most recently, who attempt to show the primacy or dominant influence of these ideas not only in the process of the formation of Afrikaner nationalism, but also in its later institutionalization. While it is clearly important to trace the impact of German Romanticism, and national socialist ideas more specifically, on these thinkers and on Afrikaner nationalism generally, it is equally important not to dismiss the influence of the specific context of South Africa in the late 1930s in which these intellectuals came of age, and which shaped the form in which those ideas came to be articulated.

To dismiss either of these dimensions – which happens all too often – would be to misunderstand the nature of the activities in which these culturalist nationalists were involved. As organic intellectuals, they were not merely involved in transposing 'foreign' ideas onto South African soil. Both Diederichs and Meyer were acutely aware of the need to graft these ideas onto the historical experience of the Afrikaner *volk* as they understood it. From the point of view of interpreting their thought as part of the creation of a new horizon of meaning, the important question is not whether they were simply unabashed fascists or not. Rather, it concerns the manner in which these ideas were inserted into the local context, the way in which they informed their understanding of the predicament of the Afrikaner at the time, and the extent to which they contributed to the construction of a new common sense. The mere fact that they drew upon the available languages of resistance does not mean, however, that one can disregard the local context and the impact this had on their formation prior to their respective periods of study in Europe. Indeed, it is quite clear that, for example, in the case of Meyer, his involvement in the AB and the FAK, and thus in the *kultuurstrewe* (cultural striving) of the *volk*, preceded his doctoral studies in Amsterdam and Germany, and cannot in any simple manner be derived from the latter. As Bloomberg correctly points out, the Afrikaner nationalist ideas on race were not acquired from the Nazis.[74] Moreover, a number of Afrikaner nationalists, while inspired by the 'dynamic spirit' of Berlin, found the Nazi tendency to glorify leader, race, blood and nation hard to swallow.[75] While it is clear, especially in the case of Meyer's writings in the 1940s, that he was profoundly influenced by national socialist ideas, it is important to address the precise manner in which the articulation between the ideas which were common currency in the 1930s and the perceived struggle of the Afrikaner took place.[76] Therefore, it is crucial to assess the extent to which the language mobilized by cultural and Scriptural nationalists was permeated by the images of national socialism, and to what extent that had become a decisive element of the new common sense established by Afrikaner nationalists.[77] In this respect, the organizational involvement of Meyer in the OB was decisive, for, more than the shirt movements, the OB came to mobilize widespread popular support. It harmonized the romantic-heroic appeal of Nazism and the mythology of the Afrikaner *Voortrekker* tradition: both stressed activism, the *volkish* character of the nation, and the *volk*'s rootedness in the fatherland's soil.

Nasionalisme as Lewensbeskouing en sy Verhouding tot die Internasionalisme (*Nationalism as Weltanschauung and Its Relation to Internationalism*), Diederichs's most important work, was published in 1936 by Nasionale Pers, the Malan-controlled press also publishing the NP mouthpiece, *Die Burger*. In this text, as well as in his other writings, a singular opposition informed Diederichs's reading of the state of Afrikaner political and cultural life: that between liberalism and nationalism. Liberal individualism, associated with what Diederichs called 'cosmopolitanism', was characterized by a conception of the pre-social individual, fully developed in himself, such that his existence in the community and society was of no real importance. It was, moreover, coupled with a doctrine of equality which negated the rights and values of nationhood. Diederichs himself drew inspiration from a number of sources foreign to the liberal tradition, ranging from the ancient Greek conception of the human as a social being, only fully human within society, to a Romanticist exultation of the nation as the highest, most all-embracing form of community life.[78] Indeed, the human, for Diederichs, is a national animal *par excellence*. However, this humanity was never given and complete in itself. Diederichs focused on life as deed, as struggle, as task never fully accomplished. In contrast to the cosmopolitan conception of the individual based upon the facticity of existence, on 'lower' material needs and desires, nationalism as *Weltanschauung* regarded human beings as capable of something higher than mere natural being, as capable of a spiritual life. The division in man between the natural and the spiritual was the source of man's brokenness, and man's task was to attempt to reconcile spirit and nature.[79]

Cultural values were what allowed man to transcend himself and to sacrifice himself in the name of the development of a super-individual order of unity, the nation.[80] What held for man, *ipso facto*, also held for the nation. For Diederichs, the essence and unity of a nation was not to be found in external characteristics, such as race, colour, descent, physique, and in attachment to land. Rather, it was located in its inner characteristics, its spiritual and cultural life, in a living, moving, growing unity.[81] The nation, thus, was not a mere facticity, something already complete; it was always in a process of becoming.[82] It is important that Diederichs drew a conceptual distinction between the nation (*nasie*) and the *volk*, where the latter designated the totality of citizens sharing in the authority of the state. A *volk*, for Diederichs, thus could contain people of different races, languages and cultures. By contrast, a real nation rested on that inner unity discussed by Diederichs in terms of a shared set of cultural values. Nationalism based on a 'common fatherland', 'common descent', and 'common political attitudes' was a false nationalism.[83] Diederichs's articulation of the term 'nation' thus corresponded only in certain respects to the meaning given to the term '*volk*' in the discourse of the Potchefstroom intellectuals. Indeed, Stoker castigated Diederichs, in a review of his book in *Die Volksblad*, on his tendency to deify the nation. Diederichs, in turn, distinguished himself from attempts to make race, land and ancestry the basis of nationalism, for they tended to pull nationalism down to the realm of the merely material, vital–biological terrain of animality. Diederichs's conception of nationhood thus cannot be understood as an endorsement of *blut und boden* nationalism.

The nation was to be conceived of as an all-embracing community, penetrating the whole of life:

> A nation does not only create itself. It participates in creation on the terrain of the universal since the nation feels itself to have a calling with regard to other peoples [*volkere*], it has a duty to participate in the building of the world process.[84]

The task of the nation on the terrain of humanity consisted not in sacrificing nationhood and that which was the nation's 'own' (*die eie*), but in building up and strengthening those aspects of existence. Since humanity was made up of nations and their constituent elements, it could only reach a higher existence insofar as nations were allowed to grow.[85] The import of Diederichs's conception of nationhood as a task in both senses – to build a nation and to build nations – cannot be underestimated, for this conception of nationhood as essential to all existence was crucial to the later development of 'grand apartheid'. It is this universalizing element in his thought which foreshadowed the development of the mythical space in which apartheid as doctrine emerged, and which was closely linked to the transformation of the specificity of the Afrikaner's position into an imaginary which was to structure all of South Africa's political landscape.

Politically, the conception of nationhood proposed by Diederichs was a continuation of his rejection of liberal individualism. He proposed a positive conception of liberty as the freedom to the accomplishment of the highest, the most real in man.[86] One was free insofar as one was not tied to the lower and the natural, insofar as one developed one's highest self, and this development, for Diederichs, was possible only within the nation. True freedom was thus conceived of as a task requiring self-sacrifice, and entailed a duty of service to the nation. Similarly, national freedom was not, in the first place, a political freedom, but cultural and spiritual freedom. A nation was free when it had freed itself by becoming itself, and by maintaining that selfhood in its purity; a nation was not free when subjected to foreign ideals which were at odds with its innermost nature. Consequently, a nation could be politically free, but spiritually enslaved. As can clearly be seen from this understanding of the relation between freedom, spirituality and nationhood, the role of the state could not be that of the fascist state out of which the right to nationhood emerged. For Diederichs, both politics and the state always had to be subjected and subordinated to the nation, and not vice versa. States and political parties had a crucial role to play in the life of a nation, but they were only means through which the nation could live out its cultural ideals.[87] Diederichs's understanding of the state as a mere means to an end – given in culturalist terms – foreshadowed the utilization of the state apparatuses under apartheid.

The role of democracy, understood in a liberal sense, is negligible in Diederichs's account. With no value attributed to the individual as such, and with the mechanisms of state reduced to mere instruments, individualist democracy could easily be discarded. That is not to say, however, that Diederichs rejected 'democracy' out of hand. To the contrary, he held that nationalism and democracy developed alongside one another, and were essential to one another: 'Nationalism could not be other than democratic. Any undemocratic, autocratic or despotic government is at odds with nationalism as discussed before, since it makes the government of the state sovereign and betrays the sovereignty of the nation.'[88] For Diederichs, the truly national or democratic government did not necessarily rest on a majoritarian principle; it was truly national insofar as it represented the values, ideals and principles of the nation. Insofar as the spirit of the nation was represented, it did not matter whether the government was by one person or many. In a sleight of hand, Diederichs subordinated democracy to the nation and subverted the force of the democratic logic in the name of a higher unity, a unity exalted as creative, as active force, based not on reason and intellect, but on feeling, intuition and emotion. Intellect may inform one on how to reach one's goals, but national goals were always set by the emotive.

This emphasis on the centrality of nationhood also inspired Diederich's rejection of communism. In this, Diederichs's analysis concurred with the position expressed from a number of other sites of enunciation: the church, the AB, the OB, the *Nasionale Raad van Trustees* (NRT, National Council of Trustees), the ANS and the G/HNP's assault on the trade unions. In 1939 the DRC published a report on communism and the trade unions, and we have seen in chapter 1 how central the struggle on this terrain was for the constitution of the Afrikaner *volk*.[89] Already in that work, the main themes of anti-communist rhetoric were apparent: a concern with the communist focus on class differences at the expense of 'national' differences; a complete rejection of the 'equalization' between white and black propagated by communists; and a demonization of communist 'agitators' working in black communities. While the contest for the soul of Afrikaner workers provided the primary context for the expansion of Afrikaner nationalism's anti-communism, this was overdetermined by a concern with black organized resistance to the passing of the Hertzog Bills of the mid-1930s. It is therefore not entirely suprising that the first publication of the HNP Information Service consisted of an analysis of 'the communist threat'.[90] In this pamphlet Eric Louw documented the National Party position on communism in contrast to that of the *laissez-faire* attitude of the Smuts government. Of particular interest is his citing of a unanimous decision by the Cape NP in 1937 where it was argued that communism had to be countered, *inter alia*, by stonger immigration laws, and by the criminalization of undesirable propaganda. The simultaneous demonization of the (Jewish) immigrant, the communist agitator and the black rioter was captured in this three-pronged attack, and it foreshadowed the extremely wide uses to which anti-communist legislation would be put.[91] This was the result of the perception of communism as a threat to the whole terrain of the *volkslewe*. As J.F.J. van Rensburg argued on the occasion of a conference hosted by the ANS in October 1937:

> Here we have to deal with a recognized, self-recognized, anti-Christian movement. Against the State, against the Church, against the *Volk*. It

> penetrates into every terrain of life, in the family, at work, in leisure. And for that reason, because it strives to a Totality, it cannot be fought only in Parliament or in the Church, or in schools. . . . [92]

Intervening in this terrain, Diederichs situated his discussion of communism in *Wat die Kommunisme werklik is* (*What Communism Really is*) in the context of the devastating effects of international capitalism on people's lives. These effects lead people to yearn for an order in which the division between capitalist and non-capitalist classes would be less acute, and in which a more equal division of material belongings would be possible. Communism, he argued, presented itself as the only order capable of ensuring freedom, equality, peace and happiness against the divisionary effects of capitalism. On closer investigation, however, communism showed itself as a total *Weltanschauung* which was absolutely incompatible with the Christian historical outlook on life: it negated the spiritual side of life in favour of lower material needs; it negated the existence of God and made religion the 'opium of the people'; it rejected moral standards of living; it inspired class hatred and class struggle; it aimed at revolution; it rejected the national idea; and it did away with the traditional division between races. Diederich's reading of communism was clearly filtered through the same lens as his reading of liberalism, and proceeded from the espousal of the centrality of the nation. It was in the denial of the centrality of the nation that the twin dangers of communism were to be found:

> All attempts to maintain and strengthen the unity of the *volk*, and all efforts to bring the different parts, groups, classes or strand of the *volk* to unamimous cooperation, are condemned in principle by him [the communist]. The idea of the '*volk*' itself is replaced by the idea of 'class'. . . . For him, no peoples exist; only classes. . . . Class hatred and class struggle are therefore the fundamental tenets of communist doctrine. The unity of society must be destroyed, and in its place, a new form of sociality has to be established.[93]

As it eradicated differences between *volkere*, so it espoused a policy of 'equalization' between white and non-white. In so doing, it attempted to 'uproot' 'non-whites' from their natural environment and created a sense of animosity between white and non-white.

As we have seen in the case of the Scripturalists, and as will become clearer in the discussion of the thought of Geoffrey Cronje, a complex logic was at work in Diederich's discussion of the dangers of communism. While his whole critique was informed and shaped by the logic of the nation or *volk*, and not by 'colour', the development of the argument proceeded by reintroducing a distinction based on 'colour': the communist danger consisted in its propagation of the idea of equality, which would do away with the traditional South African distinction between 'black' and 'white'. For all its emphasis on the cultural spiritual nature of the nation, the racial dimension was never far beneath the surface.[94] We have seen in the previous chapter how the nationalist interventions in the field of trade union activities were overlaid with this racial animosity, and how the Afrikaner women of the KWU attempted to distance themselves from that logic. It was, however, left to Piet Meyer, Diederichs's fellow culturalist, to attempt to develop the argument concerning the relation between the struggle of Afrikaner workers and that of the nation more fully.

Meyer's *Die Stryd van die Afrikanerwerker* (*The Struggle of the Afrikaner Worker*), published in 1944, set out to show the existence of a distinct Afrikaner 'socialism' and to argue for its continued pertinence to the Afrikaner's struggle.[95] At the time of its writing, Meyer was involved in both the AB and the OB. The AB, up to the end of the Second World War, saw the relation between Afrikaner and English-speakers as of overriding importance.[96] This was even more evident in the sorts of concerns around which the OB arose: the relation between Afrikaner and English-speakers, and the nature of Afrikaner unity and the ground upon which that was to be established. *Die Stryd van die Afrikanerwerker* drew together elements of both the Calvinism espoused at Potchefstroom and the nationalism of Diederichs and coupled them with aspects of national socialism. These concerns dovetailed well with those matters which Meyer regarded as crucial: the cultural and economic life of the *volk* and of Afrikaner workers. Tapping into the wider international climate, Meyer argued that the struggle of Afrikaner workers was in essence one against imperialism and capitalism, and it was only insofar as both these dimensions of struggle were prioritized, that the Afrikaner's position could be improved. Nationalism on its own operated with too narrow a conception of the *volk*, while socialism erred on the side of class; only an articulation of the two would produce a satisfactory solution.

However, within each of these domains, divisions of a political and social nature had to be overcome for they weakened the Afrikaner's position. In the process of enumeration of these divisions, Meyer strove to bring into being a new object of discourse, namely 'true Afrikaner socialism'. Afrikaner socialism came into existence against both the reformist tradition of the British-influenced and -led socialism of the Trades and Labour Council and the Labour Party, which was grounded in liberalism and aimed at protecting a labour aristocracy while supporting imperialist wars, and the attempts of the Communist Party to break down racial divisions between white and black.[97] Afrikaner socialism, while initially fostered by the British socialist tradition in South Africa, became radicalized once it became clear to Afrikaner workers that they were mere 'water-carriers and wood-cutters' to the 'foreigners who lived on the fat of the land'.[98] It was not until the rejection of capitalism was coupled with the Afrikaner's deeply held religious principles that the full force of Afrikaner socialism could be developed. Meyer argued that

> [a] stronger and deeper grounding, in terms of which the capitalist system could be experienced as wrong in essence, was his own [the Afrikaner's] Christian-social principles, principles forming the core of this own tradition. . . . this system [the capitalist system] has to be replaced with an order in which one would be the keeper and shepherd of the other.[99]

As nationalists, Afrikaner workers had to become socialists 'in a practical anti-capitalist sense', and as socialists, they had to remain nationalist in their outlook on life.[100] Afrikaner socialism was, moreover, a moral and national socialism which pre-empted the loss of the Afrikaner's 'inner nationalism'.

'Inner nationalism' was contrasted, as for Diederichs, to the nationalism of political parties and was necessary to protect Afrikaner workers against exploitation by fellow unionists.[101] Meyer constantly reminded his readers that the leaders of the Labour Party and of the trade unions, despite their 'theoretical internationalism', remained in essence English (British), and thus opposed to the inner nationalism of Afrikaner workers.[102] With the formation of the NRT under Albert Hertzog in 1936, further efforts were made to break the influence of British socialist and communist leaders over Afrikaner miners and clothing workers, and to bring Afrikaner working-class organizations under the influence of Christian nationalism.[103] While these early efforts were ultimately unsuccessful, Meyer saw the conditions of 'spiritual confusion and material poverty' which dominated since 1938 as fertile ground for the reintroduction of a truly Afrikaans method of struggle, the commando-form. Moreover, the period since the awakening in 1938 pointed ever more strongly in the direction of a recognition that party political methods of struggle within 'the imperialist-political and capitalist-economic orders' left the Afrikaner nationally divided and socially impoverished. With the outbreak of the Second World War, the OB was born out of this 'intuitive sense' that the Afrikaner had to resist the new imperialist and capitalist onslaught on the separate national and social destiny of the *volk*.[104] The OB provided the forum where Afrikaner nationalism and Afrikaner socialism could be united, not merely externally as parallel struggles, but as an integrated whole embodying the full potential of the *volkstrewe*.[105] For Meyer, its organizational form – the commando structure – had three important characteristics: it embodied the familial and labour unity of Afrikanerdom; it replaced the reformism of party politics with an all-out struggle against imperialism and capitalism in South Africa; and it put authority and discipline in the place of 'democratic irresponsibilities'. The reformist liberal-capitalist order had to be replaced with a characteristic Afrikaner national and social outlook on life.

The socialism of which Meyer was a proponent had to be distinguished from a liberal ordering of society in which the voluntarist individual took precedence. A socialist order would make society, rather than the individual, paramount. Hence, national socialism, arising in Western Europe and designating 'the revolution of the twentieth century',[106] had to replace liberal principles with social ones within national contexts. In the South African context, this meant that for Afrikaner socialism the 'socialist ordering principle, according to which human relations in the national context are structured, had to become the dominant one'. But Meyer was careful to distinguish Afrikaner socialism from 'state socialism', for the latter was not fundamentally at odds with capitalism: it merely replaced the capitalist exploiter by the state. Workers simply became the 'wage slaves' of the state.[107] By contrast, Afrikaner socialism was hailed to be an indigenous product of Afrikanerdom: it arose out of the traditions and *Weltanschauung* of the *volk*; it was anti-imperialist, anti-capitalist and did away with the negative freedoms of the democratic state. It strove to care for the *volk*, for workers, and saw to it that wealth produced would be equitably shared between those who participated in its production.[108]

During the 1940s, Meyer was not only active in the OB, but also participated actively in struggling, under the auspices of the AB, for a republic.[109] Indeed, Meyer took the most important aspect of his doctoral studies in Amsterdam to be its 'politicological' dimension. Afrikanerdom could be freed from the yoke of imperialism only if it accepted a republican state form. During this period Meyer was also an editorial board member of the *Tweede Trekreeks* (Second Trek

Series), and published *Die Afrikaner* in the series in which he set out the main characteristics of the republican state form, which corresponded closely to the views held by Stoker:

> The state ought to be truly republican, free and Christian national. It must be grounded upon the eternal legal principles of the Word of God; the clear path of development of the history of the *volk*, and the necessary adjustment of this past to modern conditions. . . . The state system should not be based upon a foreign model. It must break with everything in democracy which could be regarded as detrimental to the *volk* or false, and should facilitate strong government based upon the concepts of *volksregering* as found in the South African republics, while accommodating itself to the realities of an industrialized state in the interests of the *volk*.[110]

The OB's blueprint for an Afrikaner-dominated Christian national republic, first made public in 1940, clearly bore the imprint of Meyer's thinking. It sought to replace the Westminster system of government with a mixture of constitutional ideas drawn from Kruger's South African Republic, the Nazi doctrine of the *Volkstaat* and Mussolini's corporate system of representation. Its ideas were also characteristic of contemporary AB thinking: it contained references to an authoritarian head of state with apparently unlimited powers, exclusive Afrikaner domination, subjection of all English speakers, racially restricted citizenship, one official language, abolition of the monarchy and occupational representation.[111]

The centrality of the organicity of the *volk* continued to inform Meyer's writings, even later when he came to work within the Rembrandt group (an investment corporation with diverse interests in tobacco, liquor and coal mining) and moved away from national socialism. In 1951, Meyer became head of public relations for the Rembrandt group (under the leadership of Anton Rupert, one of the third-generation Afrikaner intellectuals who were to have a great impact on the reformist agenda from the late 1970s onwards). His first task was to report on 'The Powers Against Us'. In so doing, Meyer produced a historical account of the Afrikaner's economic backwardness, especially with regard to the mining industry. At this point, little if anything of the former concern with the frontal attack on capitalism was present. Meyer now argued that the Afrikaner's duty was to develop his economic entrepreneurship.[112] This apparent sea-change can only be adequately accounted for if it is realized that the core of the cultural nationalist philosophy consisted in a valorization of the *volk*. Whatever was seen to be harming the *volk* was evil. While during the late 1930s and the 1940s, the international context facilitated the articulation of national socialism with Afrikaner nationalism, and enabled culturalist nationalists to develop a critique of liberal capitalism and communism in principle, several other philosophies of life could occupy this position of 'other' against which the identity of the Afrikaner was to be defined. The element of the OB philosophy which would last beyond the 1940s was its fierce rejection of communism, something which the wider nationalist *volksbeweging* shared. In this sense, the shifts in emphases in Meyer's writings were indicative of the wider trends in Afrikaner nationalism, which soon after 1948 distanced itself from the influence of national socialist thinking and sought to form an alliance with capitalist forces which could be harnessed to the needs of the *volk*.

Scientific Racism: The Afrikaner *Volk* and the White Race

In addition to the emphasis in nationalist thought on the organic and culturalist nature of the *volk* during the decades of the 1930s and 1940s, a distinct 'subtradition' of explicit racist thought can be discerned in the works of writers such as Geoffrey Cronje, Gerrie Eloff, both criminologists, and C.W. Prinsloo, an anthropologist.[113] The major thrust of Eloff's work *Rasse en Rassevermenging: Die Boerevolk gesien van die standpunt van die Rasseleer* (*Race and Racial Mixing: The Boerevolk Seen from the Vantage-Point of the Racial Theory*), published in 1942 in the *Tweede Trekreeks* series, was that the *Boerevolk* could be defined as a new and distinct biological type which came into existence as a result of a mixture of white races.[114] Eloff's work was popularized both by L.J. du Plessis at Potchefstroom and Cronje, who held a professorial position in sociology at the University of Pretoria. Cronje's itinerary resembles that of the cultural nationalists who were his peers. Like Meyer, he completed his doctoral studies in Amsterdam in the early 1930s and took a great interest in the European nationalist movements of the time. On his return from Europe, he became active in the student politics of the ANS, and in the wider nationalist movement. He attended the 1934 *Volkskongres* on the poor white problem and was seminal in the founding of the Department of *Volkswelsyn* (Social Welfare). While much of his writing was abstractly concerned with the development of a sociological theory of causation, he also contributed, in much more partisan fashion, to the *Instituut vir Volkswelstand*'s mouthpiece, *Volkswelstand*, as well as to *Rassebakens* (*Racial Beacons*), the official journal of the *Afrikanerbond vir Rassestudies* (Afrikaner League for

Racial Studies), which set itself the task of addressing the problems of miscegenation, the position of the coloured and Asiatic communities, Native land ownership, urban mixed residential areas and communism. His writings of the 1940s are generally considered to be amongst the most important and comprehensive intellectual justifications for racial apartheid.[115]

Already in his inaugural lecture at the University of Pretoria a seminal element of Cronje's thought was apparent. He denied that there was something like an organic community embracing the whole human race. Humanity was made up of different national communities (*volksgemeenskappe*) based pre-eminently on cultural and sociological diversity.[116] This 'cultural–sociological difference' was, nevertheless, intimately bound up with racial difference. Racial mixing for Cronje produced 'inferior human material in biological terms (physically and mentally)'.[117] The distinctiveness of Cronje's work lies in his explicit vitriolic espousal of racial division. Following Eloff, he held that the *Boereras* (Boer race) was a composite of Dutch, German and French stock and that it formed a new racial subtype.[118] In his early writings, Cronje, like Eloff and Prinsloo, drew not only upon his sociological determinism to account for racial division, but also rooted this in the traditional attitude of the *Boere*:

> We have here a contradiction between the viewpoint of the *Voortrekkers* (*Boere*), on the one hand, and the policy of the former British government (the imperialists), on the other hand. On the one side segregation (differentiation) and on the other equalization. On the one side an indigenously grown viewpoint and on the other a foreign, *volksvreemde* viewpoint. The clash between the two directions is inevitable. The special racial consciousness of the Afrikaner nation and its abhorrence of all equalization with the non-whites was not brought to this country, but grew out of the specific conditions which obtained here.[119]

Hence Cronje's deterministic sociology served to naturalize not only the divisions between 'races' but also a racist attitude. It is in this sense that his use of history is similar to that of the cultural and Scriptural nationalists: it presented history as a consequence of a secret revealed to men about their own nature and birth, such that an imaginary fusion of the past and the present was brought about.[120]

Already in 1939 in his writings on 'racial mixing' as sociological phenomenon as well as in his analysis of the question of 'mixed marriages', a series of issues which would continue to occupy his writings were apparent. In this, his thought echoed that of the cultural and Scriptural nationalists discussed earlier. The main enemies of the distinct Afrikaner viewpoint on 'racial mixing',[121] which Cronje traced back to the early nineteenth century, were British imperialist-inspired liberalism and communism. These doctrines shared the conviction that no objections could be made against racial equality. Just as liberals such as R.F.A. Hoernlé propagated the idea of racial equality, not only in the white community but also with regard to 'non-whites', communists promulgated class struggle under the 'non-white' proletariat.[122] The problem with the doctrine of equalization was that it would lead to an increase in racial conflict: racial conflict was the necessary consequence of racial mixing which followed from racial contact.[123] Drawing on E.V. Stonequist, E.B. Reuter and Gunnar Myrdal, Cronje argued that:

> Racial mixing and racial conflict . . . are at the core of the South African racial problem, and will remain so as long as contact between whites and non-whites continues on its present pattern.[124]

Ruling out the commonly held view that miscegenation between white and 'non-white' was not very common and that it would not spread as a result of the deep-rooted white 'instinct' against it, Cronje felt that the only solution to the problem was a 'just' racial separation. 'Justness', for him, referred to the responsibility of the white race to lead 'less developed races', via a policy of trusteeship, towards development. Trusteeship, for Cronje, had to be of a temporary nature. Drawing on the UN declaration (articles 73–91), he argued not only that trusteeship arose from respect for other cultures, but also that the political aspirations of others had to be recognized and given room for development.[125] If self-determination of the Natives was the aim of trusteeship, racial apartheid had to be its other side. Of the three possibilities for solving the racial question – continued white supremacy, gradual equalization between white and non-white, and total separation of races – Cronje presented the third as the only just solution to the problem.

The distinctiveness of Cronje's account lies in the manner in which he depicted the division between races, and it is in this respect that his writings foreshadowed most clearly the ambiguities of apartheid after 1948. Cronje argued that four clearly delineated communities existed in South Africa – the white community, the Native *communities*, the coloured community and the Indian community – and that conflicts of interest exist not only between whites and non-whites, but within the non-white communities as well.[126] Of particular interest here is the precise manner in which these divisions were set up. Even though

Cronje is generally assumed to be one of the new organic intellectuals of the emerging *volksbeweging*, the remarkable fact that his account was based not on the specificity of the Afrikaner community but on an ambiguous racial division tends to be disregarded. The sorts of divisions internal to Afrikanerdom and between the Afrikaans- and English-speaking communities which occupied the attention of the Scriptural and cultural nationalists simply did not take centre-stage in his account. Cronje's arguments for radical territorial apartheid proceed wholly in terms of the need to protect the white race and its values from extinction. Apartheid, for Cronje, thus did not refer to a social ordering aimed simply at addressing the specific 'needs' and situation of the Afrikaner community. At stake was the continued existence of the white European race. Given the racial policies which were to be instituted after 1948, this is not surprising. However, if Cronje is read in terms of the wider context of the *volksbeweging* of which he was a part during the 1930s and 1940s, the specificity of his account has to be stressed. While Cronje also drew on and tried to develop what he considered to be a Christian viewpoint of the racial question, this did not lead him to the sort of views espoused by the Potchefstroom and culturalist nationalists. More than any of them, he consistently referred to the racial question as a question of colour, even though he argued that skin colour was not to be taken as the primary basis for racial consciousness and racial apartheid.[127]

This is not to say, however, that the very language of ethnicity and *volkere* did not permeate his readings, for it is only on the grounds of that discourse that his argument for the existence of 'perhaps three separate Native communities' can be accounted for.[128] Moreover, his argument for the development of 'an own identity' was reserved for Native, coloured and Indian communities, and did not affect the unity of the 'white' community. The account offered differed for each of those communities, and was premissed upon a conception of development of races from immaturity to maturity. This also led Cronje to assert that Christian trusteeship had to be a temporary phenomenon. The 'races' which had to be led to maturity included the Natives and coloureds. Indians were explicitly excluded as falling outside of the problem as defined; they were foreigners and were to be treated as such.[129] In terms of his account of Native development, it is noticeable that Cronje used terminology associated with a certain shift in perception of the 'racial' problem. He not only wrote about Natives, but also about the 'Bantu'. This term, as I will show later, was derived from anthropological work on different 'tribes' or groupings within the Native population, and would become very important in the later expansion of the 'apartheid idea' towards 'grand apartheid'. While there were similarities in their position, in that both communities had to avoid becoming 'imitated Europeans', Native development differed in kind from that of coloured development. The essence of this difference was to be found in the tribal background of the Native, in the fact that insofar as they were not detribalized, they had both a distinctive authoritarian political system and a clear sense of racial pride to draw upon. Without these, they would simply be a cultureless and directionless 'human mass'. The trajectory of their development had to build on these characteristics, for all the evils associated with Natives – magic, immorality, polygamy and cruelty – arose from a *loss* of these indigenous values.

By contrast, the position of coloureds was much less clear. Cronje argued that they lacked a sense of their own separate identity as well as an 'own' social set of ordering principles, and that the problems experienced by them – immorality and alcoholism – were a direct result of their attempts to lead their lives like 'Westerners' (whites). Their problem was that they did not want to be non-whites, and that they were not whites. They were in a position 'between heaven and earth, neither fish nor fowl, between the tree and the bark. No wonder the coloured soul was in a state of perpetual conflict.'[130] It is also for the coloured community – precisely as a result of their closeness to the white Afrikaner community – that Cronje reserved his most vitriolic language.[131] This community, which had no consciousness of themselves as a *volk*, was the non-white group which held greatest danger for racial purity.[132] Cronje consequently prescribed the same solution to them as to the Natives: the development of a separate sense as *volk*. His fiercely racist attempts to find a way in which the coloured community could be separated from the white foreshadowed the debate on the status of coloureds that would cause deep divisions in the NP by the late 1950s. Moreover, Cronje's wavering between accounting for social division in terms of racial or 'ethnic' difference would continue during the 1950s, and would ultimately not be resolved. Cronje's work, thus, in more senses than one, anticipated a series of discursive strategies and their attendant difficulties which would continue both to inform and to haunt the apartheid project.

Conclusion: The *Volkseie* as Impossible Object

The interventions discussed here contain both similarities and dissimilarities and it is customary to reduce those factors which delimit them from one another in order to be able to establish the essential unity of their thought. In this sense, much of the literature on the emerging Afrikaner nationalism of the period falls prey to the difficulties of the 'history of ideas' which Foucault has described so acutely. The history of ideas, while it recounts the by-ways and margins of history, nevertheless does so only to subordinate them to the great themes of genesis, continuity and totalization.[133] At the beginning of this chapter I have shown how, even when the express intention was to 'disaggregate' the monolith of Afrikanerdom, this was done only to reinstitute an underlying form of unity. However, problematizing such reductionism should not lead one to assume that no form of unity existed across the thought of the organic intellectuals. If that is the case, the problem to be addressed is the following: how is one to account for that unity without reducing and nullifying those differences?

Before this is discussed in any greater detail, it is necessary to specify more closely in what those similarities and differences consisted. The similarities found in the thought of the organic intellectuals discussed do not run like a thread through all of their works. Rather, they resemble more closely a complicated network of different overlapping similarities, without a common core.[134] Both the Scriptural and cultural nationalists shared a deep conviction in the role of action and struggle in the constitution of the identity of the *volk*. This is especially clear in Stoker's conception of 'action fronts' and Diederichs's spiritualized conception of the nation as in a process of becoming, such that it always had to struggle to be itself. An emphasis on struggle was also at the forefront of Meyer's thinking. But it is clear that while they shared, broadly speaking, a belief in action and struggle, the precise manner in which it was articulated in their works differs considerably, with Stoker drawing his inspiration from Kuyperianism, Diederichs from romantic nationalism and Meyer from national socialism. These intellectuals also shared a common concern in their attempts to articulate the specificity of Afrikaner nationalism *vis-à-vis* liberalism, communism and, to a lesser extent, national socialism. However, here also there were as many differences in the content given to their readings as there were similarities. For Stoker, Christian Afrikaner nationalism had to be distinguished from liberalism in its English and Afrikaans forms, as well as from fascism and national socialism, while Meyer attempted to establish closer links between Afrikaner nationalism and national socialism by developing a distinct conception of Afrikaner national socialism. In their rejection of liberalism there were stronger resemblances: they all renounced the liberal conception of the individual in favour of an insertion of the individual into the *volk*, and they consistently challenged liberal and communist calls for equality. This repudiation of equality was closely connected to the manner in which they conceived of the relation of the *volk* to other *volkere*. They argued that the champions of equality failed to take account of the material, cultural and social inequalities and differences between Afrikaners and English-speakers. For other groups, such as coloureds, Indians and the different Bantu-*volkere*, equality was rejected in overtly racist terms: different 'levels' of civilization decisively ruled out any attempt to establish equality between white and black. However, in this respect also, the context in which these ideas were put forward differed considerably. Even though Stoker, L.J. du Plessis and H. du Plessis all held that Christian unity did not entail equality and unity in this life, they disagreed in their prescriptions for the political treatment of those differences. L.J. du Plessis argued that Christian nationalism was entirely consistent with the sharpest of inequalities, while his namesake maintained that since African racial and cultural differences had a divine origin, Africans had to remain separate, but they had to be treated on a basis of equality. Cronje, despite basing his theory of difference on racial grounds, did not hesitate to argue that 'trusteeship' of 'Natives' could only be a temporary measure. These differences of interpretation foreshadowed the debates within Afrikaner nationalists on the precise nature of apartheid and its implementation, and will be discussed in more depth in the following chapter.

These differences also influenced their accounts of the specificity of the *volk*. Whereas there was broad agreement on the centrality of the *volk*, and on the need to address the divisions within Afrikanerdom, the precise location of the essential character of Afrikanerdom is described in widely varying and sometimes contradictory ways. Stoker, for example, gave attention in his conception of the *volk* – as organic creation of God – to race, blood, language and culture, while Diederichs explicitly denied the relevance of race and *blut und boden* nationalism to his conception of the nation constituted around an inner unity which could not be reduced to the 'lower' material aspects of man's existence. Meyer, on the other hand, vacillated between Diederichs's conception of the nation as organic cultural community with its own language, spiritual life and calling, and an anti-semitic, racist conception which would allow the inclusion of English-speaking whites, but which excluded 'unassimilable whites'. The cultural and Scriptural nationalists nevertheless shared an emphasis on the centrality of the *volk* that was less clearly present in the writings of Eloff and Cronje, who focused much more strongly on the *Boerevolk* as essentially a racial entity. This, we have seen, led Cronje to draw a distinction between 'white' and 'non-white' (coloureds, Natives and Indians).[135] Cronje's division of the 'non-white' group, and especially his argument that the Native population consisted in three or more Bantu groupings, nevertheless differed from segregationist discourse, which regarded 'the Native' as an essentially 'homogeneous' population category.

It is clear from the above that it would be difficult to attribute a substantial conception of unity to these writings, for even where similarities existed, variations in their articulation occurred as a result of the fact that they drew upon different and sometimes contradictory intellectual resources. We are now in a position to return to the question as to how this unity can be thought if not in positive, substantial terms. It is my contention that this unity, the unity of the *volkseie*, can only be apprehended in negative terms. I have stressed the importance of the manner in which different thinkers successively strove to establish a truly Afrikaans (Christian) nationalism. To establish the specificity of the *volkseie*, in order to purify the nation, a series of distinctions were put into place: between true Afrikaner nationalists and Afrikaners who fell out of the bounds of the *volk*; between the Afrikaner *volk* and the English-speaking population; between Afrikaners and coloureds; and between Afrikaners and Natives. Indians were treated as foreigners who had to be repatriated. Hence, it is clear that the purity of the *volkseie* could only be produced by isolating within its bosom the false elements, and by distinguishing itself from all others who could be argued to be alien to the *volk*. In all of its dimensions, a clear racist logic was at work: exclusive Afrikaner nationalism was an obsessional quest for a core of authenticity which could, however, not be found. It could only be produced, and, hence, constantly had to be reproduced, by differentiating itself from competing conceptions of ordering: an exclusive Afrikaner nationalism was what was left once British liberalism and imperialism, communism, doctrines of equality, and so forth, were all externalized as foreign to the traditions of the *volk*. It thus forged itself in terms of a series of negative operations in which the truly *volkseie*, while remaining invisible, could be inferred *a contrario* by the alleged visibility of the 'other': the non-true Afrikaner, the English, the Jew, the black, the coloured, and so forth. That process created a series of hierarchically defined 'others' that has to be accounted for in terms of the ever-present racial horizon within which the new mythical principle of ordering was inserted.

These intellectuals also sought to show the historical rootedness of a paradoxically absent identity in the experience of the *volkseie*. It is in this sense that they constructed a new myth, a new principle of ordering. They addressed the condition of the Afrikaner by weaving together ideas – both foreign and indigenous – and by rooting them in an 'experience' which was in the process of being created. The impossibility of capturing that 'experience' of the 'own', the *volkseie*, 'our way of life', in positive substantive terms shows that the element which holds together a given community cannot be reduced to a single, positive point of identification.[136] It follows that an enumeration of the fragments of the way in which the organic intellectuals each sought to construct that unity will remain constitutively inadequate, albeit crucial. For this reason it could be argued that the most important facet of their thought has to be sought for in what escaped these individual articulations: the horizon constructed as a result of that which was in excess of each of the individual interventions. This mythical horizon is what enables one to account for the unity of the discourse of the intellectuals in a non-reductionist fashion, for it designates a space of inscription marked by its own constitutive impossibility: the *volkseie* is that which is 'ours and ours alone', inaccessible to the 'other', and that which is threatened by 'others'. In this sense, the *volkseie* points not simply to the terrain in which an overdetermination of elements associated with the *volk* is constituted – the enumeration of theological, cultural and racial 'values' – but to the ultimate impossibility of the very identity of the community. For while it is crucial to capture the sense in which images proposed in these interventions offered places for identification, it is as important not to reduce the constitution of a new mythical space to those positions. If that is done, it would be impossible to grasp that which escapes the articulation of positive elements: the logic of fact that the *volkseie* is essentially a marker of the impossibility of the very constitution of the community and thus can only be shown in its negativity.

In drawing upon local and foreign ideas, these intellectuals thus brought into being a new principle of social division, articulated simultaneously around the concepts of *volk* and race, but in such a manner that their articulation differed decisively from that of segregationist discourse. As I will show in more detail in chapter 3, these concepts, especially that of the *volk*, acted as empty signifiers, uniting all the positive elements together, and giving them their meaning, a meaning which, nevertheless, only arises out of a fundamental negativity. It is also for this reason that their understanding of politics, deeply rooted in the paradoxical 'experience' of the *volkseie*, is of crucial importance. The particularity of this 'experience' led to a recasting of the idea of democracy as primarily rooted in and subordinated to the *volk*. This particularity would, nevertheless, later be universalized into a general dictum: that which is most crucial in 'our own experience' of necessity has also to be that which organizes all other communities. It is in this conception of the universalizing task and duty of the *volk* that the roots of the expansion of the myth – which inaugurated apartheid and which had its source in a particular community – into an imaginary surface of inscription – organizing the whole of the political landscape – would be found.

The final issue to be considered concerns the relation between this new principle of ordering and segregationist discourse. I have argued that structures or sedimented practices of social division are rarely entirely dislocated. A certain 'repetitiveness' is always present. Precisely how this repetition is to be understood theoretically is crucial to any analysis which aims at showing the specificity of the form of social division instituted with apartheid discourse. The work of both Foucault and Derrida may be of help in this regard: Foucault for his theorization of discontinuity and Derrida for his theorization of the notion of iterability. Foucault argues that, in contradistinction to the history of ideas, which always aims at reducing discontinuity and ruptures to continuity, we need to be able to theorize discontinuity if we are to take difference seriously.[137] Rather than arguing for a homogeneous notion of change or discontinuity, Foucault directs attention to the unevenness of processes of transformation: to the transformation of elements of a discursive formation, of the relations between elements, and of relations between discursive formations themselves. The veracity of Foucault's arguments for the new ordering principle articulated by the organic intellectuals is clear, for the formation of this myth did not proceed in an even and homogeneous manner. It retained elements of prior formations, and its institutionalization – to be discussed in chapter 3 – was uneven and affected by differences of interpretation within 'Afrikanerdom' as well as by struggles against it. Thus, to say that one discursive formation (segregation) is substituted for another (apartheid) is not to say that a whole world of new objects, enunciations and concepts had come into being. In short, their continuities as much as their discontinuities have to be taken into account, for the same, the repetitive, and the uninterrupted are no less problematic than the rupture.[138]

The precise manner in which the repetition of elements is to be understood is crucial here, for repetition is never simply a repetition of the same. The idea of repetition, or, more precisely, repeatability/iterability, involves both elements of sameness and elements of change.[139] The structure of iteration thus refers both to identity and to difference:

> Every sign, linguistic or nonlinguistic, spoken or written . . . can be *cited* . . . in so doing it can break with every given context, engendering an infinity of new contexts. . . . This citationality, . . . this iterability of the mark is neither an accident nor an anomaly, it is that . . . without which a mark could not even have a function called 'normal'.[140]

The remainder, what remains the same across repetitions, therefore is already divided, and beyond saturation by any context and every context is always open to transformation: 'There only exist contexts without any center of absolute anchoring.'[141] The absence of an absolute anchoring point is, however, not to be understood as the absence of any anchoring at all. While undermining all claims to essentiality in his reading of iterability, Derrida does not veer over to the position of a psychotic. It is not the case that all meaning vanishes or is dissolved in context, but that there can be no meaning without reference to context, even though such a context can never be fully closed and present to itself. Marks are always open to reinscription, and this reinscription makes a difference.

This characterization of iterability facilitates a rethinking of the relation between continuity and discontinuity in the discursive production of social division. Although elements of a prior formation may remain, in some minimal sense, the same – which is not to be confused with an essential sameness – the mere fact of their repetition alters them decisively. To be more precise, the mere fact of a repetition of social division in terms of racial differences, something which the new myth shared with segregationist discourse, does not mean that apartheid is essentially the same as its segregationist precursor. To argue thus would be to ignore the context in which this repetition of 'race' was to be inserted, a context where the *volkseie* came to act as a nodal point. Traditionally, the presumed 'continuity' of racism between segregation and apartheid has been used to negate the distinctiveness of apartheid discourse. One of the most serious shortcoming of these accounts of racism resides in the assumption that the history of South Africa could be conceptualized in terms of a continuous 'interaction' between different, given, 'racial' groups. In this way history was united around a single causative centre, which presumed that one and the same form of historicity operated upon economic structures, social institutions and customs, subjecting them all to the same type of transformation. This form of historical analysis tended to discount the importance of analysing the unevenness and discontinuity characteristic of political practices. It gave no serious attention to how racist attitudes and practices have developed and changed over time, to how they have varied among different groups in diverging circumstances. It ruled out, from the start, a consideration of discontinuities and breaks in the long narrative presumed to repeat itself in its sameness over the centuries. Politically and also theoretically, this resulted in an inability to come to terms with the variety and complexity of racist discourses, and their ability to assume new forms and to articulate new antagonisms.

In contrast to these sorts of accounts, I have argued that the relation between apartheid and its segregationist precursor has to take account of both their continuities and discontinuities, without, however, reducing the continuous to the same. It is thus not a matter of apartheid being in some sense essentially the same as segregation, for that would reduce difference to the same, and neither is it the case that the whole world of objects, subjects and enunciative positions changed. In the constitution of its political frontiers, certain elements around which social division was organized remained the same. But, in this very process of repetition something new was articulated by its insertion into a novel context, that of the *volkseie*. Hence, although both discursive formations – segregation and apartheid – were structured with reference to racist exclusions, the context in which this exclusion took place makes it impossible to argue for an essential similarity between the two. Segregationist discourse was ordered around a precise division between 'Europeans' and 'Natives', and treated them both as homogeneous categories. In response to this, the discourse of the *volkseie* sought to put into question the unity of the 'European' community, and extended this questioning to the homogeneity of the 'Native' community. Thus, even though the exclusionary black/white frontier was to continue to operate in the discourse of apartheid, this frontier now functioned in a context where social division was thought, in the first place, around the centrality of the *volkseie*. This is not to say that it was any less racist, but that these racist practices now operated in a context in which account had to be taken of the new organizing principle. Should one not recognize that, one would be unable to account for the effectiveness of this discourse in recasting social division and in proposing new images for identification not only for Afrikaners, but also for the wider black community. While a broad organizing principle, a new common sense, was in place by the mid-1940s, this did not mean that the detail of the project was worked out in fully fledged form. Quite the contrary: debates on the precise nature of apartheid within the Afrikaner community continued throughout the 1940s and well into the 1950s. It was only as a result of these debates, as well as of the resistance to the implementation of apartheid, that the nature of the project would begin to crystallize. It is to an investigation of these issues that I turn in chapter 3.

3

From Myth to Imaginary: The Logic of Apartheid

> A text is not a text unless it hides from the first comer, the first glance, the law of its composition and the rules of its game.[1]

> To classify means to set apart, to segregate. It means first to postulate that the world consists of discrete entities; then to postulate that each entity has a group of similar or adjacent entities with which it belongs, and with which – together – it is opposed to some entities. . . . To classify is to give the world a structure.[2]

If to classify is to give the world a structure, then it is necessary to investigate in what precisely the structures of classification inaugurated with apartheid consisted. With the HNP victory in the 1948 polls, the implementation of their distinctive vision for South Africa became a real possibility. It is, however, abundantly clear that while the new intellectuals had developed an account of the condition of the Afrikaner *volk* through their valorization of the *volkseie*, the implications of this new mythical principle for the wider ordering of society were far from worked out. As Posel has argued, no blueprint or apartheid grand plan existed by 1948. The crystallization of the apartheid project during the 1950s also did not result in such a clear 'blueprint'. Rather, it emerged in piecemeal fashion, as a response both to divisions within Afrikanerdom on the nature of apartheid and to resistance to its uneven implementation. To stress the fundamentally equivocal, undecidable nature of the project and the extent to which it was fashioned by resistance to it is not, however, to deny the fact that a certain 'vision' was in place, but to stress the fact that there was nothing predetermined in the manner in which this broad vision would be extended and implemented.

In chapter 2, I showed in a preliminary fashion that a series of incipient political frontiers operated within the thought of the organic intellectuals of the Afrikaner nationalist *volksbeweging*. These structures of division – consisting in an uneasy combination of the *volkseie* and racial categorizations – lie at the heart of apartheid. In this chapter I will show how these structures crystallized into an imaginary that reordered the whole of the political landscape; how it was institutionalized; and how both these processes depended upon a series of struggles which contributed to its formation. The slow and uneven emergence of a mythical principle of ordering was intimately related to the experiences of a particular group, and consisted in attempts to give a precise content to that impossible object: the *volkseie*. In discussing the production of this principle of ordering I have stressed the extent to which its initial articulation took place in terms of the divisions *within* Afrikanerdom, and how a true Afrikanerdom was produced by delineating true from non-true Afrikaners by reference to a specific Afrikaner principle of ordering which only was brought into being by distinguishing it from other principles of ordering. In this sense, the fundamental premisses of the new myth were based on the rejection of the homogenization of the white community in segregationism. In line with my argument on the relational character of identity it is, however, clear that this rearticulation, and the concomitant emphasis on the *volk*, could not but have an effect on the manner in which the relation between 'white' and 'black' was perceived. The change in the perception of this dimension of social division was not, however, to occur immediately, for the very regulation of the relation between white and black was a matter of great dispute within the organizations of Afrikanerdom. Just as the segregationist vision of an undifferentiated white community was regarded as a failure, apartheid theoreticians held that segregationism, with its *laissez-faire* attitude, failed to address the problem of increasing black urbanization and social integration, and that the apartheid project could offer a new answer to this problem.

In the immediate aftermath of the 1948 election, the NP not only had to give content to its election slogan – apartheid – but also faced a struggle to consolidate itself and its position in white Parliamentary politics.[3] The process of consolidation of power took up most of the first term of office (1948–53). Various measures were taken to enable the NP, which came to power with less than 50 per cent of the vote, to retain Parliamentary dominance. These ranged from legislation to improve the Parliamentary position of the NP to changes in its internal structure of organization. Apart from attempts throughout the 1950s to remove coloured voters from the voting roll, for the 50,000 coloured men eligible to vote were held responsible for the loss of seven seats in the 1948 election, the NP introduced a series of other measures to bolster its own position.[4] It introduced the South West Africa Affairs Amendment Act of 1950, which changed the balance of power in the NP–AP alliance by adding six MPs to the NP. The Asiatic Land Tenure and Indian Representation Act of 1943, which made provision for representation of the Indian population by white representatives in the Senate and House of Assembly, was repealed; the 1949 South Africa Citizenship Act, which extended domicile requirements for immigrants, had a similar effect of strengthening the Parliamentary position of the NP. In addition, the NP attempted to ensure continued support from the groups in the Afrikaner community which brought it into power: Afrikaner farmers, finance capitalists, small traders and workers all received massive hand-outs from government in the decade after 1948.[5] Farming subsidies were increased, state contracts were redirected to Afrikaner businesspersons, white workers benefited from food subsidies and civil servants gained salary increases amounting to 133 per cent between 1948 and 1958.[6] Indeed, the massive legislative programme pushed through Parliament in the 1950s served to introduce far-reaching social regulation, much of it aimed not only at securing power for a party feeling itself threatened from many directions, but also at recreating the nature of social division.

The period after the 1948 election was characterized by attempts to set in place a series of measures – far harsher than had existed ever before – to ensure the separation and regulation of the relation between 'white' and 'non-white'. During this period, what are commonly known as the four pillars of apartheid were set into place. The first consisted in the increasing restriction of the franchise and the virtual monopolization of centralized state power by Afrikaners. This involved, *inter alia*, the establishment of control over and strengthening of the repressive state apparatuses. The second consisted in what Cohen has called the enforced coincidence between spatial and 'racial' relations, both in the recasting and refinement of the regulation of urban African townships and later in the development of the 'homeland' 'grand apartheid' system.[7] The third consisted in the enforced regulation of the supply of labour to the mines, secondary industries, farms and white domestic households. The fourth consisted in the enforcement of various mechanisms of social control which involved extensive state interference in the spheres of employment, education, health, and so forth. As Cohen points out, there is some sense in seeing this aspect of apartheid – at least in intention – as a total system of social control, a 'womb to tomb' surveillance plan for the subjugated population.[8] It has, however, to be pointed out that this total system of regulation operated as much for the oppressor as for the oppressed, albeit with very different effects. Under apartheid, the lives of white South Africans were equally subjected to a similar womb-to-tomb 'streaming', instituting different schooling, educational and other institutions for Afrikaans- and English-speaking whites.

The relative weight attributed to these different dimensions of the apartheid project has been the subject of much debate and, to a large degree, positions taken on this depend on the precise characterization of the relation between the apartheid project and the development of capitalism in South Africa. The argument presented in this chapter does not aim to resolve the question as to whether economic growth shored up or eroded apartheid. As a number of commentators across the liberal/neo-Marxist divide have argued, to conceive of this relation in these terms is to use far too crude a measure which leads to overlooking the intricate complexities, both within Afrikanerdom and the state, and within the capitalist class.[9] While the question of the regulation of the labour market and the exploitation of labour can never be dissociated from the apartheid project, my argument is concerned with these dimensions only indirectly, in that it aims to show how the movement from myth to imaginary set into place a framework of knowledge which set certain limits to the possible ways in which those questions could have been addressed. In providing such an account, it is necessary to take issue with conventional interpretations of apartheid which divide its implementation into two separate and distinct phases: that of negative apartheid (1948–53) and positive apartheid (1959–61). On this view, initial apartheid legislation fell into the category of prohibitive, negative legislation, either seeking to reduce the contacts which industrialization and urbanization had induced, or to remove such rights as 'non-whites' possessed in 'European' areas. Legislation such as the Population Registration Act (1950), the Group Areas Act (1950), the Bantu Education Act (1953) and the Reservation of Separate Amenities Act (1953) are usually associated with this 'negative' phase.[10] 'Positive apartheid' legislation, on the other hand, is argued to consist in those measures which were associated with the re-creation of tribal–ethnic values and separate institutions for the expression of political rights, coinciding with the 'age of social engineering', as the 1960s is generally known. Within the Afrikaner nationalist movement, the distinction between negative and positive apartheid was associated with the distinction between 'practical' or social apartheid and 'total' apartheid, with the former focusing on the creation of separate places of work, separate amenities and residential areas while accepting territorial and economic integration, and the latter emphasizing the need for total apartheid in all areas of life, including the economic terrain. A third set distinction with which these 'phases' is associated is that between separation on an overt racial basis (*baasskap* apartheid), and separation based on 'ethnic' distinctions. In all of these cases, interpreters tend to argue for a clear-cut diachronic succession of phases of apartheid. It is my contention, however, that what characterizes the apartheid era is precisely a certain 'undecidability' between different divisionary logics which were present in its formulation and implementation from the very beginning of the apartheid era.

In chapters 1 and 2, I showed its presence in the ambiguous formulation of a new mythical principle of ordering. In the process of expansion of this myth into an imaginary, the 'undecidable' logics at the very heart of the apartheid project became ever clearer. During the first decade after the elections, the focus of the project shifted decisively from addressing the experiences of a particular group – Afrikanerdom – to acting as an imaginary surface of inscription which purported to provide an ordering principle for the whole of South African society. In order for a myth to contain the possibility of such an expansion, it is necessary that it exhibits a series of characteristics which have to be specified more closely. In the first place, it is clear that it must possess the capacity to act as a principle of reading for a specific and concrete experience of dislocation. In the second place, it must further be capable of acting as a generalizable surface of inscription. It must therefore contain both a specific content and a form which facilitates a displacement from its initial association with a specific set to wider social demands. If the dimension of specificity predominates, there will be little possibility for an expansion of the logic of the myth and its particular principle of reading to wider areas. Should, however, the conditions be such that the *form* of ordering becomes the more dominant, then, in principle, it can be transformed into a horizon of inscription for any possible social demand. An imaginary thus emerges insofar as there is a movement away from the specificity of the demands of a particular group to the very form of the metaphorical itself.[11] In the previous chapter, I gave an account of the attempts to create that impossible particular set of contents: the *volkseie*. In this chapter I will investigate the manner in which the expansion of the project involved an extension of the form of the ordering principle associated with it. It is important, however, to emphasize that the tension between its literal contents and the form of ordering is constitutive; they always stand in a relation of tension to one another, with neither of them ever managing finally and completely to assert themselves. There is always a precarious and unstable balance between the two extremes which is a precondition for thinking the hegemonization of social demands. To put it differently, if the myth remains essentially tied to the dislocations experienced by a particular group, it will not be able to extend its reading to other domains of social life. It will thus not be able to impose its vision on society, and so to become hegemonic. Alternatively, if such a new vision could be imposed fully and unequivocally, the possibility of hegemony would also be ruled out, for under such conditions society would be transparent to itself, thus excluding any struggles around its ordering principles. Indeed, this whole process is one in which struggle is central, both in the attempts to impose a new order, and in resistance to such impositions. The movement from myth to imaginary was indelibly marked by struggles, and the form it eventually took – the establishment of 'grand apartheid' – was the result of those struggles, shaped by historically contingent events.

In showing how this undecidable logic crystallized during the 1950s, I will argue that far from being only an enforcement of existing divisions, so as better to be able to exploit African labour, a new set of divisions were put into place which reshaped the form of that exploitation. Fundamental to this process was the recategorization of 'population groups' and the redefinition of their possible modes of 'interaction'. Hence, it is necessary to clarify the precise nature and operation of the racial logics at work in NP discourse. As I argued at the end of chapter 2, any attempt to come to terms with the operation of apartheid has to take account of the complexity of its operations of structuring and dividing 'population groups', especially of the differences between a more or less 'culturalist' search for authentic identity which may or may not be associated overtly with 'colour' differences, and a conception of social division based on overt 'racial' criteria. The period between the late 1940s and early 1960s witnessed a series of changes in use of 'racial' designators, indicative of shifts in the political frontiers which set the limits of apartheid as a discursive formation. Such resignification was one of the principal social mechanisms of control through which not only new modes of domination but also new interpellations were shaped. It is thus my contention that, far from being merely 'ideological', superstructural phenomena which ought to be remarked upon only to be discarded, these resignifications are crucial to any understanding of both the operation of apartheid and the effects it had on the formation of resistance strategies.

One such earlier shift has been documented by Dubow in his work on segregation. He quotes Sir Keith Hancock, who observed at the time that until the mid-1920s

> . . . the argument within the white political world about the proper relationship to be established between English- and Afrikaans-speaking South Africans had, by 'common consent', exercised priority over the argument as to the proper relationship between blacks and whites. '*In the political vocabulary of that time, the word racialism seldom if ever referred to the colour question.*'[12]

The fact that it is only during the 1920s that race became explicitly associated with 'colour' signified an important recasting of social division. As Dubow has noted, it was indicative of the intensified significance of the 'Native question' in the 1920s and 1930s which saw a vast outpouring of 'expert' writings on the subject.[13] The ambiguities in the use of this term did not, however, come to an end in the 1930s. It continued to be used to refer to 'differences' within the white population – between Afrikaans- and English-speakers – as well as to differences between 'white' and 'black'. As late as 1971 De Villiers could argue that the term 'race' designated both the cultural and physical differences between people:

> A race . . . is not only a group of people of common descent or origin: it also includes differences of outlook and attitude, of emotional values or mores. Different language groups, such as Afrikaans and English, or Nguni and Sotho, are popularly spoken of as races, but the physical differences are the most important.[14]

De Villiers's statement reflects much of official apartheid discourse after 1948, and this use had a wide currency. The expansion of the term to designate 'colour differences' did not simply displace the earlier usage of 'race' as a signifier of social division between Afrikaans- and English-speakers. Indeed, there are continued references in official discourse to the latter in terms of race well into the 1950s and even during the 1960s. It was only with the formation of a republic on the political horizon that a conscious attempt was made to construct another form of difference between these two groups. And it is not accidental that this occurred simultaneously with an official change in the designation of white South Africans from 'European' to 'white' and with an increasing substitution of the term *volk* with that of nation.[15]

Crucial to the development of the apartheid imaginary was the redefinition of other 'population categories'. The most significant of these changes were the division of the 'homogeneous' category of the 'Native' into distinct 'Bantu ethnic groups', and the attempts to decide the status of 'coloureds' *vis-à-vis* whites. Paradoxically, the precise terms of these redefinitions have not been subjected to systematic analysis. This, more than likely, results from the fact that apartheid has been regarded as an 'irrational' project which, by definition, could not be subjected to rational scrutiny. In contrast to this view, I argue that one has to give attention to variations in the articulation of racist logics so as to be able to account for their force and effects, for the forging of divisions are acts of power and violence, and these acts manifest themselves not in simple logics but in the production of complex forms of exclusion and inclusion. It is for this reason that the precise terms of the different forms of inclusion and exclusion have to be investigated for they did not operate on a clear-cut univocal basis. Racist discourses always exclude, and those exclusions are always ranked hierarchically, but they are not always the same.[16] Indeed, it is necessary to talk about a variety of forms of exclusion and inclusion which, welded together, formed the basis of apartheid discourse.

From the point of view of the victims of racism, it may be argued that these distinctions appear to be incidental, and were nothing but fine tunings which changed little in the experiences of the harsh realities of the lives of its victims. However, the point here is not to deny these realities, but to come to grips with their internal logics. The operation of apartheid not only divided the South African population, but with that division made it more difficult to foster a common sense of opposition and resistance. While at some levels coloureds, Africans and Indians did experience the same form of oppression and exclusion, at other levels, those experiences differed quite radically, fostered internal racisms and divisions between the members of oppressed communities, and led to different strategies of resistance. This resulted from the fact that the divisionary discourse of apartheid did take hold to some extent. The interpellations offered, while they excluded, at one and the same time also included differentially, causing interiorization which could not be experienced without conflict.

It is possible to attempt to systematize the various forms of racist domination without losing sight of the historically specific contexts in which they may have occurred. It is my contention that apartheid has historically combined different modes of racist division akin to both Nazism, a racism of extermination, and colonial domination, a racism of oppression.[17] The former aimed at purifying the social body of a 'stain' or of the 'danger' of 'inferior races', while the latter aimed at hierarchizing and partitioning society. These distinctions, however, are not mutually exclusive. As Balibar contends, Nazism combined extermination and deportation, and colonial racisms have practised both forced labour, ethnic separation and the systematic massacre of populations. In a similar fashion, apartheid engaged both in systematic economic exploitation and in equally systematic repression. In addition to these, it also constructed more insidious forms of racial domination, and the discourse of the *volkseie* was crucial to their production. It facilitated a combination of exteriorization and interiorization, and these forms of ambiguous exclusion and inclusion did not operate with any simple reference to empirically 'given' population groups. One could find oneself simultaneously excluded and included, depending on the subject position one occupied. The rest of this chapter will be given over to an examination of the operation of the logics, particularly as they pertained to the African and coloured populations.

Fostering Divisions: Apartheid's Early Years

The early years of apartheid were characterized not only by debates on African urbanization, but also by debates on the nature of apartheid as such. These debates went well beyond any narrow concern with the issue of African labour and urbanization. It is my contention that in a reading of the interventions of key commissions of inquiry, as well as of the different groupings within the Afrikaner nationalist movement, the significance of these 'wider' concerns will become apparent.

'Like water spreading over a plain': the meaning of African urbanization

In chapter 1, I discussed the general economic conditions during the late 1930s and the 1940s under which African urbanization took place. As with Afrikaner urbanization, African urbanization was not simply a phenomenon which already contained its meaning in itself. Its meaning was subject to a series of contestations, both within the African community, and within the dominant white community.

I also referred to the Fagan Commission's work on the operation of laws affecting 'natives' in urban and near urban areas. This commission investigated, more specifically, the workings of pass laws and the system of migratory labour in operation in the Union, all of which were set within the wider discussion of the question of African urbanization. The simile informing its analysis of African urbanization was that of water, coming from surrounding *kloofs* (ravines) and spreading out over a plain:

> Let us imagine a plain, which is divided amongst a large number of market gardeners. . . . Let us take it, too, that there is no irrigation scheme for this plain as a whole, but that it is left to each gardener, when he considers that his plot has water enough, to throw a bank around it so as to turn away the excess. . . . There may be conditions under which such a method would work well enough, e.g. if every gardener has sufficient means to control the quantity of water that reaches his plot, . . . if the amount of water is sufficient for everybody's requirements but not so great as to cause flooding. . . . Similarly, when our economic conditions were of a relatively simple type, when the population was small and the country spacious, the movement of Native labour could, without central planning, sufficiently adjust itself to the needs of both the Europeans and the Natives themselves. Experience has shown, however, that this is no longer the case. What would now appear to be urgently necessary is *a shifting of the emphasis from the local to the central authority*, so that comprehensive, co-ordinated plans for the whole terrain can be devised and put into operation. Certainly this involves an entirely new approach to the question. . . . [18]

In constructing this new approach, the Fagan Commission argued from a series of presuppositions regarding the nature of the inquiry in which it was engaged. The rhetoric employed was essentially an empiricist-objectivist one. Throughout the report, in attempting to debunk various popular myths about 'Natives' and the process and effects of 'Native urbanization', the objectivity of 'facts' was set against subjective factors such as emotion, feelings and ideologies:

> The Commission . . . does not consider itself called upon to enter into an ethical or theoretical discussion of different ideologies. It must accept facts and sentiments as it finds them and look for the practical arrangements which will suit them best.[19]

In their discussion, the writers of the report presented a series of important 'facts' upon which their analysis was based. For example, 'influx' was portrayed as a 'natural' phenomenon, occurring as a result of normal processes of development. It was in essence a purely economic phenomenon, also occurring with regard to other races, which could be regulated, but which could not be prevented. Hence, for the first time in the Union's history, the idea was envisaged of a permanent African urban population which would have to be given some measure of control over their 'own' affairs. This, for the Fagan Commission, had the advantage of ensuring a stable labour force for secondary industries and farms, while mines would continue to draw upon migratory labour. The 'Native population' was presented as a cog in a machine, and their positioning in society depended upon their function in the operation of this machine. This commission began the process of differentiation of 'Natives' into distinct categories by virtue of their places within the productive machine of the economy.[20]

While the commission report is usually hailed as the long-lost liberal opportunity for South Africa, the document remained limited in the extent to which it challenged the racial structure of division in the country.[21] This resulted both from the position it took on the question of 'race' and the mechanisms prescribed for the regulation of labour. While it tried to debunk a number of popularly held beliefs – such as the belief that 'the Natives multiply more rapidly than other sections of the population' – and while it fully recognized the devastating effects of the system of migrant labour, it did not for a moment question the principle of residential separation, which was seen as a 'fixed policy' in South Africa.[22] Whereas the report questioned race as a legitimate basis for discrimination, it did not question the legitimacy of racial separation itself.[23] Indeed, Fagan argued that differences between the 'Europeans' and the 'Bantu' were fundamental. Hence the need to continue to regulate 'contact' between them: 'there are differences between the races to which legislation has to pay due regard and which makes a measure of separation in administrative affairs necessary and advisable. . . .'[24] Legislation, it argued, should ideally not be based on racially discriminatory terms; however, there had to be 'frank recognition of the fact that today we find Natives in all stages of development and all stages of adaptation to the European way of life and thought'.[25] As a consequence, the 'wide' category of 'Natives' had to be disaggregated. In the first instance, it made a distinction between Native villages within municipal areas and Native villages outside such areas, and for each category, different regulatory measures were prescribed.[26] Moreover, in bemoaning the insensitive application of the wide term 'Native' the report argued that 'raw *kraal*' Natives amongst migrant labourers – who were strangers to

European ideas of sanitation, cleanliness and hygiene – could not be assimilated to 'Natives in a transitional state', or to those who have adapted themselves to European civilization. These differences had to be taken into account and categorizations had to be developed which would embrace only one 'class of person and no one else'.[27] Finally, a distinction was drawn between the economically productive population, and 'idlers', 'disorderly persons' and 'other lawless elements' which, the report suggested, could be dealt with under Section 29 of the Urban Areas Act.[28] They could be removed from urban areas and sent to work on farm colonies or other similar institutions.[29] These measures, it was argued, were only in an 'indirect sense' based on racial division. Primarily, it aimed at combating general 'criminal and anti-social behaviour'. In this it concurred with a new Work Colonies Bill in preparation by the Department of Social Welfare.[30] In the very movement of the disaggregation of the category of the Native, the report thus fashioned a plethora of new 'subjects' which could be controlled and disciplined on measures not 'directly' related to the regulation of the relation between races. These measures foreshadowed regulations that would, during the 1980s, attempt to regulate the flow of people to the cities in 'indirect' fashion.

In the process of establishing the veracity of its proposals, the commission analysed the feasibility of other alternatives to the regulation of the relation between white and black. It listed three such alternatives: that of total segregation, that of no racial discrimination in law and administration, and a third, placed between the two already mentioned, which recognized that European and Native communities would continue to exist permanently side by side, but advocated that differences between them had to be taken into account by legislation. The report rejected the first alternative as both economically untenable and as morally unacceptable since it was based upon a system of migrant labour which caused great economic, moral and social dislocation.[31] The second alternative was also rejected for it failed to take account of the fundamental differences between the races. The Fagan position thus emerged as the practical, middle-ground position, based on observation of 'facts' alone. As a result of political events overtaking the commission – the National Party winning the 1948 election – its recommendations were never enacted.

Before discussing the manner in which African urbanization was constructed in the discourse of Afrikaner nationalism, it is important to point out that the possibility of 'total segregation' was one not only found within Afrikaner circles. Already in 1939, in his *South African Native Policy and the Liberal Spirit*, R.F.A. Hoernlé held it up as a liberal ideal.[32] He argued that total separation

> . . . into distinct White and Black 'areas of liberty' must be considered a genuine liberal ideal, if it means that breaking-up of the present caste-society which *as a whole* can never be a free society, or a society of free men, seeing that it makes the liberties necessary for a 'good life' the exclusive privilege of the dominant caste. . . .
>
> I suggest that, from this point of view (namely that this policy may find favour with the white groups genuinely concerned for the welfare of the non-whites), total separation should be the liberal's choice. To choose total assimilation is to condemn himself to utter impotence in the face of existing race feelings: he can do nothing for the realization of greater liberty for the non-European groups if he adopts total assimilation as his professed objective. To choose parallelism is to choose a policy which will not in practice abolish racial domination: so long as Whites and non-Whites are united in the same socio-political structure, the former will not consent to surrender their dominance. Parallelism will remain domination in disguise. . . . For the Native people of the Union, at any rate, it should be clear that there is no *escape from White domination* by way of parallelism or assimilation, but only by way of total segregation.[33]

Hoernlé realized that the policy would not be practicable, since it demanded too many sacrifices by way of power, prestige, economic advantage and convenience of the white man. By 1948, in response to the Fagan report, A.W. Hoernlé argued that the ideal of total separation advocated by her husband 'envisaged an organization of the warring sections into genuinely separate self-contained, self-governing societies, each in principle homogeneous within itself, which can co-operate on a footing of mutual recognition of one another's independence'.[34] But, given that the National Party's colour policy did not contemplate sovereign independence, and given that 'everyone would agree that the Non-European groups are by no means ready to take over such an independent state even if such a thing were feasible in Southern Africa', the only alternative was 'integration of all our races into our South African state'.[35] It has, however, to be pointed out that this vision of 'integration' was a strictly limited one. While cultural assimilation had to take place as a matter of policy, and economic integration had to be stimulated, socially, she envisaged a wide use of 'parallel institutions and separate areas of residence, in the interest of the protection of racial integrity', which were 'not incompatible with Western European ideals and indeed not with Christian principles seeing that different races are not man-made but part of the given structure of the Universe'. But, in contrast to the parallelism of 'separate and unequal' institutions and relations between white and black, this parallelism had to be strictly on the basis of 'separate but equal', thus contradicting the thought of R.A.F. Hoernlé, who argued that any 'parallelism' within one structure would necessarily continue white domination.

Within Afrikaner circles, the idea of total separation was first mooted by H. du Plessis in 1935, who proposed it as the ultimate Christian national solution to South Africa's problems.[36] For him there was no middle way between the stark alternatives of assimilation and rigid apartheid. Challenging liberals who had purportedly launched a campaign to 'detribalize' the Natives and to convert them to Western civilization, he proposed that the *volk* 'sacrifice sufficient ground [land] so that [Natives] can be segregated very gradually and in the most practical way. . . . Within their own areas, they must develop under White guardianship until, after 100, 1 000, or 2000 years, they can be independent without presenting a danger to us Whites.'[37] The *Afrikanerbond vir Rassestudie* (Afrikaner League for Racial Studies), founded in 1935, favoured a similar solution. Its secretary was M.C. de Wet Nel, a Transvaal NP organizer, later to become Minister of Bantu Administration under H.F. Verwoerd; it was chaired by P.J.S de Klerk of Potchefstroom, and it also had as a member C.W. Prinsloo from Pretoria University's Department of Bantu Languages, who was later to become Chief Commissioner for Bantu Affairs. As I argued in chapters 1 and 2, the writings of Cronje and Prinsloo published in *Rassebakens* were preoccupied with putting a stop to racial integration in the cities. The *Afrikanerbond* adopted total racial separation as its slogan in order to distinguish it from the less rigourous notion of segregation.[38] The manner in which the idea of total apartheid could have entered both the writings of the *Afrikanerbond vir Rassestudie* and later SABRA's publications was through the activities of the AB, which in 1933 recommended in a secret document that 'total mass segregation' was not only an ideal but also had to be implemented as a matter of immediate practical policy.[39] It called for the settlement of 'different tribes' in separate areas, which, over time, would gain some degree of self-government. As was later to be argued in the Sauer report, temporary migrants working in towns would be encouraged to move to their own areas, or be compelled to live in separate locations.

These ideas were also found in a paper, published in 1948, by W.W.M. Eiselen.[40] The significance of Eiselen's intervention lies in the fact that he consistently denied the basis upon which arguments for inherent racial inferiority were made at the time. He stated unequivocally that

> [t]he commonplace assertion that Natives will require centuries of contact with western civilization before attaining intellectual parity with Europeans is scientifically untenable and furthermore disproved by successful careers of a number of individuals.[41]

This led him to problematize both the liberal vision as found in the Fagan report and the principle of the 'horizontal colour bar' (practical apartheid). The latter, based upon the assumption that Natives should continue to form a lower subordinate stratum of a European-centred society, was nothing but an evil system of sheer domination, tempered with trusteeship.[42] The former, he argued, contained several important statements which could, in no way, be reconciled with the aspirations of 'our Native population':

> What does the [Fagan] Commission mean by quoting with approval these words of one of the witnesses: 'We need the Natives and they need us'? Does it mean that we need them as equals or does it mean that we need them as servants and labourers and that they need us as masters and employers? The Commission supplies the answer. It says 'that whether we think it desirable or not the economic structure of South Africa is based on the one hand on European initiative, organization and technical skill, on the other hand no less on the availability of a few million Native labourers'. Is this not merely an euphemistic restatement of the familiar slogan 'white man's brain and black man's brawn?' . . . One wonders whether in their zeal to oppose the idea of separation at all costs they allowed themselves to be trapped into expressing approval of principles which smack very strongly of the domination complex.[43]

His practical recommendations for the establishment of total separation – the only sane, unbiased and honest policy for him – included the retention of a system of migrant labour for the mines; increasing mechanization of agriculture to replace Native labour, in addition to controlled immigration of agricultural labourers from overcrowded countries of Western Europe; and the decentralization of secondary industries to Native areas.[44] Many of the features of his recommendations would be found in the NP's Sauer report and in the later work of SABRA.[45]

The policy of the *Afrikaner Party*, which entered into an election pact with the HNP in March 1947, dealt with 'natives' in general, and did not concentrate on the issue of urbanization to the same extent as the HNP. One of its core principles specified that Natives were to be recognized as a *permanent* part of the country's population under the Christian trusteeship of the European races.[46] By contrast, the policy of the *Blanke Werkersparty* (BWP, White Workers' Party), under the leadership of L.T. Weichardt, held that it was committed to a policy of territorial segregation, as well as a promotion of the 'tribal life of the Native according to his own *volksaard* [*volk*'s character] and tradition'.[47] It is interesting to note that the BWP also specified that it would promote a similar policy towards coloureds such that they would develop their 'own *volksgemeenskap*' (*volk*'s communities) in a territory set aside for them. The BWP did not field its own candidates in the 1948 election and it could therefore be assumed that its votes went towards the HNP/AP candidates. In 1947, the HNP appointed its own 'Colour commission' to investigate the regulation of the relation between white and black, and it was this commission's views which were to be implemented in the post-1948 period. Its initial policy, however, was set out in the HNP's 1943 'Economic Plan for South Africa'. This document reiterated the view popularized by the *volksbeweging* that the party was neither 'capitalistic' nor 'communistic', but national. This meant that, while private property and initiative were accepted, they had to be regulated and controlled by the state so as to prevent exploitation of one group by another, and to harness the advantages of development in the interest of the *volk*. This was to be the case especially for key industries such as the gold mines, and the iron and steel industries. Moreover, the report made black urbanization a key element of its policy.[48] This was in line with the growing perception that black urbanization posed a threat to white civilization and that, as a result of the neglect of the Smuts government to act, a process of 'equalization' between black and white was underway. As *Die Transvaler* put it in a 1946 editorial: '[blacks] are crowding out whites with their unhygienic and dirty manners of living'.[49] In order to stem the 'flooding' of whites by blacks, the HNP plan argued that it was in everyone's fundamental interest that the white race and white civilization should be protected on the social and economic terrain. Following from this imperative, in similar vein to the Fagan Commission, the implications of black urbanization were treated as matter of economic calculation. 'Non-whites' were 'an important economic asset' and the use made of this asset had to be in accordance with 'essential social frontiers'.[50]

It was, however, left to the Sauer Commission to give further substance to these ideas.[51] This commission, appointed by the National Party in 1947 – consisting of P.O. Sauer, G.B.A. Gerdener, E.G. Jansen, J.J. Serfontein and M.C. de Wet Nel – had to formulate NP policy on the colour question with reference to the relation between whites, Natives, coloureds and Indians. In setting out the terms of this investigation, Malan argued that it had to investigate the implementation of apartheid in the political and industrial terrains, and also had to consider the question of residential segregation; it had to be practical, positive and constructive, rather than negative and divisionary in character.[52] A proper exegesis of the report requires that it is read not merely with a view to scrutinizing its recommendations for the regulation of relations between 'white' and 'black', but also to clarify the grounds upon which those recommendations were made. The report started out by naming two contrasting directions which policy towards 'non-white races' have taken in South Africa: that of *apartheid* and that of *equalization*. In this, it echoed the thought of the organic intellectuals discussed in chapter 2. It divided the advocates of 'equalization' into two schools of thought. The first was 'communism', which denied 'the fundamental character of the distinction between white and non-white'. The second was liberalism. While liberals were not in favour of miscegenation, and did not argue explicitly for social equalization, they, nevertheless, had taken no steps against racial mixing, and demanded equal rights regardless of race within one society. On the reading of the Sauer Commission, both these schools of thought would inexorably lead to equalization. They only differed in the manner and timing of its realization: both would have the effect of subverting and finally extinguishing the white race as an independent and governing *volk*. Apartheid, in contrast to these two schools of thought, was argued to have grown out of the indigenous experience of both Afrikaans- and English-speaking whites; was grounded upon Christian principles of right and reasonableness and upon the conviction that the separate development of white and non-white parts of the *volk* was the only basis upon which all parts of the *volk* could be treated justly and could have the chance each to develop its own *volk*'s character. It rejected any form of oppression as wrong and detrimental to the *volk*.

The report listed three main aims of the apartheid policy: first, the maintenance of the white population and a complete eradication of any racial mixing; second, the maintenance of the indigenous non-white racial groups as separate *volksgemeenskappe* by working against any influences aiming to undermine those separate identities and by facilitating opportunities to develop each according to its own *volk*'s character; third, the maintenance of the traditional principle of trusteeship, which entailed the fostering of national pride and self-respect for each group, and the encouragement of mutual respect between different racial groups. To this end, each racial group had to have its own territory in which it would be able to develop its inalienable right to self-maintenance and self-determination. In contrast to the Fagan report, it ruled out the possibility of any 'middle road' or compromise on this question, and made apartheid the only possible solution to the problems created by the slide towards equalization. 'Equalization' took on the meaning of 'racial suicide', which could only be avoided by accepting apartheid as based on the 'healthy' principles of Christian nationalism. Indeed, the report echoed almost every theme found in the discourse of the new intellectuals: the differentiation between races and peoples was divinely ordained; each race and racial group had its own character (*volksaard*), calling and destination; and any policy of oppression and exploitation of non-whites by whites was regarded as in conflict with the basic ethical and Christian grounding of the life of the *volk*.[53] As with the discourse of the organic intellectuals, the report also vacillated between the use of racial 'colour' terms and the use of the terms '*volk*', designating ethnic and cultural differences.

A reading of this report as a mere continuation of segregationism – since it envisaged the reserves to be run on the model of the Bunga system – is possible only by disregarding the traces of a wholly new conception of social division evident within it. The deepening of the second basic tenet, set out in Article E3, held that the most important *ethnic* groups should each be drawn together territorially so that each could develop as separate national units, offering a spiritual, national and economic home to the natives. It was hoped that this would encourage 'talented and progressive Natives' to move there in order to use their initiatives in the service of their own people. The best social and welfare services had to be provided in these reserves. The state form of the reserves was also clearly regarded as in a period of transition, with the Native Councils scheduled for replacement by councils for each ethnic group. The report, in fact, was permeated with the language of ethnic specificity. These references have to be placed in the network of signifiers within this report which gave them their meaning: references to mother-tongue education; the depiction of the reserves as 'cradles of nations'; the multiple references to 'national pride' and the necessity of Christian national trusteeship. In all of these matters, the report seemed to favour a policy of *total* apartheid. When dealing with Natives on farms and in the cities, the commission, however, took a different position. It advocated the continued use of Native labour on farms and held that the 'detribalized Native' had to be regarded as a 'visitor' in the cities until such time as the ideal of total apartheid could be reached. Since these Natives were only temporary visitors, they would *never* be able to claim equal political rights with whites. Moreover, cities had a 'white character' that had to be maintained. To this end, separate Native locations had to be established and steps had to be taken to diminish the number of Natives in the cities and to reinstate their tribal links. Indeed, it argued that

> . . . the urbanization of natives is in conflict with the policy of apartheid and the Native can thus never form part of the urban population. The influx into the cities has to be subjected to all possible limitations and the Native has to be informed of the disadvantages of urbanization and the advantages of an own national home.[54]

The report thus vacillated between a conception of total and practical apartheid:

> We put as final ideal and aim *total* separation between whites and natives which has to be implemented as far as is *practical* on a gradual basis, with consideration of the needs of the country and with the necessary prevention of detribalization of agriculture, industries and general interests.[55]

In contrast to the Fagan report, which held that it did not have to address the question of the position of coloureds and Indians, the Sauer report gave considerable attention to these two groups. In line with the general sentiment in the *volksbeweging* it argued that Indians were to be regarded as 'foreign' and unassimilable', had to be treated as immigrants and had to be repatriated as far as possible as a matter of policy. By contrast, coloureds were held to occupy a 'middle' position between white and black. Residential, social, industrial and political apartheid between white and coloured had to be set into place, and mixed marriages between them had to be strictly forbidden. On the political terrain, it envisaged the creation of a Coloured Representative Council to replace the existing voting rights of coloureds. Here, as elsewhere, the report hesitated between different conceptions of apartheid, and between different forms of social division: racial and cultural/national. These two sets of concerns were intimately connected and finely intertwined and arose from different intellectual and organizational positions of enunciation within the *volksbeweging*. While the total segregation position would become the option favoured by the SABRA – created by the AB in 1947 to address the status of coloureds, the rights of the urban African population and the development of reserves – it would not be until 1952 that it would publish its view in substantially elaborated form.[56] Nevertheless, the opinion expressed at the *Volkskongres* of 1950 already indicated a preference for the 'separate and distinct development' of different population groups. In the aftermath of this *Volkskongres* organized by the Afrikaans churches in 1950, *Die Kerkbode*, the mouthpiece of the DRC, reported that the reserves should be transformed into 'national homes' for the Africans, and that African labour should

> be gradually and systematically eliminated from white industrial life and integrated into their own industrial life in their own areas. . . . To this end, large sacrifices will be asked of the white population.[57]

Similarly, *Die Kerkblad*, monthly journal of the Reformed Church, reported Gerdener's opening address, stressing the difference between nations, and the divine sanctioning of those differences, with approval.[58] In a later issue of *Die Kerkblad*, Howy, one of the Reformed Church delegates, posed and answered the question 'What is apartheid?' in the following manner:

> . . . it is the separate development of the white and non-white population groups as the only foundation upon which everyone could be treated justly and in which each can have the chance to develop its peculiar character as a people.[59]

He went on to report on the address by P.J. Coertze, which set out various solutions to the problem of Natives in the cities. Coertze argued, in familiar fashion, that only three possible solutions to this problem existed: total integration or complete equalization; partial integration or the existing 'colour bar' policy; and total apartheid. While the conference was in favour of the third, Howy reported that it had stressed the fact that total separation would be an ideal solution, but one which could not be brought about within the next fifty to a hundred years. The debates at this *Volkskongres*, in many senses, ran parallel to those in SABRA, and between the NP and SABRA. Indeed, the government of the day very quickly responded to the proposals put forward by the congress, arguing that it was completely impractical, thus foreshadowing the negative response by Verwoerd to calls for total apartheid.[60]

SABRA's 1952 document, *Integration or Separate Development?*, explicitly set out to show not only the practicability of total apartheid, but also its moral superiority. Arguing against economic integration, it held that

> . . . where an individual or a minority group is . . . totally absorbed in the economy of another community, that individual or groups is ultimately assimilated in the social, political, cultural and biological society of the larger group. But if the element which is assimilated is numerically stronger and shows greater vitality than the original group, there is a real danger that it will not be the 'absorbed' group but rather the original community which will lose its identity in the new unity.[61]

Demands for the stabilization of labour in an integrated economy would lead to an inevitable increase in the urban Native population, which in turn would lead to increasing demands for political rights. SABRA, however, felt that it was unnecessary to comment on such 'fantastic' demands. Instead, it set out three other possibilities for the settlement of political rights for Natives: first, the creation of a separate parliament for Natives; second, provision for limited group representation of the Native population through the European Parliament; and, third, the granting of the vote, on a communal voters' roll together with Europeans, to those Natives who satisfied certain fixed qualifications. The first was rejected on the grounds that in an integrated society a community of interests would be created, such that it would be impossible to find a solution which would 'satisfy the political aspirations of the Native population as well as give the European Parliament final say over all the matters where European interests were also concerned'. The second, limited group representation was discarded on the grounds that there were no reasonable grounds to presume that Natives would be satisfied with this type of representation in the long run. The third possibility was also rejected on the grounds that criteria for qualification would be set either so high that the masses would not be satisfied, or so low that the security and survival of the European and his political leadership would be endangered.[62] Hence, the policy of integration was portrayed as dishonest since it created the impression that political demands would be fully satisfied, 'when in fact the integration supporters are well aware that the Europeans would never allow such a development to take place, since their political leadership must necessarily be threatened by it'.[63] The only logical solution, then, was one which made provision for the free and separate development of the two racial groups.

For SABRA its policy of total apartheid or separate development – a policy that envisaged the full development of the two groups in separate areas – also had to be distinguished from those who saw apartheid as a mechanism to ensure the continued subordination of the Bantu to the white man. SABRA argued that such local or 'social' apartheid – with its emphasis on separate places of work, separate residential areas, separate public amenities, separate entrances and exits, separate queues and so forth – with the retention of territorial and economic integration was ultimately guided by one or both of the following considerations: that the European could in the long run not maintain his dominating position and that all that could be done was to postpone the evil day as long as possible; or that the ease and comfort of the present should be paramount – future generations would have to find a lasting solution.[64] SABRA held that this form of apartheid neither eliminated the possibility of friction between the races, nor offered the possibility of full realization of national potential. Most problematically, it left unsolved the question of the political rights of Natives.

SABRA's own solution, total territorial apartheid, demanded sacrifices on the part of Europeans, but it argued that it was not impossible to attain. The reserves had to be developed so that in the long run they could absorb the whole of the Native population and become self-sufficient economic units in their own right, as opposed to being 'sub-economic appendages' to white industries. The process of extricating the existing urban African population, SABRA argued, would be a gradual process, so as not to upset the economy. Ultimately, the economy could still rely on migrant labour, but that had to be limited to 'young, unmarried' labourers. SABRA's argument, as is clear from its distancing of itself from 'local' apartheid, was not done merely in the name of white supremacy. While a discourse of racial division was explicitly present, it was overdetermined with a discourse of 'self-determination' and a concern with the destruction of the 'organic unity of the various Bantu communities'. The reserves, under a system of total apartheid, could in the long run offer a political home for the Bantu. There Bantu communities could be granted an increasing measure of control over their own affairs, which, SABRA argued, was necessary if the question of political rights were approached objectively:

> . . . whatever the Europeans do, the Bantu *must* be given the opportunity for political development. Throughout the rest of Africa constitutional

developments are following one another in fast succession – all too fast, in our opinion; it cannot be thought that such developments will not affect the Union's Bantu population, or that the Union can follow a policy which bears no relation whatsoever to occurrences in the rest of Africa.[65]

SABRA's arguments for total apartheid were echoed almost word for word by the *Instituut vir Volkswelstand*, one of the members of the *Broederbond*-controlled FAK. It concluded, like SABRA, that the detribalization accompanying the migrant labour system was problematic for it undermined tribal authority and culture; and that the urbanization of African workers signified the permanent integration of Africans into 'white' areas and had therefore to be resisted.[66] This was in contrast to the position articulated by the *Afrikaanse Handelsinstituut* (AHI, Afrikaans Commercial Institute) launched by the *Broederbond* in 1942 as one of the instruments of the economic movement.[67] As Posel points out, it regarded the alternatives to African labour offered by the 'total segregationists' as wholly unacceptable. For it, the overriding concern was a practical one. 'Non-white' workers were already an integral part of the economy, and this made total segregation 'wishful thinking'. It did, however, uphold the principle of influx control, but argued that this had to be done in conjunction with a decreasing reliance on migrant labour, for, like Fagan, it argued that secondary industries needed a stabilized, permanent labour force. The South African Agricultural Union (SAAU), on the other hand, saw increasing African urbanization as a threat to adequate labour resources on the farms. White farmers, Posel argues, were therefore drawn to the idea of apartheid as a system whereby state control over the allocation of labour would correct this 'maldistribution' of labour.[68] In this they agreed with the Sauer report, which argued that all possible means had to be used to prevent the flow of African labourers away from the farms.[69] That did not mean, however, that they opposed African urbanization as such, only that its rate had to be strictly controlled according to urban and farming needs.[70]

While it is clear that economic considerations played a crucial role in the total/practical apartheid debate – a debate which would never be completely resolved in principle or in practice – it is equally clear that the manner in which African urbanization as well as the position of coloureds were approached was set in a context which cannot merely be reduced to the economic 'interests' of different groupings within the *volksbeweging*. As was the case with the thought of the organic intellectuals discussed in the previous chapter, the debate was marked by a certain vacillation between the need to preserve 'white supremacy' and the need to recognize 'ethnic self-determination' and the self-development of *volkere* also on the economic terrain. Interpretations of this debate which focus exclusively on the economic dimensions of proposals for influx control, and which thus tend to reduce apartheid to a preoccupation with labour-related issues, can do so only by ignoring its distinctiveness from segregation, and by disregarding the extent of overdetermination established between the different interpretations. To put it differently, the complex articulation between these different interpretations can only be understood when placed in the wider symbolic horizon of apartheid which provided the framework within which measures relating to the regulation of economic life and labour were conceived. And in this framework, a series of issues far wider than economic concerns with controlling the 'influx' of Africans into the cities were at stake. This is also the reason why, for *essential* reasons, the tension between the different conceptions of apartheid was not finally resolvable: the *logic* of apartheid depended upon their mutually contradictory presence.

Refining exclusions: early apartheid legislation

It is not the case that 'positive' apartheid only came into being with the Bantu Self-Government Bill of 1959. Although the NP consistently argued that total apartheid was an ideal, but an impractical one, and much water had to run into the sea before the Bantu Self-Government Bill could be conceived and implemented, many of the measures introduced during the early 1950s contained elements of the vision contained in 'total apartheid' and more often than not displayed a decided undecidability between the two conceptions of 'difference' contained in the signifier 'apartheid'. In discussing the interlacing of these two conceptions of apartheid, I will show how the resignifications which resulted from these measures infinitely increased the scope of control over and interference in the lives of ordinary South Africans, how the boundaries of legitimate political action were redefined, how previously 'private' activities were criminalized, and how all of this came about as a result of the reorganization of social division and the establishment of a new configuration of meanings and values based upon an extension of the idea of the *volkseie* to other groups. This expansion of the myth into an imaginary was characterized by a deep unevenness in its application, which, in turn, can be attributed to bureaucratic resistance to the implementation of these measures, as well as to a more generalized resistance originating in the communities at which these measures were aimed.

Widely hailed to be one of the pillars of apartheid, the Population Registration Act (1950) and the Immorality Amendment Act (1950) followed shortly on the introduction of the Mixed Marriages Act (1949). Together they constituted the first legal attempts to regulate the relation not between Africans and whites, but between coloureds and whites. The full force of the extension of apartheid was thus first felt by the coloured population, who, on the view of the NP, constituted a 'middle position' between white and black. Insofar as apartheid was concerned with the maintenance and protection of the 'white race', it could be argued that the Mixed Marriages Act is logically and symbolically at the very heart of apartheid policy.[71] The legislation on mixed marriages, immorality and population registration formed the basis of a philosophy that saw 'racial purity' as a virtue. On this view, the maintenance of racial purity required legislation for it could be preserved only if there existed a generalized 'heightened racial consciousness'. Malan, at the 1949 Cape NP Conference, argued that even more disturbing than the UN or the communists was the fact that some whites were 'losing their colour consciousness'. This was supposed to be most evident in the occurrence of 'mixed marriages'.[72] During the debate of a private member's bill on the Prohibition of Mixed Marriages proposed in 1936, concern was repeatedly expressed about the tendency of poor whites to draw closer to the coloured population in the towns, resulting in 'mixed marriages'.[73] The argument often heard then was repeated again: our 'weaker brothers and sisters' had to be protected against themselves and against their own weaknesses.[74] This law was also seen to express the strong feeling of public opinion against mixed marriages, thus reflecting the position popularized by Cronje and others, that racial consciousness was rooted in the traditional attitude of white South Africans.

The opposition United Party was in full agreement with the NP on this matter. Miscegenation was a social evil, had to be abhorred, and mixed marriages were not to be approved.[75] However, whereas the National Party felt that legislation was needed to curb the spread of this social evil, the United Party argued that it was a domain of social conduct not amenable to legislation, and that the strong public disapproval of it would act as a sufficient deterrent. The only voices within Parliament to condemn the measures in principle were members of the Labour Party, and the (white) Natives' Representatives, especially the communist Sam Kahn, who put forward a most classical liberal defence of freedom of choice and action.[76] The United Party's opposition was based on practical considerations alone, and its failure to oppose the Bill in principle foreshadowed the nature of Parliamentary opposition to the introduction of many apartheid measures during the 1950s. The UP was concerned not with a rejection of the principles of racial hierarchization which underpinned the law, but with the fact that the law would be difficult to implement. This was the case especially since the definition of racial categorizations was unclear.

The NP and its allies, the Afrikaans churches, which urged the NP to introduce legislation in this regard, clearly did not agree with the UP on this matter. Both the 1944 and 1947 *Volkskongresse* specified the issue of miscegenation as an essential aspect of apartheid.[77] The Afrikaans churches called for legislation to combat threats to the character of the *volk*, and a number of delegations during the 1940s requested specific prohibitive legislation on the matter.[78] The response of the UP, then the government, was the same as later in 1949, that social evils could not be combated by means of legislation. In 1948, the Afrikaans churches again sent a joint deputation to the Minister of the Interior, Dr Dönges, reiterating their request. This time, in the light of the apartheid programme outlined by Sauer, the request did not fall on deaf ears. Indeed, Dönges, in his closing remarks on the debate, argued explicitly that public opinion was less effective under circumstances of 'industrialization and mixed neighbourhoods' where a 'deadening of racial consciousness' occurred.[79] Something had to be done to prevent the occurrence of 'social problems', such as family feuding and a lack of tradition, which resulted from miscegenation,[80] and the Mixed Marriages Act was to fulfil this function of countering miscegenation as far as possible, and promoting racial purity. This was seen as a first step, to be followed by the prohibition of extra-marital miscegenation.

A number of important facets of the Bill and the ensuing debate call for further comment. In the first place, the Bill did not prohibit marriages between different 'non-European' groups, and was, thus, not so much concerned with a general protection of racial purity as with the protection of the racial purity of the white nation. During the debate itself an unspecified sense of a 'need' to protect the purity of the white race was given a more specific content. The new lines of social division introduced with this bill quickly became apparent in the constant references to coloureds. They represented a limit case to the logic of apartheid. The 'coloured community' had never been clearly differentiated from the 'white' community. To a large extent, they shared a culture, religion and language with the Afrikaner population. They had voting rights in the Cape Province, and were not subjected to legislation as a group under segregation. But, as a number of investigations have revealed, the process of reconstituting an Afrikaner *volk* during the 1930s and 1940s also entailed an exclusion of coloureds who previously might have considered themselves to be Afrikaners, a purification of the Afrikaans language, as well as attempts to restrict the absorption of middle-class coloureds into the white community.[81] In both the Immorality Ammendment Act and the Population Registration Acts the status of the coloured population as a community clearly separable from the white community was thus at stake. Much of the debate was given over to the 'problem' of determining their 'racial characteristics' in order to draw the lines of division. The solution reached was that since the South Africa Act did not include a strict definition of 'European', one was not necessary here either. The criteria to be used were to be appearance, social contacts and descent, in that order. Finally, it is remarkable, given this situation, that it was deemed unnecessary explicitly to provide anything amounting to a justification of the measure to be introduced. The discursive horizon set by segregation made this largely superfluous. A measure tearing communities apart, deepening the hierarchy of privilege and introducing 'racial' division where formerly it did not exist became law without much immediate Parliamentary opposition. It 'simply fulfilled' what was promised in the Sauer report: that all marriages between 'Europeans' and 'non-Europeans' were to be prohibited.

While the white opposition press did not do much to condemn the measure and the Bill did not seem to produce strong resistance from the African and Indian communities, the radical rejection by *The Torch* captures something of the flavour and strength of opposition within the coloured community. An editorial in *The Torch* expressed their abhorrence:

> In the name of false gods – race purity, race superiority, the Voortrekker ideal, and the narrow, crushing, suffocating cant of the medieval, black-frocked, bigoted, arrogant and ignorant dominees who preside over events in South Africa . . . one more freedom is sacrificed at the shrine of Herrenvolkism. . . .[82]

Little official response was forthcoming from the Afrikaans churches, while the measure was condemned by the English-speaking churches. The event which most clearly showed the Afrikaans churches' feeling on the matter was the public response to the contemporaneous marriage of Seretse Khama in 1949. It was roundly condemned by various official church bodies, and the terms of their condemnation were telling. It was held to justify social equalization, undermine the position of whites through the production of a 'hybrid race', gradually leading to the destruction of the purity of the white race, and eventually threatening white civilization and Christendom.[83] Not much was needed to link the approval of 'mixed marriages' to the threat of communism and equalization. Indeed, much of the Parliamentary debate, echoing the general themes of NP discourse at the time, did exactly that.[84] Labour Party, UP and Communist Party members were all portrayed as in cahoots in their resistance to the Bill. The drawing of these equivalences continued in the debates on the Immorality Amendment Act of 1950, an amendment to the 1927 Immorality Act which extended the prohibition of sexual intercourse between whites and Africans to the coloured community. The Bill was thought to form a natural corollary to the Mixed Marriages Act, for 'it stood to reason' that miscegenation could not be dealt with effectively if 'illicit unions' were to be permitted.[85] Also here, liberals and communists were thrown together in one camp, working for 'total equalization' which would inevitably lead to miscegenation. Nothing could be further from the truth in the case of the UP, which, once again, did not question the need for racial purity. If any single theme present in this debate could be drawn out it was that racial purity was of paramount and unquestionable importance:

> I want to say that this act, which prohibits miscegenation between white and non-white, touches upon one of our most important racial questions, namely that of the mixing of blood . . . on this side of the House, we have always been concerned with racial diversity, the preservation of races, and racial purity. . . . [86]

Racial pride, it was argued, was a characteristic of all Afrikaners, most whites, all 'decent' coloureds and of the Bantu who valued tribal traditions.[87] But here again, the question arose as to how difference in race could be established such that a racial pride could be fostered. In this respect, a number of NP MPs argued that coloureds constituted not only a separate race, but also a separate nation. Or, at the very least, the coloured population had the potential to develop into a separate national group, and they should be given that opportunity.[88] In 1951 Erasmus argued on the question of coloured 'nationhood' that

> [w]hat it will do will be to arouse a sense of national pride in the Coloureds. In the past . . . their chief aim has been to filter into the ranks

> of the Europeans. . . . By means of the different laws we have enacted, for example, the Prohibition of Mixed Marriages Act, the door is being closed to them and they are given the opportunity in their own ranks to aspire to a higher status for themselves. . . . They will now attain a separate identity.[89]

Arguments on coloured 'nationhood', however, were put forward in the context of discussion of the apparent break-up of the coloured population. Of special concern, in this respect, were the 'more educated, developed coloureds' who distanced themselves from their 'race' and aimed at absorption into the white community.[90] 'Passing for white' had to be stopped by reintegrating these people into the parts of the coloured community 'who valued their own nationhood', thus reflecting the overdetermination established between 'racial' and cultural identity. Despite the effort to create the impression that coloureds were indeed a separate group, it was clear that the difficulties encountered in the discussion of the Mixed Marriages Act were present here also.

As a result, the notorious Population Registration Act was introduced with great urgency. Smuts, member of the opposition, immediately cut through the arguments put forward by the NP to show that the sole aim of the Bill was the expression of the policy of apartheid, and racial registration formed a fundamental part of that policy. Even more important was the fact that this law would make it easier to separate the coloured population and to remove their voting rights.[91] According to Smuts, the whole purpose of the law was to deal with the position of coloureds. The Second Reading of the Bill displayed much the same form of racist argumentation as the other Bills discussed so far. Once again, Kahn was one of the few MPs to question the very nature of the legislation, and to condemn in the strongest possible terms the celebration of racial purity.[92] Telling of the extent to which any fundamental critique of apartheid was already standing 'outside the truth', outside the realm of the sayable, is the reply by the Minister of the Interior to Kahn's speech. The Minister called it a 'dirty speech' (*'n vuil toespraak*). It was no longer possible within the established discursive horizon to question the fundamentals of apartheid. Indeed, anyone who did so was regarded as an enemy of the state. Whereas the measures to create a coloured group separate from the white population were overtly racist, and provide a good sample of the general tenor of apartheid discourse at the time, their ambiguous exclusion did not turn them automatically into enemies of the state. In fact, the processes through which the exclusion of the coloured population was to be effected had yet a long battle ahead of them, and their exclusion, as a result of their position as a 'supplement' to the white population, would never be as extreme as that of the African population. They did not constitute a numerical threat to the white community and their 'difference', which was difficult to construct in racial terms, was too close for comfort. It is precisely for this reason that their systematic exclusion would play a crucial role in the creation of the historical conditions for the disarticulation of apartheid.

In combination with the measures just discussed, the Group Areas Act of 1950 was used further to divide existing communities. Even though local government resistance to this Act placed serious obstacles in the way of its implementation, the government forged ahead with it. In many ways the most far-reaching of the early Nationalist legislation, its objective was to extend the principle of residential segregation to its ultimate conclusions. The Bill divided the South African population into three categories: white, Native and coloured. The Act, however, also made it possible to divide these groupings further on ethnic, linguistic and cultural 'criteria'. The 'coloured' group was divided into three such subgroups on 30 March 1951: the Indian, Malay and Chinese groups.[93] Similarly, Africans were divided into special groups of Pondo, Xhosa, Zulu and Sotho peoples, foreshadowing the declared policy of the government to divide all urban locations into 'ethnic wards'.[94] In the process of achieving its goal of residential segregation, a bewildering maze of administrative categories, each with its own particular rules or restrictions, was also brought into being. There were 'full group areas', where ownership, occupancy and acquisition of land were restricted to single groups; 'controlled areas', in which immovable property could not be sold without a permit to a person who was not of the same ethnic group as the owner; and 'specified areas', in which the basis of control was occupancy rather than ownership. Further categories, not based upon restrictions of ownership or occupancy, were created to 'purify' residential areas.[95] The Parliamentary debate, held under the imposition of a guillotine, clearly showed the preoccupation of the NP with retaining 'white paramountcy'. 'Mixed' residential areas were said to be the 'deathbeds of the European race' and had to be unscrambled to prevent a bloodbath which would follow inevitably from racial friction. Nevertheless, certain Nationalist MPs did try to present this Bill as 'giving justice and fair play to the non-Europeans of this country'. Coloureds, Indians and Africans were united in their opposition to it, and most of their efforts until 1954 were aimed at the government's attempts to remove 'black spots' from (white) urban areas. Despite the resistance, by 1959, 170 group areas were proclaimed, and a total of 12,971 'black spots' were removed by 1957.[96]

Both the Bantu Authorities Act (1951) and the Bantu Education Act (1953) contain some of the earliest legislative attempts to redefine and segment Africans into a number of distinct ethnic groupings.[97] The Bantu Authorities Act, abolishing the defunct Native Representative Council, and aiming to reinforce the authority of tribal chiefs in the reserves, made provision for the establishment of a series of rural local authorities, resting on tribal distinctions. The new pattern of rural local administration – combining tribal, regional and territorial councils all acting in advisory capacity to the Minister of Native Affairs – were designed to institute 'Bantu control over Bantu areas as and when it becomes possible for them to exercise that control efficiently and properly for the benefit of their own people'.[98] The first such authorities were established in the Transvaal in 1953, and the greatest 'triumph' for the new system came in April 1955, when the Bunga – the Transkei Territories General Council – unanimously accepted the principle of Bantu Authorities, even though they warned simultaneously that the stress on tribal units could split the Transkei and that the lack of popular election of councillors under the new Act was retrogressive.[99] Native townships were later to be subjected to similar measures in the process of the replacement of the Native Advisory Boards. The exigencies of the new system – which rested on a structure of appointed African officials who had to keep the confidence of their people and were responsible to the central government[100] – were shown most clearly when Chief Albert Luthuli was dismissed from his headship of a small community in Zululand because he refused to give up his membership of the African National Congress (ANC).[101] The ANC consistently opposed the Bantu Authorities Act – it was included among the six laws highlighted in the 1952 defiance campaign – on the grounds that tribalism was an enormous barrier to the sense of African unity for which the movement stood.[102] In denying the ANC's demands for greater equality, the government nevertheless hailed the bill as

> . . . taking full cognizance of the growing African Nationalism which is noticeable everywhere in the country today. . . . In dealing with this phenomenon, we must appreciate the difference between the medium of Nationalism and that of Communism in the aspirations of the Black man towards self-government. In South Africa we must allow space for the flowering of African Nationalism. It is dangerous, if not almost fatal, to try

> to curb this development. . . . Together with this unhindered development some form of separate development would remove the sense of frustration that plagues the non-Whites in South Africa, and would give them opportunities that were denied them before i.e. before 1948 in particular.[103]

Indeed, it formed part of a policy which recognized the 'socio-cultural experiences of mankind, i.e. that peoples of all creeds and colours cling to their type and traditions . . . which find expression in the principle of "self-determination"'.[104] This view was expressed also in other legislation of the period, most notably in the Bantu Education Act and the provision for ethnic divisions within township development.

As with so many of the other facets of apartheid ideology, the discourse on education served a dual purpose which contributed to the general form of undecidability in the ideology. On the one hand, it was hailed as a means of asserting Afrikanerdom's right to difference, by distinguishing itself from an imperial, English tradition, and, on the other, it functioned as a means of racial hierarchization. The struggle around education was intimately linked to the fight for official recognition of Afrikaans and for its equality with English in everyday life, and 'mother-tongue education' became one of the nodal points around which *volkseenheid* was constructed. Since education was closely linked to the cultural sphere it had to act as an instrument for cultural transference, and it had to fulfil the function of the teaching of a 'nationally conscious' history, guaranteeing the survival of Afrikanerdom.[105] A document prepared by Verwoerd for the 1943 election rejected the attempt by the UP to foster a broader unity by imposing dual-medium education on exclusively single-medium schools as an 'imperialist' action to suppress Afrikanerdom.[106] The struggle around the imposition of dual-medium schools was thus presented as touching upon the very right to existence of the Afrikaner *volk*. Van Rooy, chairperson of the AB, argued that it was not enough just to have Afrikaans as a medium of instruction, but that all 'culturally foreign' elements of education had to be rejected, such that a Christian national spirit could form the foundation of education.[107] There was to be no 'mixing' of languages, cultures, religions or races. The system of dual-medium schools had to be abandoned since the bilingual child was 'neither fish nor flesh and had no national backbone'.[108] Mother-tongue education remained a central issue up to the 1954 general election, and served as a rallying point for bringing together various sectors of the nationalist alliance by presenting an ethnic exclusivist identity as crucial to the reproduction of the Afrikaner *volk*.

This conception of the *volkseie* formed one of the main inputs into the development of 'Bantu' education. It had two explicit aims: the reversal of contemporary trends associated with an egalitarian and universalist missionary education which fostered individualism and undermined tribal bonds; and the consolidation of the key role of the Afrikaner as the guardian of the African people. The Eiselen report stressed that educational practice had to recognize 'that it has to deal with a Bantu child, i.e. a child trained and conditioned in Bantu culture'.[109] This was clear also in the discussion of the Bantu Education Act (No. 47 of 1953), designed to give expression to the propositions of the Commission. Its declared purpose was to provide a more efficient, centralized and state-controlled system of education for the Bantu. The previous education system, largely under mission control, was felt to be 'too Europeanized'.[110] The Bill was opposed by the Parliamentary opposition, as well as by the opposition press, for being in conflict with their ideal of integration. The nationalist intellectuals at Potchefstroom University, however, hailed the Bill as an example of 'positive apartheid'. Coetzee as well as Du Plessis, in their commentaries on the Bill, stated that it was the only manner in which a 'healthy development' of the national character of the Bantu could be facilitated.[111] This is also why missionary education was regarded as problematic: it had little sympathy with tribal practices.[112] If Bantu education had become too 'Europeanized', the question as to what the nature of Bantu education had to be in order to be suitable to 'Bantu culture' was immediately raised. Here the position of the National Party was unequivocal. Introducing the Second Reading of the Bantu Education Bill in 1953, the Minister of Native Affairs, H.F. Verwoerd, maintained that the 'wrong' education for the Bantu could only lead to the creation of 'frustrated persons' with 'expectations beyond what life in South Africa could offer them'.[113] This could only spoil 'good race relations'. Only certain forms of education were deemed suitable for the education of African children:

> What does it help to design a curriculum for the African child which is, in the first place, European? One in which one learns about the kings of England and how much corn Canada exports. . . . What does it help to teach a Bantu child maths, something which he could not use practically. . . . People should be educated according to the life chances of the spheres within which they live. Some Natives would have to be educated to serve their own people in the higher occupations. . . . But apart from these people who can be employed in their own communities, others would have to receive education according to their life chances.[114]

These 'life chances' were limited. African children could not be educated as teachers, typists, solicitors, and so forth, for there would be no jobs for them. It would be 'madness' to educate 'Native children' in their hundred thousands for jobs which would not be available to them. Apart from the cost involved, which was clearly a further consideration, it was generally agreed by members of the National Party that the aim was not to provide these children with a 'broad philosophical, liberal' education.[115] They had to learn only what was absolutely necessary to be 'useful' human beings. They had to learn how to live a healthy life, how to utilize and eke out an existence on the land. The task was not, as the missionary schools would have it, to produce 'black Europeans' or 'English gentlemen', to de-nationalize the Bantu. Rather, it was to prepare the African population for taking up their pre-ordained place in the hierarchy of existence in South Africa, a hierarchy not questioned by the Afrikaner nationalists. Despite large-scale African resistance to the Act, it became law in 1953.

Education remained an issue throughout the 1950s, gaining centre-stage again with the introduction of the misnamed Extension of University Education Bill of 1957. This Bill provided for the establishment of the University Colleges for 'non-white' persons, and the simultaneous limitation of the admission of 'non-white' persons to 'open' universities. The Minister of Education, J. de Klerk, argued that there was a positive need for non-whites to have their own institutions:

> We want to make provision for them in separate institutions which can develop towards independence on their *own* basis. Secondly, they must be given the opportunity to develop to the full on the basis of what is peculiarly their *own*. Thirdly, they must be the bearers of their *own* culture to stimulate that culture amongst their *own* national group. Fourthly, the future leaders should be educated and trained there, not to break down the colour bar but to retain it in the best interest of both whites and non-whites. By this measure the Government wants to give the non-whites the opportunity to develop, to be what they are and to retain their own national roots.[116]

The Bill aroused an immediate storm of protest, and was finalized only in 1959. However, it is necessary to point out that the Parliamentary opposition to the Bill was aimed only at that part of it which limited the admission of students to the 'open' universities. The opposition conceded the principle of establishing special university facilities for Africans, coloureds and Indians. As so many times before it failed to put into question the very basis of apartheid ideology. The Afrikaner nationalist community provided its defence in the same terms as before. For example, Stoker emphasized the fact that apartheid was set against the 'Europeanization' or 'de-Bantu-fication' of the African population, since as groups the European and Bantu were distinct.[117] Du Plessis stressed similar points.[118] In both these cases, the discussion of the Bill was placed in the context of separate development or 'positive apartheid'. In this manner, the undecidable quality of the character of education was reinforced. It served both as a means of asserting simple 'difference' between cultures and as a measure to reproduce the hierarchical ordering of races. In terms of the latter, the deepening of the coincidence between ethnic–racial and spatial relations was an important mechanism.

As Pirie has pointed out, socio-spatial divisions based on ethnic grounds did not assume their full effect only with the development of rural Bantustans in the late 1950s.[119] 'Ethnic' zoning of African townships officially surfaced for the first time in 1952 in government discourse, and its aim was to design ethnically uniform wards in urban black settlements. This new form of division was closely linked into the freshly promulgated Bantu Education Act, and it was the government's stated intention that 'unless ethnic grouping is practised in locations children may have to travel considerable distances to attend schools'.[120] The division of townships along ethnic lines was also deemed to be beneficial to the development of an 'intensified community spirit', and would contribute to the formation of the proposed new measures for reorganization of the Administration Boards, such that urban blacks could also participate in 'location control'.[121] Widespread opposition to the idea existed in the Administration Boards, reflected in the Johannesburg city council's view that the separation of Native races was 'psychologically unsound and encourages the emergence of arrogance and militant racial consciousness which is always fraught with a very real danger of large scale rioting and civil disorder'.[122] In response to the criticisms, the Director of Non-European Affairs in Benoni – one of the first Administration Boards on the Witwatersrand to accept the principle and ardently and voluntarily embrace the new Daveyton township divided between Shangaan-Tsonga, Xhosa, Swazi-Ndebele, Zulu and North and South Sotho wards[123] – was that 'tribal clashes' in the townships had nothing to do with tribal differences. They were 'faction fights' by opposing subsections of the same tribe arising from 'boundary disputes', disputes over chieftainship and disagreements which had their origins in the reserves. Ironically, these fights were also ascribed to the insufficient provision of leisure facilities and the unsatisfactory provision of housing.[124] The charge of psychological unsoundness was also rejected:

> The grouping together in an area of races who have similar interests, who talk the same language, who understand each other in every way because they follow one culture, . . . surely cannot be psychologically unsound.[125]

The principle of ethnic–linguistic zoning followed as a 'natural' solution to these problems for it fostered the 'natural culture' of the Bantu and prevented de-culturalization. In addition, it was argued that since the measure was a forerunner of the Urban Bantu Authorities Bill, 'whereby Natives will be given increased responsibility in respect of their ethnic group areas and a means of reintroducing the indigenous government which exercised a very real control', it would afford the opportunity of 'regulating social behaviour', of 'maintaining law and order in a natural way and of imposing a discipline which will neither tolerate lawlessness nor the transgression [*sic*] of their moral code'.[126] Here, as with the granting of parental control over schools and the reinvigoration of rural tribal authority, the burden of disciplining was shifted on the 'Bantu' community, which was increasingly being divided along ethnic lines.

While these Bills inaugurated a new division of social space into categories of 'ethnic difference', the discourse on communism was clearly premissed upon a total exclusion which operated on the basis of a denial of those very differences. As argued earlier, the NP saw communism as one of the main threats to the *volkseie*. In communism, two frontiers central to the construction of Afrikaner nationalism were combined. They were the frontiers constituting the British, liberalism and foreignness as other, as well as the overtly racist construction of the black as enemy of the *volk*. Each of the constituent elements of the nationalist alliance articulated the communist threat in a particular manner and this facilitated the emergence of the NP as torch-bearer against communism. For the Dutch Reformed Churches, communism represented 'atheistic materialism', for the culturalists it represented 'an idolatrous attempt to transcend the separate spheres of authority laid down in the ordinances of creation', and for all the Afrikaners the communist disregard for racial differences was a thrust at the very heart of their ethnic existence.[127] These articulations were repeated constantly in NP documents and pro-NP newspapers.[128] All of them were present in the Parliamentary debates held on the occasion of the Reading of the Suppression of Communism Act (No. 44 of 1950).[129]

Introducing the Second Reading of the Bill during June 1950, the Minister of Justice set the broad context for the debate: the cold war, the war of ideologies, the war of communism against Western civilization and Christianity itself.[130] The 'religion of revolt', as communism was called, was analysed with reference to various recommendations and measures proposed by the South African Communist Party (SACP). From a text setting out the aims and objectives of the SACP, the demand to 'break down race barriers' was singled out for special attention by the NP. This demand represented an alien view of social division, one which was premissed upon a 'policy of equalization, the abolishment of all discriminatory laws and equality in all areas of life'.[131] These extremely wide sets of demands, put forward by liberals and communists alike, were used to establish the familiar equivalence between the left-wing of the UP and communists.[132] This logic was expanded also to other organizations, which were labelled communist, including the Springbok Legion, the Left Club, the Democratic League, Civil Rights League, the Torch Commando and the ANC Youth League. It was left to Ms Balinger to point out that some of these organizations were in fact anti-communist.[133] This did not, however, prevent the Nationalist argument from turning into an ever expanding logic. Anyone demanding equal economic, social and political rights for all South Africans were deemed to be communist, or to be promoting the cause of communism.

In addition, as we have seen, Afrikaner nationalists were extremely fearful of the possibility of an articulation between communism and nationalism. In response, they maintained that a fundamental difference existed between the communist and the NP's understanding of nationalism:

> By 'nationalism' we understand respect for what is one's *own*; pride in one's *own* . . . and a respect for others. But the nationalism preached by communists is something quite different. It is not love of the own, but hate for the other; not solidarity with one's own people; it is people who do not want to return to serve their own communities. . . . That is not true nationalism. . . . [134]

True nationalism was rooted in the national community and, as Nel argued during the debate, if the Bantu was properly integrated into his own community, communism would have no hold over him. However, a large part of the non-white population had 'degenerated' to such an extent that communist propaganda had become a danger not only to the white population, but also to the Bantu. The worst form of communism, Nel felt, existed not only in South Africa, but was spreading like wildfire over Africa as a whole.[135] This was the form of nationalism identified by Diederichs: a Pan-African nationalism, removed from the national community.[136] Behind the smoke-screen of nationalism, Nel argued, communists upset the lives of all the 'Bantu national units in the whole of Africa'. The so-called 'Negro nationalism' was a Trojan horse within which communism hid itself.[137]

The various facets of the discourse on communism, in fact, drew together a great many elements of other discourses which informed the emerging apartheid imaginary. It is interesting to note, at this point, that certain changes occurred in the NP discourse on communism. Throughout the apartheid era 'communism' remained central to NP discourse. However, the meaning of this term became vaguer as the years went by. Whereas the discourse on communism in the late 1940s and 1950s was characterized by a certain specificity as to 'communist doctrine' and whereas it displayed some knowledge of divisions within the communist world, the later treatment of communism was increasingly without referent, designating more generally 'an enemy', an enemy which came to be defined by its opposition to apartheid. This process coincided with the move in apartheid from myth to imaginary. The more apartheid came to be not a specific policy but a general horizon in terms of which all facets of the social could be understood, the more communism lost its specificity.

The Suppression of Communism Act was enforced retroactively, enabling the government to compile a secret list of persons deemed to be communist; to order them to resign from public office; to prohibit them from attending gatherings of any kind; to order them to remain in one particular area; to enter premises at any time, without previous notice; to seize documents; to close down any newspaper and prohibit publications without prior notice; and to presume anyone to be guilty of being a member of an illegal organization or of defending its objectives, unless such a person could prove otherwise.[138] This greatly increased surveillance of political activities, as is evident in the treason trials of the mid-1950s – arising out of the greater militancy of opposition to the introduction of apartheid measures – and redefined the limits of legitimate political action. It criminalized extra-parliamentary activities, and the identification established by the prosecution between the ANC's Freedom Charter, communism and violence had the additional effect of making co-operation between elements of the white opposition and the Congress Alliance more difficult.[139] Although the trials were a failure from the government's point of view, they, nevertheless, reflected the growing ability of the NP to define the terrain of struggle and to set limits to political debate.

The significance of the nature of the political frontiers established shortly after 1948 was that they all displayed a certain 'undecidability', a tension between the formation of systems of difference, based on a discourse of ethnicity and nationhood, and a paratactical division of the social which created sets of equivalences, externalizing and redefining the 'enemy'. This undecidability would continue to characterize apartheid discourse. On the one hand, it operated vicious systems of oppression, while, on the other, it spoke a language of difference and self-determination. The latter was to become the core around which an imaginary was articulated, of which *grand apartheid* was to be the highest expression. Nevertheless, this did not diminish the fact that even, or rather, precisely, a discourse of difference could only constitute itself by forging a series of exclusions. The constitution of the figure of the 'African' as 'other' in early apartheid discourse was by no means simple and straight-forward. As with the exclusionary strategies just investigated, the debarring of African South Africans from the polity took place against the backdrop of overtly racist sets of prejudices and constructions. The African population, however, was not simply excluded *en masse*, as was evident in the increasing divisionary logic of the apartheid discourse. The figure of the 'black' was a highly overdetermined one: at once a homogeneous race and different ethnies; simultaneously noble savage and barbarous other, tribal elder and militant agitator. Overt racism provided only the initial groundwork of marginalization. Beyond that, the situation was considerably more complicated. This was particularly clear in the introduction of the Native Labour (Settlement of Disputes) Act of 1953.[140]

Historically, the measures introduced in this Act have to be set in the context of a series of events occurring in the late 1940s. This period was marked by industrial conflict, generally ascribed to the rapid increase in the African labour force, which culminated in the 1946 miners' strike and a revitalization of African trade union activities.[141] The 1946 strike, in which 76,000 African mine workers participated and which brought gold mine production on twelve mines to a standstill, came to an end only after Smuts and the Chamber of Mines intervened and broke the strike violently. This was the first large-scale strike organized by an African trade union, the African Mine Workers' Union, and it brought the dispute concerning the recognition of trade unions to the fore. The Council for Non-European Trade Unions, at this point, had 150,000 members and 119 trade unions belonged to it. The NP, as a result of the Botha Commission recommendations concerning Labour Legislation, began to submit these trade unions to strict legislation. The Botha Commission reported its findings on its investigation into the question of African trade unions in 1951. It considered three possibilities for dealing with African trade unions: admitting them to the machinery of the Industrial Conciliation Act; recognizing them, but providing separate machinery; and leaving them uncontrolled. The first and third options were rejected as 'too dangerous'. This left only the second, which the Commission recommended. The government did not follow this recommendation, arguing that it would act as a stimulus to their growth, and that unions would be used as a political weapon 'to create chaos at any time'.[142] In 1953 the Native Labour Act prohibited all 'racially mixed' trade unions, took Africans out of the definition of employee, and thus out of the official collective bargaining mechanisms, and declared all strikes by African trade unions to be illegal. While African trade unions themselves were not outlawed, they were simply not recognized by the government, an act which aimed at helping the Native trade unions to 'die a natural death'.

What were the justifications produced for this legislation, and what did that imply about the constitution of the 'African' in National Party discourse? The justification for removing existing rights to organization was overtly racist. Both the NP and the UP agreed that Africans were incapable of organizing their own trade unions. They were simply not civilized enough. The Minister of Labour, B.J. Schoeman, said in his introductory speech to the Second Reading of the Bill, that Natives had not yet reached the 'level of development' at which trade union activities could be entrusted to them.[143] Hundreds of thousands of Natives were illiterate and 'largely primitive, and did not have the know-all to run trade unions.[144] The opposition spokesperson immediately agreed with this; it was true indeed that most Natives had only recently emerged from a condition of 'half barbarism'.[145] However, the supposed inability of Africans to run trade unions was only half the story. Equally clear was the fear of communism, which was assumed to form part and parcel of the trade union movement. Forgotten was the Afrikaner's own experience of not even a decade before. Africans were portrayed as essentially gullible and susceptible to the influence of leftist agitators.[146] Quoting Third International statements, Hertzog drew a set of equivalences between communism, trade union activities and the overthrow of the state. Placing such powerful weapons as trade unions in the hands of the Natives was like allowing children to play with dynamite.[147] Communists infiltrated trade unions, and used unknowing Natives to further their cause of violence and destruction. Another NP MP supported this contention in the following manner. He argued that 'to go out on strike' for Africans meant 'to go out on strike with any weapon they could get hold of'. To strike for the African simply meant one thing: to hit, to stab and to kill.[148] Making reference to alleged events during an Industrial and Commercial Workers' Union (ICU) strike, he 'recalled' that Natives on strike even went so far as to desecrate white graves.[149] A series of very clear displacements occurred in the course of the debate. Starting from a picture of innocent and uneducated Africans, it moved on to the figure of the leftist agitator, while frequently naming prominent South African communists. From here it was but one step to link trade unionism with the overthrow of the state, and other violent activities. This already dense overdetermination was complicated even further by references to 'tribal practices' deemed unacceptable to white civilization. With this, the argument had come a full circle. The innocent black became a violent and primal being, constituting a threat to the existence of the 'small white population at the tip of Africa'. Moreover, references to events elsewhere on the continent frequently featured in this debate. For example, reference was made to a Dar-es-Salaam 'witchdoctor' who allegedly had been paid to comment on a trade union's lack of success.[150] These references to 'Africa' seemed to draw upon another imaginary of violence and barbarism present in the background of the debates, completing the multi-faceted constitution of Africans within them.

As with most of the apartheid laws, the debate in this case was more revealing of the nature of white South African identity than of the elusive 'African', bearing out Connolly's proposition that the constitution of the other as other exposes a 'sore spot' in one's identity.[151] The very discourses which had to constitute the justification of the exclusion of the African from existing industrial conciliation machinery in fact served to produce white unity, a unity which could only exist in the face of the threats posed by the imaginary figure of the 'black'. The latter was not only produced in a racist discourse. It was overlaid by many of the significant discourses structuring the formation of apartheid discourse itself: the concern with communism, with the 'detribalized Native', with race and with conflict. Bearing no relation to 'actual Africans', this symbolization went far beyond a narrow concern with the purely economic aspects of labour availability and control. While there is no doubt that the introduction of this law has to be seen in that context, there is equally no doubt that laws such as this cannot be accounted for simply in terms of the 'needs' of capitalists, farmers, and so on, as has so often been argued to be the case. It is only within the imaginary horizon of apartheid discourse that these exclusions, as well as the severity of the exclusionary practices, can begin to make sense. The sets of exclusionary discourses characteristic of the early apartheid discourse continued to inform the apartheid imaginary. Of special importance in this regard is the symbolization of the wider historical context in which grand apartheid emerged.

Forging an Imaginary: Apartheid's Babel

> O love, could thou and I with fate conspire
> To grasp this sorry scheme of things entire
> Would we not shatter it to bits and then remould it
> Nearer to our heart's desire?[152]

> While we have a multi-racial population, we have no intention of developing into a single multi-racial community. . . . We will try to develop on this multi-community basis forms of harmonious co-existence rather than run the risk of biological integration and social degeneration which many of us hold to be inherent in the multi-racial society *per se*.[153]

On 31 January 1959 the Minister of Bantu Administration and Development announced the introduction of a new bill – the Bantu Self-Government Bill – making provision for the establishment of self-governing, independent 'homelands'. Contradictory evidence exists for the precise moment in which the possibility of such self-governing 'homelands' was conceived. Though Verwoerd discussed this possibility with M.C. de Wet Nel already in 1952, according to Lazar, no evidence of this was present in the documents and statements of the Department of Native Affairs during the early 1950s.[154] It is, nevertheless, clear that its introduction in 1959 was the result of a series of contingent historical developments, rather than of a preconceived 'blueprint'. In this respect, the development of African nationalism within South Africa and the process of decolonization underway on the wider African continent played a crucial role. Having said this, it is equally clear that the debates on the nature of apartheid provided the framework within which it could become a conceivable possibility at all. The expansion of the myth of apartheid into an imaginary, that is, the movement in which the *volkseie* increasingly came to be regarded as a *universal* ordering principle, paved the way for its introduction. As I have argued in chapter 2, the conception of the *volkseie* entailed, for the Afrikaner nationalist movement, simultaneously a *duty* to extend it to other groupings. That the political form in which this duty was to be expressed was not a necessary development is clear from the fact that Verwoerd, as well as other prominent NP figures, explicitly ruled out the possibility of total segregation and the removal of Africans from the urban areas:

> Nobody has ever contended that the policy of apartheid should be identified with 'total segregation'. The apartheid policy has been described as what one can do in the direction of what you regard as ideal. Nobody will deny that for the Native as well as for the European complete separation would have been the ideal if it had developed that way historically. . . . In every field of life one has to fix one's eyes to the stars, to see how close one can come to achieving the very best. For that reason I say this: keep in view what promises to be the best for your country and try to approach it within the realm of what is practical.[155]

While the Bill did not implement 'total apartheid' as envisaged by SABRA, it nevertheless did raise expectations that something new was in the air. The annual journal *A Survey of Race Relations* hailed it as one of the most significant measures ever introduced in South Africa.[156] Similarly, another commentator pointed out that:

> In the last few months there have been clear signs of a *new interpretation* by the South African Government of the policy of apartheid, or separation of the races. Cabinet ministers, and the Afrikaans press, have been at pains to stress a change of attitude. It has been hailed as 'positive apartheid'; as 'a New Look in South Africa'; as a 'New Era'; as 'Our New Deal'; as 'Harmonious Multi-Community Development'.[157]

The crux of this Bill, based upon the division of the African population of South Africa into ethnic groups, involved a twofold change in existing policy. Firstly, Africans were no longer to be represented in Parliament by white Natives' Representatives. The only existing political rights for Africans at Parliamentary level, however limited they were, were removed. In return for the loss of indirect Parliamentary representation, it conceded to the African population a system of local government controlled by a Minister and subject to a Parliament in which it would have no representation. Secondly, the possibility of eventual independence for the African reserves was held out; it was no longer a matter to be decided by future generations. Both these aspects were criticized by the Parliamentary opposition as repugnant to the principles of natural justice, as it removed long-standing rights. Moreover, the opposition maintained that the attempt to divide South Africa into 'black states' and a 'multi-racial' state, if implemented, would involve grave dangers for all South Africans, for it would give a foothold to communists in the 'independent black states'. The leader of the Natives' Representatives opposed its Second Reading in much the same terms as the opposition. He argued that it sought to lay the foundation of a political separation of white and black, which would deprive the African population of all say in the government of the country to which it belonged and of which it formed an essential part. The Bill, he argued, introduced without consultation with and against the wishes of the African population whose future it sought to shape, was based on false premisses, supported by fallacious analogies, would bring South Africa into contempt at home and abroad, and would endanger the peace and security of the country.[158] The broad opposition thus clearly rejected the premisses of 'grand apartheid', based upon the principles of separate 'national homes' for separate 'ethnic groups'.

Reflecting the moral–theological language of the organic intellectuals of the nationalist movement, De Wet Nel – in his opening address to Parliament on the occasion of its Second Reading – argued that it was based on the three cornerstones of the 'colour policy of South Africa': that God had given a divine task and calling to every nation; that every nation had an inherent right to self-preservation as a moral right; and that the personal and national ideals of every individual and of every population group could best be developed within his own national community, or sphere.[159] The number of such ethnic groups and, thus, the number of reserves or 'homelands', as they became known in the NP doctrine, varied according to the spokesperson involved. De Wet Nel foreshadowed eight such groups, even though initially, he said, only five of them would be recognized,[160] while Eiselen thought the division would be into six or seven groups.[161] The final Bill settled on eight 'national units' and outlined a development of the structures already established under the Bantu Authorities Act (No. 68 of 1951). Its preamble stated that, since the Bantu peoples of the Union of South Africa did not constitute a homogeneous people, but formed separate national units on the basis of language and culture, it was desirable for the welfare and progress of the said peoples to afford recognition to the various national units and to provide for their gradual development within their own areas to self-governing units on the basis of Bantu systems of government. In contrast to the conception prevalent under segregation, that the African population was a homogeneous one, by 1959 the division of the 'Bantu peoples' into a number of different 'national units' had become generally accepted. As I have shown thus far, the transition from homogeneous to heterogeneous population categories did not come about suddenly. Its general acceptability was the result of a number of discourses on 'difference' acting in a mutually reinforcing manner. From the mid-1950s debates concerning social division increasingly crystallized around the notion of *ethnicity*, its meaning and implications for the 'colour question'. These included a deepening of discussions taking place in the Afrikaner community before 1948, as well as new additions to the existing arguments. In this respect, the theory of social contact which underpinned this rearticulation, and its expression in the work of the Tomlinson Commission, was of crucial importance.[162]

The Tomlinson Commission, which included a number of prominent SABRA members, was appointed in 1950 to conduct an exhaustive inquiry into

> . . . the rehabilitation of the Native areas with a view to developing within them a social structure in keeping with the culture of the Native and based on effective socio-economic planning.[163]

It offered an extensive account of 'culture contact', the consequences of such contact, and the possible responses to it. This account formed the basis of its recommendations on the rehabilitation of the 'Native areas'. While the commission dealt with what it recognized as a political problem, it abstained from making comprehensive proposals for the satisfaction of the political demands of the African community.[164] The furthest it went was to state that it wished to permit itself a prophetic look at the future, and that it

> . . . would be inclined to regard the proposed development plans as a means of bringing about a degree of political development which might serve as the forerunner of an eventual configuration in Africa under which certain parts of the continent would be reserved for Europeans, and to which the Bantu would be allowed entry as temporary migrant workers without being able to claim political rights.[165]

While not making more concrete suggestions, the report suggested that the real home of the Bantu was the reserves. Moreover, the development of the reserves was no longer to be regarded as a part of the general economic development of the country, but as part of a plan to circumscribe and confine the African people, as far as their economic rights and political aspirations were concerned, to a small portion of the country.[166] These conclusions were reached on the basis of a particular view of culture contact. An inspection of both nationalist and opposition journals revealed a general preoccupation with the notion of 'culture contact' and its effects.[167] For Tomlinson, only three possible outcomes to culture contact existed:

> Concerning the possible and also probable course of the process of contact between two peoples living within the same area, there is little if any doubt among ethnologists, sociologists, and historians. One organism is superseded by the stronger without leaving any perceptible influence behind it, or is absorbed by the stronger without altering the culture of the absorbent people in any way worth mentioning, or after a process of adaptation . . . a new organism arises from the original elements which then vanish in the new unity.[168]

This is not surprising, given the obsession of nationalist politicians with the 'inevitable' disasters consequent upon 'integration'. As I have argued, apartheid was articulated as a policy by its very opposition to integration. Tomlinson also recognized this:

> . . . two poles of thought have arisen in consequence of contact. These two poles . . . coincide to a large extent with . . . the preservation of a characteristic type of existence on the one hand, and the fusion of all existence on the other. . . . The leading groups at the head of the two formative poles now termed 'apartheid' on the one hand, and 'liberalism' on the other, are witness to the fact that in their minds, the time has already arrived for choosing between the maintenance of separate identities and the coalescence, between the traditional South African and the Neo-Western way of life.[169]

Thus, the Tomlinson account of the process of culture contact was very much situated within the broad discursive horizon already delimited by earlier debates on the nature of apartheid. The choice was between total integration or total segregation; no middle road existed.[170]

What gave it its novel impact was that this theory of culture contact was developed within the new context of a fascination with ethnicity as a basis for social division: it was no longer simply a matter of discussing the effects of cultural contact between white and black. Rather, interest was expressed in terms of the impact which different 'cultures' could have upon one another. Coetzee, for example, argued that the proper task of anthropology (*volkekunde*) was the study of the character of the cultures of peoples, the process of cultural contact and the outcome of such contact.[171] Indeed, Coetzee went so far as to argue that the condition of possibility for anthropologists to play an important role in the administration of race relations was precisely the fact that it was concerned in the first place not with race and biology, but with cultural differences between peoples.[172] It was generally agreed that assimilation and acculturation, insofar as they existed, had a limit. When this limit was reached, conflict and racial tension would come about, resulting in the destruction of the different peoples.[173] Moreover, as with the prevalent views on detribalization, it was frequently argued that acculturation, taking place as a result of contact, could only produce perverse and fraudulent beings. Potgieter, an anthropologist teaching at the University of South Africa, held that there was always a tendency of the lesser culture to attempt to take over elements of the superior culture.[174] This could only result in a 'secondary accretion', a supplement which was not integrated into the primary fundamental value system of the Bantu.[175] Indeed, it could only produce confused 'Euro-Africans', not quite succeeding in the assimilation of a selection of elements from 'European' culture. The loss of certainty incumbent upon it could only lead to a degeneration of morals, instability, a loss of principles and an increase in crime rates.[176]

This fascination with ethnicity, now no longer limited to the Afrikaner *volkseie*, and argued to be a counter to ethnocentrism, was reflected also in Afrikaans literature, where a marked change in the representation of Africans, now taking the form of an interest in the Bantu as 'tribal and national man', could be observed.[177] In addition – as was clear in De Wet Nel's remarks on the introduction to the Bantu Self-Government Bill – the formation of the discourse on ethnicity was greatly influenced by the new theologico-political language of the sovereignty of spheres, which proved to be invaluable to the justification of territorial separation along ethnic lines. As I argued in chapter 2, it was closely connected to the Calvinist emphasis on respect for the principle of diversity.[178] In the extension of this doctrine – based upon the notion of the *volkseie* – to others, the metaphor of 'Babel' took on a central articulatory role. The repeated references to Babel, found in the writings of the Potchefstroom intellectuals during the mid-1950s, contained a deep undecidability, consisting in an unresolved tension between the creation and existence of unity and diversity.[179] One of two possibilities was opened up by this reasoning. Either an African nation already existed and had to be recognized in its unity by Afrikaner nationalists, or African nationalism had to be constituted as an impossibility. The latter option was taken. The *de facto* African nationalism was argued to be a fraud, a corruption of real nationalism. As a result, the latter had to exist *de jure*. The extension of this form of ordering to other groupings thus was not only made possible, but was an imperative. Others *had* to live their real nationhood if they were to develop their full potential. The paradox arising out of this was that nations always already existed and were ordained by God, yet, at the same time, they had to fight for their existence and had to be shown their real interests, namely to exist as a nation. The image of Babel, welded together with the conceptions of freedom and equality prevalent at Potchefstroom, led to a complicated interpretation of the nature of unity and difference between 'ethnic' groups. The principle of difference was to be interpreted as a universal principle manifesting itself variedly in different historical circumstances.[180] Particularity existed, but only as a manifestation of the universal principle of diversity. What is crucially important about these theological conceptions articulated in Potchefstroom is that they were easily linked to the contemporaneous debates on the nature of apartheid. Many commentators writing in *Koers* made these connections explicit. As early as 1949 Du Toit argued that the unity found in Christ was not a unity that was relevant to 'earthly' pursuits: 'The religious Native is one with us in Christ.' But, contrary to what liberals thought, this argument could not be extended to develop a critique of apartheid.[181] As Du Plessis put it: unity in Christ as a matter of fact transcends but does not abolish all temporal diversities.[182] Attempts to do away with boundaries and particularities, to eliminate national, cultural and racial frontiers, awaited the same fate as the biblical Babel: artificial unities were doomed to implode on themselves.[183] Snyman, explicitly addressing the liberal notion of a 'multi-racial society', a society in which groups differing from one another in culture, religion, race or language could live within a single political framework, side by side but without actual racial fusion, claimed that this was an unrealistic ideal. The mere presence of different peoples within one set of boundaries was unacceptable, for integration, only up to a certain point, was not possible:

> One fatherland will, in the long or the short term, result in the formation of one people, whether as a result of fusion, peacefully or by conflict.[184]

Du Toit concluded, in similar vein to Snyman, that 'there is a point beyond which racial mixture cannot go without disaster'.[185] This was something which could not be understood by Europeans or even Americans, for they lived 'safe and secure in their own homogeneous national societies'.[186] In South Africa, however, a similar integration would 'certainly wipe out the fully established South African nation of Afrikanerdom whether Afrikaans- or English-speaking, and would immerse the developing non-European nations in tribal chaos'. As I have shown, the notion of diversity, articulated in opposition to any doctrine which advocated any form of 'equalization' or levelling, was linked, moreover, to the nationalists' peculiar conception of freedom.[187] For the purposes of relations between 'groups' a distinction was made between degrees of freedom on the basis of the 'degree of development' of human beings. This was the principle of *developmental differentiation* of human freedoms.[188] Apartheid, according to these theoreticians, did not deny freedom, but facilitated its development in different spheres according to the stage of development reached by each group. The notions of freedom and equality were thus inextricably bound up with boundaries between groups, and these principles could not be extended if such an extension implied a weakening of such boundaries.[189]

Also in anthropological writings, the key journals of SABRA, the Potchefstroom intellectuals' and government publications, a wide-ranging discussion of the division of races and tribes in Africa took place. Both Coetzee and Tomlinson drew on a key text by Seligman, *Races of Africa* (1930), to divide the peoples of Africa into the following groups: the Khoisan; Negroid peoples; eastern, northern and semi-Hamites; eastern, southern and western Bantu.[190] Moreover, it was argued that the Bantu constituted a group primarily on linguistic grounds and could therefore be further divided into Nguni (including Zulu, Xhosa, Swazi and Ndebele), Shangaan-Tsonga, Sotho and Venda groupings.[191] In this division, Schapera's collection *The Bantu-Speaking Tribes of South Africa* (1953), often quoted in debates, was used to show the objectivity and immutability of so-called 'ethno-linguistic' divisions within the Bantu population. During the later debate on the Bantu Self-Government Bill, De Wet Nel argued that, as the Tomlinson Commission had shown, the aim of 'homelands' was not simply to create more separate pieces of land, but the development of separate communities with their own traditions, in their own spheres.[192] Since Bantus had their own culture, traditions, and ways of living, they also had their own interests, interests which were integrated into the *volkstruktuur* (*volk*-structure) and which could not be linked to that of whites.[193] To provide support for this position, De Wet Nel referred to various 'experts', arguing that 'Western forms of democracy' should not be 'forced' upon the Bantu. Schapera's *The Bantu-Speaking Tribes of South Africa*, Gluckman's contribution to *African Political Systems* and Cowan's *Local Government in West Africa* were cited as such texts.[194] It is worthwhile quoting the extract used during the debate from Cowan's text, for it shows the logic of the argument very clearly:

> A place must be found, for example, in the African democratic system for the traditional rulers; this may well entail a curb on the powers of the people's representatives. But it is not incumbent on the West to judge whether an African council is meeting the standards of democracy laid down for another culture. It is sufficient that the new institutions become a part of the structure of African society, in what form is most acceptable to its members.[195]

This strategy of argumentation established an articulation between Schapera's work on the linguistic divisions within the African population, and the project of the so-called 'homelands'. In fact, Schapera stated quite explicitly that

> [o]f the Bantu as a whole it can be said that they have now been drawn . . . into the orbit of Western civilization. It is more likely that in certain directions at least, they will develop their own local variations, but these variations will be within the framework of a common South African civilization shared by both Blacks and Whites.[196]

The extract from Schapera, cited by an opposition member during the Second Reading of the Bill, clearly shows the different articulations which may have followed from Schapera's original acount. Only a wider context of articulation could provide it with a particular meaning, and in the case of the Afrikaner nationalists, this was given by the whole theory of culture contact, the importance of ethnicity and the significance of membership of a *volk*. Not only the division of the African population into different groups, but the very appellation 'Bantu' was a product of the 1950s. Whereas segregationist ideology utilized the term 'Native', apartheid ideologues, drawing on the theorizations of the anthropologists at their disposal, increasingly came to talk of the 'Bantu' as the object of policy and analysis. The NP started using the term in 1951, and in 1952 it became official policy. This change was not without significance. As Eiselen, Secretary of the Department of Bantu Administration and Development, and former Professor in Social Anthropology at Stellenbosch University, argued in 1959:

> Perhaps this is the appropriate time at which to say something about the nomenclature employed for official purposes in the Union. . . . There is no doubt that the vast majority of our [*sic*] Bantu population are firmly attached to these divisions on ethnic and linguistic lines and that they have no desire to do away with the traditional ethnic and language groups in order to form a greater Native community. . . . Because they attach so much value to their Bantu languages and also to a number of Bantu culture traits, the colourless appellation *Native* is gradually being replaced by *Bantu*, which is, moreover, an indication of the government policy to establish progressive Bantu communities.[197]

That this was not the case was clearly shown in the response of the Conference of African leaders, held in Bloemfontein in 1957 to discuss the Tomlinson report. They rejected the concept of 'national homes' for Africans in unequivocal terms, arguing that Africans were the indigenous inhabitants of the country with an indisputable claim to the whole of South Africa as their home. There was no part of the country to whose development they have not made their full contribution; homelands, as they clearly saw, would only further facilitate the exploitation and economic strangulation of the Africans, in addition to perpetuating white domination.[198] The precise meaning given to decolonization and African nationalism was deeply marked by the undecidable logic of apartheid.

Ex Africa semper aliquid novi[199]

In 1920, almost every hectare of African soil was under the control of a European imperial nation. By 1975, the continent consisted of forty-two independent nations, two colonies and two independent states under white minority rule. The events spanning these fifty years had a lasting impact on the character of social division in South Africa. Decolonization, the growth of Pan-Africanism and the rise of African nationalist discourses in South Africa itself played an immensely important part in the formation of the Afrikaner nationalist imaginary during the 1950s. Indeed, the crystallization of the apartheid project into the vision contained in 'grand apartheid' cannot be explained only with reference to the internal struggles within the Afrikaner community. I will argue in this section that events in Africa had a decisive influence on the internal struggles, and their resolution cannot be understood without placing them in the broader context of the African continent.

Before discussing the wider African context, however, it is necessary briefly to document the state of internal resistance to the expansion of the apartheid project. The decade of the 1950s was deeply marked not only by the 1952 Defiance Campaign, but even more so by the Congress of People held at Kliptown in 1955. In addition to the draconian Suppression of Communism Act, the government introduced the Criminal Law Amendment Act and the Public Safety Act (1953), both of which were designed to deal with mass defiance. At the 1953 Cape Provincial congress of the ANC, Prof. Matthews in his presidential address suggested the organization of a multi-racial 'Congress of the People' campaign in which he noted that several groups were considering 'the idea of a national convention at which all groups might be represented to consider our national problems on an all-inclusive basis'.[200] Within two months of his address, two further national organizations had been formed: the South African Coloured People's Organization (SACPO) and the South African Congress of Democrats (COD). Together with the South African Indian Congress (SAIC) and the ANC, they were to form the Congress Alliance.[201] This multi-racial alliance planned three campaigns, each of which was to come to a climax in 1955: the first was directed at the removal of some 58,000 Africans from the 'Western Areas' of Johannesburg; the second at the Bantu Education Act; and the third campaign was to hold a Congress of the People.[202] The Congress of the People was finally to meet at Kliptown on 25–26 June 1955, at which the Freedom Charter was adopted as a guiding document in the struggle against apartheid. Its preamble stated that 'South Africa belongs to all who live in it, black and white', thus signifying the multi-racial spirit of the campaign, which was aimed at establishing unity where apartheid divided. This document would have a venerable history in the resistance struggles against apartheid. Twenty-eight years after its adoption by the ANC and twenty-three years after the banning of the ANC, a new generation of resisters declared that

> [t]he Charter stands out from all other alternatives for change in South Africa, not only because of the manner in which it came into being, but also because of the demands reflected in it.[203]

This echoed the sentiment expressed by Chief Albert Luthuli, namely that the Congress of People was unique in that it 'will be the first time in the history of our multi-racial nation that its people from all walks of life will meet as equals, irrespective of race, colour and creed, to formulate a freedom charter for all people in the country'.[204] As we have seen, for the Nationalist government, these sentiments expressed nothing but a 'communist' ploy to derail the true Bantu from his 'own' path of development. A similar strategy was followed in dealing with the process of decolonization and the rise of Pan-Africanism.

The process of decolonization, as with all events, had to be symbolized in order to make sense. The symbolization of 'Africa' in the discourse of Afrikaner nationalism in the 1950s drew upon two clearly delimited symbolic funds. The first I will call a 'colonial imagination', while the second consisted of a more narrowly defined identification with the conception of nationalism as understood within the Afrikaner *volksbeweging*. The colonial imagination provided a setting within which a particular conception of nationalism could be paraded as an answer to the fears raised by the spectre of decolonization. The signifier 'Africa' thus played an immensely important role in the process of the formation of the homeland discourse: it allowed for the articulation of a vague sense of impending doom and threat, while simultaneously foreshadowing the correct solution to the problem.

The very invention of Africa as more than a geographical entity can only be understood as an outgrowth of 'European racialism'.[205] In the case of apartheid discourse this is abundantly clear. Throughout the 1950s the presence of Africa was central to discussions of the 'colour question'. 'Africa', in these writings, did not refer simply to the geographical unity of the continent. Rather, it was a complex signifier, binding together a series of discursive articulations, providing them with a unity which did not pre-exist these articulations. The symbolic value with which the signifier was weighed down, testified to its importance in the development of the particular form of difference characteristic of apartheid discourse, as well as to the constitution of the 'other' of this discourse. From the mid-1950s onwards, numerous articles appeared in journals and newspapers attempting both to provide information on 'Africa' and to situate South Africa in relation to the wider African continent. More specific questions addressed, for example, were concerned with the 'task and Christian calling of the Afrikaner in Africa', the need to understand Africanism, and the placing of Africa in an international context.

In specific discussions, as well as in articles of a more general nature, traces of what I have chosen to call the colonial imagination were present. An extreme example of this can be found in the writings of S.J. du Toit. Du Toit, in an attempt to describe the 'races of Africa', depicted the 'Semites, Hamites and the Bantu' as living in a condition of barbarism, as being ignorant and full of superstition.[206] Indeed, Africa was portrayed as incapable of sustaining any form of civilization. In the words of the Afrikaans poet, Africa was the resting place of a cursed spirit, an unknown land visited by 'doom and death'.[207] Africa was swamp-like, absorbing and drowning civilizations, and giving back nothing in return.[208] Populated by primitives, who no longer showed any respect for whites, Africa was held to be the 'dark continent' of colonial imagery.

Less extreme, but no less potent, was the imagery utilized by Coetzee, writing in *Koers* and in the *Journal for Racial Affairs*, the mouthpiece of SABRA, in the late 1950s. Starting from the premiss that the term 'dark Africa' constituted nothing but an expression of ignorance concerning the African continent, Coetzee set out to correct this state of affairs, to provide knowledge of Africa. The need for this was stated quite explicitly: (white) South Africans had to have knowledge of the continent of which, paradoxically, they were part, but which they regarded as other. Garvey's 'Africa for the Africans' was a slogan discussed without any sense of recognition; (white) South Africans were not African, not of Africa in any meaningful sense of the term. Coetzee remarked that while the white indigenous population of the Southern part of Africa claimed the inclusive name of 'Afrikaner', they remained essentially 'South-*Afrikaners*', largely isolated from the continent on which they founded a fatherland, and with which their fate would be inextricably bound up.[209] The rise of independent, indigenous African states, the 'grabbing hands and luring eyes of half-eastern and eastern states', the opening of markets and the presence of heathen peoples were amongst the other main factors listed as reasons for needing knowledge of Africa.[210]

Coetzee clearly spoke in a context in which there was a wider recognition of this craving for knowledge, reflected, *inter alia*, in the creation of the Africa Institute, of Africa study groups at several universities, including Potchefstroom, and the founding of a Department for African Affairs within the Department of Foreign Affairs. However, it has to be asked what the precise discursive context is in which this new interest in Africa emerged. Something of this was reflected in Coetzee's account of the history of Africa in terms of colonialism. The history of Africa was, for Coetzee, the history of colonialism, and yet a certain new interest in Africa was emphasized. Coetzee analysed this in telling terms. The 'spying eye' of communist Russia was portrayed as working by way of the Middle East in Africa: 'with its red fingers' it meddled in the affairs of the 'dark peoples' of Africa.[211] The rising nationalisms in Africa were seen as a perfect façade behind which Moscow could do its work.

Clearly, two central themes, which reflected wider concerns, were present in Coetzee's papers: that of the decolonization of Africa and the rise of African nationalism; and the threat of communism. As I have shown, both these themes were intimately linked to the emergence of a peculiar understanding of African nationalism taking shape within the discursive domain of Afrikaner nationalism. The accounts of the rise of African nationalism, and especially of Pan-Africanism, provided by Afrikaner nationalists, reflected the emerging consensus within the Afrikaner community on the nature of nationhood.

Pan-Africanism

The late 1950s and early 1960s witnessed a spate of articles attempting to come to terms with the event of decolonization and the rise of Pan-Africanism.[212] A series of important issues were condensed in the treatment African nationalism receives in these writings. Much of the attempt to make sense of African nationalism consisted of terminological clarification: terms such as 'Afrikaner', 'African', 'nationalism', 'ethnicity', and 'colour consciousness' were central to the inscription of the events into the Afrikaner nationalist imaginary. While some writers argued that the colour question took the form of a national question in Africa, insofar as the 'desire of yellow and black peoples' for national freedom was a desire for political self-determination,[213] others held that something more was at stake. Strauss, for example, claimed that Africa posed 'human' rather than simply racial problems. He characterized the condition of all who lived in Africa – traditional indigenous blacks, white settlers and extremist Pan-Africanists – in existential terms. Living in Africa became a symbol for a condition of uprootedness and confusion: 'The human of and in Africa is uncertain of himself.'[214] This uncertainty can be traced back to the onto-theological problem which inaugurated the apartheid project: the understanding and characterization of the *volkseie*, and its role and function in history. Africa acted as a signifier for ontological uprootedness, for its peoples had been doubly alienated from their original conditions of existence. Initially, colonialist expansion introduced the indigenous populations of Africa to an essentially foreign, Western culture. While a certain ambiguity towards the aims and effects of colonization was displayed – it was both a curse and a cure, unsettling a natural order and bringing salvation and (Western) civilization – no such ambiguity was present in the portrayal of those Africans who came 'into close contact' with white settlers. Indeed, they were the enemies of the 'real' African, that is, of the traditional African, holding on to tribal practices and shunning the emerging Pan-African consciousness. Eiselen, in a widely read and debated article in *Optima*, displayed this attitude very clearly:

> It is true that there is a class of évolués who claim that they have relinquished their Bantu loyalties and that they are building up a new comprehensive African community, which . . . claims the whole continent as its heritage.[215]

These évolués, who adopted the name 'African', were said to be frauds, for they were not rooted in any real community. Strauss claimed that Pan-Africanism was located in a 'thin top-layer of developed Africans, under European influence'.[216] It was a corruption not only of the real African identity, but also of the very nature of nationalism. Indeed, they were inseparable. Pan-Africanism lacked a 'national context and state and group patriotism', and was, therefore, essentially rootless.[217] The link between nationalism, in its true form, and national or ethnic belonging was crucial to the rejection and critique of Pan-Africanism. Pan-Africanism most consistently was portrayed as something coming from outside of Africa, whether from 'foreign' black intellectuals such as Du Bois, or from a certain complicity with colonialist settlers. It was not of Africa. Its externality corrupted identity and nationalism. Indeed, for Afrikaner intellectuals it was questionable whether Pan-Africanism could be described in terms of the category of nationalism at all. Pan-Africanism, on these analyses, was organized on the principle of 'colour consciousness'; it was not a patriotism based on the state or group.[218] Rather, it designated the awakening of an African consciousness, based on racial and social characteristics.[219]

The rejection of Pan-Africanism on the grounds of its basis in colour consciousness calls for further explanation. Why would the ideologues of apartheid reject colour as a basis for a national consciousness? Two different answers to this question come to mind. The first is clearly connected to the Afrikaner's understanding of nationalism, as based on ethnic groups, on clearly defined communities, bound together by a set of elements, of which race may be one. The second concerns the fears raised by the processes of decolonization in the white imagination. Pan-Africanism was not *simply* a form of unity based on a colour consciousness. The analysts of Pan-Africanism, above all, were acutely aware of its relational character, of the fact that it was a response to colonial exploitation and discrimination. Again and again they stated that the cohesive factor in Pan-Africanism, in the absence of a real community, was a common hatred of whites.[220] No real unity could exist across the African continent. Africa was far too divided; 'cultural, racial, political and civil heterogeneity is characteristic of Africa'.[221] Pan-Africanism, thus, had to be understood as a process in which links and alliances were forged in the face of a common enemy. These alliances were not natural, and were bound to break down. Yet, they were dangerous, and had to be countered. This was so especially in that Pan-Africanism tended to become associated with the threats of majoritarianism and communism in Africa, especially the threat of violence and conflict.

The images conjured up by the Mau Mau in Kenya, Ghanaian independence and the 1958 Accra conference were of great importance in the discourse of decolonization. For example, the portrayal of the pre-independence events in Kenya were covered by some 804 reports in *Die Burger* alone during the period 1952–55.[222] The coverage mostly painted inaccurate pictures of fearful bloodshed. Hugo argues that some idea of the reasons why this struggle retains an indelible place in the memory of white South Africans may be seen in the following extract from one report:

> . . . the [Mau Mau] oaths are: not to reveal the working of the organisation to the government or to whites . . . not to sell land to whites; not to help whites; to drive the whites out of Kenya . . . to steal weapons from whites . . . to kill whites.[223]

The Mau Mau were characterized as a phenomenon resulting from the 'concessions' made by the British Empire. Similarly, Ghana and the Accra conference symbolized something of an 'unthankfulness' on the side of Africans, as well as serving as signs of an inability and unreadiness for 'Western democracy'.[224] However, the fears raised by the manner in which independence was attained in some former African colonies did not serve to deny the recognition of a right to independence. *Die Volksblad* of 23 February 1960 put forward the position that there was something inevitable about the drive to independence, but even that acknowledgement was riddled with unarticulated fears:

> To South Africa Nyassaland demonstrates that non-whites will not be content with appeasement and clever plans. They want territories where they can eventually manage their own affairs, and if the White man fails to help them quickly in this, he is in danger of being swept away.

Die Transvaler on the same day came to a similar conclusion:

> . . . the flood of Native nationalism cannot be stopped. . . . To lead the Natives to self-government in their own territories before they demand it and of necessity take it – that is the challenge of the moment.

This challenge was to be linked to the prevention of 'detribalization', a phenomenon judged to lie at the heart of the reason why Africanism could gain a foothold in Africa. Verwoerd, introducing the Bantu Authorities Act in 1951, said:

> The tribal authority is the natural ally of the government against such rebellious movements [as the Mau Mau]. It was the chiefs with their authorities who sided with the forces of law and order and who assisted European authority.[225]

A loss of contact with one's 'own' community – detribalization – engendered all sorts of problems. These 'problems', as we have seen, were the subject of much discussion in the context of the problem of African urbanization within South Africa. Discussions took place against the background of an idealization of the rural Natives, depicted, in almost Rousseauian terms, as noble savages. Detribalization showed the corruption of the original, good Native; the best of Native life was considered to be bound up with the tribal system. Malan, in a discussion of the notion of 'development along own lines', stated this quite explicitly:

> The picture which the phrase brings to mind. . . . is that of an amicable savage, the miraculous recipient of all the virtues, and none of the vices of European civilisation, sitting contentedly in a Transkei cottage weaving homespun while his family study the Old Testament in Xhosa.[226]

'Unfortunately', as E.G. Louw, the Minister of Native Affairs, stated in 1950:

> . . . strong influences have been at work in the effort to destroy everything connected with the national character of the Natives. That steady background of his tribal consciousness and of his tribal links is gradually disappearing, and the Native is . . . suspended in mid-air; he has a feeling of instability which is nourished by people who are only too eager that he should be torn away from all his anchors, so that he can become easy prey to their propaganda.[227]

The movement to the cities, and contact with 'foreign' notions such as equality and liberalism, led to an unhealthy severing of links with 'tribal' communities. Such a denial of tradition was evident in rejection of the term 'Bantu' and in calls to use the term 'African' instead. The main commentators on events in Africa were acutely aware of this. Coetzee, for example, held that the name 'African' was adopted as a gesture of resistance to ethnic differentiation.

> Under the non-traditional leaders of the Bantu in SA it has become a symbol of the unity and power of 200 million people. To be called Bantu is to give in to a policy of division and the resulting powerlessness. The same can be said of the division into ethnic groups.[228]

This point was belaboured in much greater detail in a somewhat later intervention by Van Rooyen. He maintained that the use the term 'African' reflected the fact that the terms 'Bantu' and 'Native' were regarded as insulting terms, and that the African was breaking free from his primitive tribal context. For him, as for the National Party ideologues, the use of the term 'African' involved a dismissal of the existence of separate national Bantu groups, each with its own language and traditions. Moreover, the struggle for 'the soul of the Native' reflected another struggle, that between Afrikaner and English traditions:

> There can be no compromise. Either the Bantu takes over the best of the cultural goods of the majority of whites in South Africa, or they lean toward the integrationist whites, supported by 'Africanists' from within and outside Africa. If the choice is for the latter, the black wave of 'Africans' will push ever more threatening against the white.[229]

Detribalization and denationalization were explicitly linked in the Afrikaner nationalist imaginary. As a commentator at the time put it:

> One should not, as a matter of principle, denationalize a nation; . . . South Africa has a very special reason for refusing any attempt at denationalization. Within living memory precisely such a policy was attempted, and more than failed. . . . Attempted denationalization in the wake of military conquest triggered off an Afrikaner national movement of explosive power. . . . There is in South Africa a scorched earth on which the seeds of denationalization will not grow – whether the intended victim be Boer, Briton or Bantu.[230]

The idea of 'difference' at the heart of debates in the Afrikaner community during the 1950s constituted a response to the perceived threats to the continued existence of the Afrikaner community, and of the 'white nation'. Having exposed the 'sore spots' in their identity, Afrikaner nationalists proceeded not only to work out a specific solution to their problem, but to re-create the world in their image. And this re-creation, in the light of decolonization and the rising tide of African nationalism inside South Africa, took the form of 'grand apartheid': the division of South Africa into a white South Africa and separate, independent 'homelands' for Africans.

The measures contained in the Bantu Self-Government Bill were the topic of widespread discussion during 1959, especially since they seemed to touch upon the series of wider issues on which opinions within the Afrikaner community differed widely. One of the most important in this respect was the question of whether or not apartheid involved total territorial segregation. As I have noted, SABRA intellectuals, as well as some Dutch Reformed ministers, saw total territorial apartheid as the only *morally* acceptable solution to the colour question. The creation of homelands, which could become 'independent', thus arose in a context in which demands for a more positive thrust to apartheid were strong. Indeed, Verwoerd, who became Prime Minister in August 1958, saw it as his task to give apartheid a certain moral force and direction which were absent theretofore. Stanley Uys, an *Africa South* writer, commented on Verwoerd's inauguration in the following terms:

> Dr Verwoerd was brought in to lead the Nationalist Party almost as an act of desperation. After 10 years of Nationalist rule, during which it has become increasingly urgent to find an answer to the question 'What is Apartheid?', the Government had come to the crossroads: only Dr Verwoerd stood out as the man who claimed to know the answer.[231]

The answer consisted in a selective welding together of elements of the imaginary in the process of formation during the 1950s: the general debate as to the import of apartheid as the only alternative to 'integration'; the viewpoint of SABRA on total segregation; the input of Potchefstroom intellectuals on the nature of nationalism, nationhood and the sovereignty of spheres; the impact of the Tomlinson report; changes in naming linked to the emerging anthropological discourse on ethno-linguistic divisions in the 'Bantu' population of Southern Africa; and the wider context of decolonization and the rise of Pan-Africanism.

All of these elements were clearly present in the debate on the Second Reading of the Bill in May 1959. It is clear that not only the notion of the sovereignty of spheres, but also the conception of nationhood developed by the Calvinist and culturalist intellectuals was drawn upon to provide an account of the character of the 'South African' colour policy. Indeed, De Wet Nel argued that apartheid was not simply an ideological façade; it was a philosophy, a deeply held belief system which was rooted in three hundred years of South African history.[232] The crucial question facing South Africa was the following: should the process of formation of a people aim at the establishment of a multi-racial community, a community of unity (*eenheidsgemeenskap*), or should it aim at the development of separate peoples (*volksgroepe*)? The answer to that was clear. South Africa had rejected integration and accepted the policy of apartheid or separate development, in terms of which the right to self-determination was said to be extended to the Bantu. This 'benevolent' extension was made possible by the fact that the existence of separate 'national units' within the Bantu group had already been firmly established within anthropological discourse. Indeed, De Wet Nel maintained, a number of peoples in Africa had already gained their freedom, and some others were on their way to it. It was an irresistible force which could not be suppressed.[233] This, so it was argued, also held for the South African Bantu. The Bantu Self-Government Bill was in perfect accord with the processes of decolonization taking place in Africa.

An important displacement took place in the construction of this argument. The growing tide of African nationalism in Africa was transferred to the 'South African Bantu', only to be denied. This did not take place surreptitiously. It was stated quite bluntly; black nationalism did not exist:

> What exists is black hatred of the white man. It is the monster which will digest all the good things in Africa. But I need to ask directly, is not this creature the creation of the white man? This monster resulted from the fact that national units [*volksentiteite*] were ignored. . . . I want to say explicitly that I believe in nationalism in the case of our Bantu national groups: it is a nationalism based on the people [*volk*].[234]

The firmly held belief that nationalism had to be grounded in a people made it possible to deny the reality of African nationalism both within and outside South Africa. The argument here followed the same lines as the one analysed earlier: African nationalism was not a real nationalism. This belief in possessing access to the 'reality' of nationalism, to true nationalism, also made it possible for the National Party to ride roughshod over objections by both Africans and some members of the white opposition that they did not consult the people in whose interest this policy was supposed to have been developed. The conception of freedom involved in this understanding simply did not allow for the idea that not all persons adhered to the view of nationhood held by the organic intellectuals in the Afrikaner community. Or rather, if they did hold a different position, it was simply wrong, for true freedom and development could only be found within a community based upon an ethnos. The authoritarianism of this viewpoint did not, however, go unchallenged within the Afrikaner community. Indeed, it was another bone of contention between SABRA visionaries and the National Party. In his 1958 address to the SABRA conference on 'Our Task Concerning Race Relations in South Africa', Basson argued any racial policy was useless unless it was acceptable to non-whites, and that such acceptance was ruled out of court unless there was a fundamental change in terminology utilized by white politicians.[235] Europeans could not demand co-operation and goodwill from 'non-whites' while talking the language of 'European supremacy', and 'White man's country'. It was at this congress that the impatience of the 'visionaries' within SABRA with the continuing government rejection of the total apartheid idea as anything more than an (impractical) ideal culminated for the first time in open criticism of the Verwoerd regime.[236] That, together with the insistence of Olivier that a conference with African leaders should be organized to facilitate consultation, led to the resignation of Verwoerd from SABRA, and finally a purge of visionary intellectuals from the SABRA executive.[237]

Eiselen, Secretary of the Department of Bantu Administration and Development, challenged the view held by SABRA intellectuals and 'other radicals' that consultation was a necessary requirement for legitimacy.[238] He explicitly stated that there was 'no reason for ruling out apartheid on the grounds that the vast majority of the population in South Africa opposes it', as 'one militant church leader' (*sic*) had claimed. Since the Africans had 'traditional homes' within South Africa, that was where they belonged. Freedom could be found only in acting out the onto-theological order: in living as a member of a nation, within which one's highest aspirations could be reached and developed to the benefit of the larger community. Arguments based on liberal grounds did not hold sway. To the contrary, a liberal solution could only lead to a prolongation of white supremacy:

> What is envisaged by liberal optimism as a very gradual process must inevitably in practice become a battle of retreat in which the White man defends his supremacy and the Black man, relying on numerical superiority, tries to reverse the position by racial pressure.[239]

Echoing the widely held belief that racial integration would lead to conflict, and complementing the rejection of 'multi-racialism' with the view that cultures and races had inherent characteristics, the Minister of Bantu Administration and Development argued that the Bill had to make provision for the establishment of political forms which would reflect the specificity of the 'Bantu' culture. Indeed, for the purposes of this argument, 'Bantu culture' was presumed to be homogeneous enough to enable the government to put forward a single remedy: the restoration of forms of political representation appropriate to their culture. It was argued that 'Western democracy' was not such a form. As the traditional 'Bantu' political systems were not deemed to be inherently undemocratic, these systems could be utilized and built upon to foster a political system appropriate to the Bantu's position and culture in South Africa. 'Bantu-centric' forms of development had to take place.

Economically, this policy allowed for a tightening of controls over urban African labour. By defining the urban African townships as 'outposts of ethnic homelands', the Bantu Affairs Department could attack the concept of residential rights for the urbanized. As Posel points out, restricting the number of workers entering the cities could now be redescribed as a part of the government's 'magnanimous' drive to boost the productivity of the reserves.[240] This strategy was closely linked to the envisaged programme of industrial decentralization, which aimed to relocate labour-intensive industries from the cities to the border areas surrounding the 'homelands': industries situated on these borders could draw on migrant African labour, and thus sustain industrial expansion without increasing the urban African population.[241] These measures, together with the internal development of the reserves, were supposed to create and sustain the economic development of the 'Bantu' in his own sphere. However, as was already clear from the government's response to the Tomlinson Commission's recommendations, the government had no intention to provide the extensive allocation of funds and the much needed 'consolidation' of the 'homelands' were such a project to succeed. Rather, it is clear that SABRA was ultimately correct in its evaluation of the NP's reluctance to accept its solutions: ultimately the homelands, as established, would neither counter white domination nor fulfil the political demands of the African population.

This project, emerging in the 1950s, formed the basis for the expansion and deepening of separate development throughout the 1960s, up to the early 1970s, when the first cracks in the apparently hegemonic imaginary appeared. Separate development, the preferred term for apartheid in the 1960s, could function as an imaginary since it claimed to solve all the problems to which the emerging apartheid project was a response. On the 'positive' side, it offered certain advantages. As Verwoerd argued in 1962:

> The first is that every group would . . . at least be able to exercise control over its own people. . . . Secondly, it could offer an opportunity of developing equalities among groups. It could satisfy the desire for the recognition of human dignity.[242]

These advantages, however, were dependent upon being exercised in separate spheres. While a 'multi-racial' state would be unfair to 'minorities' (Indians, coloureds and whites), it would also constitute an injustice to Africans, since a 'ceiling' would be placed on their 'development'. The realization of the legitimate aspirations of the African population, then, was clearly not assimilable with the conception of an integrated state. Neither white nor black could realize themselves fully in such a state. By the mid-1960s, the discourse of difference had become so entrenched that it was possible to argue that separateness did not imply discrimination:

> . . . we instituted the policy of separate development, not because we consider ourselves better than others, not because we considered ourselves richer or more educated than others. We instituted the policy of separate development because we said we were different from others. We prize that difference and we are not prepared to relinquish it. That is the policy of separate development.[243]

Not only did 'positive' apartheid provide a solution to the provision of political freedoms and equality in all (separate) domains, but it also solved the 'problem' of increasing African urbanization. The 'homelands' constituted the real home of the African. Those Africans still residing in the cities could be under no illusion as to their temporary status. While apartheid did not succeed in halting African urbanization, and it never was its purpose to do so, it did considerably slow down its tempo by the introduction of a variety of influx control measures. These measures were not simply labour control mechanisms. The symbolic horizon of positive apartheid within which these measures were made possible tells a different story. Apartheid, rather than a handmaiden of capital, created the context within which capitalists, farmers, and so on, had to frame their demands. This is the real importance of the constitution of the imaginary: it made possible some things, and ruled others out. A socially and politically integrated society was ruled out. The demands of the economy had to be phrased within the symbolic horizon provided by apartheid. This imaginary, insofar as the SABRA demand for total apartheid was rejected, included a recognition of the continued presence of Africans within what was considered to be 'white' South Africa. However, this recognition was subjected to strict limitations, which makes sense only within the horizon discussed. The institution of the grand apartheid solution did not occur overnight. More importantly, the vision of a 'just apartheid' was established at great cost. The ultimate irony of apartheid was that its most 'just' moment was also its most brutal.

Resisting closure

Opposition to the proposed solution to South Africa's 'colour' policy did not come only from within black ranks, as I argued in chapter 2. The most vocal opposition from within the Afrikaner community came from B.J. Marais, C.F. Beyers Naude – who later was to be driven out of the Afrikaner community, and banned for continued resistance to apartheid – and B. Keet. Keet held that the overemphasis on difference and separation was contrary to unity in Christ. Marais wrote that the attempt to find a Scriptural basis for apartheid was doomed to failure, for all new nations were born as a result of 'a mixing of races', and if such a mixing was contrary to God's command, then the birth of all new nations, including that of the Afrikaner nation, must have been in conflict with God's will.[244] These criticisms were prevalent within the Afrikaans churches throughout the 1950s, and came to a climax with two events: the publication of *Vertraagde Aksie* (*Delayed Action*), a collection of articles by DRC theologians making public their misgivings about the application of apartheid; and the Cottesloe Convention in 1960 which stressed, *inter alia*, the disintegrating and unacceptable effects of migrant labour on the African community, deplored the low wages and working conditions of Africans in the urban areas, and argued against job reservation.[245] The NP and the AB immediately started a concerted campaign against the signatories to the Cottesloe Consultation. Verwoerd, in a New Year's message, went so far as to attack the Cottesloe delegates for misrepresenting the Afrikaner community:

> The impression created by opponents of the policy of separate development that certain churches have taken up a critical stand-point is absolutely false. In point of fact the churches have not yet spoken. Through their synods . . . the voices of the churches have yet to be heard.[246]

The press rallied opinion to crush the 'dangerous heterodoxy'. The Afrikaans churches subsequently failed to ratify the report at their synods, and voted to withdraw themselves from the World Council of Churches. A process of marginalizing the dissenting intellectuals thus began, paradoxically, at the moment when apartheid was supposed to have reached its zenith as a 'just order'.

A system of differences, a situation in which Afrikaner, English, coloured, Indian and African South Africans could live together while recognizing and institutionalizing those differences, could only be created by constituting an 'other' against which these differences could be lived as such. The systems of exclusion forged in the early years of apartheid did not fall into disuse during the 1950s. To the contrary, the 1950s were marked by a continuous deepening of those exclusions. The growth of an African nationalism and Africanism with South Africa proved to be resistant to being defined out of existence. Ironically, the most severe resistance to the implementation of the grand apartheid system with its emphasis on 'Bantu authorities' was encountered in just those areas where tribal tradition had been thought to be at its strongest. One commentator ascribed this to the fact that the system turned chiefs into 'petty despots who exercise power as a reward for implementing government policy'.[247] The final irony, perhaps, is that the disturbances which took place in so many dissimilar areas of South Africa could be related to the fact that a uniform policy was imposed on all Africans. What was supposed to have been the highest point of particularism failed precisely for enforcing the same particularism on all, without discrimination.

The case of resistances in Sekhukuneland is a telling one in this regard. From the beginning of 1955 the government struggled to gain recognition from the tribal authorities for a series of measures to be introduced in connection with the Bantu Education and Bantu Authorities Acts. The Bapedi tribe, under leadership of their Regent, twice decisively rejected the whole Bantu Authorities system. The Native Affairs Department even tried to bribe them with promises of a railway bus service, a new secondary school, a clinic, a post office and a telephone.[248] The tribe refused and a series of members of the royal family were deposed, and deported by the government. For four successive years, the introduction of these Acts was resisted. By 1958, Verwoerd, acting under a law passed in 1927, 'sealed off' the area. This meant that any person who 'verbally or in writing makes any statement which is either intended or likely to intend to subvert or interfere with the authority of any State official' became liable to a large fine and three years' imprisonment. During March of that year, the ANC was banned as an illegal organization in Sekhukuneland. Several months of unrest followed. In now familiar way, the Native Affairs Department official explained the 'real' cause of the trouble in Sekhukuneland as a conflict between the Bapedi and Baktoni tribes, and portrayed the government as the protectors of the latter.

These events were not confined to a certain part of the country. Several districts were alight with unrest and repeatedly the cause for this was given as grievances related to the introduction of the Bantu Authorities system. Resistance against the extension of passes to women and to pass laws in general also continued. On 26 March 1960 the Commissioner of Police announced a reprieve:

> In view of the fact that Bantus, as a result of intimidation, are so gripped by fear to carry reference books and are even afraid to carry any money, I have decided to relieve this tremendous tension and to prevent innocent and law-abiding Bantus from landing in trouble. I have instructed that no Bantu male or female is to be asked for his or her reference book.[249]

In both the case of the Sekhukuneland disturbances and the pass law-related unrest, the government began to draw divisions within the African community between 'good' and 'bad' behaviour. 'Goodness', in spite of the paradoxes involved here, was usually attributed to the 'tribal Bantu', the 'decent Bantu' who 'knew his place'. The essentially good community was shown, in familiar fashion, to be subject to infiltration and corruption by 'agitators'. After the Sharpeville shootings, on 6 April 1960 the organizations deemed to partake in 'intimidation' and 'agitation' were banned under the Unlawful Organizations Act (No. 34 of 1960). The activities of the ANC and the Pan-Africanist Congress (PAC) were thereby declared illegal and a threat to the security of the state. The apparent reprieve won with the relaxation of the pass laws was just that, an apparent reprieve.

During the Second Reading of the Bill, the Minister of Justice stated that the government:

> . . . has decided to call a halt to the reign of terror which the Pan-Africanist Congress and the African National Congress have been conducting recently among the Bantu peoples of South Africa, to call a halt to the activities of the terrorists, White and Non-White, who act as instigators behind the scenes without taking an active part themselves.[250]

The reasons for the introduction of the Bill were further spelled out. Cruel and barbaric intimidation, assault and threats of innocent people were behind the resistance. The same rhetorical patterns of justification were in evidence, reinforcing well-established prejudices, linking all forms of resistance to a desire to overthrow the state. The 'real Bantu' did not have anything to do with this; the culprits were instigators, communist agitators and 'nationalists' who used innocent people for their own ends. The causes of unrest were not to be found in the apartheid system. They were external, and continued to be linked to an alleged communist threat. This established a pattern which was to be repeated *ad infinitum* during the following two decades.

The events of early 1960 and the subsequent introduction of a State of Emergency produced a sense of crisis within 'white' South Africa. Reactions to this varied. The Federated Chambers of Industry (FCI) expressed the hope that the disturbances could be brought under control, so that 'law-abiding' Africans who wished to work but were threatened by intimidators could return to work. The FCI stated its strong conviction that the waves of unrest had a real basis of grievances which agitators could exploit. It urged the government to consult with leaders acceptable to the urban African population. In contrast, the AHI reaffirmed its support for separate development, and so did the Afrikaans churches. The dissident Afrikaans ministers again voiced concern and issued a statement that apartheid was unethical, unbiblical and without any Scriptural foundation. In contrast, the SABRA reaction was one of silence. Apart from a statement issued after a closed meeting, rejecting the 'distorted picture' of South Africa presented in the world media, it simply reaffirmed its demand for the consolidation of the Bantu areas, as well as of the need to enter into consultations with 'responsible Bantu leaders'.[251] The government announced that it saw no reason to depart from its policies.

The shootings at Sharpeville, and the country-wide disturbances, thus, did not succeed in shattering the belief in the 'justness' of separate development. If anything, since they were read and interpreted in terms of the already existing frontiers, the events of the late 1950s and early 1960s served to reinforce those divisions. Instead of putting into question the apartheid imaginary, they strengthened the belief in its necessity. They 'showed' the violence just below the surface of 'African life'; they 'revealed' the extent to which communists sought to undermine 'white civilization' in South Africa; and, finally, they laid bare the forces of nationalism within the country, seeking to infiltrate and destroy innocent communities. World opinion turned on South Africa, but it did not 'understand' the 'unique' position of white South Africans seeking to eke out a living at the tip of a continent threatened by the expansion of 'international communism'. The resistance was thus turned to the advantage of the Nationalist government. The repression inaugurated an era of 'peace' in which it became possible to believe that the dream of a just apartheid had been achieved.

Conclusion: The Logic of Apartheid

The nature of the classificatory logics described here, those logics giving the world a structure, captures something of the nature of apartheid discourse. It shows that inherent in the process of drawing boundaries and of producing frontiers are two moments, separable and yet inextricably intertwined: that of creating distinctive entities, or systems of difference, and that of producing a series of entities to which the differences will be opposed, thus constituting systems of exclusion. Apartheid discourse operated with precisely such a logic. The systems of difference fashioned in this discourse could only come into being by the simultaneous operation of a logic of exclusion. I have argued that in the case of apartheid this logic is essentially undecidable. This is attributable to the specific type of classificatory logic we have been investigating, namely political frontiers: neither systems of difference, nor systems of exclusion ever totally succeed in imposing themselves, ever succeed in suturing the social. They stand in a relation of tension to one another, a relation characterized by a war of position in which neither can gain the upper hand in any final sense. That is not to say that no position of dominance could be established. To the contrary, the movement from myth to imaginary in apartheid discourse depended on precisely this possibility. Apartheid reached its zenith, the impossible completion of the movement from myth to imaginary, with the introduction of 'the final law' spanning the racial pattern in South Africa in 1959.[252] The Bantu Self-Government Bill, based on the belief that the 'forces which would plough the white man under' could be contained only by a Babelish dispersion, had to carry the immense burden of providing the ultimate, the last and final solution to the 'colour question'.

I have traced the beginnings of this imaginary back to the dislocations which were at the root of the emergence of a reactionary, exclusive Afrikaner nationalism in the 1930s and the 1940s. The experiences of rapid urbanization, of fragmentation of the Afrikaans-speaking community into social classes, the continued subordination of this community to an English-speaking 'imperial' cultural, social and economic hegemony, all made it highly unlikely that the segregationist discourse of South Africanism, based upon an alleged equality between the Afrikaans- and English-speaking communities, would succeed in creating one white South African nation. The emerging organic intellectuals drew these diverse events together in a discourse which could not only make sense of them, but also produced an overdetermination between the elements, such that the solution put forward, namely the reconstitution of the *volk*, became the answer to all their problems. This included the 'Native question'. By the end of the 1940s, with the Fagan Commission moving towards an acceptance of the permanence of African urbanization, these intellectuals declared war also on 'integration'. Thus, apartheid not only was held up as the solution to the relations of subordination between the Afrikaans- and English-speaking communities, it also became the doctrine which set itself against the drift to integration. By the 1948 election and in its immediate aftermath these frontiers were inextricably intertwined. Apartheid was the watchword of the intellectuals, who were concerned both with the position of the Afrikaner *vis-à-vis* the English population, and with the relation between 'the races', now discussed under the rubric of the 'colour question'.

In its articulation of the 'colour question', apartheid both continued the frontiers already in existence under segregation and instituted a novel form of social division. That is why it is not possible to theorize the relation between segregation and apartheid in terms of either a radical rupture or a mere continuation of racist practices. Even in the instances where apartheid clearly continued in the tradition of segregation by excluding the African population *en masse* from the polity, the continuation cannot be thought in terms of a simple repetition of the same. The new historical context of articulation, that of a perceived threat of communism and the rise of African nationalism during the period of decolonization, gave the strategies of exclusion a different import; one which is crucial in accounting for the movement from myth to imaginary in apartheid discourse. Faced with what were perceived to be threats, the discourse of difference was extended to the African population. In this process, a series of subject positions were created which did not previously exist. The once 'homogeneous' African population was argued to consist of separate Bantu 'national units', or different 'ethnic' groups. The elaboration of novel forms of social division was part of an extensive debate in the wider community of Afrikaner nationalists. Different groups of intellectuals partook in the struggle to give meaning to the signifier 'apartheid'. The significance of these interventions should not be underestimated, for they facilitated the elaboration of a horizon within which it became possible to give apartheid its 'moral' overtones. The highest expression of morality, within this horizon, was the creation of self-governing 'Bantu homelands'. With this, the system of differential positions was expanded: not only the Afrikaans- and English-speaking communities could now exercise their right to difference; also the Zulu, Sotho, Venda and Xhosa 'national units' could partake in that freedom. The symbolization of the event of ethnicization of South Africa in this manner made it possible to present apartheid as natural, just and moral in the eyes of the white Afrikaner population.

By re-creating the world in their image, what was a specific solution to a very particular series of dislocations became universalized. With this, the movement from myth to imaginary was completed. Apartheid could no longer be considered as a series of *ad hoc* responses to pressing problems. It became a complete, moral vision of social division. Without taking into consideration these symbolizations, it is impossible to account for the establishment of apartheid hegemony. For what is crucial here is not, as some historians have argued, whether Verwoerd believed that he had created a just ordering of society. Even if it were possible, it would not be our task to determine his personal convictions. Rather, it is important that in the figure of Verwoerd as architect of grand apartheid a series of discourses were drawn together making it possible to present the ordering of the social as just and moral. In his name a vision was forged, one which forgot its own origins, and in this forgetting made it possible to appear to itself as natural. However, it is also true that the forgetting of the violence of institution could not be complete, not all traces of it could be covered over. The gap between the particularity of the initial response and the universality of the grand apartheid solution could not be closed entirely, since the creation of any unity involves forms of exclusion. This showed itself, in the case of the 'homelands' solution, in a variety of ways. First, it was clear in the fact that in devising forms of inclusion, exclusions were present. While the discourse privileged the production of 'ethnic difference', it, nevertheless, in one and the same moment, excluded all Africans, as a whole, from the polity. In the second place, the resistance offered to its institution was strong and continuous. Yet, even these events were representable within the apartheid imaginary. If anything, it was articulated to reinforce the already existing patterns of exclusion. Does this then mean that no resistance could be effective in undercutting the logic of apartheid? Certainly not. This is the subject matter of the following two chapters. However, a few pointers may be in order here.

For a resistance project to succeed, a logic different to that of apartheid discourse had to be developed, a logic which would not simply constitute a reversal of that project; one which could not be reabsorbed into its already existing systems of exclusions and differences. Historically, such discourses developed around two of the main axes of exclusion operated by apartheid, and both had to do with the undecidable quality of the complex sets of politico-strategic movements which constituted the internal history of apartheid. Suffice it to say that the constitutively 'undecidable' character of apartheid discourse was both its strength and a condition of its disintegration. Apartheid shrewdly operated with 'undecidable' logics. The process of its constitution, as I have shown, involved applying the central social categorizations, such as race and *volk*, in an undecidable manner. 'Apartheid' itself also portrayed these characteristics. These categories could be argued to be microcosms of the wider processes of identity constitution in this discourse, and they operated as 'hinges' in the Derridean sense.[253] *Volk* was used to distinguish between different 'peoples', such as the Zulu, Xhosa, Afrikaans- and English-speaking South Africans. At the same time, however, it was utilized in order to distinguish and hierarchize 'white' and 'black'. The category of race displayed the same uncanny undecidability, an undecidability which is at its most acute in the operation of the signifier 'apartheid' itself. Throughout the 1950s, the period of institution of apartheid, a war of position was being played out between proponents of apartheid who saw it as essentially a project to safeguard the existence of the white *volk*-race, and those who regarded it as something more, as an ideal intimately connected to a divinely ordained order of things, without which no freedom was possible. While the latter became the dominant form of official rhetoric, the former was never too far in the background.

Apartheid both operated systems of blatant discrimination and worked with an ideology of discernment. The presentation of apartheid as a project of separate freedoms, reaching its highest point in the 'grand apartheid' idea, had as its condition of possibility the brutal suppression of any discourses critical of it. The deceptive doubleness of the discourse could thus not be hidden away, covered over, for too long. While apartheid attempted to pass itself off as natural by retaining only one meaning, the 'right meaning', to paraphrase Descombes, and thereby claiming that the good is only good, my deconstructive reading has attempted not only to reveal the deceptive duplicity of this discourse, but to place its deceptiveness at the very heart of any attempt to account for its hegemonic possibilities.[254] 'Somehow the thing had to be possible.' I have argued that this possibility cannot be accounted for simply by listing laws and stipulating characteristics. Just as a process of enumeration remains unsatisfactory, so do attempts to reduce the logic of apartheid to any of its constitutive elements. The creation of 'homelands' cannot, for example, be understood simply by reference to the 'cheap labour pools' associated with them. While not denying that certain interests were at work, it is crucial to place these within the discursive horizon provided by apartheid discourse, for it is only then that the precise forms of exclusion and inclusion, the formation of new subject positions and social categorizations, can be understood. These forms constituted the horizon of possibilities within which capitalists, farmers, industrialists, and so forth, had to articulate their demands. Apartheid discourse, thus, elaborated contexts of intelligibility, domains within which certain demands and articulation of interests could make sense. Insofar as it became hegemonic, it delimited the domain of the possible. What fell outside that became unintelligible. Raising fundamental objections was still possible, but in a very real sense these were no longer heard, for they fell 'outside the truth'. Challenging apartheid would mean also, or precisely, challenging the domain of truths, the space of representation, established by this discourse.

A last question concerning these processes of identity formation still has to be addressed, one which finally has to disprove theorists arguing that apartheid simply was 'irrational'. I have shown that apartheid, far from being irrational, consistently operated with very clear logics of identity formation. The articulation of new discourses, all of which came to be related to the increasingly empty signifier of apartheid, contributed to a systematic elaboration of knowledges, and techniques of surveillance, which had precise beginnings and genealogies. The overdetermination established between these different strands or understandings of apartheid, and the undecidable quality resulting from them, cannot be accounted for in objectivist terms. Apartheid both discriminated and discerned, and its history is a history of shifts between these two undecidable poles. In the formation of an imaginary horizon, a certain decidability was established: apartheid, while becoming increasingly all things to all people, succeeded in portraying itself as a project within which many, if not all, desires could be fulfilled. That was, as long as these desires were in accord with the onto-theology inaugurating this project.

4

The Roots of an Expanding Imaginary:

From Separate Development to a Plural Society

If to classify is to give the world a structure, then the crisis of such a structure could be expected to involve a problematization of the classificatory systems upon which that structure was built. The deepening crisis evident in South Africa during the 1980s displayed exactly such a radical questioning of the systems of difference and of exclusion put into place by apartheid during the previous decades. Any investigation of the emergence of this crisis, therefore, has to be built around an account of the consecutive waves of domestic and international resistance to apartheid and the repeated attempts by the regime to restructure forms of social division which characterized it. In these attempts, two primary enlargements of the apartheid imaginary took place which were centred on the continued exclusions operative within it. The first concerned the position of coloured and, to a lesser extent, Indian South Africans, while the second concerned the position of urban blacks. While the impetus for an expansion of the apartheid imaginary can be located in events during the 1970s – from the increasing resistance by trade unions to the 1976 Soweto crisis – and can therefore be said to have arisen from a clearly definable conjuncture, the genealogies of the form of the relation of white domination to the variable, uneven systems of exclusion constitutive of it make it necessary to disaggregate the position with respect to coloureds and Indians, on the one hand, and that of urban Africans, on the other. In this and the following chapter, I trace out these trajectories separately. In the course of this discussion, the attempts by the NP to construct a new balance of forces around rearticulated political configurations and philosophies will take centre-stage.

This is not to say, however, that the nature of the reforms and adaptations, and the consequent expansion of the apartheid imaginary, can in any way be attributed solely to the internal workings of its logic. To put it differently, while the logic of apartheid – in its simultaneous operation of systems of inclusion and exclusion – contained the possibility of its expansion, the need for that expansion and the multiple revisions which it underwent during the period stretching from the 1960s to the early 1980s have to be sought in the nature of the resistance discourses which increasingly challenged those very logics. In the treatment of the transformation of apartheid discourse, two separate analytical issues are therefore at stake. The first concerns the question of the limits, and thus of the identity, of apartheid discourse. The identity of apartheid discourse was not given in a set of positively specifiable characteristics, but could be found in the boundaries or frontiers through which others were excluded. It is therefore not possible to address, through a determination of the presence or absence of a series of essential characteristics, the question regarding the point at which the apartheid imaginary entered decisively into crisis. Such an enumeration may be useful up to a point, but it cannot be used to specify the precise point at which the discourse could be said to have been challenged decisively. To attempt to do so would lead directly into the fallacy of assuming that once, for example, a set of key laws or regulations have been removed from the statute books, or certain elements of economic transformation have occurred, one has moved 'beyond' apartheid. What would be missed by such an account is precisely the central defining feature of apartheid, which exceeds any such enumerative delimitation, namely the fact that it operated with an *identitary logic* premissed upon the impossible object of the *volkseie*. This logic, while located in a precise historical context, also displayed a set of features which went beyond that context. The apartheid imaginary, in constituting itself as if it were self-sufficient and identical to itself, uncontaminated by any relation to alterity, called upon wider metaphysical and onto-theological premisses, found also in other discourses of identity.[1] That means that what appear to be alternative discourses may in fact continue to be premissed upon an identitary logic similar to that of apartheid, and, under those circumstances, the claim that one has moved 'beyond' apartheid would only be partially true.

At this point a further question arises. Does this then mean that it is no longer possible to delimit the discourse of apartheid? That there were no limits to the manner in which it could be rearticulated and transformed? The answers to these questions, quite clearly, have to be negative. Thus, there has to be a point beyond which this discourse could not be expanded without losing its identity. This point was reached when the negatively constituted object of the *volkseie* lost its potential to organize forms of social division as a result of the multiple and uneven impact that resistance discourses had on it. It is at this point that the conjunctural crisis could be said to have become an organic one.

This brings me to the second analytical point concerning the disarticulation of the apartheid project. If, as I have argued, all identity is relationally constructed in and through the production of frontier effects, then challenges to those frontiers will have subversive effects upon the dominant discourse. That is to say, the process through which forms of social division are brought into being does not depend solely on the internal logic of a discourse. On the contrary, that which has been excluded in the process of construction of social division has the capacity to question and to undermine those very frontiers. Resistance discourses, as political practices which engage in the creation and transformation of social relations, are not radically external to the field in which dominant discourses are produced. While the 1960s were characterized by the turn to underground warfare, the 1970s and 1980s saw an increasing shift in the strategy of resistance movements towards engagement in what Gramsci has called 'wars of position'. These challenges to the dominant discourse took place on a variety of terrains, starting from the emergence of the Black Consciousness movement in the late 1960s, and ranging from trade union struggles in the early 1970s to an increasing mass mobilization in the wake of Soweto 1976. During the 1980s, with the realignment of internal resistance movements under the auspices of, *inter alia*, the United Democratic Front (UDF), the challenges posed to the transformist project became more acute and forces of resistance engaged more directly in the questioning of the proposed new forms of social division. The period from the late 1970s onwards can thus rightly be characterized as one in which both the state and the forces of resistance were engaged in an arena of struggle in which move and countermove produced far-reaching effects on the organization of social division; so much so, that by the mid-1980s the very logic of apartheid was beginning to fragment. This situation produced an organic crisis, a terrain in which a general questioning of authority and hence of apartheid hegemony became visible; a site in which control slipped out of the hands of the state and opened up the space for the forging of a new national popular will. As Gramsci had known so well, when such crises occur, 'the situation becomes delicate and dangerous, because the field is open for violent solutions, for the activities of unknown forces'.[2] While the discussion of the full implications of this crisis will be treated in the following chapter, it is necessary here already to remark that there was nothing necessary to the manner in which the crisis was resolved. Its resolution depended upon a series of well-documented political struggles, both within the regime and within the forces of resistance, with no immutable logic behind them. That is to say, neither economic demands nor the logic of capitalist development had to lead to its dissolution. Rather, the position taken here is one which emphasizes the primacy of the political. The crisis into which apartheid discourse entered in the mid-1980s uncovered the political nature of this project; it challenged the naturalization of social division which became sedimented in institutional forms and so uncovered the particularity and non-necessity of this logic. In this sense, the crisis of apartheid can be located in the contraction of its imaginary horizon of intelligibility, making visible, once again, the literality and specificity of the project.

This chapter deals with the roots and, therefore, the historical conditions of possibility for the emergence of the transformist project in the late 1970s, and locates these conditions both in the logic of the discourse itself and in the form of resistance to that logic. The expansion of the basis of legitimacy of the state was limited by the particular form in which apartheid became sedimented during the 1960s. This, in turn, depended upon the silencing of resistance to it within the Afrikaner community itself. The consolidation of the logic of 'separate freedoms', following in the wake of the severe repression which characterized the early years of that decade, provides the material for the first section of this chapter. Thereafter, I pursue the anomalies opened up by this logic, specifically with reference to the positions of the coloureds and Indians, and trace out the concomitant changes and transformation of the imaginary which dominated the construction of social division during the 1970s and early 1980s. A remarkable feature of this period has been the simultaneous operation of logics of repression and reform, of coercion and co-option, on the one hand, and of resistance, on the other. It is customary to describe this relation in terms of a dialectic. That is to say, cycles of resistance and repression/reform relate to one another in a necessary manner; the one necessarily calls forth the other, for they are internally related.

To problematize this sort of account is not to say that the relation between these processes has been one of externality, for to argue thus would be to deny the premiss of the relationality of identity upon which my argument is built. Contrary, then, to attempts to think this relation in terms of either a necessary relation of mediation or one of pure externality, I will argue that what seems to appear as a necessary internal relation in fact appears in that form only as a result of the very retroactivity of judgement. As Žižek puts it in his recasting of the Hegelian dialectic: 'dialectical necessity' is always, by definition, a necessity *après coup*.[3] And it is that moment of retroactive constitution of 'what actually took place' which has to be called into question by giving centrality to the moment of articulation: a putting together of elements which have no a priori necessary belonging. Seen from this point of view, attention has to be shifted from the mere coincidence of the two processes, to the *form* they took under precise historical circumstances. To put it differently, while at a most general level the notion of a dialectical relation between these two processes may seem illuminating, it is in fact misleading when coming to account for precise historical developments and changes, for it ignores the contingency of what seems to appear as necessity. That is why it is necessary to investigate the minutiae of the operation of changes in the form of social division. Otherwise one may fall into one of two equally fallacious positions: one may either be led to assume that the dominant discourse evolved in the manner in which it did as a result of its own internal logics; or one may come to regard the changes occurring during the 1970s as a result of 'objective' historical conditions, which disregards the precise historical form of resistance discourses.

The Context of Repression: *Salus reipublicae suprema lex est*

No account of the expansion and eventual crisis of the apartheid imaginary would be adequate without placing it in the context of a series of repressive measures introduced during the early 1960s. The 'silent sixties', as this decade is popularly referred to, were premissed upon a vast expansion and use of the repressive apparatuses of the state.[4] It would not be an overstatement to say that the alleged success of the apartheid project – in the eyes of its institutors and supporters – depended precisely upon the sheer scope of the measures designed and implemented to suppress any possible resistance to it. Combined with the economic boom which characterized the 1960s, it created an illusion of peace and prosperity that was not to be ruptured until the early 1970s.[5]

The decolonization process underway on the African continent raised concerns not only about the 'rising tide' of African nationalism within South Africa, but also about the security position of South

Africa on a continent of independent African states.[6] In addition to the formation of the armed wing of the ANC, the early 1960s were characterized by the emergence of liberation movements in most of the 'buffer states' surrounding South Africa.[7] Together with a continuing fear of the spread of communism, and faced by more militant and now also underground, armed African resistance, these factors led to a revaluation and sharpening of the mechanisms of control and domination in the immediate aftermath of the Sharpeville period.[8] These measures included the Defence Amendment Act of 1961, which extended the Minister of Defence's powers to act in operations for the prevention and supression of 'internal disorder'; the Indemnity Act of 1961, which prevented detainees under emergency regulations from instituting any civil actions against the government or persons acting 'in good faith with intent to prevent or suppress disorder'; the twelve-day detention clause of the General Law Amendment Act, to be extended to ninety days in 1963; and the 1962 Sabotage Act.[9]

These measures were justified by a reinvigorated fascination with the threat of communism.[10] As I have argued earlier, the invocation of communism occurred wherever resistance to the racial policies of the regime was expressed. The increasing use of this 'threat' to justify repression thus came as no surprise in a context of growing internal and international resistance to the apartheid regime. The words of B.J. Vorster, upon the introduction of the General Law Amendment Act of 1962, made this all too clear:

> South Africa remains a prime target in the eyes of communist strategists. It represents a strong link in the line of Western defences against communism on the continent of Africa. . . . Its peoples are progressive, peaceful and law-abiding but they belong to a variety of nations. . . . They have their roots in different civilizations and are fundamentally different in their stage of development, outlook on life, culture, customs and tradition. *To sow the seeds of suspicion, to create friction between the various races and to disrupt the life-lines of South Africa's buoyant industrial economy so vital to the well-being of its peoples, have become the essential elements of communist strategy in South Africa.* Sabotage, . . . intimidation and terrorization of innocent people are the techniques employed to subvert the forces of peaceful progress and lawful government.[11]

The 'failure' of the West to support the South African anti-communist stance was attributed to the West's inability to recognize 'the obvious Communist tactics of presenting a negative picture of South Africa to the world with a view to gaining the maximum support for exercising pressure on South Africa to amend her policy'.[12] With regard to internal resistance, arguments that subversive forces were intent on destroying the achievements of the policy of separate development were frequently made and were echoed also in the contributions to the *Volkskongres* on communism held in 1964.[13] The extent to which these contributions still reflected knowledge of various doctrinal divisions within the communist world is remarkable, for this feature of the anti-communist campaign would become more and more diffuse as time went by.[14] In line with the increasing focus on Africa, much attention was given to statements by Stalin, Lenin and Mao on the need to 'destroy Europe through the loss of Africa' and to the co-operation of communists with African nationalist movements.[15] Within South Africa, the SAIC, the African People's Organization, the COD, the South African Council of Trade Unions, the ANC and the PAC were quickly singled out as front-organizations for international communism despite repeated denials of this by some of the movements concerned. This list of organizations was rapidly extended also to include liberal critics of apartheid, the World Council of Churches and the UK Anti-Apartheid Movement, to name but a few.[16] In the wake of the *Volkskongres*, the National Council Against Communism was created, and in 1966 it sponsored an 'International Symposium on Communism'. That the concern with communism was not only limited to the inner circles of the National Party, is clear from the wide dissemination which the discourse on communism received during the 1960s, a discourse which would become even more central to the maintenance of white domination during the 1970s and 1980s.

Resistance to the various measures introduced during the early 1960s came from a wide variety of sources. Not only did the liberation movements continue their campaigns against racial domination and economic exploitation, but several groupings within the white community also subjected the measures to severe criticism. For example, the 90-day clause of the General Law Amendment Act of 1963 brought into being the '*90-Dag*' *Proteskomitee* ('90-Day' Protest Committee), which drew upon the support of legal experts, psychologists, church leaders and medical professionals to denounce all aspects of this clause which made provision for the continued detention of persons in solitary confinement, with no right to legal representation or medical services, and which stated that persons so detained could be interrogated at any time and without time limit, until a response which satisfied the police had been elicited.[17] Opposition parties and the opposition press decried the measures as dictatorial in nature, as gross infringements of civil liberties. The extent to which criticism continued to fall on deaf ears, however, can be seen most clearly from the following statement, made by Vorster in 1971:

> Many black people have gone to jail in South Africa and there are many on Robben Island and in other places where they have to serve long and hard sentences, but thank God, no black person in South Africa has ever found himself in trouble because he stood up for that which is his *own*.[18]

The strengthening of the repressive state apparatuses also included a vast expansion of the South African Defence Force (SADF). In 1961 a ballot system of conscription was introduced for the first time, which, by 1964, led to a more than sixfold growth in the Citizens' Force, while the Permanent Force doubled during this period. In line with these developments, and the perceived threat from African countries, the defence budget increased fivefold, so that by 1964/65 it constituted 21 per cent of government expenditure, while the total budget for national security amounted to 26.8 per cent of government expenditure.[19] In addition to these increases in expenditure, which was also reflected in the growth of the local armaments industry in anticipation of an international arms boycott against South Africa, the intelligence services were restructured.[20] This reorganization reflected internal struggles and divisions between different visions as to the appropriate manner to deal with the internal and external threats to state security, divisions which would surface again in the mid-1980s. As O'Meara has pointed out, by the late 1960s, the Department of Defence began to play a more open role in politics, arguing for militarily defensible policies, and so aligned itself with more *verligte* (enlightened) positions within the NP, while the Security Police was aligned with the *verkrampte* (narrow-minded, unenlightened) faction within the party.[21] In 1969, the Bureau of State Security (BOSS) was set up as a complement to Military Intelligence and the Security division of the South African Police (SAP). This quickly led to a demotion of Military Intelligence, with BOSS taking command over the intelligence chiefs of the army, air force and navy to solve the internal problems of co-operation between the military and police intelligence positions.[22] The Potgieter Commission argued in this respect that the confusion of functions between Military Intelligence and the Security Police was itself a danger to 'the security of the state.[23] As a consequence of these restructurings, the Security Police took full responsibility for the containment of the armed struggle.[24] The Potgieter Commission further recommended the creation of a State Security Council (SCC). The SCC, established in 1972, was to become one of the central bodies in the formulation of the 'Total Srategy' which was to dominate South African politics during the 1970s.[25]

In addition to the repressive measures instituted during the early 1960s, other, less overt, ones were also introduced. They included the use of the resources of the South African Broadcasting Corporation (SABC) openly to attack institutions and organizations hostile to the regime – including the English language press, the Institute of Race Relations, the National Union of Students, the Defence and Aid Fund (banned in 1966) and the Christian Institute.[26] In 1963, the government also established the Publications Control Board, regulating both socially and politically 'undesirable' materials. It is in this general context of repression that debates on the further extension of the logic of apartheid into a discourse on 'separate freedoms' took place.

Consolidating 'Separate Freedoms'

The verlig–verkramp struggle

> The National Party has not been a party that stood still, but has always been on the march. It is the National Party which not only brought about changes, but has been able to meet every new situation because its principles preeminently make it possible for it *to master every situation*.[27]

The process of consolidation of the policy of 'separate freedoms' – apartheid was a term rarely used from the late 1960s onwards – opened the way for profound changes in the articulation of social and political identities in the discourse of the NP. The change from Union to republican status in 1961 was accompanied by a redefinition of the relation between Afrikaans- and English-speaking whites. This was achieved through a far-reaching rethinking of policy towards other African states, as well as by a deepening of some of the already existing frontiers. These changes in NP policy affected the Afrikaner community at large, and resulted in a serious rift between different Afrikaner organizations. During the late 1960s a schism developed between those who saw the process of consolidation as threatening to the preservation of the Afrikaner *volk* and those who argued that separate development had to be taken to its logical conclusion. The NP, during this period, found itself hovering between these alternatives, neither prepared to take the overt supremacist role prescribed to it by the far right, nor prepared to live with the consequences, limited as they were, of its policy of separate development.

The battle lines between the two groupings within the Afrikaner community were drawn around four main issues of party policy: the question of playing 'mixed' sport; immigration; the status and positions of African diplomats in South Africa; and the discourse on national unity. These four issues can be seen as nodal points, acting as areas around which a wider set of differences in the understanding of the logic of separate development were condensed. 'Separate development' seemed to offer a clear-cut set of guidelines for the elaboration of policy. However, even this apparently lucid logic constantly ran up against policy areas where it offered no clear guidelines or solutions to problems. While relative agreement existed with regard to what separate development meant for the treatment of the African population as a whole, much less clarity existed in the case of both urban Africans and coloureds, and new rules had to be invented to deal with them. Even the apparently clear position with regard to the African population did not go uncontested in the white community. Dissatisfaction with the repressive logics inherent in the exercise of separate development was voiced by some church spokespersons at Cottesloe in 1960. However, separate development was not only challenged for the atrocities committed in the name of the doctrine of 'separate freedoms'. In the early 1960s a series of far-right groupings emerged within the NP to organize against the independence granted to the Transkei in 1962. Organizations such as the *Terug na Strijdom Beweging* (Back to Strijdom Movement), the *Konserwatiewe Studiegroep* (Conservative Study Group) and *Red Suid Afrika* (Save South Africa) were active in putting forward arguments against the self-government of homelands. These groups regarded the essence of apartheid as contained not in its doctrine of 'difference', but in its supremacist strains. These groups were also strongly opposed to the emerging discourse on national unity and immigration put forward by the National Party. These divisions were contained under Verwoerd's autocratic leadership. However, in the later 1960s they became more pronounced, leading Vorster, Verwoerd's successor as Prime Minister, to marginalize the far right-wing groupings active within the Afrikaner community.

One result of the apparent success of separate development in providing answers to the dislocations facing the Afrikaner community was the fact that after the formation of a republic in 1961, a rearticulation of relations between the Afrikaans- and English-speaking population took place. The exclusivist discourse constituted around the *volk* no longer dominated National Party thinking in the same manner as before. Rather, with the main cultural and material objectives of

Afrikaner nationalism secured, the focus was being placed increasingly upon the formation of a white nation. Having resolved the 'colour question', it was possible to turn attention toward bettering relations between the two 'white' language groups. This was already abundantly clear in Verwoerd's calls for a cessation of hostilities between them during the run-up to the referendum on the Republic. Desiring to unite the Afrikaans- and English-speaking *volke* into a republic, Verwoerd sought to diminish the long-held antagonism between them. This had to be done carefully, without endangering either's language. In the process, much attention was given to the fact that the two 'language groups' – not separate *volkere* any more – could exist in a mutual space, and could even be united for political purposes. Verwoerd, at a republican rally in 1960, made very clear the purpose of such unification:

> We have been living for many years with division and strife between English- and Afrikaans-speaking people. This struggle has been born out of our history. But what is important for the people of South Africa at present is something more than history . . . besides history there is the future. . . . In that future we see the revolution of Africa and the growing problems of South Africa. For the sake of that future we must stand together as whites. We, both English- and Afrikaans-speaking people who believe in a certain colour policy, wish to work together in this direction. . . . For this reason I say we must have a republic, partially because this will take away the injuries of the past and heal our wounds.[28]

Verwoerd thus saw in the unification of these groups not only the healing of past wounds, but also the strengthening of whites' position *vis-à-vis* a series of perceived threats. The 1960s saw an elaboration of the discourse on communism and a proliferation of laws aimed at dealing with the 'internal threat' to the state. The brutal suppression of resistance in the early 1960s was accompanied by a perception of being threatened, apparent in the fact that private households were highly armed, white schoolchildren were called upon to receive training in the use of firearms, and military spending increased by some 600 per cent.[29] This perception was present across the white population. The UP supported all government bills dealing with the 'internal threat' and in the 1966 election the NP consolidated its position, taking 58 per cent of the votes cast.

The 1961 SABRA annual conference was organized on the theme of Afrikaans–English relations and explored the possibilities of co-operation between the 'two language groups' on cultural, educational and political terrain.[30] These themes were to be developed further under the leadership of Vorster, to the point where he could claim the existence of a single *nationhood* amongst white South Africans:

> . . . we should ask ourselves what the basis of our policy is . . . the cornerstone of the National Party is the retention of the identity of the White Afrikaner and the White South African. . . . We as South Africans – whether we are Afrikaners or whether we call ourselves South Africans – we are proud of our nationhood. . . . Today *the White South African nation consists of Afrikaans and English speakers*, each with a white identity of its own but bound by a common love and loyalty to South Africa. We have different outlooks but we have the same roots, the same aspirations and the same destiny in South Africa.[31]

The conception of 'nationhood' articulated here had as its precondition certain changes in the discourse of Afrikaner nationalism. These included the fact that, with the consolidation of Nationalist power over the state, material differences and inequalities between the two population groups began to diminish. In addition, the change in leadership of the NP had a significant influence, since Vorster did not come from the same 'stock' of Afrikaner leaders as Malan and Verwoerd. He was not schooled in the ethnic tradition of the 1940s and 1950s, and thus not equally committed to the ideals of Christian national exclusivism.[32] This opened the way for him to elaborate separate development into a discourse which focused less on the *volk* and more on the (white) nation. The break with a radical ethnic exclusivism occurred during the 1960s and was bound up with a continued perception of threat to the white South African population:

> In the first instance it is not a question of what language a man speaks . . . but one's view of the future. The point at issue is one's faith in the policy of separate development, one's faith in the *survival of the white man* here in South Africa – that is what is at issue and from the ranks of the people who believe thus – Afrikaans- and English-speaking alike – a nation will be built.[33]

The 'nation' did not include anyone outside the white community and was thus unequivocally a racially defined one. This articulation echoed Verwoerd's 1962 distinction between 'citizens' and members of the 'nation'. At the time Verwoerd argued that 'coloureds' could be considered as citizens, but not as 'a part of this homogeneous entity that can be described . . . as "the nation"'.[34] By the late 1960s the language of *volkism* was virtually absent from NP discourse. It was now replaced by a discourse on *multi-nationalism*, considered to be more suitable to the 'realities' of the South African situation. Multi-nationalism, however, was still opposed to multi-racialism. Emphasis was now placed on the fact that different nations could achieve 'full independence'. This particular articulation also echoed Verwoerd's idea, never fully developed, of a 'Commonwealth of States', and foreshadowed P.W. Botha's later proposal for a free association of 'sovereign' states, politically independent, but economically inter-dependent. This multi-nationalism was, moreover, being applied increasingly to coloureds and Indians. However, while the African 'nations' could reach independence, coloured and Indian 'nations' would continue to be subject to a white parliament.[35] Vorster went so far as to portray multi-nationalism as the 'third phase' of the NP programme of action. The first, apartheid, consisted of separating what had been 'intermingled'; the second, separate development, consisted of the processes through which governments were created and people were 'given status'; while in the third, people were being treated as 'equals'.[36]

During the later 1960s further resistance developed within the Afrikaner nationalist community to the policies of national unity and separate development. Organizations such as the *Genootskap vir die Handhawing van Afrikaans* (GHA, Association for the Maintenance of Afrikaans) and *Christelike Kultuuraksie* (CKA, Christian Cultural Action) sprang up and were supported by cultural leaders such as Piet Meyer, Chair of the AB, and Andries Treurnicht, who was to lead the second breakaway from the NP in 1982. They criticized the discourse of 'national unity' and co-operation between Afrikaans- and English-speaking South Africans on the grounds that it did not seek real unity, but only 'togetherness-in-whiteness'.[37] Against them Vorster argued that the term 'South African nation' was used only in a political and not cultural sense; the Afrikaner *volksgedagte* (idea of the *volk*) and South African nationhood were complementary and not in opposition to one another.[38] In addition to these issues, the right-wing of the party was also becoming more and more dissatisfied with immigration policy, which did not have, as an explicit aim, the securing of immigrants who would further the perpetuation of 'traditional Afrikaner values', and with the NP policy on sport and 'black diplomats'. The latter arose as a result of Vorster's policy of 'outward movement' in regard to other African countries. For the first time in the history of South Africa was there anything like a recognition that the country belonged to Africa and was a part of the African continent. Vorster stated this rather bluntly at Naboomspruit in 1971:

> I say to you that we do not only have a duty to ourselves, but we have too long described ourselves as Europeans to the outside world. *We are not Europeans, we are of Africa,* as any other person is of Africa. Africa is the land of our birth. We will die here in Africa.[39]

Henceforth, the move away from Afrikaner exclusivism was complemented by an attempt to break the isolation in which South Africa found itself as a result of its apartheid discourse. Vorster's more pragmatic attitude was also reflected in the NP's approach to 'mixed sport'. While under the leadership of Verwoerd, apartheid was enforced in a doctrinaire manner, Vorster was prepared to do away with its more openly discriminatory aspects in order to regain some international recognition. On 11 April 1967 Vorster announced a new sports policy in Parliament, allowing, *inter alia*, a 'mixed' South African Olympic team. However, no 'mixed' trials would take place beforehand. Similarly, foreign sports teams were asked not to include obviously 'non-white' members. In this manner Vorster tried to placate right-wing criticism of changes to Verwoerdian apartheid: 'mixed' sport could be played in an international arena, but not in South Africa. However, the Basil D'Oliviera affair in 1968 – leading to the cancellation of the MCC cricket tour to South Africa as a result of the fact that D'Oliviera was included in the MCC team – shattered any hopes that this more 'enlightened' policy would end South African isolation in the international sporting arena.

The deepening divisions within the NP were reflected in Afrikaner organizations as well as in the Afrikaans press.[40] At the 1966 SABRA Youth congress in Warmbaths this rift was labelled a division between *verlig* and *verkramp* by Prof. Willem de Klerk. *Verligtes*, according to Willem de Klerk, were liberals in a new Afrikaans form.[41] Those who were *verlig* threw all tradition overboard and wanted openness and freedom in all areas of life. In contrast, *verkramptes* were the narrow-minded Afrikaners, extremists and ultra-conservatives. While De Klerk himself rejected both the 'extremes', and argued for a positive Afrikanership which would include elements of each, the press took up these labels and accorded *verligtes* a positive value, while to be *verkramp* was designated as negative.[42] As a result, the struggle around the policy areas discussed above came to be characterized in terms of a battle for hegemony within the NP. Initially the NP avoided taking sides in the disputes, always trying to mend differences to prevent a break in the Afrikaner community. By late 1968, however, Vorster issued an ultimatum to the 'super Afrikaners' either to accept NP policy or to leave the party.[43] By then the question had become one of which tendency represented the real and true ideals of the National Party. This was finally resolved by a systematic purging of *verkramptes* and the marginalization of their organizations within the Afrikaner community. In 1969, the *verkramptes* left the NP. The breakaway of the *Herstigte Nasionale Party* (HNP) signified the extent to which a rearticulation of Afrikaner identity had already taken place. This event foreshadowed what would take place again in the early 1980s: another breakaway, on similar grounds of a return to 'Verwoerdian' ideology. The *verkrampte* camp continued to signify white supremacy, Afrikaner exclusivity, a narrow emphasis on the maintenance of traditional Afrikaner values and on racial superiority, while *verligtes* emphasized South African nationhood and rejected everlasting white domination in favour of the expansion of 'separate freedoms'. The latter involved continued demands for a quickening in pace of 'homeland' development and the granting of full independence to the 'black nations'. In addition, for the *verligtes* real separate development had no need for 'hurtful' petty apartheid measures. Whereas the *verkrampte* faction argued for a return to precisely these types of measures, *verligtes* felt that they were of a temporary nature. Once the framework of separate development was in place, petty apartheid could be done away with. For example, in its October 1968 issue *Woord en Daad* (*Word and Deed*), the journal of the Potchefstroom-based Afrikaans Calvinist Movement, rejected these apartheid measures as a permanent solution to the racial question, and described apartheid regulations as 'intolerable burdens which could be justified only if they were regarded as transitional regulations'. A call was made for the immediate improvement of homelands. As a result of the *verligte* victory within the NP and other Afrikaner organizations, the 1970s were characterized by calls for the repeal of petty apartheid measures (that is, signs such as 'whites only' on park benches, segregated hotels, theatres and restaurants) such that by 1975 R.F. Botha could state at a session of the UN Security Council that the NP

> ... does not condone discrimination *purely* on the grounds of race or colour. Discrimination based *solely* on the colour of a man's skin cannot be defended. And we shall do everything to move away from discrimination based on race and colour.[44]

The consolidation of separate development thus did not take place without a struggle in the Afrikaner community. The division between *verlig* and *verkramp* increasingly characterized differences which existed on policy issues, to the point where a rupture in the Afrikaner community and in the NP was precipitated and the *verkramptes* were marginalized. This strengthened the possibilities for 'co-operation' between the 'two language groups' and reinforced the discourse on national unity. However, not all problems were solved. One particular area of separate development had not yet been worked through. This concerned the position of coloureds and Indians in the larger order of grand apartheid. Around this issue the NP endeavoured to take the middle road between *verlig* and *verkramp*. While in the case of immigration, sports policy, black diplomats and national unity, the *verligtes* within the NP won the day, they would not succeed in turning their demands for full citizenship for coloureds into NP policy.

'Lines which would never meet'

> Desperately at a loss are we about the destiny of those bloodclose darkselves of ours – the people of mixed descent.[45]

The coloured population occupied a very peculiar place in the onto-theology of apartheid. This place was characterized by its irrepresentability within the discourse of nationhood and its concomitant territoriality. The coloured population were regarded as 'an appendix' to the white community. This made the establishment of a separate nationhood for them difficult, if not impossible. Moreover, by virtue of their closeness to the white community, their 'supplementary' status created the possibility of disarticulating the very logic of social division instituted by apartheid. This was recognized in the repeated arguments concerning the role of coloured voters *vis-à-vis* the main 'white' political parties, and led to the ending of the remaining direct representation in Parliament and their exclusion from a common voters' roll in 1956. As a result of this, throughout the 1960s and the 1970s, attempts had to be made to find a space within which the political aspirations of the coloured community could be satisfied. Whatever 'resolution' was to be found, it would be the result of continual struggles in the Afrikaner and the larger white community, as well as within the range of political organizations found in the coloured community.

The possible paths of development specified for the coloureds displayed wide-ranging differences. These were closely connected to the existing lines of division within Afrikaner nationalist politics. Separate development, with its emphasis on nationhood, offered no obvious solution to the position of the coloured population. As a result, a long-running debate occurred in the early 1970s on the application of the logic of separate development to them, resulting in three basic alternatives for the satisfaction of their political demands: a coloured 'homeland', 'parallel development' and political integration of the coloured community into 'white' politics. Within the coloured community, opinions varied from welcoming separate development to a total rejection of the appellation 'coloured'. As a result of the formation of the Coloured Person's Representative Council (CPRC) in 1964 'coloured' politics, for the first time, included organized political parties. The Labour Party and the Federal Party both participated in the CPRC. While the Labour Party's programme had as a priority the return of coloured people to common roll representation and the rejection of apartheid, the Federal Party made no secret of its support for the government's policy of separate development.[46] At this stage, neither party sought to question the existence of a distinct 'coloured' group. Thus, even though the Labour Party had declared the eradication of apartheid as its aim, it accepted its basic framework of racial categorization. The formation of political parties prepared to participate in the CPRC stood in marked contrast to a much more radical political tradition in this community. Throughout the 1950s, the South African Coloured People's Organization and the Non-European Unity Movement (NEUM) were active in organizing resistance to the extension of apartheid measures to the coloured population. Both these organizations took a non-collaborationist stance and dominated coloured politics between 1948 and 1961.[47] The issue of collaboration or boycotting of governmental bodies remained a seriously divisive issue in coloured politics and resurfaced with the introduction of the tri-cameral Parliament.

Soon after the establishment of the grand apartheid design in 1959, a certain 'restlessness' and 'disgruntledness' in the coloured community were 'reported' by white politicians. This, no doubt, was the bitter fruits of a decade of systematic political and social segregation of the coloured community.[48] Their disfranchisement and the enforcement of the Group Areas Act, especially the 'cleansing' of District Six, did not improve the relations between the coloured and the white communities. Radical opposition to all apartheid measures existed, and while the SACPO had been silenced by 1962 with many of its leaders arrested or banned, the NEUM continued its resistance. It declared the CPRC a 'mock council' and 'a shabby substitute for citizenship rights'.[49] As a result of the recognized disaffection in the coloured community, certain SABRA and Potchefstroom intellectuals decided to raise the issue of the place of coloureds in the larger order of things. On 23 July

1960, Dawie, an influential political columnist for *Die Burger*, started a fiery debate by proposing that the National Party was moving strongly in the direction of a 'radical' solution to the problem:

> The drive to a forward movement in Nationalist policy for the Coloureds is becoming more and more strong. The most dramatic idea of course is . . . that the Coloured voters must be permitted to elect white or brown members [to Parliament]. This of course is only one part of the complex of plans being discussed by thinking people. . . .

Verwoerd, in a press statement, immediately rejected this possibility.[50] He argued, in familiar fashion, that this would present a springboard for the 'integration of the races', leading to 'biological assimilation'. The NP's policy for this community was one of 'parallel development': colour streams were parallel and would remain so. Each community had to develop in its 'own stream' or in parallel lines, and these lines 'would never meet'.[51] Whereas 'full independence' would be granted to 'Bantu peoples', this was not a possibility open to the coloured community. Instead, they would be given opportunities to develop within the 'white state', firstly by means of local government, and secondly through managing their 'own affairs' in Provincial Councils. In due course, they would be given further rights of self-development. The same logic held for the Indian community.[52] With some minor modifications, this remained the NP position until the later 1970s.

Central to the NP strategy of fostering a separate coloured identity was their separation from the African population. In the mid-1950s a Coloured Labour Preference Policy (CLPP) was introduced in the Western Cape amidst a storm of criticism from the Chamber of Commerce and Industry, farmers and other employers' organizations, in order to ensure continued separation and the elimination of contact between these groups.[53] The Eiselen scheme, as it was known, regarded the 'problem' of contact between coloureds and 'Natives' as so serious that it 'demanded the attention of the general public and the Government'.[54] Miscegenation and the disappearance of 'differences in social and cultural outlook', 'moral decline' and 'economic impoverishment of the Coloured community' were cited as reasons for these measures.[55] Between 1956 and 1961, 20,000 African workers were deported from the Western Cape under the CLPP.[56] The policy was decried by the ANC as an attempt to 'divide and rule' by forcibly separating coloureds and Africans.[57] Since these measures favoured the employment prospects of coloureds, they acted as a way of hierarchization, dividing the coloured and African communities from one another and enabling the NP further to develop its policy of parallel development.

One of the clearest expressions of this policy was given in a paper delivered by the Minister of Coloured Relations and Rehoboth Affairs to the Abe Baily Institute for Inter-Group Studies in 1972. Arguing against the concept of a 'coloured homeland', on the one hand, and political integration, on the other, Dr S.W. van der Merwe stated that the NP policy, set out in 1961, remained unchanged:

> . . . the policy of parallel development as applied to the Coloureds embraces a policy of parallel administrative bodies at different levels, with continual liaison and consultation with White institutions at various levels. Control over matters affecting the Coloureds in particular is already being exercised by the Executive of the Coloured Person's Representative Council, to which several important powers and functions have been delegated . . . [58]

This statement was merely a reiteration of the May 1971 statement by the Federal Council of the NP, which took the position that the expression of a separate coloured identity required the rejection of any policy which would lead to integration. 'Integration' was rejected on the same grounds as previously: it would lead to 'unnecessary and serious friction between Whites and Coloureds'. In addition, a coloured homeland was deemed unpractical since no one historical coloured territory existed.[59] While 'White and Brown', by virtue of their 'co-existence', shared a 'sphere of mutual interest' which demanded mutual deliberation, it also had to be recognized that there were spheres in which the interests of either group were decisive. As with 'friction theory', the doctrine of spheres informing the formation of homelands for Africans underpinned the separation of coloureds into a 'parallel' position. While more of a commonality was recognized, the over-whelming emphasis still fell on the need to separate 'communities', even if it was almost impossible to justify such separation.[60] Indeed, one searches NP documents in vain for such justifications. Although references to the need for the constitution of a separate coloured identity are rife in NP materials, arguments for coloured nationhood never really took hold in the NP. Accepting the fact that coloureds fell within the 'European sphere' left the NP with few possible arguments to legitimize the exclusion of the coloured community from the polity. Even the implicit racism was no longer made explicit. Coloureds were 'simply different'. The fact that coloureds were seen to fall within the

'Western' group was, thus, a double-edged sword. On the one hand, it made the position of coloureds and their exclusion from the polity a particularly difficult one to justify. On the other hand, as I have shown, it allowed Nationalist politicians to argue for their separation from Africans. The fear of the formation of a 'non-European front' played a central role in the motivation of efforts to incorporate the coloured population at the expense of the African workers.[61] This structural undecidability in the position of coloureds, reflected also in the 'negative definition' given to them in the Population Registration Act as neither white nor black, was to remain the Achilles' heel of Nationalist politics.

The NP position did not satisfy demands from either the *verkramptes* or the *verligtes* within the party. As early as April 1960, SABRA established a committee to investigate the position of coloureds. The committee members included Profs S.P. Cilliers, Jan Sadie and Gerrit Viljoen, as well as Ds H.J. Snijders and Mr J.W. Germishuis.[62] In January 1961, a unanimous report was published arguing that a political and social structure should be set in place which would allow the coloured community to develop full citizenship. Simultaneously, the existing Union Coloured Council was rejected as a framework for political expression. Territorial and political separation or differentiation was also rejected out of hand. In addition, a call was made for the scrapping of the notorious Group Areas and Mixed Marriages Acts. The report was suppressed by Verwoerd and was one of the factors which led to the polarization of SABRA and its eventual split. As I have already pointed out, the split in SABRA led to the marginalization of the grouping of people labelled 'integrationists' and later *verligtes*. SABRA was taken over by a conservative tendency under the leadership of Prof. P.F.D. Weiss, who was later to become a leading figure in *verkrampte* circles. The different positions on the coloured question crystallized around the *verlig–verkramp* fault-line during the 1960s. What is particularly interesting in this regard is the fact that the SABRA *verligtes* who argued in favour of more radical development of the 'homelands' with respect to the African population proposed that the coloured community should be integrated, at least politically, within the 'white' community. A 'homeland' was not a possible solution to the problem of the political position of coloureds. It was the far right who tried to capture the moral high-ground with an argument for a coloured homeland. The possibility of such a solution, however, depended upon the capacity to show that the coloureds were 'a nation in the process of formation'. This was indeed the road taken. Even so, they never formulated a convincing 'plan' for territorial segregation. At the most, what they could produce was some notion of a 'homeland without geographical content'.[63] The NP repeated its rejection of both positions, holding that a homeland for coloureds was not 'practical politics', and that representation of coloureds by coloureds was not acceptable either. Any reverting to the pre-1956 position, it was argued, would lead to a situation in which white unity would be torn apart.[64] Instead, the NP insisted on its policy of parallel development.

The debate on the coloured question continued throughout the 1970s. In July 1971, following in the footsteps of calls made in 1968 from the *Woord en Daad* group at Potchefstroom, twenty-nine university professors and lecturers from the Universities of Pretoria, the Witwatersrand and South Africa repeated the call for the political integration of the coloured community.[65] This was later supported by 109 Cape academics, also demanding full and equal citizenship for the coloured community. Hence, contrary to existing interpretations, the *verlig–verkramp* division cannot be accounted for in terms of a North–South divide.[66] Support for the 'liberalization' of coloured policy was found across the regional divide of white politics. *Die Burger*, a Cape paper generally supporting the *verligte* cause, demanded that the twenty-nine set out what they meant by 'full citizenship rights'.[67] In reply, four of them spelt out a programme, consisting of the introduction of equal voting rights for coloureds, scrapping of 'negative' laws such as those enforcing group areas and job reservation, equal pay for equal work and equal access to public facilities.[68] *Die Burger*, however, rejected this on the grounds that it ignored the impact which common voting rights for whites and coloureds would have on white unity, in effect taking the position of the NP.[69]

Throughout the early 1970s there were continued reports of dissatisfaction in the coloured community. By April 1971, with the full backing of its leader, P.W. Botha, the Cape NP had organized a campaign within the NP to reverse what it regarded as the dangerous alienation of the coloured population. Vorster at first resisted the campaign. However, in January 1973, in order to contain the growing revolt in the NP, many of whom supported the *verligte* position, as well as to appease 'moderate' coloured opinion, he conceded to the appointment of a commission of inquiry. The Theron Commission reported its findings in 1976.[70] While the government never accepted its core recommendations, this investigation gave rise to yet another commission of inquiry under the leadership of P.W. Botha that would change the face of South African politics decisively. Before discussing these developments, it is important to contextualize the contents and reception of the Theron Commission report. The report had given serious attention to the description of the sense of powerlessness and frustration felt by a group whose history and cultural affiliations were 'closely allied with those of whites', and yet whose channels for expressing feelings and aspirations were abysmally inadequate, if not non-existent. The recommendations made in order to alleviate the situation included a call for the repeal of the Mixed Marriages Act and the clause of the Immorality Amendment Act prohibiting intercourse between white persons and others; the opening of commercial and industrial areas to all races; the repeal of the job reservation clauses in the Industrial Conciliation Act; the opening of all universities to coloured students; the elimination of gaps in salaries, conditions of service and social pensions between whites and coloureds; the removal of barriers to inter-racial sport at national and provincial levels; the gradual opening of spaces, facilities and beaches for use on an inter-racial basis; and provision for satisfactory forms of direct coloured representation and decision-making at the various levels of authority and government.[71] It explicitly stated that the main problems arising from the restrictions of the political and civil rights of the coloureds arose from the fact 'that the Coloureds have no share or say in the decisive, legislative governmental institutions in the country' and that the institutions on which they were represented had a 'subordinate status'.[72] While some of these recommendations deviated quite strongly from existing government policy and reflected much of the *verligte* position, the report did not for one moment question the very fact of racial categorization. Indeed, in discussing the category of 'coloured persons' it noted a number of anomalies between different laws and recommended that the sub-categories of the 'coloured' group should be scrapped. The existence of racial categorization as such was not put into question.

In response, the government White Paper stated that numerous recommendations made by the Theron Commission were acceptable to the government.[73] These included 'consultation' with coloureds on issues of 'common interest', the progressive elimination of discrimination, sharing of facilities on a wider scale and the opening of industrial areas to coloured entrepreneurs. These measures fell within the already accepted position on the repeal of 'petty apartheid' measures. The White Paper further held that the recommendations which would amount to the recognition and development of the identity of the various population groups being broken down was not conducive to the orderly and evolutionary advance of the various population groups. The government was not, therefore, prepared to change its standpoint in relation to the Mixed Marriages Act. Neither was the granting of direct representation acceptable. Commenting on the White Paper, *The Sunday Times* stated that in it *verligtes* saw both their credo and the wish that fuelled it explode yet again.[74]

More important than the content of the report, and the government's predictable response to it, was the wider context in which it was published. This highlighted the fundamental flaws of the report. In an article in *The Sunday Tribune* Dr J. Gerwel, lecturer at the University of the Western Cape, stated that:

> . . . a discussion of the position of the Coloured people which is not integrated with a consideration of the entire South African society is bound to remain superficial.[75]

He went on to argue that the recommendations of the Theron Commission represented a blueprint for the gradual integration of 'a Mulatto group into the ruling White power structure at the expense and exclusion of the Black majority'. These remarks touched upon the crucial problems of the report. While representing a certain break with the logic of apartheid, it remained caught in the racialist division of the social by accepting the parameters of that discourse. Not putting the Population Registration and the Group Areas Acts into question locked it into a logic from which it could not escape. Moreover, its failure to discuss the relation between the coloured community and the African majority made it, in the words of Labour Party leader Sonny Leon, 'an expensive exercise in futility'.[76] This was brought home unequivocally by the fact that the tabling of the report, and its subsequent discussion, took place against the backdrop of events that shook the white establishment to the core.[77] The events of Soweto 1976 followed ferment that started in the early 1970s with the re-emergence of radical trade union activities. These events came in the context of a political situation in which Black Consciousness (BC) acted as an organizing principle and motivating force for resistance. The Labour Party began to flirt with BC during the early 1970s and it led it to cast its understanding of the position of coloureds in terms of a wider struggle for *black* liberation.[78] This indicated the growing influence of BC ideology put forward by organizations like the South African Students' Organization (SASO) and the Black People's Convention (BPC) in the coloured community.[79] While the struggle within the Labour Party between BC and proponents for a separate coloured identity continued, and was only temporarily resolved in favour of the latter in the mid-1970s, it had a profound impact not only on the coloured community but also on thinking within the NP. The NP initially displayed an ambiguous attitude towards BC, seeing in it an ideology which could be used to support separate development. However, the very real possibility of an articulation between the oppressed groups posed a serious threat to the whole apartheid project which was being questioned from all directions during the 1970s. It is not surprising, then, to witness yet another change in nomenclature in the NP discourse at this point. By 1974, it was held within the NP that the term 'Bantu' had to be replaced by the term 'Black'.[80] In contrast to the use of this term in BC discourse, it referred strictly to Africans in NP parlance. This was a direct challenge to the use of the term as a collective one to include coloureds, Asians and Africans. In the wake of the 1976 uprisings, the NP began a process of reformulating their strategy of political exclusion of coloureds and Asians from the central polity. This reconstitution of social and political division precipitated yet another split within the NP in 1982. More importantly, the transformist project facilitated the emergence of a form of resistance capable of disarticulating the desperate efforts to hold apartheid society together.

The Transformist Project

The final recommendation of the Theron report provided the soil from which the transformist project would grow. It argued that if constitutional reform were to provide 'political citizenship rights' for coloureds, the Westminster system had to be adapted to the requirements peculiar to the South African *plural* population structure.[81] In the 1977 constitutional proposals, as well as in the debates during the run-up to the November general election, the NP emphasized its commitment to this recommendation, holding that the Westminster system did not have to be followed 'slavishly' in South Africa.[82] On the contrary, the right of all groups to self-determination required serious reform of the existing Parliamentary system. Starting from this basic thesis, the NP sought a new legitimizing theory, and much of the traditional apartheid logics were to be disarticulated as a result. The need to embark on the road of constitutional reform, as remarked earlier, did not simply arise from *verligte* pressure within the NP. It could very well be argued that such pressure, if isolated, might not have amounted to any change whatsoever. The NP record on appointing commissions of inquiry only to reject or ignore their recommendations is general knowledge. While the *verligte* demands for a lasting solution to the problem of coloured representation could not bring the NP to constitutional reform, it was, nevertheless, important, for it provided direction to that search. The crucial impetus for the drive to reform was given in the overdetermined conjuncture of the early to mid-1970s.

A series of changes in the emerging conditions of the early 1970s are important in this respect. The late 1960s and early 1970s saw the emergence of the BC movement, which played an important part in the radicalization of resistance politics and in the inculcation of a sense of black pride. The rapid industrial expansion of the 1960s also affected the character of the 'new' black working class: they were increasingly drawn from urban communities, were more skilled, and were integrated into the heart of the industrial economy.[83] While the 1960s were characterized by unprecedented economic expansion, in the early 1970s the South African economy began to show signs of contraction, evident in particularly high rates of inflation and the beginnings of a severe balance of payments problem. This led to pressure on the conditions of black workers, and as a result the manufacturing and mining industries were shaken by strikes. While the number of black workers involved in strike action in any one year in the 1960s never exceeded 10,000, 1973 alone saw 370 strikes involving 98,029 workers.[84] Out of these actions grew an independent trade union movement, fighting not only for the right to struggle for higher wages, but also for the right to organize.[85] The more generalized resistance culminating in the Soweto popular uprisings of 1976 decisively shattered the illusion that separate development had resolved the 'colour question'. Increasingly, it was recognized that the 'urban black problem' had to be addressed.[86]

In addition to these internal challenges to the apartheid order, regional conditions underwent marked changes. The overthrow of the Portuguese regime in 1974 led to the decolonization of Portugal's African colonies, Mozambique and Angola. These events, together with the uncertainties with regard to the former Rhodesia and South West Africa/Namibia, had an enormous impact on the NP as well as the wider white community. While they initially gave rise to a 'detente' policy under Vorster's leadership, it was clear that a serious rethinking of state policy in this area was also necessary.[87] The realization of the shortcomings of internal and external policy dimensions, coupled with mass resistance and a deepening recession, called for a concerted response. This took the form of a transformist project, in the Gramscian sense, through which the regime tried to expand its basis of legitimacy by co-opting subordinate groups in various ways.

This project was to serve as the litmus test for the separate development imaginary. If the transformist project succeeded, the imaginary would have shown itself to be capable of almost indefinite expansion. If not, the imaginary itself would recede to reveal once again its literal, ignoble beginnings.

The first element of the transformist project to be discussed here concerns the political representation of coloureds and Indians within 'white South Africa'. As I have argued, the logic of separate development did not provide a space of representation for the coloured and Indian populations. In the context of the deep alienation of these communities, and in the face of the possibility of political alliances being formed between Africans, coloureds and Indians, first in the discourse of Black Consciousness, and later in the non-racialism of the Congress tradition, the need to act in order to protect the apartheid order was clear. The co-optation of segments of the coloured and Indian population into the tri-cameral Parliament came to provide the conditions for the broadening of the basis of support for the threatened state. The second element of this project – to be discussed in chapter 5 – concerned the position of urban Africans. By the mid-1970s it was still claimed that the political position of 'blacks' in general was solved by separate development. Yet, it was clear that that of *urban* Africans required more attention. A news commentary by the state-controlled South African Broadcasting Corporation put it in the following way:

> In short, what place should the urban blacks occupy in the South African framework? First, it has to be stressed that similar to the situation in the homelands . . . the management of their own affairs is not only consistent, but is required by the South African framework. In the homelands this process has proceeded quite well, and in the Transkei it has culminated in independence. The Coloureds and Indians have their own political institutions: but progress with the urban black communities on the way to municipal self-government raises specific questions, questions which are practical rather than ideological. . . . The recent legislation on community councils offers wide scope for the exercise of local self-government: but if it is to succeed . . . work will have to be done with greater urgency and imagination than before. . . . [88]

The recognition that the 'urban African problem' was of a more general nature and could not be accommodated within the old separate development framework did not come about until the mid-1980s. Meanwhile, the government insisted that the issue to be addressed with respect to urban Africans was of a purely practical economic nature, and it appointed two commissions of inquiry to deal with what were perceived to be the most urgent problems, those of manpower utilization and influx control. The Wiehahn and Riekert Commissions had to provide direction as to the conditions under which the creation and co-optation of an urban African middle class could take place. In this manner, the strategy of transformism was articulated around the two areas to which the logic of apartheid could not provide an answer, and this project was to be elaborated in a context set by military thinking. The Total Strategy furnished a horizon in which sense could be made of, and solutions could be provided for, the multifarious problems facing white South Africa by the mid-1970s.

Total Strategy

While the idea of modern war as 'total warfare' was already present in P.W. Botha's speeches as Minister of Defence during the late 1960s, the idea of a total strategy to counter the total onslaught was first propagated by the military in the early 1970s. Since then it has acquired a far wider meaning than its initial military signification. Apart from a brief period in the mid-1980s, with the signing of the Nkomati Accord between South Africa and Mozambique, the discourse of the NP continued throughout the 1970s and 1980s to be infused with symbols and imagery associated with the 'total onslaught'.[89] The increasing centrality of this concept was due primarily to P.W. Botha, who, after becoming Prime Minster in 1978, gave it a prominence it previously lacked.[90] The threat, so it was argued, originated in Soviet expansionism and the spread of Marxist ideology. At a conference on 'Psychological Strategies', the Deputy Minister of Foreign Affairs, Louis Nel, argued in his opening address that

> [t]here has been a prolonged and relentless campaign to single us out as such. The main – and most dangerous – impetus comes from the Soviet Union; but the campaign is also generated elsewhere. . . . The purpose of this campaign is . . . the isolation of South Africa, the creation and intensification of a revolutionary climate, the subversion and ultimate destruction of the government . . . While the Soviet Union may pose the greatest real threat to the peace and stability of South Africa, we cannot ignore the machinations of the United Nations against us, particularly on the psycho-propaganda level. The UN has become a factory, churning out anti-South African resolutions. . . . UN money goes directly to our enemies, such as the ANC, to whom it accords full recognition and provides a platform.[91]

The enemy of the state was thus identified in much the same way as before. The banning of the newspaper *The World* and eighteen organizations in October 1977, many of them inspired by BC, was done in the name of the need to resist international pressure and internal armed resistance, both of which were deemed to be part of a 'greater plan' to undermine the South African state.[92] Within the borders of the country, BC organizations were now held responsible for the Soweto violence.[93] Regionally, the threat was seen to come from neighbouring states which harboured ANC camps, in addition to the fact that they aligned themselves with the Soviet Union. For each of these aspects of the threat, the 'Total Strategy' provided a solution.

Under Botha's leadership the total nature of the threat facing South Africa was continually stressed. The 1977 White Paper on Defence put it in the following terms:

> The process of ensuring and maintaining the sovereignty of a state's authority in a conflict situation has, through the evolution of warfare, shifted from a purely military to an integrated national action. . . . The resolution of conflict in the times in which we now live demands inter-dependent and co-ordinated action in all fields – military, psychological, economic, political, sociological, technological, diplomatic, ideological, cultural, etc.[94]

Since a 'multi-dimensional threat' existed, a multi-dimensional strategy was called for. The notion of strategy employed here is crucial. It is clear from the use of the term, influenced by the thinking of André Beaufre, that it was recognized that a strategy was the outcome of a choice of methods to be applied in order to attain a given political objective, and that force was only *one* of those means.[95] The multi-dimensionality of government strategies, alternating between repression and reform, developing ever more complicated systems of exclusion and inclusion, was to be crucial in the years to come. Already in 1977 it was recognized that

> [s]trategy . . . is not something constant, since a change in one of the factors must have an effect on all the others. It must be constantly adapted to changing situations in respect of, for example, the threat, manpower potential, the financial climate, domestic or foreign policies. . . .[96]

While the strategy employed had to be multi-dimensional and flexible, it had to avoid the danger of being fragmentary. Adrian Vlok, later to become Minister of Law and Order, argued in Parliament that total resistance necessitated co-ordination between the community and the state:

> Fragmentary and ad hoc efforts in any sphere are futile and pointless. The onslaught must be resisted on a national basis in all spheres, by all national groups and inhabitants of the South African continent.[97]

The need for co-ordination and rationalization of state administration in order to be able to implement the Total Strategy had far-reaching effects in all areas of South African political, social and economic life. In the name of the Total Strategy, a new alliance of forces was formed, linking together an increasingly centralized state, military apparatuses and the private sector. In the construction of this new balance of forces, official discourse underwent a series of marked shifts which were indicative of a series of wider changes occurring within sectors closely related to the state. These included new powers assigned to 'experts' serving on permanent Cabinet committees and to specialized commissions of inquiry in the wake of the reorganization of the political decision-making bodies which diminished the role of Parliament, political parties and even of the caucus. The language of ideology was replaced by a 'technocratic rationality' and a depoliticization took place of areas previously dominated by doctrinaire decision-making.[98] Each of these changes stretched apartheid discourse far beyond its original articulation. It altered the way in which identities were constructed and political and social divisions thought and lived. Most importantly, it opened up new spaces of participation which, however limited, facilitated resistance to the transformist project. To point to these changes is not, however, to deny the fact that much continuity existed within this domain of rearticulations with the imaginary fashioned by apartheid discourse. This was evident in the very discourse of the 'total onslaught' itself, a discourse which did not remain at the level of public pronunciations by the state, but which set out to interpellate subjects in an ever-expanding fashion. Attempts, for example, to foster a sense of 'vigilance' within white communities provide ample evidence of this. The discourse of the total onslaught did not function only at the level of overt attempts to eliminate the enemies of the state. A far more insiduous logic was at work here, one which increasingly normalized – in the Foucauldian sense – a series of practices aimed at exposing the enemy within. The penetration of this logic into the domain of the everyday lives of ordinary people is abundantly clear in the manner in which the regime attempted to interpellate white women and children into the discourse of the total onslaught by making them partners to an ongoing process of surveillance.

Normalizing the onslaught: the beginnings of a security psychosis

> A nation's resistance can only be as strong as the resistance which its women can offer.[99]

Aimed specifically at white women, the document 'Women Our Silent Soldiers', provides an excellent example of how the popularization and dissemination of the discourse against 'communism' operated.[100] Compiled by wives of members of Cabinet and printed by the N.G. Sendingpers, the document opened with a 'clarion call' by Mrs Tini Vorster to women to move forward with their 'menfolk' and to be aware of the 'total onslaught against us as a nation'. Women were portrayed as 'indispensable "soldiers"' and an 'invisible weapon' in the fight against the 'psychological-propagandistic onslaught' on South Africa. In this struggle, knowledge of the enemy was held to be a key weapon, and was used to incite women to inform on those living in close quarters to them:

> You cannot fight against your foe unless you know him. Make a study of Marxism *in your own family, social or political circles and you will be shocked to learn under what guise the enemy works in the circles in which you move.*[101]

This incitement to surveillance operated with a multi-dimensional strategy. In the first place, women were held to be responsible for the political education of their children:

> Educate them politically so that they will not later become part of a confused and apathetic group of young people. Get as many of them involved in party [NP] activities because this will result in only a very small number of them at university for example being drawn away from the National fold by foreign dogmas and left/liberal schools of thought.[102]

In the second place, warnings against 'suspect' organizations originating within the white community, such as Women for Peace, the Women's Movement, Women for Peace Now and *Kontak* – all organizations which set out to foster closer relations on an interpersonal basis between black and white communities and families – were issued. The bigotry of the regime's offensive was evident in the reasons provided for the attack on these women's organizations:

> Their actions are questioned because they were not long in making demands amounting to educational integration and other forms of integration, which

> most certainly will not improve relations. The names of some of the persons involved also pointed to a distinct PFP [Progressive Federal Party] connection [*sic*].[103]

Finally, 'counter-offensive' action had to be taken against domestic employees by checking their identity documents for falsification; by 'visiting' their 'dwelling places' regularly to establish whether 'strangers' were 'harboured' there; by being on the look-out for literature of a Communist origin and books containing manuals for terrorism; by inspecting the contents of suitcases and trunks for false bottoms in which machine guns could be smuggled; by paying attention to clothes not obtainable in South Africa; and in the rural areas, by being on the look-out for 'surfaces of footpaths that might have been disturbed'.[104] Lists of banned publications were provided to assist women in their quest for the safety of their kinfolk. Well aware of the doubt which might exist concerning the veracity of the onslaught, the document sought to assuage women's consciences by discussing the 'present situation' with regard to the government's 'excellent record' on matters concerning the provision of housing, facilities and labour relations. In line with this, it was argued that it was 'the privilege of every woman in the country to make her contribution for the protection of her own people in her own unassuming way'.[105]

This incitement continued into the 1980s. In 1986 another pamphlet, entitled 'The Crisis in Our Country. A Conversation between the Housewife and Her Domestic Help', was issued by Women for South Africa and it followed similar lines to the interpellative strategy outlined above.[106] This document displayed a greater urgency, asking 'housewives' to 'proceed with speed' in initiating 'discussions' with their domestic employees. In line with the widespread resistance in the country at the time, women were warned against not only the ANC, the SACP, but also the UDF, the South African Council of Churches (SACC) and other local organizations. 'Black people' were argued to be 'very confused' and not capable of understanding the reasons behind the present unrest. 'Comrades', operating in the townships, were singled out for special attention. Playing on the generational gap between the young activists and their parents, it argued that the Comrades came 'from the outside into the townships', and that they taught children all sorts of 'ugly things', including stealing, stone-throwing, burning down and destroying places, and disobedience to their parents. The second 'model conversation' provided in this pamphlet portrayed the division between the state and its enemies in terms of a metaphor of the lamb, the fox and wolf:

> The Communists are really like all these animals. They look like lambs first, soft and innocent. Then they change into the jackal, sly and underhand. When they change into wolves, they show their true colours, they show their teeth that will *cruelly rip us up*. Then you seen the *communist in his true colours*.[107]

Denouncing the promises made by the 'lamb' – including such threatening things as free housing, free books and schools, free medicine and hospitals, the provision of houses and new towns, and the care for the elderly, orphans and the sick – the story continues to show how the lamb will turn into a jackal and a wolf:

> We have seen the jackal change into a wolf in many countries, when the Communists begin to show their true colours. Then the Communists get rid of their old friends, just as the wolf devours everybody. It is estimated that the Communists have *murdered more than 100 million* people in countries which they have taken over. . . . This is happening in South Africa already, the Black people fear for their lives if they do not do exactly what the '*Comrades*' are commanding them. Many people have already suffered a '*necklace death*'.[108]

That these images of a 'total onslaught' penetrated deep into popular culture was evident also in the growth of *grensliteratuur* (border literature) which burgeoned in South Africa from the late 1970s. While the writings of a new generation of Afrikaans writers, including Etienne van Heerden, Alexander Strachan, George Weideman and Koos Prinsloo, portrayed a sense of disillusionment, nihilism and defeat, stories in popular women's magazines such as *Sarie* and *Die Huigenoot* told a different tale.[109] These personalized and depoliticized accounts tended to focus upon the experiences of young, white South African males during their 'border service', but did not display the same critical awareness as found in border literature proper. Almost invariably, the themes of patriotism and service and sacrifice to one's country against an unnamed enemy dominated these stories, and served as a further link in the chain of normalizing practices around the 'total onslaught'. This process was also supported by 'Youth Preparedness' programmes, first introduced in white secondary schools in 1972. In addition to the existing 'cadet system', which aimed at fostering awareness amongst schoolboys on the nature of the onslaught against South Africa, these programmes were used to 'educate' pupils on the nature of the threat to the South African state.[110] In the aftermath of Soweto 1976, there was a marked expansion of these programmes in white schools, which served to forge a white consensus on security issues, especially with respect to white school pupils who were on the verge of being called up for their compulsory two-year military service.[111] In all of these domains the discourse of the total onslaught, while explicitly naming the enemy, also fostered an environment in which subjects were constructed to expect the enemy in unexpected places, thus creating a culture of suspicion and mistrust towards anyone who dared to question the actions of the state.

The public articulations of the policy framework by Botha at the Natal NP Congress in August 1979 have to be seen in this context. In the face of 'grave threats to the country', the NP needed a national plan for survival, one that would present the only possible alternative to three other wholly unacceptable options. The first was an 'authoritarian Marxist-type socialist political order', which, in South Africa, would lead to chaos, dictatorship and civil war.[112] This was clearly articulated against both the perceived external threat of 'Soviet expansionism', and the increasingly more vocal anti-capitalist nature of internal resistance discourses. The second option rejected was that of the *verkrampte* vision of total separation, which Botha now argued could only lead to black–white confrontation. The third unthinkable option was that of 'black majority rule under a dictatorship'. Against these options, a more intricate and elaborate vision of apartheid reforms was furnished in the form of a twelve-point plan.[113] The significance of this plan was that it was an attempt by the NP to develop a counter-strategy within the broad parameters of its existing policy. However, each of the twelve points acted as an indicator of areas in which shifts or rearticulations of existing policy were to take place. In the following sections I will examine some of the more important changes in NP discourse with a view to investigating their implications for the constitution of identities and political frontiers.

The construction of constitutional reform in NP discourse

During the 1970s, strategic conceptions increasingly functioned as a terrain in which the emerging 'national unity' could be fostered and strengthened. The changing regional balance of forces as well as the rise of internal liberation movements made it easier to mobilize around the themes of white unity and co-operation. Co-operation and consultation became key terms in the discourse of reform. This was the case not only for the constitution of white unity, but even more so in the endeavour to construct a multi-racial alliance between whites and coloureds and Indians of a certain political persuasion.

The terrain of constitutional reform was one fraught with pitfalls for the Nationalists, who were concerned with both Afrikaner unity and the satisfaction of demands from 'moderate' coloureds and Indians. The search began for a constitutional arrangement which would, as one commentator put it, lift the ceiling of domination and 'recognize' the 'uniqueness' of the 'plural population structure' of South Africa. At the end of 1976, as a result of the Theron Commission recommendations on the inappropriateness of the Westminster system to South African conditions, a Cabinet committee under Botha's leadership was appointed. The work of this committee culminated in the 1977 constitutional proposals. These furnished the basis for the new constitutional dispensation put into place in 1984 on the grounds of a President's Council (PC) investigation.[114] Not many significant differences existed between the PC's and the 1977 constitutional proposals. In short, both involved three elective bodies, for the coloured, Indian and white 'national groups', each with jurisdiction over the interests of their own group.[115] A Cabinet council was envisaged to discuss matters of common concern. Decisions were to be reached through consensus. If that proved impossible, the State President was empowered to make final, binding decisions.[116]

With the introduction of the reform process important changes took place in the NP discourse. Debates around some of the key terms of the transformist effort can be taken as a good indicator of areas of discursive rearticulation.[117] Already in April 1978, *Deurbraak*, an oppositional journal, pointed out that terms such as 'consultation' and 'morally justifiable' formed part of a new NP discourse on the need for change. To that list one may add a continued emphasis on 'self-determination', and a greater stress on the 'multi-national', 'multi-cultural' or 'plural' nature of South African society. This process was accompanied by a concern with new constitutional models, especially consociationalism and the development of methods of consultation and co-operation. A system of 'segmental authority' was proposed with a division between 'own' and 'common' affairs in the late 1970s. Finally a debate on 'power-sharing' ensued which led to a split in the NP to the right and the formation of the *Konservatiewe Party* (KP, Conservative Party).

The terms in which the envisaged model for the 'accommodation' of coloured and Indian political aspirations at national level were legitimized have to be explored in more depth for it is through this process that the previously all-white power structures were transformed to 'include', for the first time, members of other 'racial' groups, albeit on the old terms of racial categorization. One of the most striking features of the new reformist language was that it was not underpinned by any clearly discernible concern with notions of social justice. Rather, appeals to whites were made on pragmatic grounds. For example, calls for the acceptance of change were made in the language of 'decency' and 'politeness to others'. Occasionally the inspiration of 'Christian' values were also called upon to play a legitimizing role. In this sense, the discourse of the NP in 1980 differed little from that in the 1950s. Authoritarian practices were not questioned, and it was assumed that what the NP considered to be the good was indeed so for the majority of the population. This was perhaps at its clearest in the NP's continued adherence to the notion of 'self-determination'.[118]

The principle of self-determination still provided the principal basis for the exercise of political rights.[119] Indeed, it was presented as a unique solution to a unique problem. The problem – how to ensure 'full' political rights for whites, coloureds and Indians without power-sharing and a power struggle – was to be solved by the 'exclusive right of each group to decide its *own* affairs in its own Parliament'.[120] The notion of self-determination drew together a number of reformist themes. The first was a concern with the maintenance of identity. This concern remained prevalent throughout the Vorster and Botha eras. Vorster made it one of the central issues in his interpretation of NP policy. Stating the basis of NP policy at the 1973 Orange Free State NP Congress, he argued that the 'cornerstone of the National Party is the retention of identity of the White Afrikaner and the White South African'.[121] Under Botha preservation of identity remained a central issue.[122] In 1980 he expressed it as follows:

> The principle of identity – acknowledges the composition of those who live in our country, the realization of the concept of sovereignty and own communities with the maintenance of culture and self-determination. In other words, we serve the ideal of Freedom.[123]

However, a marked shift occurred in the NP's position on *whose* identity had to be preserved, as well as in its understanding of the *manner* in which such preservation was to be guaranteed. At a first glance it seems obvious that the identity to be preserved was simply that of the coloured, Indian and white population groups. However, the issue was somewhat more complicated. The shift from a narrow concern with Afrikaner identity to the maintenance of a 'national' (white, Afrikaans and English) identity was almost total by the time Botha took over the reins of the NP. While never denying the need to serve the interests of the Afrikaner population, Botha, and NP spokespersons in general, began to focus increasingly on the unity of the (white) nation, at the expense of *volks*-unity. Adding to the production of a 'security' psychosis was the sedimentation of this unity at a political level. Increasingly, calls for Afrikaner unity were rejected in terms which would have been unthinkable during the previous three decades of NP rule. By 1985 an NP document made it abundantly clear that the term 'nation' no longer had any cultural overtones. In response to a question as to the meaning of the term 'one nation' in NP discourse, the following answer was provided:

> The concept 'nation' is purely a constitutional one, and has been described as a community of people composed of one or more nationalities and possessing a more of less defined territory and government. The State President has emphasized that the South African society is *multi-cultural* and that our nation consists of a diversity of *minority* groups.[124]

During the discussion of a Private Member's Bill, introduced by the KP leader Andries Treurnicht, affirming the 'right to self-determination of White South Africans', the NP not only questioned the relevance of nationalism based upon the *volk*, but queried its very possibility in the South African context. Branding as 'abnormal' and 'deviant' the KP argument that the new constitution brought an effective end to *volksnasionalisme*, the MP for Mosselbaai answered in the following manner that party's accusation that the NP had abandoned its 'real' policy:

> No, *volksnasionalisme* is not an out of date concept in South Africa, and the Afrikaner *volk* is not on its way out. The fact is, that insofar as the Whites, Coloureds and Indians are concerned, *volks nationalism does not exist and has never existed in South Africa*. The Honorary member knows that the term '*volk*' is a culture-historical one, while 'nation' is a constitutional one. *We have never had volks nationalism in the case of the Whites, Coloureds and Indians in South Africa.*[125]

While the existence of cultural identity was recognized, the NP now held that questions of cultural identity had no relevance whatsoever to political divisions.[126] The same point was made by the Minister of the Interior:

> To those dragging Afrikaner sentiment, Afrikaner religious life and the cultural aims of the Afrikaner into politics, I want to issue a word of warning. . . . It is the NP's policy that we struggle in the political terrain, but not in the religious and cultural spheres.[127]

The South African 'nation', in constitutional terms, now consisted of the coloured, Indian and white 'minorities'. Culture had been severed from political life, and political language had been purged of *volkist* imagery. Party unity, it was argued, had never been confused with the unity of the *volk*. The need to make this separation stemmed from the break between the NP and the KP in 1982. This break had serious repercussions in the Afrikaner community and in Afrikaner cultural organizations, where a battle similar to the one between *verlig* and *verkramp* was being played out.[128]

Self-determination thus became a question of allowing all 'minorities' constituting the 'plural' society to exercise their autonomy in their 'own spheres'.[129] Rejecting majoritarianism and the 'conflict' and 'friction' said to go hand in hand with a denial of the self-determination of population groups, the NP contended that its proposals were in accord with Article 1 of the United Nations.[130] Self-determination, however, did not quite mean what it meant in the NP discourse of the 1950s and 1960s. An important rider was now added wherever it was discussed. While the self-determination of 'white South Africans' was important, it had to be qualified by the right of other groups to the same. The right of others was held as a prerequisite for the maintenance of 'white self-determination'.[131]

The institutional form in which the right to self-determination was to be expressed was premissed on an attempt to draw a distinction between 'own' and 'general' affairs, continuing in another guise the concern with the *volkseie*. Under the new constitution, the bills dealing with own affairs were defined as those bills 'affecting the identity of a recognized population group', and depended upon the ability to categorize people into different racial groups. In areas of concern pertaining to a particular group, that group would have the right to make laws and regulate actions. 'Own' affairs included social welfare, art, education, recreation, health matters, community development, local government, agriculture, water supply, appointment of marriage officers, election of members of the relevant chamber of Parliament, and so forth. All other matters fell under the rubric of 'general affairs'. Own affairs, however, had to be administered with due regard for general laws related to them, which reinforced rather than devolved the power of central government. As the latter was dominated by the statutorily defined white group, it followed that the white majority party held control of the pace of change.[132] 'Segmental' authority was meant to be protected by this division of affairs and care was taken to present the area of 'common affairs' as well as the fact of 'common decision-making' in non-threatening language. The legitimation of the fact that coloureds and Indians could now participate in decisions affecting the white population, for example, was presented as something that any 'reasonable person' had to accept.[133] Areas of common interest existed and everyone concerned had to be able to participate in decisions touching upon them.

This distinction was drawn in the context of debates on 'power-sharing', amongst other things, and it is clear that the division between own and general affairs acted as a new articulation of the older doctrine of the sovereignty of spheres. Nevertheless, the fact that much continuity existed between the new constitutional proposals and previous NP thinking did not prevent a contestation from developing around the possible and likely effects of the reforms. Not only within the NP but in the Afrikaner community at large a struggle ensued around the meaning of the term 'power-sharing'. This acted as a condensation point for the changes introduced into NP doctrine in the course of the legitimation of the transformist project. From the first moment of constitutional reform, power-sharing was rejected by the NP. As stated earlier, the NP saw the problem to which the new constitution was to be a solution as the formation of a system in which 'full political rights' for coloureds, Indians and whites could be provided 'without power-sharing and a power struggle'.[134] Power-sharing was rejected as UP, and later as PFP, policy:

> We do not believe in sharing of power. It is a PROGFED [PFP] term which means the right of all to take decisions on all matters in a common Parliament. In contrast to this we believe in the absolute right to take decisions on own matters, each in his own Parliament. On matters of common concern we believe in consultation and co-responsibility in a Council of Cabinets for the Whites, Coloureds and Indians.[135]

However, by the beginning of the 1980s, the NP started to move away from outright rejection of 'power-sharing' such that in February 1982 it was possible for P.W. Botha to declare in the House of Assembly that power-sharing indeed was NP policy.[136] Throughout the early 1980s, confusion reigned in NP circles on whether or not power-sharing was acceptable. Several ministers continued to contend that while the NP rejected power-sharing, a division of power was acceptable. This remained the situation until the NP issued a special position paper on the subject in 1986. By then, however, the KP had split from the NP precisely because of its alleged break with 'traditional NP doctrine'. In the process of attempting to establish a clear meaning of the concept, a further gradation of the term was introduced. 'Healthy power-sharing' was now distinguished from its ordinary, non-acceptable form. While many of these debates, especially when placed in the larger South African context, appear to be pure sophistry, important effects did follow from them. For that reason I will briefly investigate the at times clumsy efforts to hegemonize the meaning of the term 'power-sharing'.

The NP position paper confronted the question of change in policy directly. It distinguished between power-sharing in a 'negative' and in a 'positive' sense. The former, equated with PFP policy, was argued to lead to nothing but a 'surrender of power'. In contrast to this, the NP used the term in a 'positive' sense:

- All South African citizens (including Whites, Blacks, Coloureds and Indians) must *participate fully* in the governmental process up to the highest level.
- This participation must take place *without domination* of one group over other groups.
- The basis upon which this can be realised, is the granting of self-determination over own affairs to each group whilst joint decision-making takes place in regard to matters of common interest.
- The structures within which this participation will take place must be *created by means of negotiation* between the leaders of all groups concerned.
- The envisaged system must guarantee *the human dignity and rights of* individuals, and must at the same time ensure *sufficient protection* to minority groups.
- The process of reform must take place in a *peaceful and orderly* manner and must establish an orderly system.

> By 'power-sharing' the National Party therefore means that all people, irrespective of race, colour, religion or sex be in possession of true political rights, but without the Whites – or any other group – coming under the domination of any other group.[137]

It is clear from the above, especially when compared to the twelve-point plan, that considerable shifts had taken place in NP doctrine during the early 1980s. I will return to this shortly. For the moment, it is important to stress the extent to which the whole debate around power-sharing acted as a condensation point for the issues at stake with regard to self-determination and the maintenance of identity. 'Healthy power-sharing' denoted a system in which segmental autonomy, or 'minority rights', could be exercised without 'domination' of one group over another. This was to be achieved by an institutionalization of the division between own and general affairs in a tri-cameral Parliament.

Much of the theoretical inspiration for this 'new dispensation' came from consociational models of constitutional development, based upon the thesis of a 'plural' society.[138] In this respect, Lijphart's work was of special significance, since he argued that 'ethnic cleavages' were a relatively permanent feature of the South African political landscape which had to be taken into account in any arrangement of political institutions.[139] While the NP at times both advocated and rejected consociationalism, it could be argued that, regardless of the rhetoric, the institutional structures envisaged displayed definite traces of such thinking.[140] In line with the 'national strategy' aiming to avoid 'Marxist authoritarianism', 'black dictatorships' and 'total separate development', consociationalism, with its emphasis on maintaining the 'distinctiveness' of each of its constituents, provided a way for the co-optation of coloured and Indian 'elites', without endangering the principle of self-determination. The only alternatives were no longer integration or separation. A third way was possible due to the success of separate development and an 'increase in knowledge'.[141] The politics of 'co-operative co-existence' fitted neatly with the increasing move towards an elitist politics. Since the early 1980s, the locus of decision-making had been highly centralized within the executive, reducing its accountability to Parliament and to the NP rank and file. The slow shift away from Cabinet government and the appointment of specialized Cabinet committees, with the SSC at its apex, not only had the effect of insulating the NP from resistance in its ranks, but also changed the whole tenor in which politics was conducted.

A change in tenor was also evident in numerous writings of 'dissident' Afrikaners during the late 1970s and early 1980s. Voices of dissent within the Afrikaner community increasingly questioned both the morality of apartheid and the terms in which this project was constructed. Willie Esterhuyse's *Apartheid Must Die*, first published in Afrikaans in 1981, is a good example of this trend. Questioning the 'friction' theory of apartheid, he argued that it was morally suspect for two reasons:

> In a multiracial society it is based upon the assumption that people are intolerant of one another because of racial prejudice . . . and must therefore

> be kept apart. . . . Its morality is suspect . . . when the measures taken to avoid friction are not regarded as temporary but as permanently preserved. . . . The 'friction' argument is still further suspect, since those measures aimed at eradicating friction often intensify it. . . . The problem is compounded when a single racial group decides where the friction lies and what measures are required.[142]

Rejecting the language of the total onslaught, Esterhuyse argued that

> [i]n Afrikaner circles a great many moral mouths are gagged by the 'enemies-of-the-people' myth, thereby ignoring the fact that racially discriminatory attitudes and practices are themselves the greater enemy, for they contain an explosive potential which could destroy the structure of the established political order.[143]

While commentators like Esterhuyse refrained from engaging in the 'new South African vogue of presenting alternative constitutions', and while arguing for structural reforms while discounting the possibility of 'black majority rule', preferring the non-political language of 'moral' analysis, it could be argued that the increasing public visibility of Afrikaner voices against apartheid played an important role in facilitating the conditions under which the apartheid imaginary could be expanded beyond what many regarded as its 'proper' limits.[144]

The depoliticization of politics

Increasingly the problems of politics were regarded as matters to be solved by experts, involved at the highest level of decision-making. This depoliticization of politics enabled the NP to present the difficulties created by apartheid as essentially non-political, and technical. The NP held no specific responsibility for them. As P.W. Botha argued:

> I do not believe in an utopian future, a man-made paradise without problems. This was not promised to us on this earth. I do, however, believe that poverty, war, violence and insecurity, which we all see around us, need not have to be our fate. We should not begin with grandiose prestige projects, but must systematically build up from the grass roots a stable, well-planned structure of co-operation. We shall have to set our goal and general aims and work out a charter for Southern Africa.[145]

Answers to the problems facing South Africa were not to be found in 'ideologies'. Practical questions had to be answered and called for pragmatic responses. In this context there was an increasing tendency to compare South Africa with the rest of Africa. This was especially so in the cases of urbanization and poverty, but it also occurred with the portrayal of resistance. 'Urban terrorism', it was contended, was 'the curse of our time'. It could rear its 'ugly head' in Cape Town, Johannesburg and Durban. After all, it occurred in New York, London, Paris and Berlin, in fact in cities 'throughout the entire world'.[146] The language of the NP also served the purpose of drawing a stark distinction between its own emphasis on co-operation and other approaches based upon a 'confrontationalist', 'ideological' politics characteristic of radical opposition. This was increasingly the case as resistance to the new constitutional proposals took on a more concerted character in the early 1980s.

With the development of the new constitutional proposals one strand of the transformist project was put into place. The attempted co-optation of coloureds and Indians into central government structures represented a break with certain aspects of earlier NP thinking. Their inclusion was facilitated both by the *rapprochement* between Afrikaans- and English-speaking South Africans as well as by the ascendancy of the *verligtes* within the NP. With the breakaway of the *verkramptes* and the formation of the KP, the NP was freed to introduce quite important changes to its policy. The 'undecidable' position of the coloured and Indian groups could be fixed in a system in which they were included 'as equals' 'at the highest level'. By 1986, the NP provided extensive arguments supporting the thesis that apartheid, itself, was dead. Stoffel van der Merwe stated that apartheid, in its 'primary sense', came to denote 'discrimination and oppression', rather than a system in which 'various peoples (nations) and population groups would live apart from one another and would develop each in its own way, with dignity and autonomy'.[147] The NP had thus 'dissociated' itself from apartheid. Its plan for the future involved, *inter alia*:

- democracy for all, with overt and effective protection of all groups;
- freedom as the cornerstone of democracy at three levels, i.e. the individual, the groups, and the State;
- the elimination of discrimination; and
- the stimulation of private enterprise and effective competition.[148]

A far cry from the *volkist* language of the previous decades, the transformist project was increasingly couched in the language of 'democracy', allowing for participation 'at the highest level'. The extent to which this shift in nomenclature took place can, in no small degree, be attributed to the effectiveness of resistance discourses from the late 1970s onwards. Botha, for example, repeatedly contested the fact that South Africa was an 'unjust society'.[149] Other terms of debate which emerged in NP discourse, only to be 'refuted' later, included 'universal franchise', an 'undivided South Africa' and 'one citizenship'. These breaks in NP doctrine were witness to a disarticulation of a number of the fundamental tenets on which the onto-theology of apartheid was premissed. They were also present in the case of the developments around the position of urban Africans in the 1980s. These breaks did not have to lead to the crisis which was undeniably present in South Africa by 1984. Nothing in the process of rearticulation or disarticulation had to induce a crisis. However, the exclusion of the African population from this settlement set the stage for an irresistible challenge to the logic of transformism. Yet, the state tried to counter any resistance by co-opting black elites via a series of economic incentives in the name of 'free enterprise'. The second leg of the transformist project, and its relation to the new links forged between the private sector and the state, is the subject of chapter 5.

Conclusion: Fault-Lines and Failures

The contours of the initial weakening of the apartheid imaginary as a result of political resistance to its expansion have been traced out in the course of this chapter, and have been located not only in the fact of resistance, but in the very form that resistance took during the 1970s and early 1980s. The increasing focus of resistance movements on the formation of unity on the grounds of a *black* identity in the wake of Soweto 1976, and largely as a result of the impact of the BC movement, in addition to the growing anti-capitalist nature of resistance, found particularly in the domain of trade union struggles, forced the regime to attempt to broaden its basis of legitimacy by co-opting 'moderate' coloured and Indians into the tri-cameral system, grounded upon a redefined discourse of consociational pluralism. However, I have argued that the conditions for this expansion have to be sought in the initial struggles occurring within the nationalist movement around its inability to find a solution to the problem of coloured representation. The project of separate development first had to be consolidated. This consolidation – which had as a condition the repression of any radical opposition to the project of separate development – involved a distancing from certain of the themes characteristic of apartheid discourse, strengthening the emphasis on 'difference' at the apparent expense of its more overt discriminatory logics. This was, furthermore, made possible by the *rapprochement* between Afrikaans- and English-speaking South Africans. The discourse of 'national unity', however, revealed its racist characteristics in the drawing of frontiers which accompanied it. The nation was white. Coloureds, Indians and Africans had no place in it. Yet, as I have argued, matters were not quite so simple, for the drawing of this frontier did not occur along neat racial lines. Those willing to participate in the 'homelands' scheme and in the coloured and Indian Representative Councils initially and later in the tri-cameral Parliament were regarded as allies, albeit on terms set down by the dominant forces. With the emergence of the 'total strategy' in the late 1970s, this tendency was confirmed. Lines of inclusion and exclusion were being drawn and redrawn in ways which complicated the initial forms of social division inaugurated by apartheid, and the manner in which this redefinition took place was only partially determined by the internal possibilities of the logic of separate development.

The limits to this logic were already apparent by the early 1970s when no coincidence could be found between 'nationhood' and 'territory' in the case of the coloured community. From the very beginning, their nationhood as such was in doubt. The fact that this community could not be represented within the logics of apartheid, however, did not prevent the ideologues of apartheid from attempting to position them within its system of differences. The emphasis on 'pure difference' made it possible for coloureds and Indians to be drawn into the folds of that system, yet without being fully included, for political representation remained premissed upon racial division. Second, developments during the early 1970s made it clear that the urban African population, contrary to what was hoped, could also find no resting place in that scheme. This realization was reinforced by continuing economic demands for integration. As a corollary to the incorporation of coloureds and Indians into a tri-cameral Parliament, urban Africans were being offered the spoils of an economic system of co-optation as well as a place in local government structures.

During this period, the political grammar of the dominant discourse underwent a series of changes which increasingly were to put into question the very core of its logic: the fact that it was premissed upon the construction and 'protection' of the *volkseie*. The language of nationhood increasingly replaced that of the *volk*: the fostering of a white nation, not least through the production of a security psychosis, gave way to a politically defined conception of nationhood, calling into question the very link between *volk*, culture and nation upon which the apartheid imaginary was grounded. Moreover, this was accompanied, on the one hand, by a shift towards representing the South African population structure in terms of a plurality of 'minority groups', and, on the other, by a depoliticization of the language of politics itself. The latter occurred in two distinct realms: in the increasing centralization of bodies of political decision-making, and the accompanying militarization of South Africa, and in the *rapprochement* between the Afrikaner establishment and the forces of private enterprise. These shifts, in their turn, were reinforced by critical voices from within the nationalist grouping, and by the very form of resistance from without.

While it was clear by the early 1980s that many of the central elements of apartheid discourse were no longer operative, the logic of apartheid was not thrown into doubt until coloureds and Indians, squatters and commuters, migrant workers and township dwellers, conscript resisters and other white democrats, to name only a few, were drawn together into an overarching political project. Only then, I would argue, did the *conjunctural* crisis turn into an *organic* one, a crisis which violently tore the ill-fitting jigsaw of apartheid asunder. This is the subject-matter of chapter 5, in which I will argue that it was only once the system of representation on which apartheid was premissed was decisively shown to be incapable of any further expansion, and frantic, *ad hoc* reforms became the order of the day, that the very structure of apartheid society began to disintegrate. From the mid-1980s onwards, NP discourse was openly haunted by the figures of resistance, forcing Nationalists to express their failing project in terms of justice and fairness, the language of rights and of citizenship, making a mockery of these terms. What began as a project of transformism ended in a state of disarticulation and crisis. Despite this, the terms in which the apartheid imaginary's expansion was articulated – involving a shift from a language of separate and parallel development to one of consociational pluralism – introduced a vocabulary which would yet have a long future ahead of it, for it provided much of the basis upon which negotiations during the 1990s would take place. In this sense the discourse on pluralism, introduced at the very moment of the failure of the apartheid imaginary, opened onto another future in which it would delimit much of the terrain of political debate.

5

A Crisis of Hegemony: From Transformism to Negotiation

The period from the mid-1980s to February 1990 was marked by an increasing inability of the regime to determine and control the constitution of political frontiers and, thus, the nature of social division upon which the political ordering of the society rested. It is during this period that the conjuctural crisis turned into a full-scale crisis of apartheid hegemony. As a result of the unsuccessful strategy of transformism, the late 1980s were witness to successive waves of resistance which, though attempts were made to contain it by the declaration of several states of emergency, decisively put into question the grounds upon which apartheid was premissed. In accounting for this crisis several dimensions have to be disaggregated. This requires a discussion of the various forces involved in contesting the reforms, both within and without the dominant bloc. However, it also presumes a theoretically infused account of what precisely a crisis of hegemony entails. For this reason, it is pertinent to start our discussion with the latter. In this respect, it is crucial to distinguish what could be characterized as a crisis of hegemony, that is, a crisis of an organic nature, from a conjunctural crisis. In contrast to the former, the latter involves for Gramsci a 'set of immediate and ephemeral characteristics of the economic situation' closely linked to immediate politics, to 'tactics' and agitation.[1] Since much depends on this distinction, it is necessary to elaborate. As Gramsci argues, conjunctural phenomena do not have any far-reaching historical significance; they give rise to political criticism of 'a minor, day-to-day character', while organic phenomena, on the other hand, give rise to socio-historical criticism, whose subject is wider social groupings. Moreover, organic crises are related to 'incurable structural contradictions' upon which forces of opposition organize:

> These forces seek to demonstrate that the necessary and sufficient conditions already exist to make possible ... the accomplishments of certain historical tasks. ... (*The demonstration in the last analysis only succeeds and is 'true' if it becomes a new reality*, if the forces of opposition triumph. . . .)[2]

In avoiding both excesses of economism and of voluntarism, it is therefore necessary correctly to specify and understand the relation between the conjunctural and the organic. However, in following Gramsci in this distinction, it is also necessary that we distance ourselves from the last 'redoubt of economism' present in his thinking. This requires, as I have argued earlier, a widening and, therefore, weakening of what has traditionally been understood by 'structural conditions'; for us, 'structural contradictions' entail the whole of the imaginary horizon which regulates both the political and economic terrains. Attention has already been given to how certain aspects of this imaginary had been put into question, and how, from a variety of sources, attempts had been made to refashion the very balance of forces articulated together in this imaginary. In this chapter, I will further extend this analysis to include the quickening of the pace of resistance arising from the manner in which the transformist project impacted upon the black community.

An important question in this respect concerns the precise weight which is attributed to resistance discourses under these conditions, especially by comparison to what is generally, though incorrectly, regarded as 'objective' economic logics. To make clear what is at stake here, I will refer to Murray's analysis of the crisis of the 1980s, which is exemplary of a broader position quite often taken by analysts of the South African political landscape. In attempting to avoid the pitfalls of explanation by enumeration, Murray has argued that a distinction has to be drawn between the inventory of observable symptoms – including meagre growth rates, recession, bankruptcies, unemployment, and so forth – which merely specifies the 'physiognomy of the organic crisis', and those elements that make up the anatomy of the crisis – the contradictions in the structural 'regime of accumulation'. This distinction, to some extent, can be taken as overlapping with one reading of the Gramscian distinction between the terrain of the conjunctural and that of the organic. In contrast to this type of account, which locates the organic features of the crisis in the economy, a terrain presumed to be unmarked by the political, I regard the distinction between the conjunctural and the organic rather as located in the differential effects which discourses of reform and resistance have had, or may have in principle, on the imaginary horizon as such. By the late 1970s, there were clear traces of a conjunctural crisis. These traces did not yet have the force to put into question the logic of apartheid, that is, the imaginary on the basis of which social division had been instituted. This situation, however, changed in the course of the 1980s, where a clear crisis of hegemony emerged. Earlier, I have argued that the force of the logic of apartheid could be located in its operation of simultaneous frontiers of inclusion and exclusion. A crisis of this hegemony would therefore have to be located in a situation in which the dominant bloc became less and less capable of maintaining and controlling these divisions. That this occurred is evident in the analysis which is to follow. However, at this point, the precise theoretical implications of this analysis need to be drawn out further.

It is important to emphasize that the proposed theoretical division between the conjunctural and organic dimensions of the crisis does not amount to a 'superstructuralism' or to a mere reversal of the relation between the 'structure' – in the traditional sense – and the superstructure. The proposed distinction runs *through* both these domains, usually characterized as external to one another. That is to say, in both cases of conjunctural and organic crises, analysis of politics and the economy is to be taken into account. In my forthcoming analysis I aim to show how the response to the economic crisis by the new organic intellectuals was articulated within the imaginary horizon of transformism, and how a new balance of forces came to be constructed as a result. Despite these attempts, the regime did not succeed in restabilizing the situation. In accounting for the resulting organic crisis of the mid-1980s, the role of resistance to these attempts was decisive.

The extent to which forces of resistance succeed in reshaping the terrain of the imaginary itself is evident in the fact that they managed to bring about a shift in the previously existing disposition of social forces. It is necessary to note that Gramsci stresses the retro-activity of this operation: what seems to be necessary only becomes so once the battle has been won, once a new reality based upon a new political grammar has been put into place. And for this to occur, there first had to be a decisive weakening of the dominant imaginary. It had to be dislocated in the theoretical sense of the term; many signifiers previously fixed within a determinate terrain had to become floating signifiers, available for rearticulation into a new imaginary. The formation of this new imaginary is still underway and, therefore, to some extent still open to contestation. I return to this in chapter 6. It is necessary, finally, to point out that the very process through which this new imaginary came into being, and sought to reshape the form in which social division was traditionally cast, is not one which can be understood in terms of the positing of an 'externality' between forces of conservatism and retention and forces of renewal and progress. To put it bluntly, insofar as the resistance discourses were premissed on an opposition to 'apartheid' – whatever that term may have meant – to that extent, they will also be fundamentally affected by the reform and breakdown of the apartheid imaginary.

This chapter sets out to analyse the overall trajectory of the second dimension of the transformist project as it related to urban Africans, as well as the deepening crisis into which the waves of reforms, resistance and repression led by the late 1980s. It aims to provide an account both of how the regime attempted to construct a new alliance of forces, and of how this was put into question by the re-emergence of resistance movements articulated around a discourse of non-racialism.

Free Enterprise, the Private Sector and the State

One of the most crucial areas of rearticulation occurring as a result of the Total Strategy was a *rapprochement* between the private sector and the state.[3] The national economic strategy formed part of the country's total national strategy and was to be

> applied within the economic system of the country. The system which we support in the RSA is that of free enterprise, based on principles such as competition, private property, private initiative . . . [4]

The closer working relation between the state and organized business was constructed on the basis of a newly held belief in 'free enterprise'. This facilitated an understanding of the private sector as an important ally against the anti-capitalist, Marxist struggle. The government went to great lengths to ensure that there could be no confusion between its economic strategy and other, more unacceptable forms of economic planning. It was stressed repeatedly that, although the economic strategy had to form part of the total strategy, this did not mean

> . . . socialism or Marxist 'planning', involving extended use of direct economic controls to regiment the private sector. On the contrary, it is precisely with a view to the successful implementation of its total strategy that the government is placing more emphasis on free enterprise. . . .[5]

The marked shift in alliances involved in this *rapprochement* becomes visible when it is set against the historical background and opinions predominating before the Botha take-over. As late as October 1976, Vorster rejected any role for the business sector in ensuring the stabilization of society. Calls from the FCI for a phasing out of the system of job reservation in 1976, and from its Transvaal regional affiliate for changes in the policies dealing with municipal government, housing and public amenities in urban townships, and with transport, education, influx control, job reservation and a number of other discriminatory measures, were all but ignored.[6] Against the demand for restructuring of the basis of society voiced by individual businesspersons and business organizations, Vorster wanted to keep business and politics strictly separated. The business community had nothing of value to contribute toward the solving of political problems. As he put it:

> . . . although I do not question the right of any businessman . . . to hold within the limits of the law to express his own views on the way in which our society should be structured, I do question. . . the propriety of using as vehicles for such viewpoints business organizations which have been constituted not for this purpose, but to represent the legitimate business of their members.[7]

For Vorster, economic advice could be given on strictly 'economic' matters, and for that there was the state Economic Advisory Council (EAC), ironically under the leadership of Riekert.[8] This situation changed drastically during the Botha years.

The immediate factor precipitating the change from Vorster to Botha was the uncovering of the misappropriation and 'misuse' of state funds which is known as the 'Muldergate' affair.[9] The effects of this change in leadership were profound. As I have pointed out in chapter 4, with the ascension of Botha the military-security complex, and more specifically the SSC, came to take on a decisive role in governmental decision-making. This was complemented by the decline in the role of Parliament, and the ascendancy of a technocratic system of Cabinet committees, staffed increasingly by 'expert' advisors from the civil service, the academic community and the private sector.[10] These changes, no doubt, were in part informed by the changing economic conditions of the late 1970s and early 1980s. How exactly the relation between these economic conditions and the rise of a free market discourse is to be understood is, therefore, crucial. There is no doubt that the need for economic adjustments, including a rethinking of state control over conditions of capital accumulation, arose initially from economic problems facing South Africa by the late 1970s.[11] Pointing to these economic conditions, however, does not constitute an adequate explanation of the shifting alliances. While such conditions indicate the need for change, they do not provide an answer to the central question at stake here, namely why these changes took the form of a *rapprochement* between Afrikaner nationalist and English business leaders.

Contrary to what some eminent analysts assume, namely that this shift can be taken as evidence for economic determination of the political process, or, to put it more crudely, as evidence that 'ideological' shifts in NP discourse could be read as a reflection of deeper, underlying changes in its 'objective' class basis, it seems that changes in the construction of political frontiers facilitated this shift. Two such changes are relevant here. The first concerns the forging of closer relations between the Afrikaans and English language groups during the Vorster years. Historically the relation between Afrikaner nationalists and 'English' capital had been a less than happy one. A change in this frontier had to precede any possible articulation between the central forces of Afrikaner nationalism and 'English capital' and this took the form of a discourse on 'national unity'. Moreover, the possibility of closer co-operation between state and private enterprise was boosted by the beginnings of dissent and criticism in Afrikaans business circles towards government intervention in the economy. A particularly vitriolic attack was launched in 1977 on government spending by Andreas Wassenaar in his book *The Assault on Private Enterprise*, in which he accused the NP of supporting 'communist' policies because of its refusal to let market forces run their course.[12] Other influential Afrikaans business organizations were equally critical of aspects of government policy, especially of the poor living conditions and extent of unemployment amongst urban Africans.

The second political condition which, together with the first, can account for the emerging *rapprochement* between the government and the business community was the fact that resistance to existing forms of social division during the 1970s began to exhibit an increasingly anti-capitalist rhetoric. The close linking of apartheid and capitalism led to a questioning of both. By 1981, this had become a key issue addressed by the new organic intellectuals, who now saw it as their task to defend capitalism. Jan Lombard, President of the Free Market Foundation, argued in 1981:

> ... we all know that the crucial battle for the minds of the South African people has begun in earnest. ... In the leading cultural institution of the Afrikaner people, the *Federasie van Afrikaanse Kultuurverenigings*, the idea of the free market economy as a political philosophy was thoroughly thrashed out as the principal theme of the annual congress less than a year ago ... the *battle lines will be drawn between the political philosophy of the free market economy, on the one hand, and the political philosophy of socialist collectivism on the other.*[13]

Part of the strategy to defend the status quo while fending off the forces of resistance was openly admitted to be the need to establish a separation between 'hurtful racial discrimination', which could easily be done away with, and a 'free enterprise' economic system, which had to be defended in order to avoid the 'Marxist' alternative. Many of the reforms introduced in order to co-opt urban Africans explicitly took a form calculated to bring about such a separation. This involved, amongst other things, the promotion of 'entrepreneurship' in the 'economically disadvantaged communities', the introduction of a freehold system, the withdrawal of the state from the provision of essential services in the townships in order to depoliticize the issue of collective consumption, and so forth.

The closer working relations between the state and the private sector received their first major impetus on the occasion of the 'Carlton Conference', held in November 1979 between the Prime Minister and business leaders. This initiative was preceded by a series of important changes in the terms in which the economic situation was viewed. Since the mid-1970s, an emphasis on 'neo-liberal' economics as a solution to the economic crisis had begun to emerge.[14] This was evident, for example, in the work of the influential economist Jan Lombard. In *Freedom, Welfare and Order*, published in 1978, Lombard argued that

> ... two basic questions have to be answered, namely *what* is to be done (including the problem for whom it is to be done) and *who* are to make the decisions and carry them out. These questions will have different detailed answers ... but according to the general economic theory of liberty, in all cases the introduction of politics into economic affairs will be governed by *a theory of limited government.*[15]

Lombard also questioned many of the prevailing economic orthodoxies from the perspective of an argument based upon the liberal principles of individual liberty and strong but limited government. He rejected the 'dualistic' view of the economic order, and insisted on the highly integrated nature of the economy.[16] Moreover, he argued that the economics of the 'new urban society' would cut across 'colour' classifications, and that this was necessary for reasons of political stability and economic productivity.[17] The impact of this view on regional policy will be discussed shortly. Suffice it to point out here that the emphasis on the logic of the 'free market' and the concomitant stress on 'individual liberty' became increasingly important in government thinking during the 1980s.

That Lombard's was not a voice in the wilderness is clear from the fact that initiatives for the improvement of urban black conditions, through the utilization of market mechanisms, emerged as early as November 1976 with the creation of the Urban Foundation (UF). The UF was set up by leading English and Afrikaans industrialists Harry Oppenheimer and Anton Rupert to address the poor quality of life in the townships, which was regarded as one of the fundamental causes of black frustration and anger. Here the beginnings of a business strategy to deracialize the economy so as to create a black middle-class 'buffer' against revolution can be detected.[18] It is also remarkable that Anton Rupert, who came of age in the 1940s in the context of the drive for Afrikaner economic independence, was one of the foremost proponents of a free enterprise system.[19] Rupert, who was active in the small business section of the RDB, argued throughout his career that all people had to be given the opportunity to develop, and that the fostering of a spirit of entrepeneurship was key to this. For Rupert, however, the free enterprise system and private initiative, while pre-eminent instruments for stimulating development over a broad front, also included a corporate social responsiblity and community involvement.[20] This philosophy of 'partnership' between business enterprise and the community was given practical form in, *inter alia*, the establishment of the Economic Development Bank for Equatorial and Southern Africa (EDESA) in 1972 and the creation of the Small Business Development Corporation (SBDC) in March 1979.[21] Since the early 1960s, Rupert argued for property rights for blacks in urban areas as a guarantee for stability, and this theme continued to inform his public interventions.[22] In 1976, shortly after the outbreak of the Soweto revolt, he warned that

> [w]e cannot survive without a free market economy, without a stable black middle class that enjoys full property rights, without personal security, or without a feeling of hope for progress in the hearts of all our people.[23]

In the wake of the Soweto riots, the UF was created, which was in no small degree responsible for the lifting of excessive government regulations, the institution of the 99-year leasehold system and the later full acceptance of property rights for blacks.

These changes, and the fact that a free enterprise philosophy – based upon a partnership between the state and organized business – was embraced by the government, arose out of the perception of a total onslaught on South Africa. This was clear in the background material sent out to participants in the Carlton Conference which stressed this theme. It was repeated in the Prime Minister's opening address. According to Botha, ideological attacks on South Africa brought to the fore a common interest in the preservation of order and stability in the Southern African region.[24] To this the private sector could make a substantial contribution. While the government was responsible for the establishment, maintenance and protection of the national order within which private enterprise could fulfil its functions, the business sector could co-operate with the government to their own advantage.[25] The economic strategy outlined aimed at the creation of more jobs, a more equitable distribution of income and the promotion of general economic development. Moreover, a rationalization of state development corporations was envisaged so that full use could be made of the skills and abilities of the private financial sector, and economic activity with the greatest possible participation by 'black entrepreneurs' could be encouraged.[26]

Ensuring 'a more equitable regional distribution of economic development in Southern Africa' was an important part of the economic strategy which could be realized through the creation of a 'constellation of states' in Southern Africa.[27] The constellation idea reflected several overlapping levels of perception. As argued earlier, the government was convinced that the 'West' did not take the threat to South Africa seriously enough. As a result, much was made of South Africa's allegedly 'neutral' position between the superpowers. However untenable that rhetoric, it could be argued that the constellation of states was in part a response to that perceived exclusion. More importantly, it had a clear political intent. South African officials grouped African countries into 'inner' and 'outer' circles, defined in terms of security, geographical proximity and political affinity.[28] The innermost circle consisted of South Africa and the 'independent homelands', the second of Namibia, and the third of the BLS (Botswana, Swaziland and Lesotho) states. The rest of the African states were grouped in a similar fashion. For example, Malawi, Zaïre and the Ivory Coast were regarded as 'moderate', while Angola and Mozambique were held to be 'radical'. The constellation was thought to be a means of expanding South African markets and establishing better working relations between Southern African states. It was also hailed as a continuation of the Verwoerdian idea of a 'Commonwealth' of Southern African states.[29] Such a constellation would be held together by common interests.[30] It would include the 'national states' or homelands and would be open to any other country 'which identifies the need to expand relationships and to co-operate in a regional context'.[31] The idea of a constellation of states was based, however, upon more than a simple desire for closer economic ties with other African states in the region. It intended to offer material progress in return for 'peaceful co-existence'.[32] It never quite got off the ground, and the idea was soon formalized in a more limited form, including only South Africa, the Transkei, Bophuthatswana, Venda and Ciskei. Other possible constellation members – Lesotho, Swaziland, Botswana and Zimbabwe – joined the Southern African Development and Co-ordination Conference (SADCC) of nine black states in a clear rejection of the Botha initiative.

The realignment of business interests and government policy around the discourse of free enterprise had to create the conditions under which urban blacks could be co-opted, could be given a 'stake in the system', in lieu of their continued exclusion from political decision-making processes.

Transformism: The Differential Inclusion of Urban Africans

From their inception, the new constitutional proposals were questioned by almost all parties outside the government. Most attacks focused on the exclusion of Africans from the central decision-making institutions of government. The Theron report was rejected for the same reasons. Now, however, the NP felt the need to defend and rationalize the exclusion of Africans from the central polity whereas before it was so secure in its position that no justification was deemed to be necessary. This did not mean that the NP position on the need for blacks to exercise political rights in the homelands changed. It remained that articulated in 1976.[33] In the political arena, as far as the NP was concerned, the issue was settled. Nevertheless, the Soweto uprisings and the increasingly vocal criticism of government policy by the business community showed that something had to be done to improve the material conditions under which urban blacks lived and worked.[34] In line with its new technicist language, the NP held that the urban black question was a practical one which could be solved by enabling 'neutral' free market principles to govern their existence. In order to ensure the smooth working of a system of economic co-optation, the Vorster government appointed two commissions of inquiry during the course of the late 1970s; they were to be to the African community what the tri-cameral Parliament was to coloureds and Indians. The reports of the Wiehahn and Riekert Commissions were to be followed by other investigations as the black political resistance to the changes introduced grew and the reform measures proved ineffective. These reform measures all concerned the status of urban blacks and their residence rights in 'white' urban areas. They amounted to a constant redrawing of the boundaries of exclusion, which had the effect of making ever more prominent the ambiguities constitutive of the discourse of apartheid. These shifts in divisions may be traced out via an investigation of the formation of, and changes in, state strategies pertaining to the 'drawing of borders'; apartheid created internal boundaries and fostered the birth of 'new states' and this territorial dimension formed an essential part of the onto-theology of apartheid. Consequently, the delegitimization of its division between 'homelands' and 'white' South Africa in the 1980s finally began to put into question the apartheid imaginary itself.

The first wave of reform measures followed in the wake of the Wiehahn and Riekert reports. The former, a commission of inquiry into labour legislation, appointed in May 1977, reported two years later. In keeping with the new commitment to depoliticize the economic order, the commission did not see its way open to investigate and comment upon matters of a political nature.[35] It was, however, very clear in its support of a free market economy, alleged to have been the policy of successive South African governments.[36] Arguing that a 'socialist way of thinking' has become evident under black workers, the report set out to ensure 'industrial peace' by proposing new legislation regulating the functioning of African/black trade unions. This aim fell squarely within the ambit of government thinking, which saw a peaceful labour force as the 'first line of practical defence' against the total onslaught.[37] The Wiehahn Commission recommended policy changes on a wide variety of labour-related issues. It proposed the establishment of a separate Industrial Court, a National Manpower Commission, the repeal of all segregation regulations from laws relating to factories, offices and shops, and the removal of all statutory job reservation. Most important were its recommendations on the regulation and registration of African trade unions. These unions emerged out of the strike wave between 1972 and 1975. While not recognized by inclusion in any collective bargaining machinery, it was clear by the mid-1970s that they were to be a permanent feature of the political landscape in South Africa.[38] Government spokespersons maintained now, in sharp contrast to their earlier position, that the only way in which conflict could be avoided was by the inclusion of these unions into a regulatory framework, a framework that would, nevertheless, per definition, exclude political issues.

The framework that the report set for itself started from a recognition of six principles of 'labour democracy'. They were the right to work, to free association, to collective bargaining, to strike, to protection and to development.[39] The commission set out to establish a framework for collective bargaining which would be true to these principles. Consequently, it rejected the premisses upon which the former system of exclusion was based. Wiehahn, very much in line with the growing influence of liberal economic thinking, argued that economic development over time had changed the position of the African workforce. Africans had reached the end of their 'industrial trek' and, in order to ensure industrial peace, they had to be incorporated in the system which formerly excluded them.[40] To facilitate such inclusion, it was recommended that African trade unions be officially recognized and allowed to register as formal and full participants in the collective bargaining system.

The government White Paper, in familiar fashion, significantly watered down these proposals. One of the most contentious issues in this regard was the extension of the definition of employee. The 1956 legislation excluded Africans from this definition, and Wiehahn recommended that this be reversed. The government, however, revised the definition in such a way that only Africans with Section 10 rights were allowed to join unions. Migrant workers and commuters from the 'homelands' were thus excluded. It was only after a storm of criticism that a ministerial exemption was issued to include migrants in the definition. The significance of this strategy will become clearer once I have discussed the recommendations of the Riekert report, published almost simultaneously. The other crucial issue concerned the exclusion of 'politics' from the domain of trade union action. While the Wiehahn report held that the inclusion of Africans into the central collective bargaining mechanisms came about as a result of 'economic developments', an awareness of the political nature of unionism was never far beneath the surface. For the government it was clear that the incorporation of the African unions had an important political function in that 'correct' unionism had to exclude political demands: industrial relations solely concerned the relationship between the parties in the work context, and politics had no place there.[41] The legislation confirmed this by outlawing 'affiliation' of a union to a political party.[42] Fears of a spill-over between labour matters and general political and social demands continued to be expressed. These fears, however, had to be subordinated to the wider concern with bringing independent African unions under control.

The debate within the African unions on registration and the possibility of co-optation was one which caused deep rifts in the independent trade union movement.[43] Paradoxically, the attempt by the government to co-opt the unions opened up a new site of struggle in which resistance began to flourish. Unions such as the Congress of South African Trade Unions (COSATU) effectively utilized this space to undercut the very nature of the system which was meant to be put into place by the Wiehahn legislation. Subject to serious strategic debate, the terrain of union activity became an important site of political struggle, especially as the other spaces opened up by the constitutional reforms were closed down in the later 1980s. The Wiehahn recommendations were supplemented by an investigation into legislation affecting the utilization of 'manpower', chaired by P.J. Riekert, the Prime Minister's Special Advisor on Economic Affairs. The terms of reference of this commission were to investigate all matters relating to the economic aspects of the utilization of manpower with a view to the elimination of 'bottlenecks' and other problems experienced by employers.

The Riekert Commission is known for the distinction it drew between 'urban insiders' and 'rural outsiders' in the process of attempting to devise a more effective form of influx control.[44] Grafting this distinction onto the existing labour-regulating practices had serious consequences for the system of social division as envisaged under apartheid. The territorial dimension of its onto-theology allocated all Africans in the final instance to a particular 'homeland'. Their presence in 'white' South Africa could only be that of 'temporary sojourners'. However, the scheme envisaged by Riekert to regulate the flow of Africans to urban areas established the seeds of an urbanization strategy which would undermine the territorial dimension of apartheid. The rationale behind the distinction was to facilitate the incorporation of urban insiders – Africans holding Section 10 rights – by offering them a number of previously unavailable concessions. In 1979, the Rikhoto case established, for the first time, the permanent right of Section 10 workers to reside in what were considered to be white urban spaces. The Riekert report now gave concrete expression to this by advocating permanent leasehold and home-ownership schemes and a relaxation of restrictions on occupational and geographical mobility. Simultaneously, controls and mechanisms of exclusion governing the presence of temporary contract and surplus labour were tightened. The quality of life for 'qualifying' urban black people would thus improve dramatically. However, they constituted only about one and a half million people together with their dependants out of a total black population of twenty million. Life for the outsiders, for thousands of men, women and children, would be made infinitely worse, even unsustainable.[45]

The split between urban insiders and rural outsiders was at the heart of a new urbanization strategy which replaced direct controls of labour movement and migration with more insidious, indirect means. In place of the notorious pass laws, Riekert proposed to manage the urban black population by regulating access to housing and employment. In this way, those regarded by law as 'idlers and undesirables' could be singled out and removed from the urban areas. Riekert maintained that

> . . . movement control that applies to all population groups and which is linked to employment and housing affords a far more acceptable and justifiable basis than the present set-up, and that it will in no way yield poorer results, but rather far better results, since control will then be concentrated on a far smaller number of strategic points – i.e. on employers and owners of premises.[46]

As is clear from the above, it was hoped that the burden of responsibility for control of the urban population would be shifted onto employers, who faced increasingly severe punitive sanctions if they engaged in 'unlawful employment practices'. This had a dual effect. It drew employers into the administration of the urban African population and served as a way to withdraw the state from direct and overt mechanisms of control, thus facilitating yet another form of depoliticization of processes which had already become deeply politicized.

The new approach differed from traditional apartheid policies insofar as it recognized, for the first time, the right of a limited group of Africans to reside permanently in the cities. However, as was clearly stated in the report, the inquiry would, in addressing the problem of manpower utilization, remain within the framework of certain parameters which were taken as given. In short, this meant the retention of the basic principle that Africans should exercise their political rights in the so-called 'homelands'. Moreover, it was assumed that Africans would continue to live in segregated areas and be subject to some form of influx control. The tentative inclusion of segments of the African population thus clearly stayed within the boundaries of traditional apartheid structures, not putting into question the distinction between 'white' South Africa and the 'homelands'.

This strategy of economic co-optation of the urban insiders, whose position was improved at the expense of the outsiders, has to be placed in the light of the broader changes in official discourse. As was the case with the Wiehahn report, Riekert took as one of its principles of departure the establishment of an effective labour market mechanism supposed to remove any obstacles to the exploitation of so-called 'market forces'. In addition, a clear attempt was made to depoliticize the remaining measures of control. This was presented as a normal part of the regulation of the economic life of the country. It was regarded as a purely economic phenomenon 'necessarily' following from the development of the secondary and tertiary sectors. Hence, the changes were argued to have little to do with NP policies. The depoliticization of questions concerning urbanization, poverty and living conditions in general reflected a wider establishment consensus. Urbanization, during the late 1970s, was portrayed as a 'challenge for modern communities everywhere', in Africa, Asia, Europe and the United States of America.[47] The problem and traumas of urbanization in South Africa were ascribed to its 'high degree of urbanization' and the 'attraction of its sophisticated cities'.[48] The growth of large squatter communities on the urban periphery, and the need to provide adequate housing, in similar fashion, were held to be normal problems of a developing society. In solving these 'problems', the private sector, it was argued, had a responsibility to make a substantial contribution.[49] The private sector did in fact have a substantial input into government commissions of inquiry dealing, *inter alia*, with the urban African housing crisis, which emerged as result of the government's decision to put a halt to the provision of housing in 1968. In addition, corporations such as SANLAM, the Anglo-American Corporation and the Standard Building Society put up large sums of money to finance housing projects.[50]

The report of the Riekert Commission itself was seen as an important contribution to 'the retention and extension of the free market system'.[51] While the emphasis on free enterprise involved a much closer co-operation between the state and big business, it simultaneously necessitated the construction of a black middle class with a stake in the system. In this way it facilitated the delimitation of a space in which an 'acceptable' blackness could exist legitimately within the boundaries of 'white' South Africa. A black middle class was seen as the urban corollary of the 'good tribal African' who knew and accepted his position in the system of differences delineated by the apartheid system. Ideally, such a stabilized middle class would constitute a moderate antipode to 'radical elements' bent on the overthrow of apartheid and of the capitalist system. Riekert contended that the most important advantage of the distinction between urban insiders and rural outsiders was the fact that it 'strengthened the position of established black communities in the white areas'.[52] Botha stated the reason for developing such a stable middle class in no uncertain terms:

> We hope to create a middle class among the nations of South Africa. Because, if a man has possessions and is able to build his family life around those possessions, then one already has laid the foundation for resisting Communism.[53]

At the forefront of the endeavour to create a black middle class was the establishment of home-ownership in the urban communities. The Minister of Co-operation and Development, Piet Koornhof, emphasized this, and argued that the 99-year leasehold system may lead

> ... to the erection of many houses by the private sector which may contribute to *greater differentiation* in housing on *social and economic lines* ... this would be an important factor in the creation of a black middle class.[54]

This project was supported by the SABC's television and radio services. The construction of 'legitimate' identities differed considerably between media with predominantly rural or predominantly urban listeners and viewers. Tomaselli and others have pointed out that while Radio Bantu (*sic*), with its audience which is located mainly in the homelands, extolled the benefits of rural life, TV2/3, the 'black' TV channels, were geared in a rather crude way towards constructing an urban-based black middle-class identity.[55] For example, in the late 1970s TV2/3 concentrated on propagating the desirability of home-ownership, of landscaped gardens, and so forth, in programmes with a clear emphasis on production and consumption. This was in sharp contrast to radio plays which emphasized traditional values by focusing on the problems of urban life, and by stressing, in the case of urban workers, a sense of nostalgia and a yearning to return to the rural areas. Moreover, black TV programmes presented an idealized image of urban life-styles. Most striking of all, perhaps, was the fact that families in these programmes were presented as units. The effects of the labour migration system were completely written out of this attempt to portray an image of the 'legitimate', 'non-political', urban black engaged in education and taking a 'stake in the system'.[56] These images should be contrasted with two other sets of portrayals. The first is that of apartheid discourse in the 1960s, where, as I have shown, African urbanization was associated with 'the dangers of detribalization' and 'a loss of values'. The second is that of an increasingly negative portrayal of the 'unionized' and therefore 'politicized' urban black working class. As both Koornhof and Botha made clear, the formation of a black middle class had a precise political aim: the production of a groups of 'moderate' urban blacks who could take their place alongside the traditionalist 'homeland leaders' within the system, while all 'radical elements' were simultaneously excluded.

The creation of a black, property-owning middle class was further facilitated by a number of other strategies to foster a spirit of 'entrepreneurship' in the African community. In the wake of the Carlton Conference, and on the recommendation of Anton Rupert, a national SBDC was established.[57] While stressing the key role the private sector was supposed to play in the management of the SBDC, Botha also emphasized the redistributive potential of the endeavour:

> . . . given our unique population composition and dualistic economy, the promotion of small business should assist us in distributing the benefits of economic growth and prosperity to as many people as possible and in supporting the spread of private business enterprise among our developing communities.[58]

To this was added an attempt to open up the informal sector, since it was regarded as a 'provider of income and employment opportunities and particularly as the breeding ground for entrepreneurial talent among members of the economically less developed [*sic*] communities'.[59]

The success of this strategy, and of the Riekert distinction between urban insiders and rural outsiders, depended upon the ability to maintain a clear insider–outsider distinction and, in this respect, its economic viability and political legitimacy were of the utmost importance. A series of factors, however, worked against the maintenance of this distinction, as well as against the logic underpinning it, namely the division between the 'homelands' and white South Africa. As a result of its acceptance of the homeland–white South Africa division, the Riekert Commission could not address changes in the reproductive economy which undermined the very possibility of making any clear-cut distinction between the urban and rural African workforce. One of the most salient changes taking place in the later 1970s was the rapid growth of an urban population in the homelands dependent upon metropolitan employment. The fast-developing sector of cross-border commuters, according to De Clercq, presented an anomaly for the traditional apartheid division assumed to be in existence by Riekert.[60] It also reflected a new regional stabilization of the African labour supply in which there was a *de facto* incorporation of parts of the homelands population into some ('white') suburban peripheries and deconcentration points.[61] Further, the Riekert Commission did not take into account the ever-growing rural poverty in the homelands which contributed to the massive increase in movement from the countryside to the cities. Neither did it address the mushrooming of peri-urban squatter areas. Both of these sectors – the cross-border commuters and the squatter populations – carried the potential of undercutting the maintenance of an insider–outsider distinction. The fact that they did not fit into any of the official apartheid categories caused endless problems for its reproduction.

By early 1981 significant changes in policy had been introduced, reinforcing the processes outlined above. The closer ties established between the state and the private sector were strengthened by a further conference, the 'Good Hope Conference', at which a series of far-reaching changes to government policy were made public. The rejection of the constellation idea on a Southern African scale, together with the acknowledgement that the 'homeland' economies were dismal failures and could not be regarded as autonomous economic units, led the government to propose a form of regional economic co-operation which cut across political borders within South Africa. Simon Brand, Chief of Financial Policy in the Department of Finance at the time, placed the government's rethinking of regional economic policy in the wider context of the constitutional reforms already underway. Constitutional development in South Africa consisted of setting up separate political structures for different 'ethnic or national groups' and involved a 'devolution' of authority away from the centre. This approach had been developed furthest in the 'national states'. However, the geographical areas assigned to the jurisdiction of these 'decentralized' political structures coincided 'with the relatively stagnant economic regions of the country'. He argued:

> It was realized ... that the decentralization of authority to political structures with jurisdiction over territories that would remain outside the

> mainstream of economic development ... *could not lead to a constitutional dispensation that would meet the criteria of acceptability and stability.*[62]

In order to overcome this problem, 'functional economic units' – often cutting across 'national borders' – had to be established such that 'co-operation in regional development policy between different states' could be advantageous to all.[63] Nevertheless, Brand made it clear that so-called 'decentralized political structures' in the 'national states' had to remain the focal point for the accommodation of the constitutional aspiration of Africans.[64] However, the recognition of the common economic system for all population groups that fell outside the national states did have the 'inescapable consequence' that

> ... members of different population groups will be living in close proximity to each other, albeit in separate communities. This brings about a need for the development of institutionalized liaison between such local authorities on matters of common interest.[65]

The creation of new regional 'functional units', the division of the country into eight such regions, would have serious implications for the territorial premisses upon which apartheid was built. Not disregarding this fact, Brand concluded in these words:

> ... if appropriate constitutional responses to situations brought about by economic reforms are not forthcoming, social and political tension could well be intensified rather than relaxed.[66]

This was exactly what occurred. However, in the late 1970s and the early 1980s, the government still believed that black resistance could be contained and the middle class co-opted by economic reforms.

The new regional development plan moved away from industrial decentralization, aimed at the relocation of industries close to homeland borders and based on the premiss of the homeland–white South Africa division. This plan, appropriately described as a 'soft borders' approach, was, however, based upon premisses fundamentally different to that developed under apartheid. According to it, development had to take place within regions free of constraints imposed by political borders, thus breaking down the territorial division characteristic of apartheid and replacing it with regional sub-economies, which were to form the basis of the construction of new local and regional authorities from the mid-1980s.[67] While these economic changes were important in that they undercut the territorial divisions upon which apartheid was built, and produced increasingly larger groups of people who simply did not fit into the logics upon which apartheid discourse was premissed, they could not, in and of themselves, effect their disarticulation.

It is here that the political factors working against the implementation of both the Riekert strategy and the tri-cameral reforms assume their centrality. The three areas of black resistance were of particular importance in this regard. The trade union movement played a decisive role in subverting the insider–outsider distinction. By refusing to admit the division of the African working class and by deliberately setting out to organize migrants, commuters and settled workers alike into single organizations, they contested that distinction.[68] They also challenged wage differentials between migrant and settled labour, and thus destroyed employers' attempts to reserve unskilled lower-paid jobs for migrant labourers. The second set of challenges which made the implementation of the strategy difficult developed around the growing squatter communities, who offered strong resistance to removals and resettlement by the state.[69] While the permanence of Africans had been accepted since the Rikhoto judgement in 1979, it is undoubtedly true that the squatter resistance further undermined the insider–outsider division.

The third set of resistances were located in the African townships. The recommendations of the Riekert Commission came in the wake of an emerging local government crisis manifesting itself in a proliferation of community-based grassroots movements.[70] These movements were organized around issues of collective consumption. However, it was not until the early 1980s, with the NP's attempt to reform the constitution, that the inchoate resistance forces began to coagulate into relatively united and nationally defined political blocs.[71] The launching of the UDF and the National Forum in 1983 saw the formation of legal and nationally mass-based political organization for the first time since the 1950s. These developments were paralleled on the trade union front with the emergence of new forms of unity, culminating in the formation of the COSATU in 1985.[72] The UDF, formed to organize resistance to the tri-cameral Parliament and to reforms aimed at urban Africans, filled the space opened up for political organization by the elections following in the wake of the constitutional reforms. Its initial platform was consolidated around the issue of the exclusion of Africans from the tri-cameral Parliament. The UDF quickly became a national force, articulating local township grievances into a broader anti-apartheid discourse.[73] This was abundantly clear from the statement issued on the occasion of the launching of the UDF at Mitchell's Plain on 20 August 1983:

> In accordance with these noble ideals, . . . we join hands as trade union, community, women's, students', religious, sporting and other organisations to say no to Apartheid. We say NO to the Republic of South Africa Constitution Bill – a bill which will create yet another undemocratic constitution in the country of our birth; We say NO to the Koornhof Bills which will deprive more and more African people of their birthright. We say yes to the United Democratic Front on this historic day; . . . we commit ourselves to uniting all our people wherever they may be in the cities and countryside, the factories and mines, schools, colleges and universities, housing and sports fields, churches, mosques and temples, to fight for our freedom.[74]

Not only did the UDF work against any division within the urban African community, but its opposition was predicated upon a discourse aiming to construct a form of unity which cut across all racial divisions, thus having the potential to undermine the very logic upon which the social division of apartheid was based. Hence, the significance of the sets of struggles condensed around the UDF was that it forcefully revealed the particularistic nature of the transformist project. While the NP and its allies presented this project in 'neutral', non-political, universalist terms, the articulation of resistance around the fact of the exclusion of Africans showed its origins in the project of a very precise endeavour to broaden the basis of the state without endangering the apartheid order. As a result of the growing militant and unified opposition, it became more difficult for the state to hold on to and utilize its discourse, still premissed on a dichotomization of political and social spaces.

Constitutional Reform Revisited

In order to make clear the nature of the contestation offered by the UDF to the incorporation of coloureds and Indians into the tricameral Parliament, and the exclusion of Africans from the central polity, it is enlightening to look at the battle around the meaning attributed to the constitutional proposals and 'Koornhof Bills'. The Koornhof Bills, originally tabled in 1980, consisted of three interconnected Bills, the centrepiece of which was the Orderly Movement and Settlement of Black Persons Bill, scrapped in 1983 as a result of the fierce protest which it called forth. The other two Bills dealt with the provision of social services – the Black Communities Development Bill – and black local authority elections in the urban African townships. These proposals followed on from the largely discredited

Community Councils, first introduced in 1977, which aimed at offering Africans a form of self-government parallel to that of the 'self-governing' homelands. By the mid-1980s the Department of Co-operation and Development reported that a total of 200 Community Councils in 238 black urban residential areas had been elected, albeit on polls of as low as 6 per cent.[75] The 1982 Black Local Authorities (BLAs) Act reconstituted the Community Councils into town or village councils, and transferred the bulk of powers formerly allocated to the Administration Boards to the new local authorities. This was clearly an attempt to defuse national black political claims through the substitution of power at the grassroots level.[76] However, the fact that the new BLAs were to be self-financing, in contrast to the old Administration Boards, which were partially funded by profits the boards made on sales of sorghum beer and levies they charged employers for their registered workers, was to be one of the core factors which were to lead to the increasing politicization of the provision of services.[77]

The UDF's campaign against both the tri-cameral system and the BLAs – for which an election was scheduled in late 1983 – made this abundantly clear:

> DON'T VOTE FOR KOORNHOF'S COUNCILS.
>
> *What is the government doing?* It is making new plans. The government calls one of these new plans the Black Local Authorities Act. They tell us that it will give us a say in how our community is run. . . .
>
> *But what does the Local Authorities Act mean?*
>
> - The council will be under Koornhof and will have no power.
> - They are the same as the community councils but only have a new name.
> - They cannot solve our housing problems, blocked drains, high rent or transport problems. . . . The councils will only help making apartheid strong.
>
> WE SAY NO TO APARTHEID![78]

This pamphlet, as other UDF documents, began to establish a clear set of equivalences between the proposed reforms, the continued exclusion of Africans from the polity, continued repression and apartheid in such a manner that those taking part in the 'system' were shown to collude in their own oppression. A document issued by the Ad-Hoc Anti-PC (President's Council) Committee made this only too clear in arguing that the (coloured) Labour Party was selling out by its decision 'to side with the government and to implement Apartheid'.[79] It went on to argue that 'joining the system to fight the system' means:

- attacking some of our trade unions in their struggle for a living wage;
- attacking Dr Allan Boesak for the courage and successful struggle to have Apartheid declared a heresy; . . .
- that our children will be forced to fight on the borders defending white privilege. They will be given guns and sent into our townships (as in 1976 and 1981) to search our homes, harass our mothers, scatter our children. . . . [80]

Resistance, in contrast to participation in the system, meant fighting for a free, non-racial and democratic future for South Africa.[81] Drawing on a longer tradition of non-racialism, Patrick Lekota argued already in 1984 that

> *The UDF is, indeed, the future non-racial and democratic South Africa in embryo.* It is because of their uncompromising commitment to racial discrimination . . . that the Nats and their ilk feel threatened by the UDF. The front is opposed to the domination of blacks by whites. It is equally opposed to the domination of whites, including Afrikaners, by all blacks. We realise that, over many centuries of interaction, the people of South Africa have shaped the landscape of this country into what it is today, they have built and cemented unbreakable social and cultural links of blood, history, language and customs; they have become an inseparable part of each other. . . . *We claim this country for all of them.*[82]

The government strategy, by sharp contrast, aimed to depoliticize the issue of black local authority elections, presenting its case almost entirely in terms of the need to provide 'a safe life for children', 'decent housing', 'good streets', electricity and clean water.[83] This was entirely in line with the wider attempt to defuse issues of collective consumption, around which the UDF and other organizations coagulated, and was a strategy extended to general township 'improvement' measures in the mid-1980s.

The strategy of depoliticizing the terrain of labour relations was also fiercely contested during the mid-1980s. Struggles on the labour front built upon the history of trade union resistance evident in the country since the early 1970s. COSATU took a lead on this terrain. While there were tensions between the community-based movements, organizing under the auspices of the UDF, and COSATU on matters of strategy and on the leadership role of the organized working class in the struggle for liberation, as well as divisions within COSATU between 'populists' and 'workerists', like the UDF, COSATU accepted the Freedom Charter as a guiding document which reflected the views and aspirations of the majority of the oppressed and exploited in their struggle against national oppression and economic exploitation in 1987.[84] The period of the mid-1980s witnessed a series of deepening struggles between the unions and the state. In February 1988, as a result of these struggles, the government issued restrictions which 'legally' limited COSATU's activities to a narrow range of factory-floor trade unionism. The 1988 Labour Relations Amendment Bill also substantially limited workers' right to strike, outlawed solidarity action in industrial disputes and opened trade unions to civil action for losses incurred by their members' actions.[85] These restrictions followed in the wake of continued harassment of labour leaders, including the bombing of COSATU House in May 1987, and the dismissal of more than twenty thousand workers for taking part in industrial action during 1987 and early 1988.[86]

Despite these restrictions, COSATU played a crucial role in delegitimizing the state's attempts to depoliticize labour relations and to drive a wedge between so-called 'moderates' and 'radicals' by encouraging debate within its ranks on socialism and democracy, and by working towards a 'working-class understanding of the Freedom Charter'. In 1987 COSATU adopted a strategy of 'disciplined alliances' – based on the retention of organizational autonomy – with the mass-based, democratic, non-racial community organizations, and in the wake of the banning of the UDF in 1988, it had to take on a leading role in the struggle against apartheid. In addition, COSATU could draw on a tradition of internal democracy to strengthen oppositional movements in the community and to disseminate the language of socialism. As Jay Naidoo argued in 1987:

> The interests of the working class can only be advanced by us locating ourselves in the hub of the struggle for democratisation of society, by building working-class power as the foundation of the organs of people's power.[87]

Apart from working within the black trade union movement and the townships, COSATU, like the UDF, also set out to create informal alliances with the liberal section of the white community so as to isolate the apartheid regime and to strengthen and broaden the unity of anti-apartheid forces. The combination of the politics of the organized working class with that of the national democratic, community-based organizations, which tended to reinforce one another, both contributed decisively to the subversion of the transformist project of the early 1980s.

The Dimensions of the Crisis

From reform to counter-revolution

Between 1984 and 1988 the country entered deeper and deeper into a state of crisis, evident in all spheres of the society: in the resistance to the political reforms associated with the tri-cameral Parliament; in the increasingly reactive nature of the second wave of reforms which were coupled with extreme measures of repression under the consecutive states of emergency since 1985; in the state of the economy; and in the fragmentation of the dominant bloc. Together, the overdetermination between these dimensions induced an organic crisis: a situation in which the state no longer was able to determine and control the nature and forms of social division, and in which a greater and greater set of core terms were taking on the character of floating signifiers, that is, of signifiers open to contestation and available for rearticulation amongst different discursive attempts to re-suture the fluid, inchoate prevailing conditions.

During this period, a battle was fought out between reformers and securocrats concerning the strategy to be employed to curb resistance and to create the conditions for the implementation of further reforms. The change from a more reformist to a security-oriented strategy occurred in mid-1986 when it became apparent that the measures implemented thus far were insufficient to stem the growing tide of resistance. It is important, by contrast to existing analyses, to stress that this shift did not involve a radical break in strategy, and that neither the 'reformist' nor the 'securocrat' camps were homogeneous blocs.[88] The reforms of the early to mid-1980s were part and parcel of the carefully planned Total Strategy discussed in chapter 5. In addition to the attempts at forging a new historic bloc around the alliance between the state, private enterprise and the security forces, a reorganization of state departments took place in 1982. As a result of this process, a new department – the Department of Constitutional Development and Planning (DCDP) – was created under minister Chris Heunis. Over the next three years, the functions of the department dealing with the administration of black affairs – the Department of Co-operation and Development – were taken over increasingly by the DCDP. This organizational change was accompanied by a certain measure of 'deracialization' of the structures falling under its ambit, and with it came the introduction of what is generally known as the 'second wave' of reforms.[89]

In the face of the developing crisis in the townships in the wake of the implementation of the tri-cameral system in 1984, the state abandoned any attempt at implementing the Riekert influx controls. By April 1986, the pass system was scrapped in its entirety, and influx control was replaced with a policy of planned or orderly urbanization. The rationalization for this, once more, was presented in terms of developmental logics.[90] It was also made clear that influx control no longer had any 'constitutional' function; it had to be replaced since it was not working. In a political advertisement, popular during the reform process, P.W. Botha proudly proclaimed its abolishment:

> Influx control has been abolished. The pass laws have gone. The prisons are emptied of the victims of this unhappy system. No South African will ever suffer the indignity of arrest for a pass offence again. A new era of freedom has begun.[91]

The measures provided in its place shifted away from direct prohibitions over movement, residence and employment, to the use of indirect ones. These included regionally differentiated financial penalties and 'positive' incentives, such as tax reliefs and the waiving of health standards in places of employment in order to influence settlement patterns.[92] This method of control over urbanization was said to be 'positive', since it allowed for the 'use of market forces, subsidies and development' to encourage people 'to settle in certain suitable areas rather than forbidding them to move to urban areas'.[93] The racially 'neutral' and indirect character of the measures, however, did not mean that all direct controls were given up. More insidious methods were also utilized. An example of this is the controlling of housing on the basis of legislation dealing with health and trespass laws. Nevertheless, a certain opening up of the situation and modification of the insider–outsider distinction occurred with the acceptance of differentiated accommodation. A far greater urban population was now legally resident in what was formerly 'white' South Africa.

The orderly urbanization strategy no longer relied on the homeland–white South Africa distinction. Instead it was linked to the new 'regional industrial dispersal strategy' which aimed at a relocation of industrial activities away from metropolitan areas to 'deconcentration' points. These points coincided with the development regions envisaged under the 'Good Hope' plan. The whole of South Africa was divided into nine development regions which cut across homeland borders in some cases, and which formed the basis of the framework for a variety of state institutions, such as the Development Bank and Regional Development Advisory Committees. From 1985 onwards each development region incorporated certain metropolitan regions which were governed by Regional Services Councils (RSCs). Thus, the orderly urbanization strategy formed part of a series of measures to contain the deepening crisis by trying to depoliticize the provision of services, and to introduce a measure of political legitimacy at the local state level. The Black Local Authorities, which had all but collapsed, were given representation on the RSCs together with 'white' municipalities.[94] These councils performed on a political level what the Development Regions did on an economic one: they cut across the 'white' South Africa homeland borders. The second wave of state reforms thus constituted a complete rejection of the idea that the homelands formed independent political and economic units, and in that sense the formulation of state strategies, from Riekert to orderly urbanization, involved an increasing dissolution of the historical premisses of apartheid. By 1985 the government acknowledged openly that the 'homelands' policy was a failure and that it would restore citizenship to all Africans residing permanently in 'white' South Africa. Moreover, it marked a change in the presentation of the reforms around the tri-cameral system. It was conceded that it was not a final solution, but only one step in a longer evolutionary process which would eventually lead to 'democracy for all'.

The need to reformulate policy was attributed to the existence of three problems, namely that of the 'development' of the 'national states', and international and domestic opposition. Stoffel van der Merwe presented as points of 'fact' that it had become apparent to the NP that it was not possible to accommodate all of the black people in independent states.[95] As a result, it had to be recognized that 'the policy of separate states' did not, as was hoped for, 'turn out to be the complete solution to the problem'.[96] A solution, which had to provide security, protect self-determination, avoid 'group domination' and fulfil the aim of a 'just society', had to be found. In addition to envisaging a review of the question of citizenship for blacks, it was stated that political rights could not be withheld from black people for ever'.[97] The possibilities spelt out for such an exercising of rights ranged from extending the powers of the 'national states' over some of the areas outside their borders, to the creation of a national assembly of black people outside the 'national states'.[98] For the first time now it was held as a prerequisite that any plan had to be acceptable to 'a significant number of black people'. To this end it had become 'an urgent need . . . to enter into discussion with the black people for the purpose of reaching agreement on the form in which their political rights may be realised'.[99] An informal, non-statutory forum for these discussions was envisaged.[100] With these proposals the NP acknowledged on a political level what had been evident in its economic planning for some time. As with the regional development plan, these proposals undercut the autonomy of the 'national states', and recognized publicly for the first time that they did not satisfy the political demands of the African majority. These plans came too late to have any impact within either the African or the white community. Not recognizing demands for a complete dissolution of the 'homelands' system and a re-unification of South Africa under a one-person–one-vote system, the scheme never got off the ground.

The limits of these reform measures quickly became apparent. By mid-1985 the situation, from the perspective of the state, was clearly out of control, and a partial state of emergency was introduced, to be followed by a national State of Emergency declared in June 1986, one month after the Commonwealth's Eminent Persons' Group mission was wrecked by SADF raids on Botswana, Zambia and Zimbabwe. In mid-1986 the securocrats gained control over strategic decisions on how to deal with the reform process. It is in this context that the National Security Management System (NSMS) was activated, and began to play a central role in the structuration of policy. The roots of this system lay in the reorganization of the security complex in 1972, with the creation of the SSC. The SSC, a permanent Cabinet committee, functioning during the Botha years as a sort of 'inner Cabinet' with a special status, came to assume a central role in the NSMS which operated through twelve Joint Management Centres (JMCs), which in turn were divided into sixty sub-JMCs and 450 mini-regions. Each of these bodies had an excecutive committee, and consisted of a committee for security, for constitutional, economic and social affairs, and for communications.[101] Participation in these committees reflected the interpenetration of the elements of the new historic bloc: membership ranged from military and intelligence personnel to representatives of local authorities and businesses.

The rise of the NSMS reflected a dissatisfaction with the strategy of the reformers, located in Heunis's Department of Constitutional Development and Planning, which relied on 'soft repression' and limited coercion in addition to constitutional reforms as outlined in the Total Strategy.[102] Now, the discourse shifted to one concerned with 'counter-revolutionary warfare', which adapted and turned revolutionary strategy on its head. Inspired by John J. McCuen's *The Art of Counter-Revolutionary Warfare* (1986) and Frank Kitson's *Low-Intensity Operations* (1971), strategists argued that the idea that 'the business of normal goverment and the business of the Emergency are two separate entities should be killed once and for all', so deepening the already existing interpenetration of security and socio-economic concerns.[103] Kitson's work, especially, warned against the absence of 'conscious planning' in counter-revolutionary action, and the JMCs were hailed as the mechanism through which this 'important shortcoming' – *ad hoc* responses and unco-ordinated decisions – could be countered. Thus, the shift to counter-revolutionary warfare did not involve a complete break with the Total Strategy, which also emphasized the 'political line' developed by Beaufre, but rather a deepening of it. This was evident in the three-stage counter-revolutionary theory adopted: the first dimension of this strategy involved the re-establishment of law and order in the townships, and in this the JMCs and mini-JMCs were to play a crucial role; the second consisted in an emphasis on the socio-economic reconstruction of the townships, so removing the causes of unrest and undermining the activists by eliminating the grievances around which they mobilized the communities; and the third stage consisted in constitutional reforms.

The re-establishment of 'law and order' in the townships took place largely through a series of repressive measures, ranging from the elimination of activists to the use of overt force in situations of unrest. In the period from 1984 to 1988, 35,000 SADF troops were deployed in the townships, some 45,000 persons were detained without trial and numerous activists were killed under 'mysterious' circumstances.[104] The offices of the Black Sash and the SACC, as well as the headquarters of the South African Catholic Bishops' Council, were bombed in 1988. As became clear in the early 1990s, the state operated with three more or less distinct categories of persons and organizations targeted: the first included 'legitimate' ANC targets like Ruth First, and involved military attacks on neighbouring countries; the second category consisted of 'domestic' political activists; and the third seemed to be individuals targeted for no particular reason. While the latter grouping could possibly be ascribed to 'maverick' individuals within both the SAP and the SADF, the first two categories were officially approved at the highest level of the SSC. In addition to the state-sponsored death squads, late 1985 also saw the rise of right-wing vigilante groups in urban townships as well as in the 'homelands' responsible for what was portrayed as 'black-on-black' violence. During this period, 3,574 persons were killed. Of these, 73 per cent of the deaths occurred in the townships, and 59 per cent were the result of 'internecine' warfare, while 41 per cent were the result of overt security action.

The activities of the vigilantes clearly worked in concert with the state's repressive policies, achieving what the SADF and the SAP could not as a result of limitations placed on them by potential publicity and legal restrictions.[105] While vigilante groups clearly had regionally specific characteristics, they also shared a series of common features: these groups all emerged in late 1985; they all targeted members of leaders of groups associated with resistance to apartheid or homeland rule; and they operated openly, believing, correctly, that they enjoyed police support.[106] In the townships, community activists, often associated with the UDF, and in the homelands those who were involved in non-ethnic forms of organization which threatened the support basis of homeland leaders, were singled out as targets. Vigilante groups often also exploited and exacerbated existing divisions within the communities in a manner strikingly similar to the state. In the townships on the Reef, the battles between insiders and outsiders – between township residents and hostel dwellers – became a regular feature of the political landscape, with police consistently being accused of siding with the more conservative, traditional hostel residents. In the squatter camps as well as in the townships, inter-generational conflicts emerged between parents and children, founded upon the prominent role the youth (comrades) played in formulating strategies and making decisions for the community.[107] In this case also, it was clear that the police sided with the parents against the radicalized youth. A similar process was underway in the homelands, where the power of traditional rulers was threatened by non-racial forms of organization. Possibly one of the single most important factors in the state-sponsored violence in Natal was the creation of the Inkatha-supported United Workers' Union of South Africa (UWUSA) in May 1986, six months after COSATU's launch. The government spent some R1.5 million on its activities, which, according to government spokespersons, was earmarked for activities 'combating sanctions' and thus clearly had the political aim of countering the growing influence of COSATU and its discourse on non-racialism and socialism.

This process was furthered by attempts to undermine grassroots resistance in the townships by bolstering the political and financial position of the town councils through their inclusion into the well-funded JMCs. It was hoped that the creation of so-called 'model townships', by upgrading housing, infrastructures, services and facilities, would undercut resistance and 'win over the hearts and minds' (WHAM) of the people. Government strategists associated with the WHAM strategy believed that only 20 per cent of Africans were politically militant, 30 per cent moderate and 50 per cent undecided, and the strategy was aimed at isolating 'radicals' and drawing 'moderates' into the system.[108] Government strategists thus knew that the success of reform measures depended upon their ability to make inroads into the unity displayed by the resistance movements. Drawing upon ANC documents, Botha argued in Parliament that

> [t]he concern with which the South African Communist Party and its demonstrated pawn, the ANC, regards the Government's reform initiative, is apparent . . . from a discussion held during the ANC's national conference. . . . It was inter alia argued: 'The danger of introducing reformist illusions among sections of our people remains. . . . The need to cement the unity of the broad democratic movement, and to broaden as well as deepen its base, is made more imperative by the urgent task we face of defeating the enemy's new offensive.'[109]

The second leg of the 'counter-revolutionary' strategy thus consisted of bolstering reforms and building up a strong economy.[110] General Malan, Minister of Defence, argued that in a situation in which forces of resistance were bent on creating chaos, the security of the state had to take precedence, and for this six very important requirements had to be met. The first was the establishment of law and order, to which end the security forces were deployed in the townships. The second concerned the structures in the urban black communities in particular. Malan held that

> [t]he third level of government is the basis of South African democracy. If it fails at this level, the cracks will spread upwards. I therefore consider it to be of the utmost importance that these third-level structures be established and that the function effectively. . . . The functioning of these structures is a target identified by the enemy.[111]

The third requirement had to do with housing: 'Give someone the opportunity to own his own house, and he has something to lose.'[112] The following two had to do with job opportunities and education and training, especially with countering 'people's education', once again reflecting the extent to which the agenda was now being set by the mass democratic movement. The final requirement was the achievement of labour peace.[113] Meeting these requirements meant that the national JMCs had to be activated in order to regulate co-ordinated action at grassroots level.[114] The WHAM strategy, involving selective control and containment, complemented the shift in thinking away from traditional influx control, to controls within the urban areas. By means of a combination of selective allocation of resources to bolster conservative elites and vigilante forces, and the repression of the democratic community organizations, the government attempted to maintain control.[115] It divided townships into one of three categories: they were classified as 'ungovernable' when authorities were unable to provide essential services; they were classified as 'stable' when services could be provided, but an armed escort was needed; finally, 'normal' townships were those where services could be provided without 'harassment by citizens in the process of conducting the revolution'. A 'security' mode was employed to transform an ungovernable community into a stable one. Once this situation was reached, the 'welfare' mode came into play with the tarring of streets, provision of housing, telephones and other services so as to re-establish 'normal' conditions in the townships.[116] This was to prepare the ground for further reforms, implemented in the absence of issues around which 'radical' activists could mobilize:

> The activist seizes on a problem area in order to incite people against government. On the other hand, the government identifies problem areas in order to deal with them and eliminate them. By removing socio-economic problem areas opportunities are taken away from the activist.[117]

Major rejuvenation programmes took place in so-called 'trouble spots' such as Alexandra, Lingelihle, Bhongolethu and Duncan Village. These programmes were allocated on the basis of strategic decisions, not on need, and were not limited to the actual provision of services, but also proceeded through attempts to interpellate the population. This was abundantly clear in the materials distributed in the effort to create divisions, and to foster support for 'moderate' forces. A cartoon, depicting a conversation between township youths and 'Comrade Rat', situated the infrastructural improvements in the following manner:

> *Friendly township youth (1):* They are busy putting in a new sewerage system.
> *Comrade Rat:* Hmff!!! It's going to take years!!
> *Township youth (1):* I've got a surprise for you Comrade Rat. . . . The workers decided to work during the whole December holiday!!

Township youth (2): But Alex, what will this mean for us, the people of Alexandra?

Township youth (1): This will mean that about a third of the houses in Alex will be able to use flushing toilets in the future . . .

Comrade Rat: What about the *rest* of Alexandra?

Township youth (1): Another two major sewerage systems have been planned for the future!!![118]

This conversation, built upon the negative image of 'comrades' constructed in official discourse, aimed to interpellate urban Africans into the reform process via the same depoliticized language of 'service provision' utilized with respect to the BLA elections. It went further, however, by attempting to depict 'workers' and 'the people' in a positive, co-operative light. The inclusion of these figures, no doubt, has to be attributed to the extent to which resistance discourses in the early 1980s already succeeded in constructing a set of equivalences between workers, trade unionists, the people, local community-based organizations, and so forth, which the government tried to disaggregate by differential inclusion of 'moderate' Africans, workers and township people.

From the mid- to later 1980s, in the context of the State of Emergency, there was a proliferation of 'enemies' of the state, and it became more difficult to maintain clear and consistent lines of inclusion and exclusion. The strategy increasingly became one of emphasizing the separation between 'moderates' and 'radicals', although this division itself was becoming more problematic to maintain:

> The National Party commits itself to the vigorous implementation of a national strategy to enable the RSA to repulse decisively the total onslaught of Soviet expansionism. . . . Consequently, *the government does not view the struggle as one between White and non-White, but as a struggle between the forces of chaos, violence and suppression on the one hand, and a Christian civilisation of law, order and justice on the other.*[119]

This was especially clear in the portrayal of violence occurring during uprisings. Posel argues that one of the main intentions in the depiction of violence had been to contest representations of the township violence as a people's war, 'a mass-based struggle, with an articulate and democratic leadership and a clear programme and strategy'.[120] The state, in its interventions, fell back on an agitator theory: external agitators, such as the ANC and the SACP, were said to have infiltrated the otherwise calm townships, and sparked off mindless and destructive violence. The violence, nevertheless, was not portrayed in simple black–white terms. As Posel remarks, while the discourse on violence played on the long-standing white fears of the 'black mob', it simultaneously had to override any crude racial depictions, for the whole of the transformist strategy depended upon the state's ability to co-opt support from 'moderate' blacks and exclude 'radicals' and 'communists', while selling the idea of 'power-sharing' to the white population.[121] Posel's findings are confirmed by an investigation into the use of other media in the portrayal of 'the enemy' and the concomitant drawing of political frontiers as well as in the proliferation of 'treason' trials from 1985 onwards.

The activities of the UDF were targeted in particular. The UDF was quickly shown to belong to the domain of exclusion. While it continually denied that it was a mere front-organization for the ANC, the state argued that the UDF had the same 'revolutionary aims' as the ANC. The Minister of Law and Order, Louis Le Grange, soon after its inception, made this contention by drawing a set of telling equivalences. Paraphrasing him, the SABC Radio service reported that

> [i]t is understandable that the UDF has no open links with the ANC. Nevertheless, it is telling to see what company an organization keeps. . . . Even a brief investigation brings the following to light: the UDF associates itself with the 'Freedom Charter' approved by the ANC; more than 90 per cent of the organization's members were members of the ANC or the banned South African Communist Party; at a UDF meeting, homage was paid to the former Soviet leader, Yuri Andropov; banned publications such as *The African Communist* and the ANC journal *Umkhonto we Sizwe* are giving publicity to the UDF as an ally in the struggle; that the UDF, like the ANC, is committed to extra-parliamentary methods to bring about change, even though it proclaims itself to be against the use of violence; that the UDF was actively involved in organizing protest marches during the Coloured and Indian elections [to the tri-cameral Parliament], protests which led to widespread violence and the arrest of more than two hundred UDF supporters. . . .[122]

These and other similar reports also refrained from using overt racial references. The emphasis now had shifted almost entirely to an opposition between the forces of resistance, intent upon radical change by revolutionary, violent methods, and moderates, working hard for 'evolutionary' change, through consultation and negotiation. 'Radicals' were regularly portrayed as 'murderers', 'criminals' and 'intimidators' with a 'cynical disregard for elementary rights'.[123] They all strove for the violent overthrow of the 'present RSA system' and wanted to replace it with 'a so-called (Black) majority government within a unitary state in which a dictatorial elite will rule the masses'.[124] On 28 March 1985 a statement was issued by the Deputy Minister of Foreign Affairs, Louis Nel, following on the massacre at Uitenhage on 21 March. In line with other attempts to present South Africa as simply one more country with some internal problems, he echoed John Vorster's 1977 claim that 'urban terrorism was the curse of our time':

> In general I would like to state that violence is not unique to South Africa. It is a universal phenomenon. One only has to think of the hundreds of people killed during violent clashes following the assassination . . . of . . . Mrs Indhira Ghandi. Or of the innocent policemen killed . . . in Ulster; or for that matter, of the deaths, damage and destruction during the riots in Miami some four or five years ago. . . . In fact, examples of violence are innumerable.[125]

The riots within the black townships were, once again, portrayed as the result of actions of radicals instigated by the ANC and SACP, who reject 'negotiation and consultation', and who continue to 'threaten, intimidate and murder any of their black brothers who show a willingness to work towards peaceful reform'. These trends in the constitution of political frontiers continued, and were solidified during the consecutive states of emergency introduced from 1985 onwards; they were also evident in the political reforms introduced during the period from 1985. This included measures such as introduction of stringent squatter controls, the redefinition of the Group Areas Act, as well as the creation of 'free settlement' areas, all of which aimed to make reforms more attractive to 'moderates'.

Theoretically, it is important to consider some of the evaluations of these changes. In contrast to those who argue that the crisis could be attributed in large measure to the state of the economy, I have argued that its origins were to be found in the political terrain, and, more specifically, in the consecutive waves of resistance following in the wake of the implementation of the tri-cameral system. Both the disarticulation of this project by wider and wider elements and the scale of international criticism contributed to the inducing of an economic crisis of enormous proportions. While it was hoped that the transformist strategy would be legitimized by an increasing withdrawal from direct intervention, leaving the terrain open for 'neutral market forces' to do their work, this depoliticization was not allowed to take place. Both the 'free enterprise' discourse and the continued racial exclusiveness of the reforms were being challenged. In this respect, Cobbett and others have argued that the new reforms went 'beyond the political and territorial premises of apartheid, though not necessarily [beyond] those of race or ethnicity'. This requires further comment.[126] While it is clear that the reforms of the mid-1980s went well beyond what could be understood as the historically specific social divisions instituted by apartheid, I have argued that for these changes to become effective, they had to be articulated to wider resistance discourses. The so-called 'structural' disarticulation of apartheid logics, while important in itself, was not sufficient to bring about the disarticulation of the political logics which had shaped the society. A dislocated structure merely opened the space for a multitude of possibilities of rearticulations which were, by definition, indeterminate. That is why the political factors working against state strategies are to be given a certain primacy, for it is only from there that the construction of an alternative order can be addressed. In this respect, it is necessary to take a closer look at the nature of resistance discourses during the mid-1980s, and their role in the fragmentation of 'white unity'.

The fragmentation of white unity: the re-emergence of the far right

Resistance to the reform strategies aimed at the co-optation of sections of the urban African community, as well as the incorporation of coloured and Indian collaborative elites, did not only come from the black communities. From both the white right and left dissent was registered. Despite attempts to organize consent in the 'white' community for both the incorporationist and repressive aspects of the transformist project, by the mid-1980s cracks began to appear in that community. The formative efforts of the early 1980s brought about profound changes in the relation between the NP and white workers, between the state and the business community, and between Parliamentary and extra-parliamentary political movements.

Whereas much of the initial articulation of Afrikaner nationalism was deeply concerned with the plight of Afrikaner workers, and whereas up to 1970, for example, a complete issue of *Stryd*, the official organ of the NP in Transvaal, had been devoted to the position of the 'white worker', by 1979 the NP no longer saw these people as a central part of its constituency. This change accompanied the shift away from *volkist* themes, and was reinforced by the recommendations of the Wiehahn report. On the publication of the report's recommendation that job reservation should be abolished and African trade unions recognized, attempts were made to placate white unions. This was done, however, in the neutral language of 'economic needs'. All references to the changes in the racial structure of labour were avoided.[127] In addition, the government newspaper, *The Citizen*, portrayed the reaction of the white Mine Workers' Union against the Wiehahn recommendations as a *verkrampte* 'backlash' and an 'anachronism in these days of enlightenment'.[128] It was quite clear that white workers could no longer expect any privileged treatment:

> . . . the Black worker must be advanced whether the White *reactionary* workers care or not, for the simple reason that there is no alternative. We need the Black man. We need him at the bottom rung of labour. . . . But we also need him in semi-skilled or skilled work.[129]

Little effort was put into reincorporating white workers into the reformed NP. They were left largely unprepared for the changes envisaged in the labour field. In addition, neither their unions nor their employers tried to gauge their feelings, nor did they prepare white workers to co-operate in the task of eliminating the economic gap between black and white. It is no surprise, then, that the KP drew support mainly from disaffected white workers and farming communities, both of which were hard-hit not only by the formal changes introduced in the labour field, but also by the redistributive efforts of the government.[130] The attitudes of these workers also reflected their adherence to the old apartheid doctrine. One of the few studies done on this subject showed an extremely negative attitude towards vertical occupational mobility of African workers.[131] Instead of being led in the direction of alliances with the black working class, these workers gravitated to the KP, who now defended their pledge in precisely the terms shed by the NP.

While the KP in the early 1980s did not make much progress by way of winning electoral support, by the mid-1980s this situation changed drastically. This period, deeply marked by the declaration of a nationwide State of Emergency in 1986, following on from the partial 1985 Emergency, not only undermined the political confidence of the poorer rural white voters, but also drastically affected their material well-being. By the mid-1980s the economy was characterized by stagnation and decline as a result of the combined effects of sanctions, the sharp fall in international confidence in South Africa in the aftermath of P.W. Botha's disastrous 'Rubicon' speech, disinvestment campaigns, the recall of outstanding short-term loans by major international banks, sizeable foreign capital outflows and the costs of its domestic and regional security policies.[132] The effects of this situation on white workers could be seen, *inter alia*, in the dramatic rise in unemployment figures for whites – from 6,000 in 1981 to over 32,000 in 1986 – as well as in the 26 per cent fall in real wages for artisans, and 42 per cent for farmers between 1974 and 1984. It is in this context that the KP began to make inroads into the traditional NP constituency. In the general election of May 1987, the combined support for the right-wing increased from about 14 per cent of the total vote in 1981 to almost 30 per cent, and the number of right-wing Parliamentary seats had increased from zero to twenty-two over the same period.[133] As a result, the KP replaced the PFP as official opposition. This trend was to continue in local and by-elections throughout the late 1980s. While the NP typically used 'strong-arm' tactics in the run-up to local and by-elections – by, for example, a raid into Angola shortly before the by-elections in March 1988 – and tended to focus its campaigns on security issues, the tactics proved to be impotent in the face of the worsening situation confronted by the white, predominantly rural, poor.[134] The mid-1980s also saw the re-emergence of more vocal extra-parliamentary, para-military hard right political movements, of which the *Afrikaner Weerstandsbeweging* (AWB, Afrikaner Resistance Movement) under the leadership of Eugene Terreblanche was the most prominent. Whilst the KP concentrated on the restoration of the pre-Botha apartheid order, the AWB, with its emotive rhetoric, gave far greater centrality to the concept of the Afrikaner *volk*'s right to govern itself in an all-white state.

Analytically, these changes are usually depicted to underline the extent to which the unity fostered by the NP had been nothing but an uneasy alliance of classes. However, as I have argued, the nationalist project was one which precisely cut across class divisions to construct a society based around the *volkist* mythology dominant in Afrikaner nationalist circles. With the move toward (white) national unity, and the need to enter into a transformist project, the focus of NP discourse changed drastically. In this regard the important question is that of the political *identification* of these groupings. The mere fact of a split along 'class lines' is not necessarily an indication of the nature of the political project either leading to or following from the split. While the NP's transformist endeavour during the 1980s had distinctive 'middle-class' overtones, any judgement of the political project emerging in the wake of the transformist project will have to take into account other important factors in its articulation. The increasing emphasis on 'stability', 'law and order' and 'evolutionary change' is as important as any overt effort to construct a 'middle class'. Indeed, it has to be kept in mind that the latter endeavour proceeded from a desire to maintain a deracialized order: the deracialization 'necessitated' by economic demands but made possible by changes in the construction of political frontiers; and the emphasis on order resulting from the strong stress on stability in NP discourse. (The continuity between these themes and the later NP discourse on negotiation should also not be underestimated. Indeed, these themes contain many of the conditions for the unbanning of the ANC and the SACP in February 1990.) It is precisely in the space left by these changes that the far right could mobilize and agitate against the NP, so contesting its right to speak for whites and for the Afrikaner community while the NP, paradoxically, still implicitly relied on a *volkist* loyalty.

'A grotesque ritual of irrelevance': the demise of Parliamentary politics and the fragmentation of the dominant bloc

The formative efforts of the early 1980s also brought about considerable change in the relation between Parliamentary and extra-parliamentary politics. By the late 1980s, the white Parliamentary and extra-parliamentary unity was about to be fractured beyond repair. The most significant developments in this respect included the resignation of the leader of the opposition, Frederick van Zyl Slabbert, in 1986, indicting the white Parliament as a farcical institution, leading to the formation of the Institute for a Democratic Alternative for South Africa (IDASA) under his leadership; and the breakaway of the Independents (New Nats) from the NP just before the 1987 general election. One of the first IDASA initiatives was the organization of a meeting between sixty-one mainly Afrikaans-speaking whites and coloureds with the ANC in Dakar in July 1987, following in the footsteps of a series of other meetings with the ANC by a growing number of whites from within South Africa. Major industrialists, white parliamentarians, students, church leaders and business organizations participated in this 'trek to Lusaka' from September 1985. The political consequences of this third 'trek' led to a de-demonization of the ANC, and it directly challenged the state's attempts to isolate the organization, thus both reflecting and fostering an erosion of government control.[135] As one of the participants in a meeting between the ANC and business leaders was to point out:

> It was difficult to view the group [ANC delegates] as hardline Marxists or bloodthirsty terrorists who were interested in reducing South Africa

> to anarchy and seizing power, with a hatred of whites. . . . the latter stereotype (which is probably the impression that most white South Africans have of the ANC) certainly did not come through at all. . . . I believe that they are people with whom serious negotiations can be undertaken and with whom a certain amount of common ground could be found.[136]

As Price points out, it was significant that the business community – the segment of South African white society upon whom the indirect effects of the insurrection of the mid-1980s had the most immediate impact – led the way in initiating contacts with the ANC.[137] Tony Bloom of Premier Milling, Anglo-American's Gavin Relly and Zac de Beer were the first business leaders to meet with the ANC, and in the wake of this meeting in Lusaka in September 1985 the business community began to be increasingly vocal in their criticism of the government's 'reform' strategy. In 1985, not only the FCI, the Chamber of Mines and the Associated Chambers of Commerce (Assocom) spoke out against the goverment, but the AHI joined them in their condemnation of repression and detention without trial.

During this period a new form of political campaigning also took root: the use of newspaper advertisements. In September 1985, ninety businessmen led by Tony Bloom sponsored an advertisement, 'There is a better way'. Throughout the 1980s, businesses placed advertisements in alternative newspapers such as the *Weekly Mail.* Shell took the lead on this, regularly placing ads in response to political developments of the day. In response to the February 1988 banning of seventeen organizations and eighteen individuals, its ad, for instance, stated that '[e]veryone has the right to freedom of thought, conscience and belief, and the right to express those beliefs'.[138] Similarly, in the wake of the banning of the newspaper *South* it stated in a full-page ad: 'You can silence the press. You can't silence the people. . .' These phenomena provide stark evidence of the extent to which the discourse of resistance began to set the agenda, and infiltrated the language of those traditionally considered to be 'the enemy'. This was also evident in the comments of a business leader shortly after the 'Broederstroom encounter' between the leaders of the democratic movements, including COSATU, and prominent business persons. Eschewing the 'non-political' nature of business, Christo Nel argued that

> [b]y 1986, it had become abundantly clear that it was no longer a question of whether business should become politically involved, but rather of how they should respond to their obvious involvement.[139]

As a result of this meeting, a Consultative Business Movement was set up which declared itself dedicated to the principles of *non-racial democracy*, economic growth and a just redistribution of wealth.

A similar process was underway with respect to the churches. While the Anglican and Catholic churches were traditionally vocal in their opposition to apartheid, by the late 1980s this resistance had also spread to the Afrikaans churches. One of the most important interventions by the churches during this period was the publication of the *Kairos Document* in September 1985 by fifty theologians working in and around Soweto, providing a theological comment on the political crisis in South Africa.[140] This document offered a critique of the state's use of the concepts 'law and order', the 'threat of communism', and called upon Christians to participate in the struggle for liberation. Within the Afrikaans DRC, a much more cautious sense of revision was also underway. In its 1986 *Church and Society. A Witness of the DRC*, it was argued that the DRC was convinced that 'the application of apartheid as a political and social system by which human dignity is adversely affected, and whereby one political group is detrimentally suppressed by another, cannot be accepted on Christian-ethical grounds' and that its members 'confess their participation in apartheid with humility and sorrow'. While this qualified criticism of 'negative' aspects of apartheid fell far short of a thorough-going critique, and while the church now denounced its (former) role as political 'pressure group', it was the first salvo in an ongoing debate which would eventually lead the DRC in 1989 unequivocally to reject apartheid.[141]

Winning the moral high-ground: the role of JODAC and the ECC

Apart from these developments, 'white' extra-parliamentary organizations played a crucial role in further fragmenting what was once 'white South Africa'. The late 1980s saw a proliferation of democratic extra-parliamentary movements working within the white community for democratic change, challenging the NP's fledgeling reformism. The sheer range of these movements is indicative of the crisis within the dominant bloc: the Detainees' Parents' Support Committee (DPSC), the Democratic Lawyers' Association, Jews for Social Justice, Five Freedoms Forum (FFF), the Johannesburg Democratic Action Committee (JODAC) and the End Conscription Campaign (ECC) were the most prominent during the late 1980s. While some of these movements openly aligned themselves with the UDF, others chose, as a matter of strategy, to forgo such affiliation in order better to be able to reach whites who were dissatisfied with the repression, but who were not ready to align themselves with the UDF.

JODAC, founded in August 1983, was formed in order to forge a sense of unity within the disparate 'white left' in Johannesburg. Its formation was closely related to that of the UDF, and resulted from an attempt to work through the meaning of the UDF's resistance to the white tri-cameral Parliament for white democrats. JODAC brought together members of other white organizations such as the Black Sash, a variety of professionals including democratically inclined lawyers and academics, individuals from church-based organizations, as well as what was called the 'Rockey Street' constituency (young punks, disaffected youths, women, and so forth).[142] While there were expectations from within the rank and file membership of JODAC to become directly involved in the escalating struggle in the black townships, JODAC was quite clear that the time for whites to work as 'organizers' in the black communities was over.[143] Instead, JODAC saw its constituency as the white community, and recognized that its real political work had to be done there. This is not to say, however, that JODAC spurned contacts with the UDF. There was close co-operation between JODAC and the UDF, and JODAC's work was greatly boosted by the UDF's 1986 'Call to Whites' campaign which appealed to whites to contribute to the building of a non-racial democracy.[144] However, the main focus of campaigns was on the building of a non-racial political imaginary in the white community.

JODAC's analysis of the fracturing of the dominant bloc – evident in the demise of the PFP, the divisions within the traditional Afrikaner nationalist constituency, the rise of new groupings such as IDASA, and increasing dissidence amongst churches, business leaders, intellectuals and the white youth – was acute. In this it saw the potential to weaken and isolate the apartheid regime, and at the same time to win broad support for the democratic movement by

> taking the message of the democratic movement into the white arena, and thus into the ruling bloc, and partly by exposing and campaigning against the brutalities of state repression.[145]

In developing its strategy, JODAC faced a series of difficulties, not least the perception on the left that getting involved with 'reformist forces' could run the risk of being hi-jacked by those very groupings they were trying to win over. To this JODAC responded with verve, arguing that the political alignment of the 'middle ground' was not set in stone, and while it could easily fit into 'an imperialist agenda', it could also be 'incorporated into a democratic agenda'.[146] As a result, JODAC did not scorn the opportunities opened up by the crisis. It, for example, argued that 'the interests of big business and the apartheid state' do not always coincide, and that white democrats needed to exacerbate existing divisions so as to be able to 'win hegemony and undermine the social base of the present order'.[147]

While underwriting the key goals of the democratic movement – the establishment of a non-racial democratic society based on the Freedom Charter which envisaged a considerable degree of redistribution of wealth – the organization also took cognizance of the specificity of the terrain of white politics, of the fact that while a broad layer of whites opposed apartheid, they did not necessarily support a one-person–one-vote, non-racial democracy; of their insecurities concerning the future; of their general commitment to Parliamentary reformist politics; and of their belief in 'free enterprise capitalism'.[148] As a result they focused on winning the moral and ideological struggle against the regime, so as to establish the hegemony of the democratic movement:

> Ultimately, this means demonstrating – even to those who disagree with us – that it is the only force capable of resolving the political and economic crisis facing the nation. We must show that the broad democratic movement is the only political force that can lead the nation to peace, justice and democracy, and heal the ravages of civil war, racial hatred and fear.[149]

In order to do so, JODAC entered into broad anti-apartheid alliances, once again shunning any 'theoretical objection to building broad alliances in white politics'. JODAC played a key role in the formation of the Five Freedoms Forum in March 1987, an umbrella organization uniting anti-apartheid organizations in the white community; and it supported the formation of Concerned Citizens (CC), founded by the Black Sash.[150] The FFF was a campaign-based organization aiming to unite white opposition and to prepare them for negotiation. Both the FFF and JODAC participated in campaigns such as 'Christmas against the Emergency', 'Free the Children' and '101 Ways to End Apartheid'. The FFF also held a series of sucessful conferences aimed at whites who approved of change, but had no appropriate means of acting on their beliefs.[151]

Organizations such as these played a crucial role in addressing the position of whites in a new South Africa, so extending the struggle into the white community. They questioned the very basis upon which the division of the social had been constructed. No recognizable horizon of agreement within the white community existed any longer. The locus of politics had shifted decisively to the extra-parliamentary domain. An increasing articulation took place between resistance movements such as the UDF and later the Mass Democratic Movement (MDM), located largely in the domain of black resistance politics, and 'white' extra-parliamentary activity, such that the government, once again, was compelled to address this relation. One of the clearest examples of the regime's attempt to close off the possibilities opened up by the new white resistance movements can be found in its reponse to the ECC.

Of the extra-parliamentary movements, the ECC was regarded as particularly pernicious in that it questioned the fundamental tenets upon which the whole discourse of a total onslaught rested. Consequently, much government energy was spent on delegitimizing one of the potentially most 'destructive' forms of resistance emanating from the white community. The ECC emerged in the context of the drive to militarization which characterized the early 1980s. During this period, South Africa's war against the front-line states took the form of intensive military campaigns in Angola, Namibia and Mozambique, ostensibly to neutralize SWAPO and MK bases, and in support of both UNITA and RENAMO.[152] One of the numerous excursions into Angola, named Operation Askari – which involved over ten thousand white troops and which was to support a UNITA push northwards – proved to be particularly damaging for the SADF. More than twenty white conscripts died in the operation, and it provoked for the first time a really critical reaction from the white public.[153] Increasing disquiet within the white community with South Africa's continued military involvement in the sub-continent and on the home-front arose in the period between 1979 and 1982, but was expressed largely within the confines of the government's definition of 'conscientious objection', allowed only on religious grounds. In this period, fifteen such objectors were imprisoned for refusing to do military service.

As a result of their activities, a Conscientious Objector Support Group (COSG) was formed in 1980. By 1983, the government reacted to mounting pressure by amending the Defence Act to broaden the category of conscientious objectors to include religious pacifists outside of the 'peace churches' in a move designed to contain the number of resisters.[154] This amendment provided for a six-year maximum jail sentence for objectors refusing to serve. A Board for Religious Objection was also set up to adjudicate claims for religious-objector status. Objectors were given several alternatives: to accept non-combatant service in the SADF for the same period as military service; to perform non-combatant service in the SADF in non-military uniform, in which case the period to be served was extended to one and a half times the ordinary period; or to do community service in a state department for the same period of time.[155] These measures had the opposite effect to what the SADF intended: it united the resistance from the English churches, who reiterated their belief that all resisters should be recognized; from other organizations, most notably the Black Sash and the COSG; as well as from NUSAS activists on English-speaking university campuses.[156] The ECC was formed in 1983.[157]

The ECC aimed to increase awareness of and resistance to the increasing militarization of society, and the deployment of SADF troops in 1984 to quell resistance in the black townships provided fertile ground for its campaign.[158] Between 1984 and mid-1986, when the national State of Emergency was declared, the ECC campaign reached its peak, growing into a national movement with twelve branches, about a thousand active members and a large support base.[159] The ECC's strategy of calling for an end to compulsory military service – without making further political prescriptions – allowed it to develop a broad strategy of resistance, and to interpellate a wide swathe of opposition groupings, ranging from pacifists and religious objectors to anti-apartheid radicals.[160] In its campaigns, the ECC also used a wide range of methods. 'Hard-edged' campaigns – such as those concentrating on getting the troops out of the townships – were complemented by campaigns with a 'peace thrust' (candlelight vigils), as well as by cultural activities, including the production of a 'Forces Favourites' music tape. Both its broad base and the variety of campaigning methods used by the ECC allowed it to develop into a forceful movement, drawing support not only from the English-speaking community, but increasingly also from the Afrikaans community.

The ECC campaigns against conscription made it clear that conscription was used 'to implement and defend apartheid policies', to maintain South Africa's illegal occupation of Namibia, to destabilize neighbouring states', and that it conditioned people to accept militarization in addition to violating the internationally recognized right to freedom of conscience in relation to military service.[161] Furthermore, it began openly to challenge the state's strategy of securing peace 'by preparing for war' with its own belief in 'achieving peace through justice'.[162] Although demands for a 'just peace' were never fully articulated, various ECC members demanded as necessary preconditions the dismantling of apartheid and security legislation, the unbanning of organizations and the release of detainees and political prisoners, thus clearly expressing wider demands which were increasingly made elsewhere in the resistance movements. While the ECC never officially became an affiliate of the UDF – arguing that such a linkage would potentially damage its position within the white community – it was broadly perceived to participate in that wider resistance. By the mid-1980s, the strength of the ECC campaigns became apparent, and severe embarrassment was caused by the trials and sentencing of two activists in the late 1980s, as well as by the public declarations of consecutive groups of conscript resisters – 23 in 1987, 143 in 1988 and 771 in 1989 – who refused to do military service. On one such occasion, they issued the following joint statement, clearly contesting the SADF's construal of resisters:

> As loyal South Africans, we wish to contribute to the building of a peaceful and just society. The SADF violently maintains and propagates a fundamentally unjust and oppressive system. We cannot make a contribution to justice and peace and at the same time be part of the SADF.[163]

The response of the state to the ECC was brutal. More than a hundred activists were detained from periods ranging from a day to a year, while the organization itself was restricted under the Emergency measures and finally banned in November 1988. The state's offensive, however, did not go unchallenged. In April 1988, the Supreme Court issued a restraining order to the SADF restricting it from harassing the ECC. The overt harassment, however, was coupled with a series of covert measures characteristic of the repression of the late 1980s. In addition to the propaganda offensive, as one activist recalls, houses were petrol-bombed, vehicles sabotaged.[164] This took place in conditions in which there was a full-blown security psychosis, evident, *inter alia*, in the growth of 'airport-style' detectors in use at shopping malls, in the proliferation of local 'security firms' designed to protect white households, in the incitement to check under restaurant tables for possible bombs, and so forth. One of the documents disseminated during this period, entitled 'The Dangerous Game (of the ECC/END to End Conscription). A Conversation with Our Women and Our Young People' set the ECC campaign in the context of 1968 and American anti-Vietnam protests, arguing that

> [w]hat appears today like an innocent movement working for a 'just peace' or initiating 'constructive projects' in the community will be proved tomorrow as the cunning fraud of a hidden agenda to weaken the SADF so that Marxists can bring about the country's downfall, as they did in

> Vietnam. It is not surprising that the ECC is called the Peace and Freeze Movement. It reminds one of the protest marches in Europe two years ago under the banner: 'Better Red, than Dead.'[165]

In familiar fashion, the pamphlet drew equivalences between organizations as diverse as the SACC, headed by Dr Beyers Naude, the Black Sash, the South African Catholic Bishops' Council, NUSAS, the Anglican and Methodist churches, the UDF, the PFP Youth, SWAPO, the ANC and the SACP.[166] The basis for these equivalences were said to be an 'undergound agenda' of conflict and destruction coupled with an 'above-ground' agenda of 'flattery and fine-sounding words like "peace" and "justice"' bound to fool 'the Christian, the uninformed, gullible person'. Analysing the motives and emblems of the ECC, mothers were called upon to alert their children and young people to the 'onslaught on the white mind', consisting in ECC arguments that 'border warfare' in South Africa was unjust, and that conscription was 'unchristian and unbiblical', and to join a Support National Service campaign. In 'The Rape of Peace', Veterans for Victory offered a similar analysis of the ECC, arguing that the SADF protected 'all we believe in and without this force the country would be vulnerable to anarchy and revolution, leading to a minority African style dictatorship'.[167] It claimed to unmask the ECC as a collection of 'misguided individuals and clergy who are being used as pawns in the international web of intrigue constituting the "peace movement"', which could be traced back to the 'World Peace Council . . . linked to Moscow' thus playing on the old set of overdeterminations established between any resistance to apartheid and the 'total onslaught'.

After providing a 'history' of war resistance and of international connections between war and conscription resister organizations, the intimate organizational links between the ANC, the UDF, JODAC and the ECC was used to deligitimate the campaign against conscription.[168] What is evident in all these materials is that the need to respond to the challenge of an 'unjust', 'unchristian' war by the ECC struck deep in the white community and forced those defending the system into falling back onto the old constructions of the communist-inspired enemy. The strength of the ECC campaigns and the degree of the state's reaction, however, make it abundantly clear that a discursive parading of 'enemies of the state' no longer had the effect it once had.

That these portrayals were by no means isolated left-overs from a previous era was clear in government and government-sponsored documents on 'negotiation with the enemy'. In June 1986, a year after the government already started engaging in secret 'talks' with Nelson

Mandela, the government issued a document entitled 'Talking with the ANC . . .' which offered an analysis of the ANC/SACP alliance's strategy of a two-stage revolution and set the government's views on violence over and against that of the alliance in a manner which re-emphasized the division between 'moderates' and 'radicals'.[169] Quoting a statement made by Joe Modise on 1 December 1985 on Radio Freedom, which called for the identification and killing of collaborators and enemy agents, the Bureau for Information contrasted the state's use of legitimate means to 'maintain order' to that of the ANC, who were 'instigators of unrest':

> It is common knowledge that innocent and moderate people are the victims of the so-called 'necklace' executions in public, people who do not support the violent aims of the ANC. . . . They are the ones who are being coerced and intimidated to toe the line of violence. In the name of freedom and democracy, moderate Blacks are being robbed of their freedom of choice – for peace. . . . From the start of the unrest in September 1984 until 22 April 1986, 508 people, mostly moderate Blacks, were brutally murdered by radical Blacks. . . . Since September 1984 no less than 1 417 Black owned businesses, 4435 private homes . . . 28 churches, 54 community centres, . . . all serving the Black community – were either totally destroyed or badly damaged.[170]

In what was a direct response to the ANC's setting of conditions for negotiations, the document argued that negotiations 'will not be conducted with the SACP, international or national terrorist groups or other fanatics'.[171] Moreover, it argued that 'all reasonable people would like to see peaceful and negotiated solutions to the problems of our country', thus contributing to the construction of opposition forces as somehow irrational and bent on destruction of good order. Similarly, on the occasion of the renewal of the State of Emergency in 1986, and later again in 1989, it was argued that the emergency regulations were not aimed at the 'normal activities of law-abiding citizens', but at radical and revolutionary 'elements', such as the 'faceless comrades' in the townships, the ANC, SACP, UDF and COSATU. The fact of the unbanning of the ANC and the SACP in February 1990, taken in the context of the ongoing demonization of the resistance movements, thus calls for further explanation.

Towards negotiations: explaining De Klerk

The unbannings of 2 February 1990 have to be put into the wider context of challenges facing an increasingly divided state in the late

1980s. Foremost amongst these were the already mentioned international sanctions and disinvestment campaigns, the increasing inability of the state to contain the domestic waves of resistance, the military defeat at Cuito Cuanavale in Angola and the growing dominance of the revived Congress tradition, with its language of non-racialism, within both the black and white extra-parliamentary arenas. By the late 1980s, the dominant bloc was faced with the failure of the transformist project, and it lost support both to the left and to the right. It was beginning to become clear that it had lost the battle for legitimacy within the white community. Moreover, there were significant divisions within the NP itself which once again began to surface.

As on previous occasions, the different factions in the NP were divided on the question of the extent, tempo and content of reforms to be implemented. This time, however, a small group of 'radical reformers' wanted to change the status quo by means of a new basic philosophy and new procedures, moving towards real negotiations with black leaders.[172] By contrast to the 'conservative reformers' who were satisfied with the pace of progress, this group felt that attempts to get significant black leaders to the negotiation table appeared to have reached a stalemate, which the National Statutory Council announced in 1988 could not overcome.[173] The main characteristic of the approach by the radical reformers was 'an openness to a multiplicity of possibilities': they were prepared to compromise on matters previously considered to fall outside of the realm of the negotiable. They argued for a negotiation process in which the government of the day would fully recognize its transitory status, that is, the fact that it was to be replaced by a representative government. Moreover, they argued that negotiation should take place not on the basis of racial groups, but on the grounds of free association and disassociation around differing ideas and philosophies.[174] Negotiation, in their view, would aim to find a constitutional model which would protect rights by means of a bill of rights and a constitutional court, and which would be based upon a decentralization of power to regional governments, together with a federative pattern in one Parliament. When De Klerk took over from Botha, however, first as party leader and later as State President, it was clear that he was not considered to be one of the group of radical reformers.

Before discussing the changes wrought under De Klerk's leadership, which would culminate in the unbannings of 2 February 1990, it is necessary briefly to evaluate the overall effects of the waves of resistance and repression which wrecked the unity of 'white politics' and which began to dissolve the alliance between the business community, the state and the security apparatuses. While the foregoing account may lead one to think that the events of February 1990 were a foregone conclusion, such an evaluation would be misleading. By the end of 1988, a mood of despondency characterized the country. With most activists imprisoned, detained or killed, with restrictions on the press harsher than ever before, there was a feeling that the state's repressive strategies had, to some extent, succeeded. The democratic movement was driven underground, and was forced to rethink its strategy. While during the mid-1980s it was generally assumed that the regime's fall was imminent, this possibility now seemed far removed from reality. This situation was, however, not to be permanent. South Africa was under pressure from its traditional Western allies to enter into a negotiation process with the ANC; negotiations after the military defeat in Angola were underway for Namibian independence; and the detrimental effects of sanctions on the economy continued. Internally, the pressure from resistance movements was again being stepped up in the course of 1989. Most important in this respect was the defiance campaign launched in August 1989 by the MDM. Even though organizational networks had not recovered from the years under the State of Emergency, political consciousness was such that large numbers of people could be mobilized in their absence.

The defiance campaign consisted of the 'self-unbanning' of organizations outlawed under the State of Emergency and challenged racially segregated institutions such as hospitals. In September 1989, a legal, peaceful protest march was held in the streets of Johannesburg for the first time in over forty years, and similar mass demonstrations took place in Cape Town and Pretoria. Significantly, at almost all the events associated with the defiance campaign, the self-unbanning of internal organizations occurred together with a defiance of the ban placed on the ANC. As one commentator remarked at the time:

> Where people unbanned the Congress of South African Students (COSAS), they also unbanned the ANC. Where they illegally flaunted their UDF T-shirts and banners, they also unfurled the black, green and gold flag.[175]

This was further evidence of the extent to which the language of nonracialism, associated historically with the Congress tradition and with the UDF in the mid-1980s, had succeeded in becoming the dominant political language in which to express resistance across communities traditionally divided by apartheid. In this sense, a new regime of truth was in the process of being established. The forces of opposition triumphed in that they succeeded in capturing the moral and intellectual high-ground of the struggle.

The same year, 1989, also saw the fall of the Berlin Wall and the collapse of the former Soviet Union. While its consequences were not immediately apparent within South Africa – neither with respect to the effect it would have on the resistance movement, nor on the NP – it clearly played a most significant role in the thinking which led to the unbanning of the ANC and SACP. For this to become a reality, De Klerk had to take over the reins of the NP and the government. In this respect, it has to be made clear that while De Klerk, as an individual, certainly played an important and even crucial part in the process of unbanning, the space for his emergence was created by conditions largely outside of his control. That this is so is evident in the numerous articles appearing in the wake of the unbannings which sought in vain for evidence in his earlier political career of an 'enlightened' attitude. Indeed, he was held to be a cautious, albeit, pragmatic leader, and it is the latter facet of his leadership style which predominated in the context of the late 1980s. Given the failure of the security-dominated strategy to set into place the conditions necessary for peace in South Africa, it is not insignificant that De Klerk's political career followed a trajectory very different from that of Botha and Vorster before him. One of the first, and potentially most radical, acts of De Klerk was to dismantle the NSMS and to reinstitute 'civilian' control over the political process, with the Department of Constitutional Planning and Development once again taking a lead in the process of policy formulation. However, as was evident in the years between the unbanning of the ANC and the April 1994 elections, De Klerk's relation to the security establishment remained riddled with tensions, for he could not afford to alienate it and neither could it be ruled out as a fall-back option should negotiations fail. It is in this context that the moribund features of the interregnum appeared, with the number of politically related deaths soaring to heights outstripping the worst periods of repression under apartheid, and in which speculation about the operation of a 'third force' was rife. These and other features of the period preceding the first non-racial general elections will be discussed in chapter 6. Suffice it to say here that although De Klerk's courageous, proactive step on 2 February 1990 opened a wholly new phase in South African politics, it was to be marked by many of the old features of the regime. The unbanning of the ANC, SACP and other proscribed organizations by De Klerk, thus, was not the result simply of a single individual's actions. While De Klerk has to be credited with taking the step that would place South Africa on the path to full democratization, he occupied an enunciative space which was created by conditions both without and within the country. In that sense, 'De Klerk' is nothing but a signifier around which irresistible pressures for reform coagulated, a space which would be marked by all the tensions of a project of radical change in conditions open to articulation in a variety of directions.

Conclusion

In conclusion, it is necessary to draw out the analytical and theoretical consequences of my analysis of the organic crisis. Contrary to an account which locates the core of the organic crisis in the 'structural' contradictions in the economy, I have argued that those conditions did not and could not produce an organic crisis in and of themselves. They only contributed to the production of a series of dislocatory logics which had to be politically articulated into a project capable of challenging the logic upon which the apartheid imaginary was founded. It is, therefore, only once this basic logic was put into question that the possibility of the creation of a new myth, capable of accounting for the dislocations, and thus of establishing a new principle of reading which could suture those dislocations, came into being.

The production of such a myth had to fulfil two interrelated functions. On the one hand, it had to articulate a new project, capable of introducing a new mode of social division, and, on the other, it had to disarticulate the form of social division upon which the apartheid imaginary was based. It therefore had to engage simultaneously in a process of articulation and disarticulation. For the latter to be possible, elements of the old imaginary had to become floating signifiers, available for rearticulation. This became a possibility as a result of the failure of the transformist project launched by the NP in the late 1970s. This project depended upon the capacity to construct a new 'historic bloc', consisting of a new alliance forged around an increasingly deracialized political discourse, in defence of 'free enterprise' and security, and resting upon the unity between the forces of 'moderation' – all of those elements of the political formation included in the systems of difference articulated by the transformist project: the sections of the coloured and Indian population taking part in the tri-cameral Parliament, moderate black 'homeland' leaders, the urban black middle class supported by the conservative Black Local Authorities, the business community and, finally, the white population.

While it was apparent from the early 1980s that the wider black community rejected the reforms aimed at co-opting them, it was not until the launch of the drive to disarticulate the elements drawn together into the 'white' section of the dominant bloc that the force of the new language of non-racialism became apparent. The business community increasingly came to distance themselves from the regime in the mid-1980s. Their resistance to apartheid – conceived in the limited form of racial domination – could be argued to have strengthened the defence of capitalism and free enterprise in the dominant discourse and therefore contributed to the dimension of limited deracialization present in the discourse of the regime. The fact that their vocal resistance waned by 1988, when it seemed that the repression had been at least minimally successful, contributes to this reading. Nevertheless, their continued contact with the ANC and the UDF/MDM did remove or at least weaken their fears of a future ANC-dominated polity. In this sense, the de-demonization of the ANC/SACP alliance did serve to open possibilities previously absent.

The disarticulation of the ambiguous security discourse, which attempted to produce 'white unity' while simultaneously fostering alliances between moderates across the racial divide, was decisive in subverting the logic of apartheid. Throughout the 1980s, increasingly more complex political frontiers were contructed around this ambiguous discourse. The security discourse did not only contain the tension of an 'undecidability' between white unity and the construction of alliances of moderates, but at times entered into explicit contradiction of other dimensions of the faltering reform process. While one of the crucial elements of the reform process consisted in the creation and sustaining of a settled, urban black middle class, support for vigilante groups more often than not led to a situation in which migrant workers were supported against township dwellers, so undermining the strategy of fostering a compliant settled urban population which increasingly aligned itself with the non-racialism of the UDF and COSATU. In countering this tendency through the WHAM strategy, further resentment was fuelled against the very population at which the strategy of incorporation was aimed. The process of construction of a white security psychosis had similar contradictory effects. The combined effects of the absence of an attempt to interpellate white workers into the transformist project and the creation of a security psychosis in the white community were to lead to an increasing bleeding of support to the right of the NP. Attempts to stem this phenomenon by focusing on 'law and order' and by cracking down on resistance movements in the context of elections did not and could not supplant the absence of a more intensive drive to incorporate them into the reformist discourse. Similar tensions marked the nature of the discourse through which women were to be interpellated into the security discourse: the construction of the 'enemy' included not only the traditional figures of the ANC, 'Marxists', and so forth, but also mainstream white movements such as Women for Peace. It is also in this terrain that the contestation between the churches and the regime increasingly took place, with the extra-parliamentary movements quickly gaining the upper hand in the battle for moral victory.

In the face of the severe repression and violence which tore the country apart between 1984 and 1988, and in the face of campaigns around, for instance, the detention of children, it was no longer possible for the regime to justify its repressive policies in the name of the annihilation of an increasingly ambiguous 'enemy'. In the absence of a successful strategy for creating the conditions necessary for further reforms, and in a context in which many of the reforms themselves were beginning to put into question the territorial and spatial aspects of the apartheid imaginary, the impotence of that imaginary became increasingly apparent to all those who were supposed to form the central elements of the new historic bloc. Reforms and modes of repression became more and more reactive, and the regime appeared to have lost the initiative in restructuring the social and political terrains. Under these conditions, a number of central signifiers around which reform was constructed became available for rearticulation. The contestation around the terms 'justice', 'democracy for all', 'normalcy' and 'reasonableness', to name but a few, bears witness to this. Indeed, it could be argued that the very appearance of those terms in the political language of the regime is evidence of the extent to which it was forced to respond to the newly dominant language of non-racialism. Attempts to construct its township-upgrading efforts in the name of the 'workers' and the 'people' provide further support of the shifting grammar of politics.

It is in this context that the activities of the UDF/MDM within the white community have to be seen. The discourse of non-racialism articulated around the Freedom Charter and in the tradition of the Congress movement first became the dominant political language in black communities in the early 1980s, supplanting the language of Black Consciousness. Through the actions of extra-parliamentary movements working within white communities this discourse increasingly succeeded in articulating those who were disaffected with the regime to the project of a democratic South Africa. While it would be wrong to argue that the language of non-racialism became dominant *tout court* in the white community, it did succeed in interpellating active sections of the community, and decisively contributed to the deligitimation of the regime. It is as a result of this loosening of traditional allegiances that the relative success of De Klerk's unbannings and the fact that he succeeded in taking the bulk of the white population with him have to be seen. The February 1990 unbannings took place in a context in which the ANC/SACP/MDM/COSATU alliance was still demonized by the regime. Overnight the enemy of the state was transformed into an ally at the negotiation tables. Not having prepared the ground for this decisive action could have had disastrous consequences. Paradoxically, the ground for it was already prepared by the MDM as a result of the delegitimation of the regime. There was general dissatisfaction with the economic conditions in the country; the lives of most urban whites as well as those of farmers living in remote areas had become almost impossibly limited by fears of attacks, and there was a widespread sense that the NP had lost the initiative to the forces of resistance. In this context, De Klerk appeared as the figure who could regain this initiative. In this respect, his conservative background and pragmatism served him well. They allowed him to construct a discourse of change which would nevertheless protect the values of 'white society'. In the stalemate of the late 1980s, he could occupy the ground prepared by the alliance of internal resistance movements, presenting an alternative to the project of non-racialism.

In conclusion, it could be argued that insofar as apartheid could be regarded as exemplary of the modern desire for order and for cultural unity, it produced the conditions of its own disarticulation.[176] If, as Bauman proposes, we think of modernity as a time when order became a matter of thought, of a practice aware of itself, then it is also clear that the very notion could only become central insofar as the problem of order appeared. To put it differently, if an order is deeply sedimented, no problem of order is present. However, should such an order be shown to be but 'an order', its political nature will have been revealed and it may become a matter of contestation. No doubt it was hoped that separate development would be able to efface its own conditions of possibility, and therewith its particularity as a political project. Apartheid, under those circumstances, would have succeeded in becoming and remaining an imaginary horizon, providing an ever-expanding field of vision for the solving of societal crises.

The putting into question of that order, however, could not occur simply by opposing to it its diametrical other. The struggle for order feeds upon its other, chaos. This was abundantly clear in the situation of deepening crisis in the mid-1980s. As I have argued, any attempt to institute an alternative order presupposes a large degree of disarticulation of that pre-existing it. The generation of different principles for the shaping of society first had to undo the 'dialectically' related order–chaos polarity. This is precisely what occurred during the 1980s in South Africa. The conjunctural overdetermination increasingly produced phenomena which could no longer be represented in terms of the logic of apartheid, phenomena which escaped even its complex forms of simultaneous inclusion and exclusion. The political articulation of indeterminate elements finally succeeded in throwing the logic of apartheid into crisis.

Indeterminacy, thus, had a subversive potential precisely because it undermined the very logic of identity upon which the order–chaos polarity is founded. It resisted reduction to either of the categories, and thus subverted the very principle of oppositionality. However, as I have maintained, the production of indeterminacy in itself was not a sufficient condition for the transformation of conjunctural problems into an organic crisis. The possibility at least existed in principle that the ideologues of apartheid could have succeeded in bringing about a deracialization of social division without inducing a crisis. Were it not for the forces of resistance which drew attention to the particularistic nature of the transformist project, forcing the imaginary to contract, to expose its limits, making it impossible for the dominant discourse to determine the lines of inclusion and exclusion according to which the identity of the social was constituted, this may have been a possibility. However, the situation of indeterminacy was given a new articulating principle – that of a non-racial conception of identity – so providing a new principle of social division, and the seeds of a new imaginary around which a post-apartheid order could be reconstructed.

6

Competing Myths: In Search of a New Identity?

During the late 1980s, a context in which the failure of the transformist project and the disarticulation of the logic of apartheid became ever more evident, a number of myths competed in the attempt to re-suture the dislocated structure of the old, dying imaginary. In this chapter I aim to provide an overview of the various forms these myths took, and of their impact on the process of transition. The symbolic representation of forms of unity, and thus also of social division articulated in the discourses of the new NP, the far right and the Inkatha Freedom Party (IFP), all can be read – in varying degrees – as attempts to present alternative principles of ordering to the discourse of non-racialism associated with the ANC. The myths articulated by the new NP, the IFP and the far right all share a certain family resemblance which distances them from the vision of a post-apartheid society favoured by the ANC. It would, however, be a mistake to assume some essential continuity in those discourses, for it is precisely to the extent in which they succeed in resituating themselves within the horizon of a non-racial South Africa that their force and relevance for the period of transition, and beyond, is to be found. The discourse of non-racialism, clearly dominant in the construction of a post-apartheid order, will have to contend with and take account of these alternatives myths if a successful transition to democracy is to be instituted. For this reason, it is necessary to investigate more closely the manner in which these alternative myths were inserted into the changing domestic and international context of the late 1980s and early 1990s.

Associative Conceptions of Identity: The Non-Naturalness of Nationhood

> . . . one of the most important shifts in NP policy is the acceptance of the idea of one nation in an undivided South Africa. The process of nation-building in South Africa has been a long and painful one. It tended to be exclusive before it became inclusive. . . . With the implementation of the 1983 constitution, the South African nation became multi-racial, including also our Brown and Asian citizens. We accept now that the final step must be taken, namely, to replace this constitution with a new one which . . . will complete the broadening of nationhood to include all South Africans, regardless of racial or ethnic origin.[1]

This argument, presented by the Minister of Constitutional Affairs during the debate which followed the announcements of 2 February 1992, encapsulates many aspects of the new NP policy and vision for South Africa, which were to be fleshed out during the process of negotiation leading up to the April 1994 elections. Most importantly, it entailed a weakening of the intimate, necessary link between nationhood, ethno-racial difference and territoriality. As I have argued, this has been a process long in the making. However, whereas the NP construed it as the outcome of a natural, albeit painful, process, there was nothing natural or necessary about it. It occurred as the result of a long process of struggle over the nature of social division, and represented not a teleological culmination of history, but a final recognition of the untenability of continued racial division and discrimination, and of the inability to maintain the order based upon it.[2]

Both the NP, and some commentators on the event, have tended to present 2 February 1990 as a surprising moment, a moment of a break with the past. However, many of the elements which were to make up the discourse of the new NP were already present on the horizon during the mid-1980s. Foremost amongst these was the reformulation of the status of the 'group', one of the nodal points around which NP discourse was organized, which emerged as early as 1985.[3] From a position of absolute centrality, the idea of the group – based upon an *organic* conception of the *volkseie* – was increasingly marginalized during the later 1980s, to the point where it could be argued openly that while group rights had to be constitutionally protected, the position of the NP on this matter was by no means set in stone. Instead of a 'rigid attachment to race and colour as the basis for a definition of the group', there was a 'new realism' in the ranks of the NP.[4] This realism – which formed one of the core elements around which the increasingly pragmatic NP discourse was articulated – included a rejection of 'group domination', as well as of 'ideologically motivated obsessions with racial prejudice'.[5] These themes echoed the terms in which the redrawing of frontiers occurred with respect to the transformist project: already during the 1980s, ideology was opposed to a pragmatist stance which took account of the 'reality' of the situation. 'Reality', in NP discourse, determined the recognition of a multiplicity of groups, but the NP argued that it did not have any preconceived ideas as to the detail of a commonly acceptable framework for the protection of such multiplicity.

The formation of groups was no longer portrayed as amenable to legislation; rather, they had to be formed on the basis of freedom of association and individual choice. An 'open group' was envisaged for those individuals who would choose not to belong to any group.[6] Thus, instead of imposing 'group' boundaries from on high, the role of the state was now to offer legal protection to groups only once they were formed on a 'voluntary' basis. This emphasis on legality coincided with the argument that a balance had to be struck between the rights of groups and those of individuals, and this had to be based upon the elimination of discrimination on the grounds of race, colour or religion, or any other basis.[7] There is no denying of the equivocation in NP discourse, given the context of apartheid. The absurdity of the idea of individuals 'choosing' their group membership in that context is apparent. It is important, however, that the equivocation – based upon a simultaneous affirmation and problematization of the idea and status of 'groups' – facilitated the hegemonization of divergent demands present on the political landscape. It allowed the NP to retain white allegiance, while also accommodating the demands of those who saw 'group membership' as nothing but a foil for discrimination. This continued emphasis on the importance of the group – now supplemented by individual rights – also allowed the NP to mobilize support from segments of the coloured population. This was most apparent in the 1994 election materials distributed in the coloured community, which played upon the ambiguous relation between coloured and African.[8]

These strategic manoeuvrings were possible as a result of the ambiguity of the term 'groups', which tended to be deployed interchangeably with 'minorities', while being carefully distanced from 'racial' categorizations. De Klerk, for example, argued that

> [e]thnicity is a reality. . . . In South Africa, it will be important to ensure that all minorities – and South Africa is a country of minorities – feel

secure and that they should have the right to maintain and develop their respective identities. However, . . . because of our recent history, it is neither desirable not feasible to define minorities in purely ethnic terms. Accordingly, when we talk of the protection of minorities we are referring to linguistic, cultural, political, religious and social groups, and not to racial groups.[9]

While there was a clear retention of the ethnicist discourse of old, this was tempered, on the one hand, by the introduction of a discourse on 'individual rights' and, on the other, by arguments for the absence of a natural basis for nation-building:

The natural binding of one language and one culture, which is usually the cornerstone of nationhood, is absent here. Therefore, we will have to rely on the other cornerstone – that of communal values and ideals.[10]

In the absence of such a 'natural basis', the South African nation had to be built. It is this dimension of the discourse which increasingly led to a focus on an associative conception of the new nation, in the process of being born. In this manner, two contradictory elements were drawn together: existing (natural) cultural and linguistic divisions served as the basis from which a (non-natural) nation had to be built. The latter had to be fashioned on the basis of 'communal values' which were themselves in the process of formation. Moreover, those values – justice, and a recognition of basic freedoms for both individuals and groups – were articulated in the context of a precise determination: the need to eliminate the domination of one group over another.

At this point of intersection, the ambiguous discourse on 'group' identity was linked to democracy. In that discursive domain a conception of democracy had to be articulated which fulfilled two interrelated functions: it had to offer protection to 'minorities', while also forestalling the majoritarian system favoured by the ANC.[11] Thus, real democracy came to be seen as not simply based upon a universal franchise:

We talk about democracy . . . but the question is, what do we mean by it? . . . Sometimes it is described as . . . 'universal adult suffrage', 'one man, one vote' of as 'government by the majority'. . . . Those descriptions . . . may be facets of a democracy, but not one of them is adequate. In other words, the presence of a simple general right to vote is not sufficient to bring democracy into being. . . . It contains no deep moral justification for the will of the majority. Majorities also sometimes exercise oppression. . . . Oppression by a majority is as immoral and unacceptable as oppression by a minority.[12]

In this manner, the importance of 'minorities' and of the protection of their rights was weaved into the very substance of democracy in order to foreclose its radically egalitarian thrust. Moreover, it is important to note that the other side of the idea of a South Africa made up of a series of 'minorities' was a presumed 'majoritarian threat' constituting a danger to the continued existence of those minorities.

The process through which the consensus of values had to be attained also reflected earlier discursive mechanisms. Throughout the period of negotiation, the NP stressed the need to engage in consultation so as to reach consensus within a 'normalized' political process. One may argue that that is precisely what a process of negotiation entails. However, the very assumption of a 'level playing-field' on which different actors could engage was, of course, highly questionable. More important, though, was the underlying assumption of the function of negotiation which dovetailed with the recognition of the non-existence of a natural basis for nationhood. Negotiation had to produce that absent consensus, and it had to take place through the bringing together of leaders of different communities, of all those reasonable persons who rejected violence and conflict as a solution.[13] In this, the NP merely reactivated the grounds of existing frontiers. As I have argued, during the 1980s, the grounds for exclusion were increasingly deracialized, and a clear frontier was drawn between those who were reasonable, against violence, and working for evolutionary change, and those who were intent on destruction and conflict as a means to bring about a new order. Even with the ANC and other proscribed organizations unbanned – including the hard right *Blanke Bevrydingsbeweging* (White Liberation Movement) – this frontier did not lose its relevance, since it was refashioned to suit the new context. Hence, a strategy based upon reasonable negotiation now excluded 'radicals' not only on the left, but also on the right. The Minister of Law and Order made this abundantly clear in his contribution to the debate during the second session of Parliament in February 1990:

> . . . I want to focus attention on a very worrying phenomenon. . . . It is the presence of violence in various forms, from left-radical sources, but also particularly from right-reactionary ranks. The one is as dangerous and destructive as the other. I want to issue a warning. It is an abyss of chaos, bloodshed and limitless misery. . . .[14]

Negotiation could only take place once parties realized that they could, in the long run, 'not win the battle against their opponents by means of violence'.[15] The ANC, in particular, continued to be associated with violence in NP discourse, not only in terms of its past resistance strategies, but also in terms of what an ANC-led government would mean for the future of South Africa. While it was now argued that the ANC could no longer be regarded as a mere pawn of international communism, it was still associated with an unacceptable ideological position. Against that 'fanatical unreason', reason had to prevail.[16] And reason, in essence, was opposed to ideological dogmatism, which, as events is Eastern Europe had shown, was doomed to failure.[17]

In the redeployment of this frontier, the NP walked a tightrope with regard to its own past and the role of the past in the construction of a new order. In certain cases, it was claimed that the past was completed and, thus, had become irrelevant. Invocation of the past, in this respect, was positively harmful, since claims of 'injustice or alleged injustice' did not bring the country closer to a solution.[18] What all reasonable South Africans – the 'silent majority' – needed was hope, and suspicion and fears based upon the past worked against the fostering of hope. Moreover, with the events of 1989 a new order came into existence. That order vindicated the completion of the past in that it showed the failure of alternative conceptions of ordering the social. All action had, therefore, to be future-oriented, for if South Africans dwelt on the 'real or imagined sins of the past', they would never be able to find one another in the present. The emphasis on the present and future – at the expense of a recognition of past evils – played another key function. It allowed the NP to proclaim itself as the instigator of change. When Nelson Mandela lit a flame of freedom on Robben Island on 2 February 1994, a full-page advertisement proclaimed: 'Today Mr Mandela honours President De Klerk.'[19] The unbanning of the ANC and the process of negotiation were paraded as achievements of the NP, and this necessitated a foreclosure of the reasons why that unbanning was necessary in the first place.

In other circumstances, however, invoking the past was necessary insofar as it functioned as a means to establish the 'reality' of the South African political landscape. I have already shown how this was accomplished with respect to the pertinence of 'group' differences. A similar argumentative strategy was used with regard to the ANC, though, producing the opposite effect: the ANC's past referred to its history as a movement unscrupulous in its use of violence. Its continued allegiance to 'outdated ideologies' reinforced that image. The past was thus relevant where it was useful, either in establishing the structure of reality, or in discrediting opponents. Even as violence mounted during the four years of transition, this structure of argumentation stayed in place. Evidence of the operation of a government-sponsored 'third force' was denied, and the reasons for violence were ascribed to those old images informing the 'colonial imaginary', only now more closely articulated to the presence of ideological dogmatism:[20]

> I am worried about the continued political intolerance and the inciting rhetoric which stimulates violence. . . . Those who tell their supporters that they could take by violent means what they could not attain through negotiation are at the forefront of those who want to blame the government. . . . As long as we seek to place the blame elsewhere, and as long as we do not engage in questioning and disciplining ourselves, the violence will not come to an end. As long as the ANC and Inkatha accuse one another and tell their supporters that it is the other which is threatening them . . . violence will not end.[21]

While the causes of violence tended to be treated in a relatively neutral fashion, this neutrality was belied when it came to naming the perpetrators of violence: those who differed *ideologically* from one another in the black community; hostel dwellers, squatters and other inhabitants of black townships; *rebellious* citizens who resisted actions of the security forces; and white right-wing individuals and groups.[22] While it was rarely made explicit, it is clear that the construal of violence traded upon images associated with the absence of reasonableness and associated with some inherent inability to act in a tolerant manner.[23] In the same fashion, public protests and mass meetings were declared to be inimical to democracy and the forces of peace and goodwill.[24] All forms of 'conflict' were argued to be 'unnecessary', since all 'reasonable aims' could be attained through peaceful negotiations.[25] Indeed, it was argued that the true democratic nature of negotiation was under threat

> . . . when mass action and related activities are used as blackmailing mechanisms. Negotiation implies that parties try to convince one another by means of the exchange of arguments in a debate. . . . To use force in the form of mass action or boycotts of participation . . . when you do not get your own way is to disregard the true meaning of negotiation.[26]

The rejection of ideological dogmatism also referred to the central question concerning the modelling of a future economic order. Here, as well, the events of 1989 played a crucial role in discrediting any alternative to the model of free marketeering which was so ardently embraced by the NP during the dying years of apartheid:

In Africa and Eastern Europe the socialist/communist economic order has failed miserably. Our neighbouring state Mozambique has officially altered its policy. Other neighbouring states are moving either quietly or openly away from Marxism, because their people are hungry. There is calamity in the economic domain. The ANC and others who associate with it will either have to distance themselves from that failed economic system, or will have to defend it.[27]

Despite the stark changes in context marking the early 1990s, the extent to which the central political frontiers which informed the NP's discourse had been refashioned remained limited and premissed upon many of the presuppositions informing the last phases of the reform process. While it is no doubt true that the legal entrenchment of racial privilege had decisively come to an end and, in that respect, a radical break with apartheid orthodoxy finally was instituted, it is equally true that the continuities in the discourse of the new NP with that of the old remain a potent force.

From Apartheid to *Volkstaat*

South Africa is being treated to intimidating and often bizarre displays of right-wing anger and aggression. Vigilantes have attacked black protest marches. Sjambok wielding 'Wit Wolve' [White Wolves] hoot like owls while on night patrol in white suburbs. Calls are made for 'a million weapons for a million whites'. Pig's heads and pot-shots have been aimed at the country's Jewry and the British embassy respectively. A child's coffin and 30 pieces of silver has been cast down on the doorsteps of the State President's office in the Union Buildings.[28]

As was the case in the immediate aftermath of the Second World War, South Africa since the late 1980s has been witness to a proliferation of 'weird and wonderful' extra-parliamentary right-wing groupings.[29] Fears of a right-wing *coup* or at the least of extremely disruptive activities on the side of the white right just before the April 1994 elections, in the wake of the abortive 'battle for Bop', were frequently expressed, both by political leaders and by the press. The fact that these fears did not materialize, and that resistance activities were limited to a number of car-bomb attacks during the election period itself, can, at least in part, be attributed to the decision by the *Vryheidsfront* (VF, Freedom Front) to participate in the general election. What is of importance here is the question of the vision of a future South Africa which informed that decision, for it is this which has the potential to make of the contemporary hard white right not an irritating, temporary hindrance on the road to a non-racial society – one which will gradually become irrelevant and will eventually disappear as processes of creating a non-racial society and of nation-building gain momentum – but a relatively permanent feature of the political landscape in the foreseeable future.[30]

In order to provide an account of the nature of the myth informing the discourse of the contemporary white right it is necessary, first, to relate it to the 'tradition' of Afrikaner nationalism.[31] There are several reasons why situating an account of the re-emergence and force of the far right in that tradition may be enlightening.[32] Foremost amongst these is the fact that twentieth-century white South African political history has displayed a marked tendency to fragment to the right, producing a proliferation of groupings who regard themselves as the true inheritors of 'Afrikaner nationalism'. This tendency was not only apparent in the aftermath of the Second World War, but continued throughout the period of apartheid rule. Moreover, the rapid shifts in NP discourse away from its traditional concern with the *volkseie* during the 1980s can correctly be argued to provide support for the argument that the veritable proliferation of hard right movements since the late 1980s has to be interpreted in the light of certain continuities in white political history. The discourses of many of the hard right movements, like that of the NP earlier, have also been dominated by anti-semitism, anti-capitalism of a national socialist variety, biblical apocalyptic imagery and an espousal of the allegedly 'true' values of the white Afrikaner *volk*. Seen from the perspective of an increasing movement of the NP towards the middle-ground of white politics, and towards an associative rather than an organic conception of identity, these movements can be read as attempting in turn to reoccupy the ground left by consecutive shifts in NP discourse. The argument for historical continuity, namely that these movements have to be understood primarily in terms of the history of the far right in South African politics, does, however, have severe limitations. One of the most important of these is the fact that an emphasis solely on historical continuity runs the risk of losing sight of the specificity, and thus of the dimensions of novelty, of these discourses.

While most analyses of contemporary hard right discourses give attention to the significance therein of ideas of 'self-determination' and the maintenance of identity, they generally fail to take note of the fact that in these discourses a new historical object came into being: that of a *volkstaat*. Most often, the idea of a *volkstaat* is treated as a mere continuation of the 'homelands' discourse of the NP. Such arguments hold that a certain section of Afrikaners, in the face of changing circumstances within the country, are now simply demanding a separate territorially based state which differs little from that of the earlier NP discourse of 'separate development'. This characterization, if applied to the now practically defunct KP, may be accurate, for its proposals for an independent Afrikaner state carry the same overt racist assumptions as the NP's discourse of old.[33] It would, however, be misleading simply to view the *volkstaat* idea in these continuist terms. In order to counter this argument, it is necessary to look more closely at the emergence of the *volkstaat* discourse on which the myth of the right is based.[34]

In April 1993, shortly after the assassination of Chris Hani, an umbrella organization, the *Afrikaner Volksfront* (AVF, Afrikaner People's Front), was launched in Pretoria under the leadership of a number of generals, in order to co-ordinate right-wing attempts to establish a *volkstaat*.[35] The presence of a significant number of generals in these ranks led to a sea-change in the manner in which right-wing ideology was perceived.[36] No longer regarded as the delusions of a conglomeration of marginal, bearded, noisy fanatics, the *volkstaat* idea gained greater legitimacy under the mainstream right, not least because one of the prominent public figures involved in it – General Constand Viljoen – was considered to be a military leader of excellence, and commanded widespread support from former white conscripts and para-military organizations, as well as from substantial sections of the SAP and the SADF.

Concerted efforts were being made to draw the far right into a negotiation process. A Conservative Dialogue programme was created by IDASA under the leadership of General Viljoen's brother, Braam Viljoen, aiming to bring together the ANC and the AVF in negotiation. Soon after the initial round of negotiations, the process broke down as a result of the unacceptability of the AVF proposals to the ANC.[37] Problems were of both a practical and an ideological character: Who were the 'Afrikaners' to be included in such a *volkstaat*? What was to happen to Afrikaners outside that territory, were it to be established? What about 'non-Afrikaners' within such a territory? How would it be practically possible to test the mandate of the AVF?[38] As the general elections which were to mark the formal end to apartheid drew closer, these issues became ever more pressing, and eventually led to a split within the AVF between those who were prepared to participate in the elections and hardliners who refused. This split produced another organization, the VF, under the leadership of Constand Viljoen.[39] In order to understand something of the similarities and difference between these two groupings, it is necessary to take a closer look at their respective views on strategy, geographical location and the composition of a *volkstaat*.

The AVF, which initially could claim the support of twenty-one right-wing organizations, including the powerful Transvaal and Orange Free State Agricultural Unions, argues for continued extra-parliamentary resistance and a struggle for self-determination outside of the negotiation and electoral processes, based upon a principled decision not to take part in forums and elections which have no legitimacy in its eyes.[40] Its vision for a future South Africa, which echoes the KP proposals for a confederation of Southern African states, is based upon a rejection of both apartheid and a unitary state as a solution to the plight of Afrikaners. Drawing freely on examples from contemporary politics, ranging from Bosnia and Rwanda to Northern Ireland and Palestine, it argues in the familiar rhetoric of the old National Party that peace and stability can only be gained in a context where peoples (*volkere*) are separated. As a result it holds a rather apocalyptic vision of the new non-racial South Africa, stating that it will inevitably fail. Here it points to the war in KwaZulu/Natal. In the case of the AVF it is easy to expose the rhetoric, and to find overt expressions of racism which render the articulation problematic. For instance, in response to a question on the definition of Afrikanerhood, an AVF spokesperson made it clear that the issue of membership could easily be settled by applying a language pronunciation test.[41] This test, reminiscent of tests under apartheid for the determination of racial identity, was clearly designed to exclude coloured South Africans from a *volkstaat*.

The situation with regard to the VF is somewhat more complicated. Like the AVF, this organization situates itself self-consciously in the present. This, however, is based on a far more informed analysis of changes in the international context. Referring to the recently won 'self-governing status' of Palestine, the VF holds that its struggle today, far from being anachronistic, is wholly in step with developments in our contemporary world.[42] Moreover, it tends to distance itself from earlier nationalist attempts to establish ethnically based 'democracies'.[43] The problem with those attempts, according to the VF, is that they were based upon blatant racism. In contrast to this, the VF has attempted to draw a distinction between the illegitimate racial basis of apartheid and legitimate ethnic forms of identification in our contemporary world.[44]

Shortly before the April elections, General Constand Viljoen negotiated a deal to the effect that the issue of self-determination be written into the constitution.[45] This concession was described by the VF as 'wrenching open a door for the continuation of ethnic politics in South Africa'.[46] Another measure agreed upon between the NP, ANC and the VF shortly before the April 1994 elections made provision for the formation of a statutory council, a *Volkstaatraad*, with the task of reporting to the Constituent Assembly on the feasibility of creating a *volkstaat*. In this respect it is important to note that the VF is already working on what is called the 'internationalization of the Afrikaner question' – an attempt to get international recognition of Afrikaners as a threatened minority – and has embarked upon a programme of establishing contacts with senior members of the UN, of the Commonwealth and the Organization of African Unity in order to create the climate in which the fifty-fourth independent state in Africa may be created via constitutional means. Since the elections, the idea of full independence has, however, been dropped. In its stead, the VF has engaged in a series of fact-finding missions to Belgium and Switzerland to investigate alternative methods of establishing Afrikaner 'territories', short of full independence. In outlining the practical implementation of such 'territories', Viljoen has argued for a 'canton' system to be employed in combination with elected councils for Afrikaners outside of these areas.

In all of this, the vexed question remains as to who the members of such an 'Afrikaner *volkstaat*' would be. While the AVF and other far right organizations affiliated to it have been vocal about the need for a racial component to this identity, the VF has been less forthcoming on this point. It insists on the fact that it is a 'non-racial' organization (simply not taking 'race' as a criterion of qualification) and that it therefore is quite at home in contemporary South Africa.[47] This view has been reinforced in their recent proposals for the basis upon which councils should be elected. Viljoen has explicitly rejected a racial basis for an electoral roll, favouring instead 'occupation groups', and has argued on numerous occasions that the 'old politics of race' has to be rejected.[48] This, however, is not the whole story, for representatives of the organization have also argued that the *volk* will have to decide the issue of membership, thus leaving the door open to racial politics.[49] This suspicion is further reinforced by the emphasis in their discourse on 'non-artificial', that is, 'organic', forms of ethnicity and community, as well as in their open denial of full citizenship rights to 'others' who may find themselves within the boundaries of such a *volkstaat*.

Situated, then, in the overdetermined context of the failure of apartheid, the emergence of ethno-nationalism in our contemporary world and the beginnings of a process of democratization underway on the African continent, the far right in some respects continues the tradition of identitary politics found in its most extreme form in apartheid. However, as I have argued, this has been rearticulated to 'fit' the context of a radically altered international situation. This, in my view, problematizes a simple continuist interpretation of the politics of the far right. The emergence of these groupings in the context of the late 1980s introduced an element of discontinuity which is crucial to understand if one is to come to terms with the possible impact these discourses may have on the transition to democracy underway in South Africa today. While it is quite clear that there is no singular understanding of what a *volkstaat* entails, of where it could be situated, and even of whether it should take a territorial form, I would argue that the idea of a *volkstaat* plays a similar role in hard right discourse to that which the *volkseie* played in NP discourse up to the mid-1980s.[50] That is, despite the differences in interpretation, it now functions as an empty signifier, binding together a series of disparate and sometimes conflicting elements into a coherent discourse which attempts to provide a principle of reading for the dislocations experienced by large sections of the white South African population during the late 1980s. Out of a conglomeration of white right-wing groupings, a project has been consolidated around the idea of the *volkstaat* which cannot be regarded as a mere continuation of racist politics. The *volkstaat* idea acts as a new myth in which a rearticulated conception of ethnicity, as distinct from race, has found a place. And it is precisely the new context in which it is asserted which makes it a far more ambiguous conception of (ethnic) difference than the explicitly racist form which ethnicism took under apartheid. It is this dimension which is crucial to understanding the contemporary significance of this movement, and it is also this which tends to be overlooked in analyses which focus only on continuities in the discourse of the far right. The mere fact of a certain repetition of 'ethnicist' elements in the discourse of the far right should not, therefore, lead one to assume that the form this discourse takes can be regarded as simply another articulation of apartheid. Such a reading would miss the crucial factors which may lead this discourse to gain some legitimacy in the context of a contemporary non-racial South Africa.[51]

Whether or not it will prove a dead-end for the hard right will largely depend upon three factors: firstly, the support it can muster from a broad cross-section of whites; secondly, the question as to whether a truly non-racial, non-discriminatory conception of identity could be developed on which a *volkstaat* is to be based; and thirdly, on whether an acceptable constitutional form for it can be found within the confines of a unitary state. In the shorter term, it could be argued to fulfil a positive function insofar as it has marginalized those elements of the hard right which have been intent on starting a 'third war of liberation'. In the longer term, its viability will depend on the degree to which non-racialism succeeds in providing a mechanism for drawing together the disparate elements of South African society. It is only in the unlikely event of a total failure of that project that the gloomy scenario sketched by elements of the far right may become a reality.

The Spectre of 'Tribalism'

> Because we have conquered at the level of KwaZulu and at the level of local government, . . . we have developed a position of strength. We have created a springboard from which we can go forth to conquer in ever widening circles.[52]

The possibility of a successful institution of a non-racial imaginary depends crucially on its ability to negotiate a long-term settlement with forces opposed to that project. In addition to those discussed above, one such force is Inkatha. Several commentators on the prospects for democracy in a post-apartheid South Africa have argued that the emergence of the 'tribal' factor in 1990 poses serious questions for the period of transition to democracy.[53] By contrast to the commonly held opinion of the late 1980s and early 1990s that Inkatha was the chief instigator of the violence and the force which unilaterally aimed at preventing a democratic settlement, more nuanced accounts of the role of Inkatha and its relation to the ANC/NP-dominated negotiation process are now emerging.[54] These accounts invariably deal with the violence which wracked KwaZulu/Natal and then later the townships on the Witwatersrand, and they question the all too easy assumption that the violence could be accounted for wholly with reference to the role of 'tribalism'.[55] In explaining the violence associated with Inkatha, it is necessary to take into consideration a complex overdetermination of factors: political differences and competition between Inkatha and the ANC; class and ethnic divisions re-emerging with the weakening of apartheid in conjunction with a competition for the allocation of resources; the weakening of and challenges to 'traditional values' by young urban activists (comrades); the 'culture of violence' driven by a cycle of feuding over territory and resources; the presence of a 'third force' in the fuelling of violence; and the political presence of a tradition of separatism in the Natal region.

In any consideration of these factors, it is crucial to focus not only on the conjunctural deepening of the complex rivalries, but also on their genealogies and their continued importance for the future of a post-apartheid South Africa.[56] In this respect, it is useful to situate each of the elements in relation to the construction and dissolution of the complex frontiers around which apartheid was articulated. Apartheid clearly fostered and exploited ethnic divisions. As I have argued, it is crucial that those divisions are seen as neither archaic, primordial elements ingrained in the texture of South African politics and, therefore, impervious to change, nor as mere creations of the apartheid project which would vanish with its demise. Both of these readings fail to recognize that the pertinent questions here concern the reinvention and contestation of 'tradition', and the conditions under which they assume political relevance.[57] I have argued with respect to the construction of ethnicity in the Afrikaner nationalist movement that the articulation of a series of dislocations was crucial to the emergence and formation of ethnic forms of social division. The same is true for the more recent politicization of ethnicity and its relation to violence in the discourse of Inkatha: almost all the accounts of the violence stress the impact of the dislocations brought about by urbanization, high levels of unemployment and the breakdown of the traditional authority structures.[58] As Adam and Moodley argue, the call for cultural revival and the invocation of a mythical past and images of pride and success in battle offered a source of dignity and identity to the rural poor, the hostel dwellers and unemployed migrants.[59] Indeed, it is clear that much of the lines of division between warring factions – urban insiders and outsiders, inter-generational differences, ethnic divisions, and so forth – display an uncanny resemblance to the domains in which divisions were fostered during the apartheid era. It comes as no surprise, then, that as those divisions became increasingly tangled and complex – to the point of disintegration – antagonisms increasingly arose around them.

The important point in this respect concerns the political articulation given to them, and it is here that ideologico-political differences between the ANC and Inkatha, and their shifting positions on the national political stage, are of crucial importance, for they provide the frame within which social conflict took shape.[60] The decision of Inkatha in July 1990 to become a 'national' political force, rather than to remain active primarily in the KwaZulu/Natal region, resulted both from the perceived inroads the ANC succeeded in making in Natal and the increasing importance of the ANC's position as primary partner in negotiation with the NP. Both of these factors contributed to a sense that Inkatha's demands would remain unaddressed where negotiation took place between the two main players. Inkatha's long-standing commitment to a 'federal' solution – in contrast to the ANC's insistence on the need for a unitary state form – was endangered by the centrality which the ANC assumed in the transition period.[61] This situation was not improved by the fact that Buthelezi's ambiguous alliance with the NP – based on his assumption of the position of a 'moderate outsider' – was under threat as a result of the incorporation of 'radicals' in the negotiation process.

Inkatha's position with regard to its preference for the form of the future dispensation has remained virtually unchanged since its inception.[62] Buthelezi has consistently argued for a 'federal' solution, entailing strong regional autonomy, not only for the KwaZulu/Natal region, but for South Africa as a whole. It is this position which first brought him into conflict with the ANC and which continues to be a serious bone of contention. This is so not only because of the form of the proposed solution, but also as a result of its tendency to undercut uniform, national-based forms of resistance to apartheid by advocating a 'special status' for the region.[63] The roots of this emphasis on the region's special status cannot be dissociated from the other elements to which it has been articulated: the nature of the democracy to be instituted and the need to take account of the imperative to avoid the domination of 'one group over another'. Buthelezi's increasing use of the 'tribal card' did not, therefore, come as a surprise.[64] The stress on a separate Zulu identity started very early in the life of the KwaZulu authority.[65] From the early 1970s Buthelezi, while arguing against the divisiveness of apartheid, maintained a strong emphasis on ethnic identity, and during the 1980s this was increasingly linked to a conception of Zulu nationhood.[66] This discourse contained a tension, reflective of the emphasis on representing both a regional ethnic constituency and black resistance to apartheid more generally. This doubling allowed Buthelezi to claim allegiance to the tradition of the founding fathers of the ANC, such that Inkatha became its real representative:

> Inkatha is structured on the ideals of the banned ANC as promoted in 1912. [Selby Msimang's] membership of Inkatha testified to the fact that it was not us in Inkatha who have deviated from the ideals [of the

> founding fathers]. The ideals of the founding fathers who were descendants of black warriors were structured on the foundation of non-violence and negotiations.[67]

For Buthelezi, the 'Mission in Exile', as the ANC was referred to during the period in which it was banned, was not the real ANC. Inkatha, with its preference for 'non-violent struggle, represented the values of that tradition.[68] This ambiguity in the discourse of Inkatha is what gave it the possibility to appeal to 'black unity' while simultaneously acting in terms of an extremely divisive 'Zulu nationalism'.[69]

In addition to this emphasis on Zulu separateness, Inkatha's position on both the economic front and the form of opposition to apartheid increasingly distanced it from the ANC, with whose approval it was intially set up. These issues also served to draw Inkatha deeper into the system which it proclaimed to fight. For Buthelezi, working 'within the system' meant that he could claim the establishment of 'liberated zones' within the borders of South Africa, while opposing that very order. However, instead of breaking with the system of social division associated with apartheid, the emphasis on regionalism and federalism – associated with an exclusive Zulu nationalism – drew Buthelezi into the ranks of 'moderates' while simultaneously distancing Inkatha from the wider national liberation movement. This became particularly apparent in the labour field after the launch of the United Workers' Union of South Africa by Inkatha. Already in 1987, Buthelezi laid the blame for the outbreak of violence around Pietermaritzburg at the feet of the ANC:

> In our Black townships the ANC Mission in Exile, working through surrogates (a term then used for the UDF, COSATU . . .), try and tip the South African scales in favour of violent solutions which will ensconse a Marxist one-party State in South Africa. You [the KwaZulu Police] will be serving in Black townships where the politics of intimidation combine with all kinds of criminal elements to sow discord and chaos.[70]

Inkatha thus echoed the construction of violence in the discourse of the regime. This starkly coincided with a growing intolerance towards any opposition in KwaZulu.[71] Inkatha's opposition to the UDF/COSATU alliance did not stem only from the threat it posed to its regional power base, but also from the very terms in which opposition was conceived. For Inkatha, the Marxism of the ANC 'surrogates' stood in direct opposition to its own espousal of capitalist free-marketeering. The latter was closely linked to its strategy of working within the system. Liberation, for Inkatha, was synonymous with upward mobility for blacks, and this required a strategy of 'infiltrating the economy'.[72] The implications of this strategy soon became clear as the full impact of the sanctions debate hit South Africa in the mid-1980s. Buthelezi held not only that workers would suffer as a result of any withdrawal of foreign investment, but that foreign investment would benefit the struggle for liberation. Consequently, Buthelezi placed himself in the camp of the most conservative foreign governments and sections of the business community.[73]

While all of these elements of Inkatha's discourse seemed to predispose it to remain an ally of the NP, the events of the early 1990s served to draw them apart. As the NP was drawn into bi-lateral 'talks about talks' with the ANC, Inkatha started making overtures to the hard right, who increasingly seemed to be its 'natural' partner in the negotiation process.[74] As Adam and Moodley have remarked, ideologically the black and white ethnic fundamentalists mirror each other in their intransigence to compromise, their advocacy of confrontation and their single-mindedness.[75] In October 1992, Inkatha participated in the formation of Concerned South Africans Group (COSAG) to protest against the bilateral agreements between the NP and the ANC. By October 1993, this group was transformed into the Freedom Alliance – comprising the AVF, the IFP and the administrations of Ciskei, Bophuthatswana and KwaZulu – organized around the issue of the 'right to self-determination'.[76] What bound these groups together was not only their common espousal of ethnicity, but also their fundamental belief in the non-viability of a non-racial future for South Africa. The dissolution of the homeland system, with its deeply embedded relations of patronage and clientelism, threatened the power base and authoritarian traditions of the old homeland leaders.[77] This raises the more general question concerning the survival and impact of forces of 'traditionalism' in a democratic post-apartheid South Africa. They represent the entrenchment of values deeply inimical to the extension of democratization into wider fields of social relations.[78] Insofar as their spheres of influence coincide with the rural/urban divide, they pose serious questions for the ANC-led government, which will have to contend with their continued presence and which will have to find a space within which 'traditionalism' may be articulated with democracy, rather than against it. This will require a disarticulation of ethnicity and its politicization, of traditionalism and authoritarianism, in the very context in which many forces seem to tend in the opposite direction.[79]

Non-Racialism and Post-Apartheid

> We give the last word to freedom, yet we know not what it is. This is the central irony of the deep and passionate struggle in South Africa – that *it is for something that exists only in relation to what it seeks to eliminate.*[80]

Non-racialism, a tradition deeply embedded in the venerable history of resistance to apartheid, is in the process of being instituted as a new imaginary form of social division, a form which takes as one of its central preoccupations the invention of a democratic post-apartheid order.[81] Non-racialism, as is clear from Albie Sachs's comment above, is defined not only by what it positively seeks to promote, but equally by what it wishes to overcome. In this sense, the 'other' of non-racialism is apartheid, a highly overdetermined signifier linking together forms of racial oppression and economic exploitation. If, as I have argued, apartheid is not only a precise and historically determinate mode of social division, but also an identitary logic which attempts to resist the never-ending quest for identification by fixing boundaries between identities for all time, then the central question with regard to non-racialism concerns the extent to which it will be able to foster and sustain difference in such a manner as to keep open spaces for identification within a democratic order.[82] That these questions are not unnecessarily esoteric is evident from the character of the central debates around the form of democracy to be instituted in the aftermath of apartheid.[83] These debates, in a variety of spheres, all touch upon the possibility and viability of an open democratic order, while taking account of past injustices in order to redress them.[84]

It is within the framework set by the Freedom Charter that the ANC sought to address the vexed question concerning the perpetrators and the legacy of apartheid. In stark contrast to the NP, which insisted that the past was irrelevant to the future of the country and that 'alleged injustices' had to be left behind if the wounds of the apartheid era were to heal, the ANC argued that no such healing could take place without bringing the crimes of the past into the light of day. This required a strategy of reconciliation without a covering over of past attrocities.[85] The theme of reconciliation and healing remained a key issue throughout the transition period, and was reiterated in Mandela's inaugural speech on 11 May 1994:

> The time for the healing of wounds has come. The moment to bridge the chasms that divide us has come. The time to build is upon us. . . . We enter

> into a covenant that we shall build the society in which all South Africans, both black and white, will be able to walk tall, without any fear in their hearts, assured of their inalienable right to human dignity – a rainbow nation at peace with itself and the world.[86]

The theme of reconciliation, which many commentators have felt played too central a role in the ANC's discourse, has been closely associated with the need to address 'white fears'.[87] And the manner in which this was done was in line with the sentiments already articulated in the Freedom Charter: equal rights for all South Africans, irrespective of race, colour, gender or creed, required that 'whiteness' had constitutional relevance only 'in terms of its inappropriateness; it is relevant because it is irrelevant'.[88] 'Whiteness' could be taken neither as a justification for privilege and domination, nor as a basis for humilation and vengeance. Indeed, it is only once white supremacy is destroyed that the true interests of whites *as citizens* can be protected. In this manner, the ANC has attempted to eliminate race as a defining feature from the political terrain, while keeping open the space for expression of cultural – rather than racial or ethnic – diversity:

> The Freedom Charter has long recognized that cultural, linguistic, and religious pluralism are not only permissible, but also desirable – South Africa is a better, not a worse, country for being populated by people of many languages, traits, and creeds.[89]

This commitment to cultural diversity expressed the struggle for difference, a possiblity once it became liberated from its association with domination and subordination. It has, however, to be based upon political equality, a struggle for the 'right to be the same', the right to equal citizenship. In this domain – arising from the quest for equality – a further set of issues concerning the institution of a post-apartheid order were articulated.

The intersection between the discourse of non-racialism and the redress of economic inequalities was and is not without its tensions, especially insofar as the latter is closely associated with a commitment to affirmative action. As Sachs has argued, non-racialism presupposes a colour-blind constitution, while affirmative action requires a conscious look at the realities between the life chances of whites and blacks.[90] That this redress is necessary goes without saying. The whole tradition built upon the Freedom Charter not only presupposed the moderate form of arguments for 'affirmative action' in the public, health, education and housing sectors, in access to and ownership of land, but also envisaged a much more radical reconstitution of the economic order.[91] Before discussing this further, it is necessary to make reference to some of the implications of the affirmative action programme. The most serious challenge to the viability of an affirmative action programme emerged from the perception of a hierarchization of the 'oppressed'. Discussion of affirmative action within the ANC proceeded almost entirely within the parameters of the oppressor/oppressed distinction. The unity of 'the people' invariably informed the discussion without due regard and sensitivity to possibly divisive factors.[92] That this is not an accidental feature of the discourse of non-racialism is clear. Non-racialism was constituted on the basis of creating equivalences between different oppressed 'groups' in order to foster a common opposition to apartheid articulated around 'the people'. An emphasis on 'cultural diversity' tended to emerge only in areas of debate where the problem of 'whiteness' was at stake. However, soon after the unbanning of the ANC, it became clear that communities which had some historical allegiance to non-racialism were increasingly dissatisfied with the lack of attention to cultural specificity and regional variations in conditions of everyday life. This concern was expressed especially by members of the coloured community, who increasingly felt themselves to be vulnerable *vis-à-vis* the African population. It was this sense of threat which the NP exploited to its advantage during the 1994 election.[93] But it has to be stressed that while these fears were exploited and manipulated in that conjuncture, they also had deeper roots in the inability of the ANC properly to address the position of coloureds within the black liberation struggle.[94] One commentator argued during the election period that anti-apartheid crusaders

> ... have been ... deficient in how they organise coloureds. They seem unable to grasp the potency of ethnicity as a force that shapes thinking, solidarity and political choice. Perhaps this is because their political positions – whether anti-apartheid, Marxist or Africanist – have a history of belittling ethnicity or rejecting it as mere fiction and appearance.[95]

Combined with the emphasis on affirmative action, the coloured community, once again, was perceived to be in a position where they did not quite 'fit the bill'. Under apartheid they were not 'white' enough, and it seemed that in a post-apartheid order they might not be 'black' enough. While perhaps over-accommodating to 'white fears', the ANC did too little to address the specificity of the coloured community in the Western Cape.[96] And this fact has to temper a too glowing reading of the ANC's position of the practicalities of creating space for cultural diversity.

The affirmative action programme, nevertheless, is a crucial part of the creation of a society in which equality takes pride of place.[97] As Sachs has pointed out, it is difficult to see how a truly non-racial society can be built without at least one generation of accelerated progress being achieved under the principles of affirmative action.[98] Affirmative action is, however, only one of the mechanisms to address inequality: the other main mechanisms include the principle of 'equal protection' as enshrined in Article 1(3) of the constitution, equal opportunity and the maintenance of minimum standards in areas such as health care, education and unemployment.[99] The depth of this programme, however, falls far short of the socialist demands which became increasingly dominant during the latter part of the 1980s.[100] While accepting the principles of the Charter of Workers' Rights – including the right to form trade unions, the right to collective bargaining and the right to strike[101] – it could be argued that the 1994 election marked the end of 'radical' politics: 'in seven days [the election period] South Africa became hostile territory for the radicals and ideologues of the Left and Right'.[102] This evaluation was echoed in Mandela's statement that the days of mass protest 'are over' and that people had to wait 'three to five years before we can really see to it that needs are met'.[103] While the task facing the government of national unity is an enormous one and most difficult to achieve given the expectations created by the very fact of the 1994 election, the developing tensions between the government and the labour movement ought not to be underestimated.[104] While it could be argued that the SACP – which portrays itself as the guardian of the workers and the poor within the ranks of the ANC – will ensure that the interest of 'the workers' and the poor will remain on the agenda, it is more likely that the organized working class will increasingly come into confrontation with the more liberalized ANC-led government.[105] In addition to this, there are a very substantial number of unemployed persons who, as a result of the legacy of the years of struggle, may not only remain unemployed, but may even be 'unemployable'.[106] While the Reconstruction and Development Programme (RDP) seeks to address these problems, it remains an open question as to whether the ANC, given the constraints of the economy, will succeed in moving towards a society in which equality can truly become a governing principle. The spectre of an entrenchment of class divisions haunts the South Africa of the future and has the potential to subvert the deepening of a democratic culture.[107]

While this may seem a pessimistic evaluation of the prospects for an extension of democracy to wider domains of the social, it has to be placed within the framework of both the existing constraints on the government of national unity and the continued presence of demands for economic equality from below. Moreover, the non-racial imaginary itself, even while considerably 'liberalized' over the past five years, continues to act as a surface on which those demands may be inscribed, and to the present date there is no suggestion that it does not remain the serious intention of the ANC to hold those demands in the highest regard. In this, the importance of the articulation of a democratic post-apartheid order lies: insofar as apartheid remains as its other, the inequalities resulting from that system will remain on the agenda, and will remain open to contestation. It is in this openness to contestation that the essence of democracy is to be found, and that the possibility for a democratic process of 'nation-building' lies.

Conclusion

The forging of a new imaginary around which social division will occur in a post-apartheid South Africa is still in the making, and it is important, in this respect, to point out that the very process of forging a new South African nation is not an unambiguous one. As I have argued, much will depend on how the discourse of non-racialism finally becomes embedded in pratice. In principle, there are at least two possible scenarios open here. If the conception of the people as a homogeneous unity is to predominate, then the prospects for a truly plural, open process of nation-building would seem to be limited. In this case, the existing lines of division, especially those associated with the far right and Inkatha, are most likely to become further embedded, leading to a scenario in which the future of South Africa will be one which will continue to be marked by deepening conflicts. If, however, the emphasis on the final impossibility of nationhood implicit in *non*-racialism becomes dominant, becomes a central articulating principle – that is, insofar as the non-closure of identity takes centre-stage – South Africa may avoid some of the worst pitfalls characteristic of processes of post-colonial nation-building. For this to become a reality, however, a series of conditions have to be seen to be in place such that there will be fewer and fewer grounds for constituencies to feel themselves marginalized. This holds not only for forces which may become politically marginalized, but also for the urban underclasses, the long-term unemployed and the rural poor. These conditions thus include not only the institutionalization of an ethos of democracy, but also the elimination of gross material inequalities. In the absence of either of them, the consolidation and institutionalization of a democratic, post-apartheid social order will be difficult, if not impossible.

Conclusion
Towards a Post-Apartheid Society

> . . . the recognition of who we are and what we value, of where we are and what we face, of 'our present commitments and responsibilities', is the only genuinely solid foundation for successful action and meaningful change.[1]

The questions as to who we are and what we value are being revalued in South Africa today. It is on this terrain that the legacy of apartheid, and its implications for the future development of a post-apartheid society, have to be addressed. It is also with these issues in mind that the logic of apartheid has to be re-examined, so as to draw out its wider implications for processes of identity formation. If a social and political order which is truly 'beyond' apartheid is to be instituted, then that order will have to break not only with the historically specific features of apartheid, but also with the logic informing and shaping its instituted modes of social division.

While my analysis of apartheid discourse offered a contextual reading of the specificity of its grammar and logic, it is possible, tentatively, to draw out wider theoretical insights concerning the general mechanisms through which collective political identities are forged. In that respect, the study of apartheid discourse can, potentially, make visible the effects of an identitary logic not reducible to its historically specific conditions. In drawing out those wider logics, it is necessary to reiterate the main points of the argument concerning the logic of the construction of apartheid hegemony.

Apartheid, as a new myth of social division, emerged as a result of the articulation given to a series of dislocations occurring during the 1930s and 1940s. Viewed from this perspective, the significance of the myth of the *volkseie* lies not only in the effects of its later expansion into an imaginary, but also in the fact that the very project that had to liberate Afrikaners from what was perceived as a continuation of imperial domination in segregationism had immediate disciplinary effects on the Afrikaans-speaking community. It sought to regulate, refashion and limit what could be understood by 'Afrikanerdom', and, consequently, produced a variety of forms of resistance emanating from the larger Afrikaans-speaking community.[2] Initially, resistance took the form of a struggle over the meaning of the traditional symbols of Afrikaner nationalism and a questioning of the narrow strictures imposed on it by the *volksbeweging*. The actions of the Afrikaner women in the KWU, for example, are a case in point. However, as the apartheid project crystallized and penetrated into more and more areas of everyday life, it became increasingly difficult to question its parameters. One either stayed within the horizon delineated by apartheid discourse, or one fell outside of it; one either engaged in 'loyal resistance', or one became a traitor to the Afrikaner cause. It was only during the 1980s – during the period in which apartheid hegemony entered into crisis – that a rearticulation of the meaning of Afrikanerhood became a practicable possibility once again.[3] The limits on resistance imposed by apartheid hegemony did not operate only with reference to the 'Afrikaner community', but were also evident in the lack of resistance to the fundamental tenets of that project by, for example, the majority of Parliamentary parties. More often that not, dissent was expressed not about its direction, but about the manner of its implementation. Outside the formal structures of political representation, more blatant forms of repression were used to gain and maintain some degree of acquiescence.

One could argue that the closures instituted by apartheid hegemony – the continuous need to regulate and dominate – stemmed from the very logic of the discourse of the *volkseie*: the fact that its very 'essence' continued to escape attempts to define and delimit it; that that which was considered to be the innermost characteristic of the *volk* – its *own*, 'organic' way of life – could not be grasped and defined in a process of enumeration of characteristics, features, ceremonies, and so forth. It could only come into being by a process of differentiation from a series of 'others': from Afrikaners who were not truly Afrikaners, from Jews, from liberals, from communists, from English-speaking whites. Once this discourse of authentic organicity became an imaginary horizon structuring all social relations, this process could only be replicated *ad nauseam*: the 1970s and 1980s were witness to an almost interminable process of proliferation of 'enemies'. In addition to the naming and prosecution of such 'enemies', it had the effect of an incitement to self-regulation, and of observation and judgement of the conduct of others.

Resistance to these forms of regulation also increased, and it forced a continual redefinition of the nature of the apartheid project. 'Apartheid' developed into 'separate development' when its emphasis on the *volkseie* was extended to Africans; it became 'parallel development' where the coloured community was concerned; the status of the *volkseie vis-à-vis* 'nationhood' underwent a series of marked changes, especially with regard to the relation between Afrikaans- and English-speaking whites; the discourse of the total onslaught continued the focus on 'self-determination', but this was set within a context where division between the dominant bloc and those externalized as other could be posed less and less in racial terms. These changes were markers of the effects of resistance on the discourse of apartheid. During the 1980s, the multiplication of forms of resistance began to disarticulate the apartheid imaginary: it could no longer act as a horizon of inscription, became incapable of integrating the multiplicity of dislocations and the demands arising from them, and was, consequently, re-literalized. This process makes visible the double movement governing the constitution of collective identities. As Laclau has argued, insofar as the moment of the imaginary as horizon of inscription predominates, the literal content of the original demands which gave rise to it will be deformed and transformed through the addition of many social demands; alternatively, if it fails to act as a horizon, its literality, its mythical character, will be foregrounded again, and its ability to hegemonize social and political demands will tend to decrease.[4] Under such conditions, a proliferation of elements, which no longer make sense of the dislocated structure, become available for rearticulation and contestation. During the latter part of the 1980s, this is exactly what occurred. As was the case with apartheid, a series of discourses emerged which attempted to re-suture the dislocated structure of apartheid discourse. The discourses of the far right, of Inkatha, of the new NP and of the UDF/ANC/SACP all participated in the struggle to provide a reading which could make sense of those dislocations.

It is possible, from this analysis, to draw out a wider understanding of the nature of dislocatory events, and the conditions under which new myths and imaginaries arise. If the dislocation of a structure is not always already given, but is the result of a series of contestatory processes which make visible the structure's constitutive non-suturedness, then everything depends upon the particularity of the context in which such dislocations erupt: on the depth of the dislocation, on what is dislocated, and on the nature of the discourses available to take up the task of re-suturing, or re-centring, the structure. It is also clear that the greater the dislocation, the wider the field of elements that will be available for rearticulation, and vice versa. A central condition for the institution of new myths would, thus, be a large degree of dislocation. It is, however, only in the limit case of the complete breakdown of a structure that a 'total refoundation' of the social becomes possible.[5] More often than not, the terrain of elements which have become floating signifiers will be limited, and the extent of rearticulation possible will consequently also be narrower. This is not to say, however, that in the latter case there is a mere 'reorganization' of elements. Even more limited forms of rearticulation may have quite far-reaching effects on the form of social division, to the extent that one may be warranted in speaking of the formation of a new imaginary horizon in which elements may be inscribed. This was the case with the conditions under which the myth of the *volkseie* emerged. Similar conditions were in place during the late 1980s and early 1990s, although it could be argued that the extent and depth of dislocations were considerably wider. The rearticulation of those dislocations, moreover, depended upon the concrete available alternatives to apartheid. Of these myths, non-racialism seems to have won the battle: it is set to become the new imaginary ordering social division in a post-apartheid South Africa.

It is worthwhile reflecting on the extent to which the discourse of non-racialism contains the possibility to go beyond apartheid, beyond the logic informing that discourse. Apartheid discourse was premissed upon the construction of closed, organic identities, still evident today, in varying degrees, in the discourses of the far right, Inkatha and the new NP. As I have argued, the process in which these identities was constituted relied upon a logic of exclusion that acted as a condition for its constitution, and that made it essentially vulnerable to resistance. Thus, the formation of collective forms of identification is relational in character, relies on a moment of exclusion and, consequently, is bound to evoke resistance. In terms of the institution of a post-apartheid form of social division, the problem of the limits of that discourse – that is, the moment at which something has to be excluded in order to forge that impossible object of identity – is of crucial significance. Hence, it is necessary to reflect further upon the logic of exclusion structuring any process of identity formation. Starting from the apparent need to 'exclude' something in the process of identity formation – the need to establish security of identity by defining the other that exposes the 'sore spots' in one's identity as 'evil' or 'irrational' – I would argue, following Connolly, that while this is a structural phenomenon, it is a *temptation* rather than a necessity: 'a temptation rather than an implication, and a structural temptation rather than simply a psychological disposition'.[6] The structure of identity formation requires that identity is formed through differentiation, but it does not follow from this that all 'differences' have to be excluded as 'other', as 'evil'. Consequently, one has here a site of indeterminacy that opens up the space for considering a variety of ways in which the relation between self and other may be conceived. From this site, it becomes possible to think of social division in terms other than merely defining a friend/foe relation.[7] What is important, from this perspective, is precisely the possibility of relating to those who are 'different' without simply excluding them as 'enemies'. This was precisely what was not possible under the discourse of apartheid, for it was premissed upon a conception of organic identities which ruled out, by law, any other form of identification. More precisely, this question concerns the possibility of consolidation of identity through the constitution of difference, rather than otherness.[8] This would involve doing justice to both sameness and difference, to conceive and develop practices in which it is possible to recognize the instability of identity, and to respect the otherness of the other.[9]

Such an alternative way of relating to difference is closely bound up with the institution of democracy, for it is within a horizon which foregrounds the impossibility of suturing the gap between the place of power and the occupation of that place that the possibility for the extension of the space of difference is opened up.[10] As Connolly argues, a democratic politics of difference, in which conventional standards sealed in 'transcendental mortar' are loosened through contestation, is a politics which would refuse to resign itself unambiguously to limits imposed by the structural requirements of any particular order. It is a politics alert to 'the tragic gap between the imperatives of organization in the order it idealizes and admirable possibilities of life that exceed those imperatives'.[11] In other words, instead of succumbing to the temptation to convert difference into otherness, into evil, a democratic politics ought to ensure that as many differences as possible are drawn in before the inevitable moment of closure arrives.

While it is clear that the drawing of a limit is necessary, even in a democratic society, what is at stake here is the point at which such exclusions become operative and the terms in which they are justified.

One can immediately rule out the possible justification of such limits by an appeal to the ideal of 'community', for that ideal tends to push its adherents to treat 'harmonious membership' and 'consensus' not as contestable ends to be interrogated by the most creative means at their disposal, but as vehicles of elevation drawing the community closer to the harmony of being.[12] This appeal to the good of the community, or the people, remains a danger in a 'post-colonial', post-apartheid South Africa, especially insofar as 'the people', which has traditionally been regarded as a homogeneous bloc, is imbued with moral virtue by the very fact of occupying the position of the oppressed.[13]

In countering such tendencies to justify exclusions, it is necessary to take account of the fact that the call for a regard for 'pluralism', for a regard for difference, is made here in terms of a radical conception of pluralism. Radical pluralism does not start from given and sedimented forms of identity simply in order to reassert them; it calls forth a responsibility for keeping open the space of contestation of identification. It is premissed neither on status nor on other ascriptive factors, nor on class or utilitarian interests.[14] Pluralism is radical only to the extent that it avoids the temptation to ground itself on those factors. However, such a radical politics of difference is likely to flourish only where a politics of 'generalized resentment' is subdued, for in conditions where there is severe material deprivation, and an absence of general access to economic, educational and cultural opportunities, reactive demands to dogmatize conventional identities are likely to be intensified.[15] Where communities perceive themselves to be under threat, and where they have lost out in their dealings with the state, this is an even greater danger.[16]

This brings me, finally, to a consideration of the discourse of non-racialism, which, on the one hand, subverts the quest for a natural identity and, on the other, seems to reassert it in its affirmation of a 'common humanity' which grounds the idea of 'the people'. I have discussed some of the problems with regard to non-racialism, and the limitations of its conception of 'the people' in chapter 6. Here I would like to focus on the possible logic contained, implicitly if not explicitly, in the discourse of non-racialism from the perspective of the imperative to cultivate 'difference'. Taking as a starting-point the impossibility of closure of any identity, it is clear that when compared to apartheid discourse, which attempted to efface the gap between identity and identification, non-racialism has the distinct advantage that it has been articulated in opposition to the identitary logic informing apartheid. Its emphasis on *non*-racialism holds out the possibility of recognizing the non-sutured nature of identity and the need to maintain the possibility of contestation. This much has been evident in the degree of consultation which took place during the process of negotiation. If the process of negotiation weakened some of the more radical demands of the resistance movements, it also began to institute a democratic ethos.[17] The importance of the struggle for non-racialism, both within the internal resistance movements and trade unions and within the 'exile movement' – apart from its practical manifestation, and the many problems that those aiming to implement it no doubt still will have to face – is that it has created a symbolic space in which democracy may be deepened and the struggle for difference may be extended.[18] And in this struggle, there can be no retreat to the illusory certainties of metanarratives. Democracy cannot be guaranteed. To sustain and deepen that order one needs to get back to the rough ground, as Wittgenstein would argue, to develop institutional forms which may sustain those possibilities.[19] In the terrain in which democracy is being institutionalized in South Africa today, we have, more than ever, to assume responsiblity for our actions and interventions, whatever form they may take. However, the efforts to institute and maintain a democratic order may never be severed from the question of equality, for, as I have argued, the presence of gross material inequalities may severely limit the conditions necessary for the deepening of democracy. Insofar as non-racialism is also premissed upon a discourse of equality, drawn from the socialist tradition, it could provide a horizon which conceives of democracy as a never-ending process of extending the demands for equality to greater and greater areas of social life. It is only on condition that the new democracy is articulated around the protection and fostering of difference, and the eradication of material inequalities, that one could truly argue to have gone beyond apartheid.

Notes

Introduction

1. See, for example, M. Lipton, *Capitalism and Apartheid. South Africa, 1910–1986*, Aldershot 1986, p. 10. The problem here concerns not only the periodization of South African history in general, and apartheid in particular, but also the related problem of its characterization. In what follows, I deal in very general terms with the manner in which the debate concerning the correct theoretical characterization of apartheid has proceeded. In the forthcoming chapters, I address more specific issues and interpretations.

2. This debate dominated South African historiography during the 1970s and 1980s. For a general overview of these debates, see, *inter alia*, C. Saunders, 'Historians and Apartheid', in J. Lonsdale (ed.), *South Africa in Question*, London 1986, pp. 13–32; and H. Wright, *The Burden of the Present*, Cape Town 1977. For a recent affirmation of the neo-Marxist terms of the debate, see P. Bonner, P. Delius and D. Posel, 'The Shaping of Apartheid: Contradiction, Continuity and Popular Struggle', in P. Bonner, P. Delius and D. Posel (eds), *Apartheid's Genesis 1935–1962*, Johannesburg 1993, p. 1. For examples of more recent work engaging with the questions excluded from this debate, see J. Robinson, '(Dis)locating Historical Narrative: Writing, Space and Gender in South African Social History', *South African Historical Journal*, no. 30, 1994, pp. 144–57; as well as the following papers presented at the *Journal of Southern African Studies* Conference: 'Paradigms Lost, Paradigms Regained? Southern African Studies in the 1990s', University of York, 9–11 September 1994: L. de Kock, 'Reading History as Cultural Text'; R. Greenstein, 'South African Studies and the Politics of Theory: Old Challenges and New Paradigms'.

3. My argument here proceeds by analogy to Wittgenstein's approach to the problems of philosophy. Wittgenstein argues that many of the problems of philosophy arise from confusions, and that once we see that, the problems are not solved, but dissolved. For a discussion of Wittgenstein's conception of the nature of philosophy, see G.P. Backer and P.M.S. Hacker, *Essays on the Philosophical Investigations*, Vol. 1, Oxford 1980, pp. 259–94.

4. Here I follow Wittgenstein, who argues against the metaphysical search for depth, against our tendency to be mesmerized by form. See L. Wittgenstein, *Philosophical Investigations*, Oxford 1953, remark 89, p. 42e.

5. My use of the term 'discourse' derives from the work of Laclau and Mouffe. The term 'discourse', like that of language game in Wittgenstein, embraces both linguistic and non-linguistic elements. See E. Laclau and C. Mouffe, *Hegemony and Socialist Strategy. Towards a Radical Democratic Politics*, London 1985, pp. 107–8.

6. For a discussion of methodological problems in explicating 'context', see, *inter alia*, Q. Skinner, 'Meaning and Understanding in the History of Ideas', in J. Tully (ed.), *Meaning and Context. Quentin Skinner and His Critics*, Oxford 1988, pp. 29–67.

7. It is, of course, the case that variations occur on the precise substantive claims made. The structure of argumentation, however, remains constant. Posel first noted and discussed the either/or terms in which the debate proceeded. See D. Posel, 'Rethinking the "Race–Class Debate" in Southern African Historiography', *Social Dynamics*, vol. 9, no. 1, pp. 50–66. Posel, however, neglects the extent to which both sides of the debate share certain presuppositions with regard to the analysis of forms of social division.

8. I discuss these presuppositions in more depth in forthcoming chapters.

9. The idea of a 'pure description' is, of course, untenable. Descriptions are always already representations. My argument is that one needs theoretical tools with which to approach the analysis of a discourse, but these tools should not predetermine in substantive terms what is to be the result of the analysis. Categories such as identity, political frontier, dislocation, myth and imaginary employed in this text fulfil that function without making substantive claims about the 'contents' which fill these categories. In each of the chapters to follow, I systematically introduce and discuss these categories.

10. On the interpretation provided here, neither the idea of a 'pre-discursive', unmediated experience nor that of 'objective interests' makes sense. If all of reality is symbolically mediated, then both 'experience' and 'interests' have to be articulated discursively.

11. The term 'contingency', as it is used here, does not imply that a 'contingency' is always something that can be changed through will or decision. As Connolly argues, there are 'obdurate contingencies' and it is a mistake to assume that the constructed character of a self-identity automatically implies its susceptibility to reconstruction. See W.E. Connolly, *Identity\Difference. Democratic Negotiations of Political Paradox*, Ithaca, New York 1991, p. 176.

12. Foucault argues that this form of power 'applies itself to the immediate everyday life which categorizes the individual, marks him by his own individuality, attaches him to his identity, imposes a law of truth on him which he must recognize and which others have to recognize in him. It is a form of power which makes individuals subjects.' Moreover, for Foucault, the exercise of power cannot be separated from freedom, since 'freedom must exist for power to be exerted, and also its permanent support, since without the possibility of recalcitrance, power would be equivalent to physical determination'. M. Foucault, 'The Subject and Power', in H.L. Dreyfus and P. Rabinow (eds), *Michel Foucault. Beyond Structuralism and Hermeneutics*, Brighton 1982, pp. 212 and 221.

13. In my theorization of hegemony, I draw on Gramscian and post-Gramscian theories of hegemony, especially on the post-Marxist articulation given to it by Laclau and Mouffe. It follows that a hegemonic formation also embraces what it opposes. In terms of resistance to a hegemonic formation, the argument would be that insofar as 'the opposing force accepts the system of basic articulations of that formation as something it negates', the place of the negation is defined by the internal parameters of the formation itself. See Laclau and Mouffe, *Hegemony and Socialist Strategy*, p. 139.

14. Arguing that a discourse is hegemonic, of course, does not entail a value judgement of the particular form and content of such a discourse.

15. Even the manufacturing of 'consent' involves a dimension of force insofar as it makes available only certain possibilities of identification, and rules out others.

16. Lefort further points out that this is the function of ideology, understood here not as false consciousness, but as the sequence of representations which have the function of re-establishing the dimension of society 'without history' at the very heart of 'historical society'. That is, ideology serves to naturalize that which is the contingent product of historical articulation. C. Lefort, *The Political Forms of Modern Society. Bureaucracy, Democracy, Totalitarianism*, Cambridge 1986, p. 191.

17. I draw my discussion of political frontiers from the work of Laclau and Mouffe, who extended the linguistic argument on the paradigmatic and syntagmatic axes of language to the structuring of social reality. They argue that political frontiers

operate both through the articulation of differential (syntagmatic) positions, and through the creation of equivalences between positions (paradigmatic). See Laclau and Mouffe, *Hegemony and Socialist Strategy*, pp. 127–34.

18. Lefort, *The Political Forms of Modern Society*, p. 198. Foucault makes a similar point, arguing that what is interesting is not so much the question as to how a society can hold individuals together, but the question of the systems of exclusion, the creation of divisions and games of negation and rejection through which a society can begin to function. See, M. Foucault, 'Michel Foucault on Attica', *Telos*, vol. 19, 1974, pp. 155–6.

19. E. Laclau, *New Reflections on the Revolution of Our Time*, London 1990, p. 65. I draw my discussion of 'dislocation' from this work. However, whereas for Laclau, 'every identity is dislocated insofar as it depends upon an outside which both denies that identity and provides its condition of possibility at the same time', I argue that dislocation makes visible the non-sutured nature of identity. Thus, while every identity may be constitutively non-sutured, it is not the case that every identity is always already dislocated. See ibid., p. 39

20. As with other Afrikaans terms, the term '*volkseie*' is notoriously difficult to translate. It designates that which is particular to the *volk* (the people) and to the *volk* alone; literally, that which is the 'own' of the *volk*.

21. I do not assume that this community has always already been in existence. In chapters 1 and 2, I investigate the precise mechanisms through which a particular conception of the Afrikaner *volk* has been produced.

22. The precise relation between capitalism and apartheid is a subject debated at length in South African historiography. However, protagonists from both sides of the divide tend to agree now that the relation was neither one of simple complementarity, nor simply one of contradiction.

23. Since one of the aims of this study is to analyse the manner in which identities are contructed in and through apartheid discourse, it is not possible to avoid using controversial terminology. I do not italicize such terms, nor do I always place them between inverted commas, since the context in which they are deployed should make it clear that those terms are labels designed to construct and interpellate subjects. There are, nevertheless, two particular terms which need further commentary: the terms 'black' and 'coloured'. Where the former is used, it normally designates the manner in which this term has been deployed in resistance discourse, namely to include African, coloured and Indian South Africans. Since the latter is particularly problematic, I have opted not to capitalize it, and not to use the common prefix 'so-called'.

24. Foucault makes a similar argument concerning the deployment of 'sexuality'. Sexual controls were not targeted at the working classes in the first place; rather, they were applied first, and with the greatest intensity, in the economically privileged and politically dominant classes. M. Foucault, *The History of Sexuality. An Introduction*, Harmondsworth 1979, p. 120.

25. The conception of identity as relational – that is, the idea that the identity of a term is not positively constituted, but given in its difference from other terms – is drawn from the work of Saussure. The idea of the relationality of identity is now widely accepted in post-structuralist literature. This dimension of the formation of social and political identities has been widely disregarded in literature on apartheid.

26. Such exclusion thus act as condition of both possibility and impossibility of the constitution of identity.

27. I discuss both the concepts of 'myth' and 'imaginary' – drawn from Laclau's work in detail in chapters 2 and 3.

28. Laclau, *New Reflections*, pp. 61–8.

29. I draw the idea of 'undecidability' from the work of Derrida. Derrida very clearly specifies that undecidability is not concerned simply with 'indeterminacy'. Rather, it designates 'a *determinate* oscillation between possibilities' which are themselves 'highly *determined* in strictly *defined* situations'. See J. Derrida, *Limited Inc.*, Evanston, Ill. 1988, p. 148.

30. Derrida argues that what is important with respect to 'undecidability' is not the lexical richness or semantic infiniteness of a word or a concept, but its syntactical deployment. See J. Derrida, *Dissemination*, Chicago, 1981 p. 220.

31. In this sense, undecidability should not be regarded either as a precondition for the exercise of hegemony, or as opposed to hegemony. The precondition for the exercise of hegemony is the non-sutured nature of the social, the fact that no element has a necessary relation to another, and articulation of elements with no necessary relation between them thus becomes possible. Undecidability should also not be opposed to hegemony, since hegemonic politics quite often find their expression in contexts where 'decidability' is suspended.

1 Dislocated Identities

1. D.P. van Huyssteen, 'Openingsrede', in P. du Toit (ed.), *Verslag van die Volkskongres oor die Armblankevraagstuk gehou ter Kimberley, 2 tot 5 Okt.1934*, Kaapstad 1934, p. 27. All translations from Afrikaans, unless otherwise indicated, are mine.

2. This point is made by analogy to Wittgenstein's argument against a metaphysical search for the 'essence' of language. Instead, he argues that we need to look at how words function, and that this does not involve a 'penetrative' activity, but attention to the 'scene of language', to the occurrence of a word and the context in which it functions.

3. Lefort, *The Political Forms of Modern Society*, Cambridge 1986, p. 204.

4. Delivering the opening lecture to the *Volkskongres* on the poor white problem, Ds D.P. van Huyssteen argued that these two issues were 'enormous mountains' which sent cold shivers down the backs of those contemplating them. Van Huyssteen, 'Openingsrede', p. 26.

5. See, for example, D. O'Meara, 'Analysing Afrikaner Nationalism: The "Christian National" Assault on White Trade Unionism in South Africa, 1934–1958', *African Affairs*, vol. 3, no. 2, 1978, pp. 45–72; R.H. Davies, *Capital, State and White Labour in South Africa 1900–1960*, Brighton 1979.

6. See O'Meara, 'Analysing Afrikaner Nationalism', pp. 48–9, and Davies, *Capital, State and White Labour*, p. 255. The fact that semi-skilled places were produced at a rate slower than the overall rate of industrial expansion, and that industry slowly started to shun its prejudice in favour of white operatives, increased the pressure on white labour. Following a period of struggle between industrial capital and the state, the issue was resolved in favour of a 'civilized labour policy' encouraging the employment of white labour to counter the effects of the changes in employment structure and practice.

7. O'Meara, 'Analysing Afrikaner Nationalism', p. 48. O'Meara points out that of the 339,895, only 230,980 were white.

8. See D. O'Meara, 'The 1946 African Mine Workers' Strike and the Political Economy of South Africa', in P. Kallaway and T. Adler (eds), *Contemporary Southern African Studies: Research Papers*, vol. II, Johannesburg 1978, pp. 57–92. Davies points out that the number of blacks involved in strikes grew from 300 in 1933 to 4,800 in 1939. Davies, *Capital, State and White Labour*, p. 262.

9. For a discussion of the unevenness of these processes in the context of a problematization of the 'cheap labour thesis', see S. Dubow, *Racial Segregation and the Origins of Apartheid in South Africa, 1919–1936*, Oxford 1989, pp. 51–74. Bonner, Delius and Posel point out that the movement of African women to the cities expanded during the 1930s and 1940s with the opening up of possibilities of domestic service employment. In Johannesburg alone, domestic employees rose from 5,000 in 1932 to 22,765 in 1938. See P. Bonner, P. Delius and D. Posel, 'The Shaping of Apartheid: Contradiction, Continuity and Popular Struggle', in Bonner, Delius and Posel (eds), *Apartheid's Genesis 1935–1962*, Johannesburg 1993, pp. 14–15.

10. UG 16–1944, *Verslag van die Verrigtinge van die Naturelle-Verteenwoordigende Raad vir 1943*, p. 3, quoted in J.P.C. Mosterd, 'Die Tweede Wereldoorlog: Impetus vir Versnelde Swart Verstedeliking in Suid-Afrika', *Journal for Contemporary History*, vol. 11, no. 2, 1986, p. 42. While Mosterd's article in places reads like an apology for apartheid, it does contain interesting information on the regional differences in rates of urbanization.

11. For a discussion of the construction of the 'Native question' in the report of the Fagan Commission, see A. Ashforth, *The Politics of Official Discourse in Twentieth-Century South Africa*, Oxford 1990, pp. 114–48.

12. Ibid., p. 117. The contributions of Delius, Lambert and Sapire to *Apartheid's Genesis* all question the dominance attributed to the African National Congress (ANC) in literature on resistance, arguing that the Communist Party of South Africa (CPSA) played a pivotal role in this period. See P. Delius, 'Migrant Organisation, the Communist Party, the ANC and the Sekhukuneland Revolt, 1940–1958', pp. 126–59; R.V. Lambert, 'Trade Unionism, Race, Class and Nationalism in the 1950s Resistance Movement', pp. 275–95; and H. Sapire, 'African Political Organisations in Brakpan in the 1950s', pp. 252–74, in Bonner, Delius and Posel, *Apartheid's Genesis*.

13. See, for example, Delius, 'Migrant Organisation'; as well as C. Bundy, 'Land and Liberation: Popular Rural Protest and the National Liberation Movements in South Africa, 1920–1960', in S. Marks and S. Trapido (eds), *The Politics of Race, Class and Nationalism in Twentieth-Century South Africa*, London 1987, pp. 254–85.

14. For a brief account of resistance in this respect, see G.M. Carter, *The Politics of Inequality. South Africa since 1948*, London 1959, especially chapter 14.

15. Bonner, Delius and Posel, 'The Shaping of Apartheid', pp. 10–16.

16. De Villiers discusses the subdivision of farms and the effects it had on the ownership structure of agricultural land. He shows that whereas a family farm usually would be between 5,000 and 10,000 morgen, it was not unusual to find farms as small as 300 to 1,500 morgen as a result of subdivision over generations (morgen = 2.2 acres). For anyone not wanting to become a share-cropper, the only alternative was to move to the cities. T.C. de Villiers, 'Die Afrikaner se Landelike Herkoms en sy Verstedeliking', in J.R. Albertyn (ed.), *Die Stadwaartse Trek van die Afrikaner-Nasie. Referate en Besluite van die Volkskongres*, organized by the Federal Welfare Council of the Dutch Reformed Churches, held in Johannesburg, 1–14 July 1947, p. 16.

17. J.R. Albertyn, P. du Toit and H.S. Theron, *Kerk en Stad, Verslag van die Kommissie van Ondersoek van die Gereformeerde N.G.Kerke na Kerklike en Godsdienstige Toestande in die Nege Stede van die Unie van Suid-Afrika*, Stellenbosch 1948, p. 50. It is interesting to note that the calculations of the number of Afrikaners in the cities at the time was made by using church census materials, indicating the extent to which the church played a pivotal role in the construction of community. It is also important to note the concern with Afrikaners attending English-speaking churches in the cities.

18. Albertyn, *Die Stadwaartse Trek*, p. 2.

19. J.R. Albertyn, 'Openingsrede: Die Opkoms van die Arbeiderstand in Suid-Afrika', in Albertyn, *Die Stadwaartse Trek*, p. 8.

20. Both O'Meara and Davies remark, on the grounds of a 1940 Department of Labour report, that the poor white problem had been solved. See O'Meara, 'Analysing Afrikaner Nationalism', p. 51; and Davies, *Capital, State and White Labour*, pp. 260–61.

21. E.L.P. Stals (ed.), *Afrikaners in die Goudstad. Deel 2: 1924–1961*, Pretoria 1986, p. 30.

22. Verwoerd, in a publication document for the socio-economic committee, remarked that unemployment was one of the most serious causes of poverty and one of the most urgent problems to be addressed. H.F. Verwoerd, 'Die Sosiologiese-Ekonomiese Komitee', in no editor, *Volkskongres oor die Armblanke Vraagstuk*, Kimberley 1934, p. 9.

23. No complete survey of all these articulations is possible. What follows, of necessity, has to have the character of an overview, concentrating on some of the most

important issues and moments of rupture during these tumultuous decades. The interventions of specific organic intellectuals are the subject-matter of chapter 2.

24. This was evident in a number of NP policy documents during the 1930s and 1940s. The 1934 NP Programme of Action, for example, declared the 'economic well-being' of the people as the most important issue to be addressed. Its agricultural policy also reflected the recommendations of the report, putting forward suggestions for the reorganization of agricultural credit, mortgage redemption plans, and so forth. In 1936 the party called for 'political and territorial segregation of Natives' and the abolishing of the coloured vote.

25. The tradition of holding conferences on central 'problems' affecting the *volk* was continued in the following decades. For example, the *Suid-Afrikaanse Buro vir Rasse-Aangeleenthede* (SABRA) held annual conferences during the 1950s on the 'Native Question', 'Natives in South African Industrial Life', 'Group and Neighbourhood Segregation', 'Native Education', 'The Native in South African Agriculture' and on the 'Coloured in South African Society'.

26. See, for example, T.D. Moodie, *The Rise of Afrikanerdom. Power, Apartheid and the Afrikaner Civil Religion*, Berkeley 1975; D. O'Meara, *Volkskapitalisme. Class, Capital and Ideology in the Development of Afrikaner Nationalism, 1934–1948*, Johannesburg 1983; H. Giliomee, 'Constructing Afrikaner Nationalism', in H. Adam (ed.), *South Africa. The Limits of Reform Politics*, Leiden 1983, pp. 21–54; D. Posel, 'The Meaning of Apartheid before 1948: Conflicting Interests and Forces within the Afrikaner Nationalist Alliance', *Journal of Southern African Studies*, vol. 14, no. 1, 1987, pp. 123–39; and P.J. Furlong, *Between Crown and Swastika. The Impact of the Radical Right on the Afrikaner Nationalist Movement in the Fascist Era*, Johannesburg 1991. See also the debate in the wake of the publication of Furlong's book in the *South African Historical Journal*, no. 27, 1992.

27. I will return to this issue at the end of this chapter. However, it is important to point out the extent of the reductionist readings to which the *volksbeweging* has been subjected. Neither Davis nor O'Meara has any difficulty in reducing the variety of struggles of Afrikaner nationalists to the need of an Afrikaner 'petty bourgeoisie' to secure for themselves a mass base. Writers, as a result, also tend to engage in extraordinary contortions to produce a 'fit' between reality and their analytical categories. See Davies, *Capital, State and White Labour*, p. 283; and O'Meara, *Volkskapitalisme*, p. 51.

28. Ashforth analyses the tradition of inquiries into the 'Native question' in depth. See Ashforth, *Politics of Official Discourse*.

29. Fourie, quoted in P.W. Coetzer and J.H. Le Roux (eds), *Die Nasionale Party Deel 4. Die 'Gesuiwerde' Nasionale Party, 1934–1940*, Bloemfontein 1986, p. 96.

30. Verwoerd argues that preference for 'civilized labour', and consequently discrimination against Natives, is acceptable since if differences in living standards between whites and Natives are taken into account, it is more economic for the country that Natives should be unemployed! H.F. Verwoerd, 'Die Bestryding van Armoede en die Herorganisasie van Welfaartswerk', in Du Toit, *Verslag van die Volkskongres*, p. 31.

31. The articulation of social division did not, however, stay at a simple white/black level. The conference also resolved that 'the tribal Native from Native Reserves competes unfairly in urban employment with Poor Whites, the Coloured, and detribalized Natives, since their work is "subsidized", as it were, by their possessions in the Reserves, and they can therefore work for lower wages. . . . ' Du Toit, *Verslag van die Volkskongres*, p. 301, resolution 49.

32. I discuss the position of SABRA in depth in chapter 3.

33. Verwoerd, 'Die Bestryding van Armoede', p. 32.

34. As a result of the work of the continuation committee of the conference under the leadership of P. du Toit and H.F. Verwoerd, the *Instituut vir Volkswelstand* (Institute for *Volk*'s Welfare) came into being in 1936, and a separate government Department of *Volkswelsyn* (Social Welfare) was created in 1937.

35. See resolutions 9, 42 and 56, in Du Toit, *Verslag van die Volkskongres*, pp. 293, 299–300, and 302–303.

36. See Albertyn, *Die Stadwaartse Trek*, as well as Albertyn, Du Toit and Theron, *Kerk en Stad*. Apart from dealing explicitly with labour-related issues, many papers addressed issues of wider concern: religion, the family, women in the city, leisure activities and questions of 'moral dislocation' accompanying urbanization and proletarianization.

37. Albertyn, 'Die Opkoms van die Arbeiderstand', in *Die Stadwaartse Trek*, p. 6. The same sentiment is echoed in other contributions to the conference.

38. It is therefore patently not the case that the re-emerging Afrikaner nationalism was infused with a simple nostalgia for *platteland*.

39. D.F. Malan, 'Die Nuwe Groot Trek. Suid-Afrika se Noodroep', gelewer te Bloedrivier 16 Desember 1938, Kaapstad 1938 [Bloemfontein, Instituut vir Eietydse Geskiedenis (henceforth: INEG) P30.19]. In this speech there is already an incipient undecidability between race and *volk*. For a discussion of the 'tradition' of celebrating the Day of the Vow as a 'Sunday', see F.A. van Jaarsveld, 'Die Eerste Openbare Viering van 16 Desember', *Tydskrif vir Geesteswetenskappe*, vol. 27, no. 1, 1987, pp. 42–9.

40. Malan, 'Die Nuwe Groot Trek', p. 7.

41. These themes are present in the writings of Afrikaner nationalists at the time. Diederichs lists what was regarded as a set of fundamental differences between the urban and rural areas, and emphasizes the 'shock' of the movement from rural to urban areas, a shock which could have detrimental effects on two to three generations. N. Diederichs, 'Die Invloed van die Stad op die Lewensbeskouing van 'n Volk', *Volkswelstand*, vol. 2, no. 4, 1941, pp. 140–50.

42. Ibid., p. 150.

43. S. Pauw, 'Die Taak van die Afrikaner in die Stad', in Albertyn, *Die Stadwaartse Trek*, p. 22. Many of the conference papers addressed themselves to the dangers of the city, which included a threat of that which is foreign, loss of traditions of the *volk*, subversion of family life, immorality, misuse of alchohol and women, gambling, and so forth. Indeed these themes form a consistent part of the rhetoric of the era, reinforcing our earlier point that a reduction of the response of the Afrikaner nationalist movement to economic motives alone is entirely misplaced.

44. This was the slogan of the *Volkskongres*: 'Daar's 'n stryd te stry,/Daar's 'n nasie te lei,/Daar's werk!'

45. Malan, 'Die Nuwe Groot Trek', p. 11. Albertyn asks whether, having been informed of the conditions leading to the poor white problem, Afrikaners could still 'throw stones' at their co-Afrikaners in the slums of the large cities. Albertyn, 'Openingsrede', p. 6.

46. H. Cornelius, 'Die Offerhande', *Klerewerker*, vol. 3, no. 10, 1942, pp. 3–6.

47. Coetzee suggests that this was the case. J.M. Coetzee, 'The Mind of Apartheid: Geoffrey Conje (1907–)', *Social Dynamics*, vol. 17, no. 1, 1991, p. 5.

48. Cornelius, 'Die Offerhande', p. 4.

49. N. Diederichs, 'Beroepsarbeid', in Albertyn, *Die Stadwaartse Trek*, p. 92.

50. Of particular concern in this regard were the closed shop agreements, which the nationalist ideologues did not reject out of hand, but argued that they could be applied 'conditionally', that is, with regard to the different 'nationalities' of workers. For an example of this argument, see H.P. Wolmarans, *Kommunisme en die Suid-Afrikaanse Vakunies*, Johannesburg 1939, pp. 47–53. This issue was the terrain of a bitter struggle between Afrikaner nationalists and non-nationalist trade unions.

51. Albertyn, 'Openingsrede', p. 8; A. Hertzog, 'Arbeidsbeweginge', in Albertyn, *Die Stadwaartse Trek*, p. 96.

52. The 1944 social and economic policy of the NP presented the party as 'neither capitalist nor communist'. 'The Social and Economic Policy of the National Party', *c.*1944 [INEG P24.303]. In this, the document echoed sentiments of national socialist intellectuals such as P.J. Meyer for whom Afrikaner socialism was directed against both (state) communism and capitalism. See P.J. Meyer, *Die Stryd van die Afrikanerwerker*.

Die Vooraand van ons Sosiale Vrywording, Stellenbosch 1944. These issues will be addressed in more depth in chapter 2.

53. Albertyn, Du Toit and Theron, *Kerk en Stad*, p. 337.

54. Ibid., pp. 335–6.

55. The writers of the report express concern about the rates of white youth crime, and the position of women in society, especially of those who turned to prostitution as a way of life. These concerns are also found in other literature of the period, and are indicative of a wide-ranging anxiety about the general effects of urbanization. Several organizations were formed to attend to each of the specific sectors' work: ranging from the *Nasionale Jeugbond*, to women's groups within the National Party and the churches, such as the *Afrikaanse Christelike Vrouevereniging*.

56. Du Toit, *Verslag van die Volkskongres*, p. 297.

57. Van Zyl Smit discusses the broad context and outlines of their thought and their impact upon Afrikaner nationalism. He does not, however, go into much detail concerning the precise relation between Cronje's emphasis on racial determinism, on the one hand, and his stress on *volksgebondenheid* (being bound by the *volk*), on the other. Van Zyl Smit, like Posel, neglects the crucial ambiguities of his thought and therefore cannot properly assess his impact on the articulation of apartheid ideology. See, D. van Zyl Smit, 'Adopting and Adapting Criminological Ideas', *Contemporary Crises*, vol. 13, 1989, pp. 227–51.

58. Ibid., p. 238.

59. See Van Zyl Smit for a discussion of Cronje's ideas on the crimes of Natives, coloureds and Asians, which were not attributed to conditions of poverty but, reflecting the general racist horizon of thought on the subject, were attributed to racial-biological characteristics. Ibid., pp. 239–42.

60. H. Cornelius, 'Woons ons Werkers in Agterbuurtes en Waarom?', *Klerewerker*, vol. 1, no. 2, 1938, p. 3. For a discussion of the provision of housing in the cities, see S. Parnell and C. Hart, 'Church, State and the Shelter of Working-Class Women in Johannesburg, 1920–1955', *South African Geographical Journal*, vol. 71, 1989, pp. 25–31.

61. E.S. Sachs, *Garment Workers in Action*, Johannesburg 1957, p. 19. This description held for all those who lived in Johannesburg's slums, Europeans, coloureds, Indians and Africans, who lived in 'filth and squalor': 'These hovels were often shared by several families. I remember visiting the home of a garment worker in 1931, a widow with six children, who lived in a one-roomed house with no windows at all, only a door and a roof of hessian.' These housing conditions existed not far from Parktown, where affluence and ostentation ruled.

62. G. Cronje, 'Rassevermenging as Maatskaplike Vraagstuk', *Rasssebakens*, 1939, p. 52.

63. C.W. Prinsloo, 'Die Bloedvermenging-Vraagstuk', *Rassebakens*, 1939, p. 35.

64. This did not, however, prevent nationalists from engaging in lurid descriptions of the 'possibilities' of such working conditions.

65. Contrary to the overstrong emphasis Coetzee puts on the discourse on women, the literature frequently also includes references to men overstepping social limits. See Coetzee, 'The Mind of Apartheid'. Prinsloo, for example quotes the case of a certain J.D.S. Blom who, in 1938, had intercourse with a 'Native woman', who subsequently fell pregnant. Blom murdered the woman. In recalling this case, Prinsloo shows no repugnance at the murder, but merely uses the tale as an opportunity to mention that Blom, in his defence, held that he had lived a fair distance from whites of his own age. Prinsloo argues that this is not an isolated case, but that the act of inter-racial intercourse (and not murder) is a 'selfish and irresponsible' one, which does damage to the nation. Prinsloo, 'Die Bloedvermenging-Vraagstuk', p. 34.

66. There was also a proliferation of discussions of the problems of alcoholism, involving a similar double strategy. The *Kerk en Stad* report, for example, argued that three quarters of 'sexually transmitted diseases, one quarter of cases of madness and three quarters of all cases of violent crime could be ascribed to misuse of alcohol.' Albertyn, Theron and Du Toit, *Kerk en Stad*, p. 323.

67. Sedimentation is here used to indicate a 'forgetting' of the moment of the institution of the social, such that its contingent character is covered over. For a further elaboration, see Laclau, *New Reflections*, pp. 34–5.

68. O'Meara, *Volkskapitalisme*, p. 11 and p. 16.

69. I use the term 'new revisionism' here to designate those social and intellectual historians who were influenced by neo-Marxism, but who tended to avoid the excessive reductionism of the earlier neo-Marxists.

70. The most nuanced account of segregation is that offered by Dubow's *Racial Segregation*.

71. See in this regard Dubow, *Racial Segregation*, p. 3, as well as S. Marks' important work on segregation, *The Ambiguities of Dependence in South Africa. Class, Nationalism, and the State in Twentieth-Century Natal*, Johannesburg 1986. Cell also focuses on the importance of the malleability of segregation. See J.W. Cell, *The Highest Stage of White Supremacy. The Origins of Segregation in South Africa and the American South*, Cambridge 1982.

72. See H. Wolpe, 'Capitalism and Cheap Labour-Power in South Africa: From Segregation to Apartheid', *Economy and Society*, vol. 1, no. 4, 1972, pp. 425–56; as well as M. Legassick, 'Legislation, Ideology and Economy in Post-1948 South Africa', *Journal of Southern African Studies*, vol. 1, no. 1, 1974, pp. 5–35.

73. This argument, to be elaborated upon in chapter 4, is based on the critique of a topographical conception of the social as developed by Laclau and Mouffe, *Hegemony and Socialist Strategy*.

74. The details of these processes are discussed in chapters 2 and 4.

75. Marks, *The Ambiguities of Dependence*, p. 14.

76. For a further discussion of the relation between liberalism and segregation, see P. Rich, *White Power and the Liberal Conscience. Racial Segregation and South African Liberalism*, Johannesburg 1984.

77. Dubow, *Racial Segregation*, p. 34.

78. These currents of thought were reinforced by the tradition of paternalism which rationalized white domination in terms of a 'civilizing mission'. Paternalism, moreover, presented white supremacy as part of the natural order of things, thus obviating the need for explicit theories of racial superiority. See Dubow, *Racial Segregation*, p. 47. While this may have been the case generally, specific instances of scientific racism did, of course, appear.

79. Ibid., p. 44.

80. Cell in *The Highest Stage of White Supremacy*, Marks in *The Ambiguities of Dependence* and Dubow in *Racial Segregation* are all in agreement that this is a key element of the effectivity of segregationism. However, they address neither the theoretical premisses, nor the analytical consequences of the emphasis on 'ambiguity' for our understanding of the workings of ideology and the production of subjectivity.

81. The term 'segregation' was first introduced in a paper by J.M. Pim in 1905. Pim, influenced by eugenics, held the view that Africans would degenerate morally in an urban environment, and they should therefore be excluded from white civilization. A debate by 'liberal friends of the Natives' was waged in a number of newspapers and journals such as the *African Monthly*, the *Transvaal Reader* and the *Cape Times* on segregation and the search for a policy 'for a modern South Africa'. Dubow correctly cautions against giving too much attention to the origins of the term, arguing that what should not be obscured is the more significant point that segregation became a political keyword in the first two decades of the twentieth century. Dubow, *Racial Segregation*, p. 35.

82. These included a sharpening of African political awareness after the First World War, expressed not only in township-based resistance, and in events such as the 1920 miners' strike and the 1922 Bulhoek affair, but also in a growing militancy in the countryside.

83. As Dubow points out, Booker T. Washington's ideas on the naturalness of social differentiation aided arguments that Africans were suited only to a rural existence

where they could be shielded from the harsh world of industrialism. Similarly, eugenics, with its idea that the degeneracy and poverty of the urban proletariat could be counteracted through the deliberate manipulation of genetic pools, came to exercise a powerful hold over segregationists. Anthropology, with its focus on cultural adaptation, also took on an increasingly important role, for it provided liberal thinkers with a theory of 'culture contact' which recognized the complexity and distinctiveness of African culture and society, and gave them a way to argue for the preservation of what was distinctly 'African' on segregationist rather than assimilative grounds. See Dubow, *Racial Segregation*, pp. 7–34. For a further discussion of the continued political significance of anthropology in South Africa, see A. Kuper, 'Anthropology and Apartheid', in J. Lonsdale (ed.), *South Africa in Question*, London 1988, pp. 35–51. See also J. Sharp, 'The Roots and Development of Volkekunde in South Africa', *Journal of Southern African Studies*, vol. 8, 1981, pp. 4–5.

84. As with the discourse of apartheid, there never was any question about the superiority of whiteness in segregationist thinking. The United Party Programme of Principles made this abundantly clear: while every endeavour would be made 'to arrive at a satisfactory solution to the Native question', this had to happen along lines which recognized as 'paramount the essentials of European civilization'. See United South African National Party, 'Programme of Principles', reproduced in Carter, *The Politics of Inequality*, p. 474.

85. Dubow points out that until the mid-1920s the political vocabulary of race seldom if ever referred to the 'colour question'. It is only during the 1920s that race becomes explicitly associated with 'colour', and this new association Dubow links to the intensified significance of the Native question at the time. See Dubow, *Racial Segregation*, p. 4.

86. In the discussion of the Native question during the segregationist period, I draw strongly on the seminal work of Ashforth, who investigated the construction of the 'problem' in government commissions of inquiry in his book *The Politics of Official Discourse*. Ashforth's work easily lends itself to this, for his analysis is informed by a Foucauldian perspective on the relation between the construction of subjectivity and knowledge. This is not to suggest, however, that discourses on the 'Native' preceding that of segregation can be ignored. A proper investigation of colonial discourses is necessary in this regard.

87. The position of Africans differed greatly in the territories which were to form the Union of South Africa in 1910. In the Transvaal and the Orange River colony the franchise was restricted to white male adults, while in the Cape Colony the franchise depended upon property qualifications. In Natal, political equality between white and black was accepted in theory, but it had little practical effect. At the time of the formation of the Union, the Cape had thousands of African voters on the electoral roll.

88. Quoted in Ashforth, *The Politics of Official Discourse*, p. 33.

89. Ibid., p. 42, emphasis added.

90. Ibid., p. 37. The laws structuring the relations between the 'European' and the 'Native' during the early decades of the twentieth century included the 1913 Land Act, which made reserves the basis for Native policy; the Native Affairs Act of 1920, and the Natives (Urban Areas) Act of 1923, which systematized influx control and segregated residence in towns; the Industrial Conciliation Act of 1924, which excluded 'Natives' from the definition of employee so that they had no right to strike; the Native Taxation and Development Act of 1925 and the Mines and Works Act of 1911, which established the industrial colour bar and job reservation for whites; and the Native Administration Act of 1927, which forged the recognition of 'Native law', established Native civil courts, introduced a *uniform* Native administration established on reconstructed tribalism, and made legal provision for the establishment of the Native Affairs Department (NAD).

91. Ibid., p. 78.

92. Union of South Africa, *Report of the Native Economic Commission 1930–32*, Pretoria 1932, UG 22/1932, Annexure 11.

93. Ashforth, *The Politics of Official Discourse*, p. 87.

94. Ibid., p. 86.

95. Union of South Africa, *Report of the Native Economic Commission*, para. 525.

96. Ibid., para. 13.

97. Marks' work on the different responses to the so-called dissolution of 'tribal' links is enlightening. It shows not only how the government at the time utilized the notion of retribalization, but also how sections of the African male community sought to reverse the trends of women becoming 'detribalized'. See Marks, *The Ambiguities of Dependence*, pp. 215–40.

98. For a discussion of the slumyard culture in Johannesburg of the latter group, see E. Koch, '"Without Visible Means of Subsistence": Slumyard Culture in Johannesburg 1918–1940', in B. Bozzoli (ed.), *Town and Countryside in the Transvaal. Capitalist Penetration and Popular Response*, Johannesburg 1983, pp. 151–75.

99. B. Bozzoli with M. Nkotsoe, *Women of Phokeng. Consciousness, Life Strategy, and Migrancy in South Africa, 1900–1983*, Johannesburg 1991, p. 75.

100. Dubow, *Racial Segregation*, p. 272.

101. Ashforth, *The Politics of Official Discourse*, p. 69.

102. Drawing on Saussure, most post-structuralist theorizations of subjectivity now accept the argument on the essential relationality of identity.

103. 'Black Peril and Colour Bar', n.d., p. 15. Pamphlet [INEG P4.62].

104. Sachs, *Garment Workers in Action*, p. 101.

105. For a discussion of the significance of the second language movement, see I. Hofmeyer, 'Building a Nation from Words: Afrikaans Language, Literature and Ethnic Identity, 1902–1924', in Marks and Trapido, *The Politics of Race*, pp. 95–123.

106. The term 'civil religion' as it is used here is drawn from the analysis of T. Moodie, *The Rise of Afrikanerdom*, p. 36. For a detailed discussion of the different uses of the term 'Afrikaner' between 1850 and 1915, see H. Giliomee, 'The Beginnings of Afrikaner Ethnic Consciousness, 1850–1915', in L. Vail (ed.), *The Creation of Tribalism in Southern Africa*, London 1989, pp. 21–54.

107. This point is also stressed by S. Marks and S. Trapido, 'The Politics of Race, Class and Nationalism', in Marks and Trapido, *The Politics of Race*, p. 17.

108. For a discussion of Fusion, stressing the economic changes and alliances between different sectors, see O'Meara, *Volkskapitalisme*.

109. United South African National Party, 'Programme of Principles', in Carter, *The Politics of Inequality*, p. 472.

110. The National Party underwent a number of name changes between 1934 and 1951. In 1934, the National Party (NP), under the leadership of Hertzog, and the South African Party, led by Smuts, joined forces to form the United South African National Party, or the United Party (UP), as they became known. This alliance was known as the Fusion government. In protest, Malan broke away and formed the *Gesuiwerde* NP (GNP, Purified NP) in 1934. In 1939 Hertzog refused to sanction a South African declaration of war against Germany and joined the GNP, which then became known as the *Herenigde* NP (HNP, Reunited NP). Hertzog soon left to form the Afrikaner Party (AP), which joined forces with the HNP to win the 1948 election. This alliance changed its name to become the National Party in 1951.

111. Moodie describes the figure of Hoggenheimer as follows: 'After the discovery of gold in 1886, imperialism became linked in the Afrikaner mind with capitalism. Capitalist interests, especially mining interests, were clearly epitomized in the gross cartoon figure, "Hoggenheimer", who was English-speaking, imperialist, and clearly Jewish.' Moodie, *The Rise of Afrikanerdom*, p. 15. For a brief discussion of the origins of the cartoon figure, see also M. Shain, 'Hoggenheimer – The Making of a Myth', *Jewish Affairs*, vol. 36, 1981, pp. 112–16. The influence of anti-semitism on the Afrikaner nationalist movement is discussed in a later section of this chapter.

112. Furlong, *Between Crown and Swastika*, p. 47.

113. Shain points out that much of the new historiography either denied or ignored

the many instances of hospitality accorded Jews in South Africa. In this regard, he focuses especially on the figure of the *smous* (hawker), and thus succeeds in drawing out by contrast the severity of the growing anti-semitic movement in the 1930s. M. Shain, 'Anti-Semitism and South African Society: Reappraising the 1930s and 1940s', *South African Historical Journal*, no. 27, 1992, p. 189.

114. A 1935 GNP pamphlet, *Laat die Feite Praat*, addressed the issue of coalition and Fusion in depth. Nasionale Party van Suid-Afrika, *Laat die Feite Praat*, 1935 [INEG, P24.464].

115. Moodie, *The Rise of Afrikanerdom*, p. 131.

116. H. Cornelius, 'Ons en die Voortrekker-Eeufees!', *Klerewerker*, vol. 1, no. 3, 1938, p. 4.

117. Coetzer and Le Roux, *Die Nasionale Party, Deel* 4, pp. 212–13.

118. These were Malan's words: '. . . get rid of the inferiority complex *vis-à-vis* others, our ancestors and the *Voortrekkers*. Believe in God, believe in your *volk*, believe in yourself.'

119. 'Die volk moet homself red.' The call to start what was to become known as the *Reddingsdaadbond*, literally League for the Act of Rescue, was first made by J.D. Kestell early in 1938, and was repeated in his speech in Bloemfontein during the symbolic Trek.

120. It is important to note here that Dr N.J. van der Merwe, who played a crucial role in the formation of the *Nasionale Kultuurraad*, which made it clear that it thought that playing 'God save the Queen' would doom the celebrations, was also a member of the *Afrikaner Broederbond* (AB). By this time, the AB had firmly shifted allegiance from Hertzog to Malan.

121. The cornerstones were laid by Mrs D.P. Ackerman (*née* Potgieter) as representative of Kmdt-Gen. A.H. Potgieter; Mrs J.C. Muller (*née* Pretorius) as representative of K-Gen. A.W.J. Pretorius; and Mrs G. Preller (*née* Pretorius) as representative of Piet Retief. *Die Volksblad*, 18/10/1938.

122. Coetzer and Le Roux, *Die Nasionale Party, Deel* 4, p. 223.

123. The Afrikaans-speaking female members of the union resented the fact that the nationalist press, especially *Die Transvaler*, whenever it attacked their union, used the English rather than the Afrikaans form of its name. It is also important to note that the English and Afrikaans editions of the *Garment Worker/Klerewerker* differed subtantially in terms of content, with the *Klerewerker* regularly carrying articles on issues pertinent to Afrikaans-speaking women which were not reproduced in the English version. These included discussions of the Centenary celebrations in particular, and Afrikaner nationalist politics more generally.

124. Cornelius, 'Ons en die Voortrekker-Eeufees!', p. 4. Translated literally, *niggies* would mean cousins or nieces. Traditionally, in Afrikaner circles such forms of address, however, are quite often between people who have no familial relation.

125. Ibid.

126. M. Kruger, 'Voortrekker Eeufees', *Klerewerker*, vol. 1, no. 3, 1983, p. 7.

127. Other unions proved less resistant to the onslaught of Afrikaner nationalism. For a discussion of the *Spoorbond* and the *Mynwerkersunie*, see O'Meara, 'Analysing Afrikaner Nationalism', pp. 64–70.

128. The *Klerewerkersunie* had suffered severe setbacks in the early 1930s, and especially with the 1931 and 1923 general strikes. For a brief account of the history of attacks on the KWU, see Sachs, *Garment Workers in Action*.

129. See Wolmarans, *Kommunisme en die Suid-Afrikaanse Vakunies*, pp. 43–7.

130. Letter from D.B.H. Grobbelaar to E.S. Sachs, reprinted in the *Garment Worker*, vol. 1, no. 4, 1938, p. 9.

131. Nasionale Party, *Verkiesingsmanifes: Algemene Verkiesing 1938*, Artikel 4.

132. Conceptually this distinction overlaps with that presented in chapter 1 in terms of the differential and equivalential dimensions of the construction of political frontiers.

133. Here I agree with Balibar that the nature of so-called 'new racism' can be

traced back to anti-semitism and also to the 'culturalist racism' of the Afrikaner *volksbeweging*. See E. Balibar, 'Is There a "Neo-Racism"?', in E. Balibar and I. Wallerstein (eds), *Race, Nation, Class. Ambiguous Identities*, London 1991, pp. 17–28.

134. On 19 February 1936, Malan proposed a motion to place 'Cape Coloureds', like Africans, on a separate voters' roll. His motion was unsuccessful.

135. The 1938 GNP congress resolved to endeavour to establish legal measures forbidding 'mixed marriages', miscegenation and 'mixed' residential areas. It also proposed economic as well as political segregation between whites and 'non-whites'.

136. Coetzer and Le Roux, *Die Nasionale Party. Deel* 4, p. 67.

137. Prinsloo, 'Die Bloedvermenging-Vraagstuk', p. 23.

138. Cronje, 'Rassevermenging as Maatskaplike Vraagstuk', p. 50–51. Cronje makes a similar argument elsewhere, pointing out that: 'When our poor, who are to a large extent already outcasts of the privileged, get into debt to Asians, they are further humiliated. And have not their debts been written off once one of their daughters becomes the wife of the creditor?' See G. Cronje, 'Rasvermening en Gemengde Huwelike', *Volkswelstand*, vol. 1, no. 3, 1940, p. 121.

139. D.W. Kruger, *The Making of a Nation. A History of the Union of South Africa 1910–1961*, Johannesburg 1969, p. 181. By 1936, the Jewish population formed no less than 4.5 per cent of the total white population.

140. Hansard, cited in Coetzer and Le Roux, *Die Nasionale Party. Deel* 4, p. 81.

141. This is the term used to describe their position by Furlong, *Between Crown and Swastika*, p. 62.

142. Speech delivered to a Stellenbosch audience in April 1937, cited in ibid., p. 65.

143. Ibid.

144. Shain, 'Anti-Semitism and South African Society', p. 191.

145. Ibid., p. 192.

146. Oswald Pirow, quoted in Coetzer and Le Roux, *Die Nasionale Party. Deel* 4, p. 271.

147. For the history of the reunification, see ibid., chapter 7.

148. O'Meara, *Volkskapitalisme*, p. 125.

149. Ibid.

150. For an excellent discussion of the character of the OB's politics, see C. Marx, 'The Ossewabrandwag as a Mass Movement, 1939–1941', *Journal of Southern African Studies*, vol. 20, no. 2, 1994, pp. 195–219.

151. *Die Volksblad*, 6/2/1939, emphasis added. Furlong argues that the use of the term '*Diets-Afrikaans*' in the OB inaugural oath reflected not the more recent ethnicism of the *volksbeweging*, but referred to a 'more distant past, a reference to . . . *all* the Dutch, Flemings, and Afrikaners in the broadest sense, an anachronistic usage from medieval times'. This, for Furlong, is evidence of a link between outspokenly fascist organizations in Belgium which had advocated a '*Dietsch Volk*'. Furlong, *Between Crown and Swastika*, p. 140.

152. Furlong argues that the shirt movements arose in what amounted to a political vacuum for militant nationalists in the period between Fusion and the GNP breakaway. Ibid., p. 33.

153. L.T. Weichardt, 'Blank Suid-Afrika', 31 January 1948 [INEG P24.173].

154. These include the Brownshirts (*Bruinhemde, Nasionale Werkersbond van Suid-Afrika*), the Greyshirts, later resurrected as the *Blanke Werkersparty* (White Workers' Party) under the leadership of Weichardt, the *Blanke Werkers Beskermingsbond* (White Workers' Protection League), and later the *N-S Boerenasie* (N-S Boere Nation), formed in 1940 by Gen. Manie Maritz, who also founded the South African Anglo-Nordic Union, and the *Anti-Kommunistiese Front* (AKF, Anti-Communist Front) under the leadership of Robbie Leibrandt.

155. Furlong, *Between Crown and Swastika*, pp. 34–5.

156. Furlong points out that known anti-semites such as A.J. Werth did not trust Malan's new party. Ibid., p. 33.

157. Weichardt, 'Blank Suid-Afrika', p. 4.

158. While many of these splinter groupings did not have much influence on white politics, the Greyshirts, later to form the BWP, did exercise some influence, and these movements certainly contributed to the formation of a certain horizon of meaning which would structure the discourse of the GNP.

159. Cited in Furlong, *Between Crown and Swastika*, p. 162.

160. The most significant contest in this regard took place around the draft republican constitution, with strong national socialist overtones, published by the OB in April 1940.

161. Malan's election as *volksleier* was accepted by the OB and the AB.

162. For a detailed analysis of the relation between the OB, Oswald Pirow's New Order and the NP, see Furlong, *Between Crown and Swastika*, chapters 5–8.

163. The proponents of a republic were located primarily in the Transvaal, and Malan would only reluctantly move in that direction.

164. It has to be made clear that the argument presented does not proceed from a mere rejection of the main neo-Marxist theses. Rather, I attempt to rearticulate the precise status of elements of the analysis, and to weaken the claims to 'objectivity'. This is not to say, however, that I proceed from a 'subjectivist' point of view. To the contrary: my analysis seeks to circumvent that distinction by focusing on the production and sedimentation of social and political frontiers through which what are essentially contingent acts appear as 'natural' and 'objective'.

165. O'Meara, *Volkskapitalisme*, p. 120.

166. While the argument is not developed in this chapter, it does not exclude the possibility of making precisely the same argument with regard to, for example, the position of farmers.

2 Apartheid as Myth

Materials presented in this chapter draw on my article 'Decolonization, Demonization and Difference: The Difficult Constitution of a Nation' published in *Philosophy and Social Criticism*, vol. 21, no. 3, 1995, pp. 31–51.

1. A. Gramsci, quoted in B. Fontana, *Hegemony and Power. On the Relation between Gramsci and Machiavelli*, Minneapolis 1993, p. 21.

2. M. Foucault, 'Nietzsche, Genealogy, History', in *Language, Counter-Memory, Practice. Selected Essays and Interviews*, edited with an introduction by D.F. Bouchard, Ithaca, New York 1977, p. 142.

3. Ibid., pp. 139–64.

4. Foucault's critique of the history of ideas is developed at length in *The Archaeology of Knowledge*, London 1972.

5. Foucault, 'Nietzsche, Genealogy, History', p. 147.

6. I use the term 'beginnings' in order to distinguish my account for a search for origins.

7. The notion of articulation is used in opposition to the idea of mediation. It presupposes a set of relations with no necessary belonging between them.

8. See, in this regard, O'Meara, *Volkskapitalisme*, and D. Posel, *The Making of Apartheid 1948–1961. Conflict and Compromise*, Oxford 1991.

9. O'Meara, *Volkskapitalisme*, pp. 1–17.

10. For a detailed review of *The Making of Apartheid*, see A.J. Norval, 'Searching for a Method in the Madness. Apartheid and Influx Control', *South African Historical Journal*, no. 29, 1993, pp. 234–45.

11. In this sense liberal and neo-Marxist historiographies shared more than was initially apparent. For a fuller discussion of this reading of the debate, see A.J. Norval, 'Accounting for Apartheid: Its Emergence, Crisis and Logic', PhD thesis, University of Essex 1994, pp. 16–61.

12. For a discussion of this problem in the context of Southern African studies more generally, see A.J. Norval, 'The 'Boerewors Curtain' and the 'Metropole'. Twenty Years of Southern African Studies', *South African Historical Journal*, no. 31, 1994, pp. 198–204.

13. Bonner, Delius and Posel. 'The Shaping of Apartheid', pp. 10–16. For an excellent review of *Apartheid's Genesis*, see Robinson, '(Dis)locating Historical Narrative'.

14. I draw here on the idea of 'supplementarity' as developed by Derrida in his reading of Rousseau. See J. Derrida, *Of Grammatology*, Baltimore 1976, p. 145.

15. Lefort, *The Political Forms of Modern Society*, p. 196.

16. Laclau and Mouffe, *Hegemony and Socialist Strategy*, p. 153.

17. Foucault, 'Nietzsche, Genealogy, History', pp. 151–2.

18. Gramsci, quoted in Fontana, *Hegemony and Power*, p. 23.

19. In fact, the very question of their relation was one which was crucial to the whole discussion.

20. I do not, therefore, attempt to provide a complete overview of the writing of the organic intellectuals under consideration. That is a task which falls beyond the scope of this chapter.

21. One of the few authors who addresses this problem is O'Meara in *Volkskapitalisme*. However, in line with his neo-Marxist approach, he regards these intellectuals as nothing more than petty bourgeois intellectuals who sought to form a mass base of support in order to further their own interests.

22. Laclau, *New Reflections*, p. 39.

23. E. Laclau and L. Zac, 'Minding the Gap', in E. Laclau (ed.), *The Making of Political Identities*, London 1994, p. 37.

24. S. Žižek, 'Beyond Discourse Analysis', in Laclau, *New Reflections*, pp. 251–2.

25. I do not agree that the theoretical focus on an external enemy, as Žižek argues, necessarily entails the illusion that after the annihilation of the external enemy I will 'arrive at an identity with myself'. Žižek simply asserts this, without taking into account the anti-humanist thrust of the argument already present in the concept of subject positions. See S. Žižek, *The Sublime Object of Ideology*, London 1989, p. 2.

26. C. Lévi-Strauss, *The Savage Mind*, London 1966, p. 18.

27. R.C. Poole, 'Introduction', in C. Lévi-Strauss, *Totemism*, Harmondsworth 1973, p. 52.

28. M. Foucault, 'What Is an Author?', in P. Rabinow (ed.), *The Foucault Reader*, Harmondsworth 1984, p. 114.

29. For example, the fact that a number of them studied abroad – in the Europe of the 1930s – is considered to be important, because this contributed to a widening of their horizons of reference beyond the parochiality of the local context. This is, of course, not to agree with the content of that 'widening', but simply to stress the sense in which studying abroad was influential in the rearticulation of their experiences in the narrower South African context.

30. A. Gramsci, *Selections from the Prison Notebooks*, London 1971, p. 338.

31. Ibid., p. 340.

32. Laclau, *New Reflections*, p. 61.

33. The transformation of mythical spaces into imaginaries will be discussed in chapter 4.

34. See, for example, J. Kinghorn, *Die NG Kerk en Apartheid*, Johannesburg 1986; J.A. Loubser, *The Apartheid Bible. A Critical Review of Racial Theology in South Africa*, Cape Town 1987; C. Ngcokovane, *Demons of Apartheid*, Braamfontein 1989; M. Prozesky (ed.), *Christianity Amidst Apartheid: Selected Perspectives on the Church in South Africa*, London 1990; and S. Dubow, 'Afrikaner Nationalism, Apartheid and the Conceptualization of "Race"', *Journal of African History*, vol. 33, 1992, pp. 209–37.

35. Ngockovane remarks that this was the case also earlier in the history of Afrikaner nationalism. For example, in the post-war reconstruction period after the Anglo-Boer War, religious leaders helped in building schools and rebuilt churches.

Ngockovane, *Demons of Apartheid*, p. 43. For a discussion of the role of the churches in the early formation of Christian national education, see J.D. Shingler, 'Education and Political Order in South Africa, 1902–1961', PhD thesis, Yale University 1973.

36. Some of these issues will be discussed in chapter 3.

37. Bloomberg argues that the concept of separate development was shaped by four major Christian nationalist ideas, namely that: (1) God created all national, cultural, linguistic and ethnic groups and desires them to retain their peculiar characteristics; (2) variety is the hallmark of creation; (3) black Africans have a special role in God's master-plan; and (4) the Afrikaner's task was not to 'Europeanize' Africans and to to rob them of their ancestral culture, but to 'Christian-Nationalize' the inner forms and values of that culture. C. Bloomberg, *Christian-Nationalism and the Rise of the Afrikaner Broederbond in South Africa, 1918–48*, edited by S. Dubow, London 1990, p. 131.

38. Dubow, 'Afrikaner Nationalism', p. 211. In this respect, it is important to note, as Dubow points out, that 'Christian nationalism' was by no means a monolithic doctrine. Much of the debate between the 1930s and 1950s consisted precisely in attempting to establish a set of core principles which, nevertheless, was open to interpretation and reinterpretation.

39. Several important Afrikaner intellectuals studied at the Free University of Amsterdam, including J.D. du Toit, E.P. Groenewald, L.J. du Plessis, H.J. Strauss and N.J. van der Merwe.

40. In discussions of Afrikaner nationalism, Stoker's work rarely receives independent treatment, and the development of political concepts in his work tend to be neglected.

41. H.G. Stoker, *Die Stryd om die Ordes*, Pretoria 1942, p. 234.

42. Kuyper's thought strongly influenced the *verzuiling* (pillarization) policy of the Netherlands.

43. A. Kuyper, *Pro Rege III*, pp. 257–8, quoted in F.J.M. Potgieter, 'Veelvormige Ontwikkeling en die Wil van God', *Journal for Racial Affairs*, vol. 10, no. 1, 1958, p. 7.

44. Bloomberg, *Christian-Nationalism*, p. 9.

45. Dubow, 'Afrikaner Nationalism', p. 219.

46. This is not to reduce the whole of his theology to politics, something which would be inadmissible in terms of Stoker's Calvinism, but rather to stress the importance which he himself gave to the precise political context in which *Die Stryd om die Ordes* was written.

47. These calls emanated primarily from the *Nuwe Orde Studie Kring* and the OB, as discussed in chapter 1.

48. Dubow, 'Afrikaner Nationalism', p. 217.

49. Stoker quoted in Bloomberg, *Christian-Nationalism*, p. 146.

50. Stoker argues repeatedly that the *volk* had to be saved from the 'marsh of British imperialist liberalism in which it is drowning'. See *Die Stryd om die Ordes*, p. 106.

51. Ibid., p. 250.

52. Ibid., p. 275.

53. Ibid., p. 238.

54. S.J. du Toit, 'Openbaringslig op die Apartheidsvraagstuk, *Koers*, vol. XVII, no.1, 1949, p. 17.

55. W.J. Snyman, 'Rasseverhoudinge in die Skrif', *Koers*, vol. XXV, no. 3, 1957, p. 167.

56. Bloomberg, *Christian-Nationalism*, p. 132.

57. Stoker, *Die Stryd om die Ordes*, p. 265.

58. T. Flemming, 'Die Vroue en Vroueorganisasies', in J.D. Vorster and H.G. Stoker (eds), *Uit Vroue-harte*, Bloemfontein 1950, p. 278.

59. Ibid.

60. Tini Vorster was the wife of B.J. Vorster, who was interned during the 1940s for his activities in the OB, and who was later to become South Africa's prime minister.

61. H.S. Brink, 'Die Boerevrou', in Vorster and Stoker, *Uit Vroue-harte*, p. 248.

62. E. Steyn du Toit, 'Bouster van 'n Nasie', in ibid., p. 232.

63. B.J. Marais, *Die Kleurkrisis in die Weste*, Johannesburg 1952.

64. B.B. Keet, quoted in Loubser, *The Apartheid Bible*, pp. 74–5.

65. Ibid., p. 75. In addition to the fact that these individuals lacked a power base, Loubser further attributes their failure to the fact that they did not have a strong enough theological frame of reference which could serve as an alternative to the Kuyperian theory of creation ordinances.

66. As argued earlier, it is important to keep in mind that while these thinkers held their struggle to be a 'cultural' one, it did in fact lead to a series of interventions on the terrain of politics to which Malan was staunchly opposed.

67. Stals points out that the *Arbeidslaers* never really became a force to be reckoned with. Stals, *Afrikaners in die Goudstad*, p. 98.

68. Furlong argues that Meyer is an example of how 'one man could effectively propagate his own rather extravagant beliefs across a wide spectrum of society. Extraordinarily ambitious, he went far beyond the usual role of a mere minutes-keeper to ensure the realization of his vision of Afrikanerdom.' Furlong, *Between Crown and Swastika*, p. 109.

69. The ANS in effect acted as a youth wing for the OB. The extent of the similarities between this break away and that of the later Black Consciousness-inspired one is remarkable.

70. Founding statement of the ANS, quoted in Bloomberg, *Christian-Nationalism*, p. 97.

71. In contrast to the usual designation of these thinkers as 'neo-Fichtean' nationalists, I prefer to use the term culturalist, for it captures more precisely the terrain in which they intervened.

72. Furlong, *Between Crown and Swastika*, p. 110. Furlong does not attempt to investigate the precise *nature of the articulation* established in Meyer's thought between the so-called 'neo-Fichteanism', Kuyperianism and his 'home-grown' national socialism. Even more seriously, he does not take account of the Afrikaans–English relation as a crucial context for this articulation.

73. A. du Toit, 'The Problem of Intellectual History in (Post)colonial Societies: The Case of South Africa', *Politikon*, vol. 18, no. 2, 1991, p. 15.

74. Bloomberg, *Christian-Nationalism*, p. 143.

75. Ibid., p. 150. Bloomberg argues that, as a result, two distinct schools of thought emerged among 1930s Christian nationalists: that represented by L.J. du Plessis – who promoted a partyless authoritarian dictatorship and the total destruction of liberal-capitalist democracy – and that represented by writers such as A.H. van der Walt and J.D. Vorster, who found the idolatrous tendencies of Nazism offensive.

76. This question concerns the proper contextualization of culturalist Afrikaner nationalism. It is clear that mere reference to fascist ideas does not provide an automatic guarantee of proper context.

77. I would conclude that it did not become decisive. The cultural nationalism of the 1920s and 1930s remained important and was reinforced by Scriptural readings. However, the socialist element of Afrikaner thought, and thus also its articulation with cultural nationalism, was clearly short-lived. Nevertheless, one still has to agree with Furlong that the NP emerged a more authoritarian party at the end of the 1940s.

78. N. Diederichs, *Nasionalisme as Lewensbeskouing en sy Verhouding tot die Internasionalisme*, Bloemfontein 1936, p. 18.

79. Ibid., p. 15.

80. Ibid., p. 18.

81. Ibid., p. 38. It is in this sense that Diederichs's thought on nationalism combines Romanticism with 'fascist' doctrines: in his emphasis on the spiritualized conception of man and of nationhood; in his rejection of the materialistic conception of man and community; in his conception of life as a struggle in which man conquers himself to become what is truly worthy.

82. In all these dimensions, Diederichs's conception of nationalism could be argued to be deeply influenced not only by German Romanticism, but also by other thinkers, such as Nietzsche.
83. Ibid., pp. 25–45.
84. Ibid., p. 40.
85. Ibid., p. 49.
86. Ibid., p. 52.
87. Ibid., p. 45.
88. Ibid., pp. 55–6.
89. Wolmarans, *Kommunisme en die Suid-Afrikaanse Vakunies*. It is interesting to note that three of the five photographs accompanying the text contained material supposed to show the 'appalling' conditions of white women in Russia, ranging from having to work with 'non-whites' to having to do hard physical labour alongside men. The fourth was a picture of the Trades and Labour Council, described as 'being of all sorts: Jews, English, Afrikaans, kaffirs, coloureds, etc.' For the writer this depicted the future of South Africa as communists saw it: with no distinction to be made between nation, race and colour.
90. E. Louw, *Die Kommunistiese Gevaar*. Publication of the Information Service of the HNP, no. 1, Cape Town n.d. [INEG P20.105].
91. It is quite clear, in contrast to the position held by writers such as Van Deventer and Nel, that right from the start anti-communism was a signifier which could be used to stifle any resistance to the dominant order in South Africa. A. van Deventer and P. Nel, 'The State and "die Volk" versus Communism, 1922–1941', *Politikon*, vol. 17, no. 2, 1990, p. 65.
92. J.F.J. van Rensburg, 'Die Taktiek van die Kommintern' in N. Diederichs and P. Meyer (eds), *Hedendaagse Staatkundige Strominge*, Johannesburg 1937. Quoted in Van Deventer and Nel, 'The State and "die Volk"', p. 34.
93. N. Diederichs, *Wat die Kommunisme werklik is*, Bloemfontein 1946, pp. 9–10 and 14. This document was produced under the auspices of the *Sinodale Kommissie vir die Bestryding van Maatskaplike Euwels* (Synodal Commission for the Combating of Social Evils) of the Dutch Reformed Churches.
94. This is not to say, however, that nationalist thought can be reduced to either of these dimensions.
95. Meyer, *Die Stryd van die Afrikanerwerker*.
96. It is simply not the case that their concern during the mid-1930s was focused primarily on 'race relations policies', except in so far as the term 'race' is used to designate not only black/white relations, but also the relation between Afrikaners and English-speaking South Africans. It was well into the 1960s before the 'difference' between Afrikaner and English-speaker was no longer described in terms of racial categories.
97. For Meyer, the tradition of non-European trade unionism represented an 'own coloured and Native nationalism' acting as a bulwark against communism. Meyer, *Die Stryd van die Afrikanerwerker*, p. 68.
98. Ibid., p. 77.
99. Ibid., p. 78–9. It is important to be clear about the import of this statement. Furlong's argues that this shows that 'as in Fascist-ruled Italy and Nazi-ruled Germany, where employer and employee belonged to a single umbrella body in the interest of national unity, the worker would be co-opted into the national movement and the class divide would be bridged by organizations stressing a common nationhood or ethnicity rather than class conflict.' Furlong, *Between Crown and Swastika*, p. 94. Furlong fails to see that attempts to prevent social division along class lines are typical of all nationalist movements. He provides no argument as to why, in this case, it should be considered *fascist*.
100. Meyer, *Die Stryd van die Afrikanerwerker*, p. 79. This conception of nationalism as 'an outlook on life' clearly is a reference to Diederich's *Nasionalisme as Lewensbeskouing*.

101. It is important to see this remark in the context of both the AB's and the OB's role in trying to establish unity within the 'Afrikaner *volk*' across differences between political parties.

102. The real existence of this socialism, for Meyer, could be traced back to 1922, with the formation of the first mining workers' commandos which contributed later to the formation of the *Spoorbond* and the railway workers' commandos.

103. Meyer, *Die Stryd van die Afrikanerwerker*, p. 83. Meyer ascribed the lack of success of these organizations to 'enemy propaganda' and the united efforts of the British socialists and communists.

104. Ibid., p. 85.

105. Ibid.

106. This echoes the title of the National Party's information secretary Otto du Plessis's booklet *The New South Africa – The Revolution of the Twentieth Century*, published in 1940. This booklet proclaimed that Western democracy was doomed and hailed the emergence of a Nazi New Order.

107. Meyer, *Die Stryd van die Afrikanerwerker*, p. 93.

108. Meyer continually stressed the indigenous nature of this project – thus also the need to link its history back to 1922 – even though the Afrikaners themselves were not 'conscious' of it.

109. In 1940–41 Meyer was a member of the AB executive policy committee which had to formulate the AB's position on the question of the republican ideal. The AB argued for the replacement of the senate with an advisory *gemeenskapsraad* (community council) in which different *volksgroepe* would be represented. This, in essence, was an argument for corporate representation.

110. P.J. Meyer, *Nog Nie Ver Genoeg Nie. 'n Persoonlike Rekenskap van Vyftig Jaar Georganizeerde Afrikanerskap*, Johannesburg 1984, p. 50.

111. Bloomberg, *Christian-Nationalism*, p. 167.

112. He subsequently organized a management school in April 1959 in Belville.

113. Dubow, 'Afrikaner Nationalism', p. 226.

114. For a discussion of the influences on Eloff and his rejection of black/white 'intermixing', see ibid., pp. 227–8.

115. They included *'n Tuiste vir die Nageslag* (1945), *Afrika sonder die Asiaat* (1946), *Regverdige Rasseapartheid* (1947) and *Voogdyskap en Apartheid* (1948).

116. Cronje, quoted in Dubow's 'Afrikaner Nationalism', p. 233.

117. G. Cronje, *'n Tuiste vir die Nageslag*, Johannesburg 1945, p. 74. Cronje, in line with the emerging consensus of the wider *volksbeweging*, found the main cause of such miscegenation to lie in the 'mixed living areas' of poor whites. The major cause of social problems was capitalist-induced poverty.

118. Whether or not 'pure' races existed did not matter for Coetzee: 'suffice it to say that differences, and often deep differences, do exist between races and that these differences . . . are so important that account has to be taken of them.' G. Cronje, *Voogdyskap en Apartheid*, Pretoria 1948, p. 31.

119. Cronje, 'Rassevermenging as Maatskaplike Vraagstuk', p. 44.

120. I draw here upon the work of Balibar. See E. Balibar, 'Racism and nationalism', in E. Balibar and Wallerstein (eds), *Race, Nation, Class. Ambiguous Identities*, London 1991, pp. 37–67.

121. Cronje, 'Rassevermenging as Maatskaplike Vraagstuk', pp. 42–6.

122. G. Cronje, *Regverdige Rasse-Apartheid*, Stellenbosch 1947, pp. 92–6.

123. Ibid., p. 71. This theory of racial contact was later to be echoed in official pronouncements, both by individuals and by the Tomlinson Commission of Inquiry.

124. Ibid.

125. Ibid., p. 127.

126. For example, it was argued that the coloured community was dissatisfied with the penetration of Natives into coloured areas, and that the Natives resisted their exploitation by the Indian community.

127. Cronje, *Reverdige Rasse-Apartheid*, p. 76.

128. Ibid., p. 157.
129. Ibid., p. 203.
130. Ibid., p. 87.
131. In his characteristic language Cronje wrote that mixed marriages between coloureds and whites – for him the result of political equalization between coloured and whites in the nineteenth-century Cape – were nothing other than 'the symptoms of the horrible exploding places [*uitbarsplekke*] of the cancerous, corroding process of miscegenation.' Ibid., p. 42.
132. Cronje, 'Rasvermenging as Maatskaplike Vraagstuk', p. 55.
133. Foucault, *The Archaeology of Knowledge*, pp. 136–8.
134. Here I draw on the later Wittgenstein's conception of family resemblances in a language game.
135. This is in contrast to the conception of later nationalists for whom coloureds formed part of the 'European' bloc. This will be discussed in more depth in chapter 4.
136. For a psychoanalytic reading of this process, see S. Žižek, *Tarrying with the Negative. Kant, Hegel, and the Critique of Ideology*, Durham, North Carolina 1993, pp. 200–37.
137. Although Foucault is generally regarded as replacing continuist forms of history with a discontinuist one, this is not the case. Foucault argues that 'there is absolutely no question here of substituting the category of the "discontinuous" for the no less abstract and general one of the continuous. I am attempting to show that discontinuity is not a monotonous and unthinkable void between events . . . but that it is a play of specific transformations, each one different from the next. . . .' M. Foucault, 'Politics and the Study of Discourse', in G. Burchell, C. Gordon and P. Miller (eds), *The Foucault Effect. Studies in Governmentality*, London 1991, pp. 58–9.
138. Foucault, *The Archaeology of Knowledge*, p. 174.
139. *Iter*, the Sanskrit term, refers both to what remains the same in the process of repetition, and to what changes as a result of it.
140. Derrida, *Limited Inc.*, p. 12.
141. Ibid.

3 From Myth to Imaginary

1. Derrida, *Dissemination*, Chicago 1981, p. 63.
2. Bauman, *Modernity and Ambivalence*, Oxford 1991, p. 1.
3. The HNP, under the leadership of Malan, and the AP, under the leadership of Hertzog, formed an electoral alliance in the 1948 election. In 1951 they merged to become the NP.
4. No evidence exists to show that the UP gave any special attention to the coloured vote.
5. J. Lazar, 'Conformity and Conflict. Afrikaner Nationalist Politics in South Africa 1948–1961', unpublished DPhil thesis, Balliol College, Oxford University 1987, p. 37.
6. Ibid., p. 91.
7. R. Cohen, *Endgame in South Africa?*, London 1986, p. 8.
8. Ibid., p. 9.
9. See Lipton, *Capitalism and Apartheid*, pp. 1–13; H. Wolpe, *Race, Class and the Apartheid State*, London 1988, pp. 8–10.
10. Posel, for example, characterizes the division between these two 'phases' in this manner. See Posel, *The Making of Apartheid*, p. 1. This is also the convention in more traditional histories of Afrikaner nationalism.
11. Laclau, *New Reflections*, pp. 60–67.
12. Dubow, *Racial Segregation*, p. 4 (emphasis added).

13. Ibid., p. 15.

14. R. de Villiers, 'Afrikaner Nationalism', in M. Wilson and L. Thompson (eds) *The Oxford History of South Africa*, vol. II, Oxford 1971, p. 373.

15. In 1959, the Transvaal NP annual congress requested the Union government and the Provincial Administrations to replace the term 'European' with 'white' in all official documents. 'Agenda of the Annual Conference of the NP of Transvaal, 16–18 September 1959', p. 23.

16. I. Wallerstein, 'The Ideological Tensions of Capitalism. Universalism versus Racism and Sexism', in E. Balibar and I. Wallerstein (eds), *Race, Nation, Class. Ambiguous Identities*, London 1991, p. 34.

17. E. Balibar, 'Racism and Nationalism', in ibid., pp. 39–40.

18. *Report of the Native Laws Commission 1946–48*, Department of Native Affairs, Union of South Africa, Pretoria 1948, UG No. 28-1948, p. 5 (original emphasis) (Chair: Fagan).

19. *Native Laws Commission*, p. 20.

20. For an analysis of the operation of this metaphor in the Fagan report, see Ashforth, *The Politics of Official Discourse*, p. 122.

21. Ibid., p. 132. The fact that the Fagan report is regarded as a 'lost liberal opportunity' actually says much about the nature of South African liberalism and its complicity in maintaining racial division.

22. *Native Laws Commission*, p. 26.

23. Here the limitedness of their insistence on 'factual' questions only is shown most clearly. In trying to undermine the position that 'commingling between black and white is undesirable', the report rejects the argument on 'purely logical grounds', and points out, in addition, that the real reason for holding this position is still 'racial difference', without questioning the very presupposition of that argument.

24. *Native Laws Commission*, p. 48.

25. Ibid., p. 27.

26. Ibid., pp. 22–4.

27. Ibid., p. 27.

28. Ibid.

29. Ibid., p. 45.

30. The Work Colonies Act (No. 25 of 1949) indeed made provision for the regulation of behaviour of 'won't works' who failed to provide for their families, as well as for a 'wider group of socially maladjusted persons', including those over nineteen years of age found guilty of contravening vagrancy laws, innebriates and drug addicts, and thiefs.

31. *Native Laws Commission*, pp. 14–19.

32. R.F.A. Hoernlé, cited in W.M.M. Eiselen, 'The Meaning of Apartheid', *Race Relations Journal*, vol. XV, no. 3, 1948, pp. 76–7.

33. Ibid. (emphasis added).

34. A.W. Hoernlé, 'Alternatives to Apartheid', *Race Relations Journal*, vol. XV, no. 3, 1948, p. 93.

35. Ibid., p. 93 and pp. 98–9.

36. Bloomberg, *Christian-Nationalism*, p. 133.

37. Quoted in ibid., p. 134.

38. Dubow, 'Afrikaner Nationalism', p. 211.

39. Ibid., p. 212.

40. Eiselen, 'The Meaning of Apartheid'.

41. Ibid., p. 72.

42. Ibid., p. 74.

43. Ibid., p. 76.

44. Ibid., pp. 83–4.

45. Posel drew attention to the divisions within Afrikanerdom on this question. Posel, 'The Meaning of Apartheid before 1948', pp. 123–39.

46. J.P.C. Mosterd, 'Swart Verstedeliking in die Algemene Verkiesing van 1948', *Journal for Contemporary History*, vol. 10, no. 3, 1985, p. 44.

47. Blanke Werkersparty, *Grondbeginsels van die Program van die Blanke Werkersparty*, 1947, p. 7 [INEG P24.1.5].

48. As Mosterd points out, black urbanization was a key issue in the by-elections in Hottentots-Holland, Kimberley district, Wolmaranstad, Zululand and Wakkerstroom between 1945 and 1947. See Mosterd, 'Swart Verstedeliking', p. 30.

49. Quoted in ibid., p. 33.

50. 'H.N.P. se Ekonomiese Plan vir Suid Afrika', *Stryd*, vol. 5, no. 4, 1946.

51. *Verslag van die Kleurvraagstuk Kommissie van die HNP*, 1947 (Chair: Sauer) (hereafter: Sauer report).

52. These were the instructions given to the Commission by D.F. Malan. Quoted in Mosterd, 'Swart Verstedeliking', pp. 36–7.

53. In this respect, the report seemed to adopt the position of H. du Plessis, rather than of L.J. du Plessis, who argued that 'the sharpest of inequalities' was compatible with a Christian outlook.

54. Sauer report, E36.

55. Ibid., B7 (emphasis in original).

56. Hence, there is a problem in Posel's attribution of the 'total apartheid' position to SABRA *as an influence on* the Sauer report.

57. Lazar, 'Conformity and Conflict', p. 226.

58. *Die Kerkblad*, 23/6/1950.

59. Howy, *Die Kerkblad*, 7/7/1950.

60. Malan, *Hansard* HAD, 1950, cols 4144–4142.

61. South African Bureau for Racial Affairs, *Integration or Separate Development?*, Stellenbosch 1952, p. 4.

62. Ibid., pp. 8–9.

63. Ibid., p. 9.

64. Ibid., pp. 15–16.

65. Ibid., p. 34 (emphasis in original).

66. Posel, 'The Meaning of Apartheid before 1948', pp. 128–9.

67. Ibid., pp. 129–30.

68. Ibid., p. 131.

69. Sauer report, E21–15.

70. Posel, 'The Meaning of Apartheid before 1948', p. 132.

71. P. Furlong, 'The Mixed Marriages Act. An Historical and Theological Study', *Communications*, no. 8, 1983, p. 89.

72. The actual number of 'mixed marriages' increased by one during the period cited by Dönges. From 1928–37, 912 marriages between coloured and white took place; from 1938–47, 913 such unions were made. This Dönges called a 'steady increase'. HAD, 1949, col. 6171. Other statistical evidence shows that the number of such marriages had decreased relative to the size of each of the groups.

73. HAD, 1936, cols 2864–70.

74. HAD, 1949, cols 6303, 6556.

75. HAD, 1948, cols 6311, 6539.

76. HAD, 1949, cols 6557–67.

77. G. Cronje, W. Nicol and E.P. Groenewald, *Regverdige Rasse-Apartheid*, Stellenbosch 1947, pp. 41–2.

78. Furlong, 'The Mixed Marriages Act', p. 16.

79. HAD, 1949, col. 6304.

80. Reference to two novels, one Afrikaans and one English, were made at this point in the debate. They are Sarah Gertrude Millen's *God's Stepchildren*, and Regina Neser's *Kinders van Ismael*.

81. See I. Hofmeyer, 'Building a Nation from Words: Afrikaans Language, Literature and Ethnic Identity, 1902–1924', in S. Marks and S. Trapido (eds), *The Politics of Race, Class and Nationalism in Twentieth-Century South Africa*, London 1987, pp. 95–123.

82. *The Torch*, 2/5/1949.

83. *Die Gereformeerde Vaandel*, June 1949.
84. HAD, 1949, col. 6118.
85. HAD, Mr Potgieter (NP), col. 2344.
86. Ibid., col. 2276.
87. Ibid., col. 2277.
88. Ibid., col. 2263.
89. HAD, 1951, col. 2703.
90. HAD, 1950, col. 2263.
91. Ibid., cols 2603–4.
92. Ibid., col. 3197–205.
93. Carter, *The Politics of Inequality*, p. 85.
94. A. Paton, *The People Wept . . . The Story of the Group Areas Act*, Durban n.d., p. 13.
95. Ibid., p. 86.
96. For an account of the forced removal of peoples during this period, see L. Platzky and C. Walker, *Surplus People Project. Forced Removals in South Africa*, Johannesburg 1985. See also the document 'Blackspots: A Study of Apartheid in Action' published by the Liberal Party (1963) [INEG P2.84].
97. K.G. Coleman, 'South Africa is Giving Greater Responsibility to Native Rural Authorities', Native Affairs Administration II, South African State Information Service, 1952, p. 3 [INEG PV27: 4/2/1/1/1].
98. Verwoerd, quoted in Carter, *The Politics of Inequality*, p. 92.
99. Ibid., p. 95.
100. The government argued that appointed leaders were necessary to ensure that chiefs did not 'only represent the illiterate and traditional Natives', but also the 'more educated and sophisticated sections of the community'. Coleman, 'South Africa is Giving Greater Responsibility', p. 2.
101. Carter, *The Politics of Inequality*, p. 95.
102. These laws were the Pass Laws, the Stock Limitation Laws, the Group Areas Act, the Suppression of Communism Act, and the Coloured Voters Act. See, 'Letter Calling for Repeal of Repressive Legislation and Threatening a Defiance Campaign, from Dr J.S. Moroka and W.M. Sizulu to Prime Minister D.F. Malan, January 21, 1952', in T. Karis and G.M. Carter (eds), *From Protest to Challenge. A Documentary History of African Politics in South Africa 1882–1964*, vol. 2, Stanford 1973, p. 476.
103. Eric van Dyk, 'Statement of Policy by the Hon. Minister of Native Affairs (National Party Government) 1952–1953', the Cape Parliamentary Debating Society, 1953, p. 3 [INEG PV27: 4/2/1/1/1.].
104. Ibid., p. 4.
105. Nel in Moodie, *The Rise of Afrikanerdom*, p. 240.
106. Nasionale Party van Suid Afrika, 'Red die Afrikaans-Medium Skole. HNP Bepleit Moedertaalonderwys' (compiled by H.F. Verwoerd), n.d., p. 3.
107. B. Bunting, *The Rise of the South African Reich*, Harmondsworth 1964, p. 245.
108. Ibid., p. 251.
109. Union of South Africa, *Report of the Commission on Native Education, 1945–51*, UG No. 53/1951 (Chair: Eiselen).
110. Kruger, *The Making of a Nation*, p. 283.
111. J.H. Coetzee, 'Die Wet op Bantoe-Onderwys', *Koers*, vol. XXI, no. 4, 1954, p. 176; and L.J. du Plessis, 'Is Kerklike Bepaling van die Christelike Karakter van ons Openbare Onderwys Prinsipiëel of Prakties wenslik?', *Koers*, vol. XXIII, no. 1, 1955, pp. 27–8.
112. Coetzee, 'Die Wet op Bantoe-Onderwys', p. 177.
113. HAD, 1953, col. 3824.
114. Ibid., cols 3834–5.
115. Ibid., cols 4336 and 4360.
116. J. de Klerk in Kruger, *The Making of a Nation*, pp. 319–20 (emphasis added).

117. H.G. Stoker, 'At the Crossroads. Apartheid and University Freedom in South Africa', *Race Relations Journal*, vol. XXIV, no. 3, p. 3.
118. L.J. du Plessis, 'Separate University Education', *Journal for Racial Affairs*, vol. 9, no. 3, 1958, pp. 3–10.
119. G.H. Pirie, 'Ethno–Linguistic Zoning in South African Black Townships', *Area*, vol. 16, no. 4, 1984, p. 291.
120. *Report of the Non-European Affairs Committee*, 1954, quoted in ibid., p. 293.
121. Ibid. This measure was regarded as the forerunner to the Urban Bantu Authorities Bill.
122. Ibid., p. 293.
123. Ibid., p. 292.
124. J.E. Matthewson, 'Ethnic Grouping with Reference to Bantu Township Planning', *Journal for Racial Affairs*, vol. 7, no. 4, 1956, pp. 160–1.
125. Ibid., p. 164.
126. Ibid., p. 165.
127. Moodie, *The Rise of Afrikanerdom*, p. 251.
128. *Die Kruithoring*, a regular NP publication, continuously stressed these themes during the early 1950s. In 1952 there was a particularly dense spate of publications on and discussion of the issue in the newspapers in the face of the Defiance Campaign.
129. Communism was defined as the doctrine of Marxist socialism as interpreted by Lenin and Trotsky, the Third Communist International (Comintern) of the Communist Bureau of Information (the Cominform) or any related form of that doctrine.
130. HAD, 1950, col. 9178.
131. Diederichs, ibid., col. 9236.
132. Ibid., cols 9331–2.
133. Ibid., col. 9426.
134. Diederichs, ibid., col. 9236, emphasis added.
135. Ibid., col. 9286.
136. Ibid., col. 9285.
137. Ibid., col. 9286.
138. A. Hepple, *Trade Unions in Travail. The Story of the Broederbond–Nationalist Plan to Control the South African Unions*, Johannesburg 1954, pp. 58–9.
139. C. Albertyn, 'The Political Trial and the Construction of Apartheid: 1952–1964', unpublished paper delivered to the 'The Societies of Southern Africa in the 19th and 20th Centuries', Postgraduate Seminar, Institute of Commonwealth Studies, 21 October 1988, p. 8.
140. HAD, 1953, cols 931–1761.
141. References to the labour unrest of the 1940s abound in the debates. See ibid., cols 988, 1004–6, 1026, 1662 and 1674.
142. Carter, *The Politics of Inequality*, p. 115.
143. HAD, 1953, col. 934.
144. Ibid., cols 932 and 934.
145. Ibid., col. 942.
146. Ibid., cols 934, 980, 983, 984.
147. Ibid., col. 986.
148. Ibid., col. 1006.
149. Ibid., col. 1005.
150. Ibid., col. 934.
151. Connolly, *Identity\Difference*, p. 8.
152. Omar Khayyam, quoted during a Parliamentary debate, HAD, 1959, col. 6542.
153. W.W.M. Eiselen, 'Harmonious Multi-Community Development', *Optima* vol. 9, no. 1, 1959, p. 3.
154. J. Lazar, 'The Role of the South African Bureau for Racial Affairs (SABRA) in the Formulation of Apartheid Ideology, 1948–1961', *The Societies of Southern Africa in the 19th and 20th Centuries*, vol. 14, no. 37, p. 99.

155. Verwoerd 3/9/1948, reproduced in E.H. Brookes, *Apartheid. A Documentary Study of Modern South Africa*, London 1968, pp. 7–8.

156. M. Horrel (compiler), *A Survey of Race Relations, 1958–59*, Johannesburg 1960, p. 48.

157. A. Sampson, 'Old Fallacies with a New Look: Ignoring the Africans', in Institute of Race Relations, *South Africa. Two Views of Separate Development*, London 1960, p. 33 (emphasis added).

158. HAD, 1959, cols 6125–6.

159. Ibid., col. 6289.

160. *Die Transvaler*, 31/1/1959.

161. Eiselen, 'Harmonious Multi-Community Development', pp. 2 and 7.

162. Union of South Africa, *Report of the Commission of Inquiry for the Socio-Economic Development of the Bantu Areas within the Union of South Africa*, Pretoria 1955. (Chairperson: Tomlinson); and Union of South Africa, *Summary of the Report of the Commission for the Socio-Economic Development of the Bantu Areas within the Union of South Africa*, Pretoria, UG 61/1955.

163. Union of South Africa, *Summary of the Report*, p. xviii. Verwoerd had a rather acrimonious relationship with Tomlinson. Shortly after the completion of the report, a document of some eighteen volumes, Verwoerd forbade Tomlinson to speak on more than one occasion on the topic during a lecture tour in the Netherlands. Verwoerd also refused to make the necessary funds available for the whole of the report to be printed. Instead, only an abridged version was printed and distributed. Tomlinson, fearing a suppression of the report, deposited a complete version of it in Amsterdam. The Verwoerd government also did not take up the central recommendations of the report. Of the £104,000,000 recommended for the economic development of the reserves, the government made only £500,000 available. The White Paper published in 1956 also rejected the proposed abolishment of a tribal land tenure system. Similarly, the recommended use of 'European' capital to help with industrial development of the Bantu Areas was explicitly ruled out by the government. It can be said with safety that the really important impact of the Tomlinson report was symbolic: it provided the regime with a clear justification for the 'grand apartheid' project. However, very few of the actual measures needed to make such a system work were accepted.

164. For a contemporaneous discussion of the report, see L.M. Thompson, 'The Political Implications of the Tomlinson Report', *Race Relations Journal*, vol. XXVIII, no. 2, 1956, pp. 9–12.

165. Union of South Africa, *Report of the Commission of Inquiry for the Socio-Economic Development*, p. 211.

166. Z.K. Matthews and D.G.S. M'Timkulu, 'The Future in the Light of the Tomlinson Report', *Race Relations Journal*, vol. XXIV, no. 1, 1957, p. 17.

167. J.H. Coetzee, 'Die Volkekunde in U Lig', *Koers*, vol. XXIII, no. 6, 1956, pp. 319–37; T.S. van Rooyen, ''n Nuwe Benaderingmetode in verband met die Studie van die Kontak tussen Blank en Bantoe', *Koers*, vol. XXII, no. 4, 1955, pp. 226–33; E.F. Potgieter, 'The Problem of Objectivity in the Study of Ethnic Relations in South Africa', *Journal for Racial Affairs*, vol. 8, no. 3, 1957, pp. 121–30; W.A. Landman, 'Voorsittersrede', *Journal for Racial Affairs*, vol. 8, no. 4, 1957, pp. 148–56; N.N.J. Olivier, 'Ons Stedelike Naturellebevolking', *Journal for Racial Affairs*, vol. 10, no. 2, 1959, pp. 33–45.

168. Union of South Africa, *Summary of the Report*, chapter 2, par. 69.

169. Ibid., chapter 3, para. 29.

170. Ibid., chapter 25, para. 42.

171. Coetzee, 'Die Volkekunde in U Lig', p. 322.

172. Criticism of this position did exist. Hellman, for example, argued that the prevalent notion of culture conflict had to be criticized, for there were no signs that the Bantu displayed any resistance to Western culture. Rather, conflict had to be regarded as *racial* conflict, since the appearance of conflict was 'due to the fact that cultural differences are associated with two major racial groups . . . one which is striving to

maintain its position of dominance while the other rejects the inferior economic, political, and social position to which it had been relegated'. E. Hellman, 'Culture Contacts and Social Change', *Race Relations Journal*, vol. XV, no. 1, 1948, p. 35.

173. Landman, 'Voorsittersrede'; B. Duvenhage, 'Nie-Blanke Arbeid as Een van die Kernvraagstukke in Ons Rasseverhoudinge', *Journal for Racial Affairs*, vol. 9, no. 3, 1958, p. 7.

174. E.F. Potgieter, 'Kontak in Suidelike Afrika. Enkele Gevolge en Kenmerke van die Proses', *Journal for Racial Affairs*, vol. 7, no. 2, 1956, p. 58.

175. Ibid., p. 59.

176. Olivier, 'Ons Stedelike Naturellebevolking', p. 42.

177. F.I.J. van Rensburg, 'Etnisiteit in Afrikaanse Letterkunde in Historise Perspektief', in C. Malan (ed.), *Race and Literature. Ras en Literatuur*, Pinetown 1987, pp. 77–88.

178. H.G. Stoker, 'Calvinisme as Wortel van Ons Volksbestaan', *Koers*, vol. XIX, no. 4, 1952, pp. 199–207; and H.G. Stoker, 'Antropologiese Wetenskappe en die Beeld van God', *Koers*, vol. XXXVI, no. 1, pp. 15–20.

179. Du Toit, 'Openbaringslig op die Apartheidsvraagstuk', p. 18; Coetzee, 'Die Volkekunde in U lig', p. 326; Snyman, 'Rasseverhoudinge in die Skrif', p. 163.

180. 'The fundamental principles and grounding of Calvinism are universal and the same everywhere. In its historical manifestation, however, it is varied, and develops in each people its specific character.' Stoker, 'Calvinisme', p. 168.

181. Du Toit, 'Openbaringslig', p. 22.

182. Du Plessis, 'Separate University Education', p. 67. Snyman also argued that while unity in Christ was universal, and cuts across national boundaries, it did not eliminate them. Snyman, 'Rasseverhoudinge', p. 169.

183. Snyman, 'Rasseverhoudinge', p. 163.

184. Ibid., p. 172.

185. Du Toit argued from a different angle that racial mixing as such was not a sin; it only became a sin when religious and cultural issues were taken into account; that is, when integration led to a 'lowering' to the level of a heathen people, or if a highly regarded culture was 'pulled down' to the *niveau* of barbarism. *Die Transvaler*, 8/9/1959.

186. Du Plessis, 'Separate University Education', p. 69.

187. Stoker, 'At the Crossroads', p. 2. Three irreducible principles of freedom and equality could be discerned according to Stoker. The two others, discussed in chapter 2, were, firstly, that human beings were equally free as such or before God. This was the principle of universal equality of freedom. Secondly, distinct freedoms of human beings – artistic, academic, religious, and so on – were of equal worth. This was the principle of equivalent differentiation of freedoms.

188. Ibid.

189. Stoker's principles had a wider resonance. Louw would later argue, along much the same lines, that unity was possible only between similar groups, since attempts to forge unity between different groups would inevitably result in a process of equalization; that is, in the destruction of religious and racial groupings. The concepts of freedom and equality cannot be used in the same breath. Equality can only be bought at the cost of freedom. W. Louw, 'Die Eenheidskonsep', *Journal for Racial Affairs*, vol. 14, no. 2, 1965, p. 148.

190. J.H. Coetzee, 'Die Indeling en Verspreiding van die Volke van Afrika', *Koers*, vol. XXV, no. 4, 1958, p. 279. In some cases the division was slightly different (Hamites, Semites, Negroids, Bantu and Khoisan). However, there seemed to be agreement on the fact that the 'Bantu peoples' could be said to occupy territory to the south of an imaginary line drawn across the African continent: 'With the exception of a few tribes, people of the Bantu group inhabit the whole area south of an imaginary line drawn from the bulge of the West African coast to the south of Nigeria eastwards through French Equatorial Africa to Lake Albert then swinging southwards to the lower end of Lake Victoria and there, crookedly eastwards through Tanganjika to the

mouth of the Tana river on the east coast.' Ibid., p. 279. This formulation was taken from the Tomlinson report.

191. Matthewson, 'Ethnic Grouping', p. 159; and G.M.K. Schuler, ''n Oorsig oor die Volke van Afrika', *Journal for Racial Affairs*, vol. 7, no. 4, 1956, p. 173.

192. HAD, 1959, col. 6300. See also Union of South Africa, *Summary of the Report*, chapter 1, II, 7 and chapter 25, XIII, 42.

193. A similar point was made by Matthewson in his defence of the 'tribal' division of the administration of the townships. He stated that a group would be best represented by a member of that group, since tribal customs, retributions and penalties were applicable insofar as they did not come into conflict with public policy. Matthewson, 'Ethnic Grouping', p. 161.

194. De Wet Nel, HAD, 1959, col. 6304; I. Schapera (ed.), *The Bantu-Speaking Tribes of South Africa*, Cape Town 1959; M. Gluckman, 'The Kingdom of the Zulu of South Africa', in M. Fortes and E. Evans-Pritchard (eds), *African Political Systems*, London 1940, pp. 25–55, L.G. Cowan, *Local Government in West Africa*, New York 1958. Considerable difference existed on the interpretation of the 'traditional' African system of government, especially on whether it was inherently democratic or authoritarian.

195. Ibid., col. 6305.

196. Ibid., col. 6356.

197. Eiselen, 'Multi-Community Development', p. 2 (emphasis in the original).

198. Matthews and M'Timkulu, 'The Future in the Light of the Tomlinson Report', p. 16.

199. This expression was used by J.H. Coetzee, 'Die Onbekende Afrika', *Koers*, vol. XXV, no. 3, 1957, p. 174.

200. Karis and Carter, *From Protest to Challenge*, vol. 3, p. 11.

201. Dissatisfaction with the increasing use of the language of multi-racialism led to open dissension with the ANC Youth League in Transvaal, and some Africanist members were expelled. See ibid., pp. 16–8 for a discussion of the emergence of Africanism within the ANC.

202. For a discussion of these campaigns, see ibid., pp. 24–35.

203. Statement issued by the South African Allied Workers' Union, the Congress of South African Students, the General and Allied Workers' Union, and the Azanian Students' Organization, quoted in African National Congress, *Selected Writings on the Freedom Charter 1955–1985*, London 1985, p. iii.

204. Luthuli cited by N. Mandela, 'Freedom in Our Lifetime', *Liberation* 1956, reprinted in ibid., p. 23.

205. K.A. Appiah, 'Out of Africa: Topologies of Nativism', in D. LaCapra (ed.), *The Bounds of Race. Perspectives on Hegemony and Resistance*, Ithaca 1991, p. 149.

206. S. du Toit, 'Die Christelike Roeping van die Afrikaner in Afrika', *Koers*, vol. XIX, no. 3, p. 85.

207. Ibid.

208. Ibid.

209. Coetzee, 'Die Onbekende Afrika', p. 182.

210. Ibid., p. 183.

211. Ibid., p. 178.

212. Coetzee, 'Die Indeling', pp. 275–88, and 'Nasionalisme in Afrika', *Koers*, vol. XXVI, no. 10, 1959, pp. 351–61; W. Louw, 'Pan-Afrikanisme', *Journal of Racial Affairs*, vol. 13, no. 4, 1962, pp. 211–27, and 'Die Eenheidskonsep', pp. 147–9; P.O. Sauer, 'Openingsrede', *Journal for Racial Affairs*, vol. 9, no. 4, 1958, pp. 129–36; J. Strauss, 'Die Mens en Menslike Verhoudinge in Afrika', *Journal for Racial Affairs*, vol. 13, no. 4, 1962, pp. 228–36; and T.S. van Rooyen, 'Die Stryd om die Siel van die Bantu', *Journal for Racial Affairs*, vol. 14, no. 3, 1963, pp. 163–72.

213. Coetzee, 'Nasionalisme in Afrika', p. 325.

214. Strauss, 'Die Mens en Menslike Verhoudinge', p. 236.

215. Eiselen, 'Harmonious Multi-Community Development', p. 2.

216. Strauss, 'Die Mens en Menslike Verhoudinge', p. 235.
217. Ibid.
218. Louw, 'Pan-Afrikanisme', p. 212.
219. Strauss, 'Die Mens en Menslike Verhoudinge', p. 325.
220. Louw, 'Pan-Afrikanisme', p. 219; Strauss, 'Die Mens en Menslike Verhoudinge', p. 235.
221. Coetzee, 'Nasionalisme in Afrika', p. 352.
222. P. Hugo, 'Towards Darkness and Death. Racial Demonology in South Africa', *Journal of Modern African Studies*, vol. 26, no. 4, 1988, p. 571.
223. *Die Burger*, 24/10/1952, in ibid.
224. Sauer, 'Openingsrede', pp. 131–2.
225. Quoted in S. Uys, 'Dr Hendrik Frensch Verwoerd, Prime Minister of South Africa', *Africa South*, vol. 3, no. 2, 1959, p. 11.
226. Quoted in E.P. Dvorin, *Racial Separation in South Africa*, Chicago 1952, p. 97.
227. Ibid.
228. Coetzee, 'Nasionalisme in Afrika', p. 354.
229. Van Rooyen, 'Die Stryd om die Siel', p. 172.
230. S. Pienaar, 'Safeguarding the Nations of South Africa', in Institute of Race Relations (ed.), *South Africa. Two Views of Separate Development*, Oxford 1960, p. 10.
231. Uys, 'Dr Hendrik Frensch Verwoerd', pp. 1–11. Similarly, the *Rand Daily Mail* claimed that the introduction of grand apartheid had given apartheid a much more definite form and direction: 'It now has a tidiness and substance it lacked before. Furthermore, it has acquired a new sense of moral justification.'
232. HAD, 1959, col. 6290.
233. Ibid., col. 6295.
234. Ibid.
235. J. du P. Basson, 'Die Taak van die Blanke Politikus t.o.v. Rasseverhoudinge in Suid-Afrika', *Journal for Racial Affairs*, vol. 9, no. 4, p. 209.
236. *Institute of Race Relations News*, 1958, p. 1.
237. L.J. du Plessis, soon after the 1958 congress, echoed Basson's thoughts. Speaking to the Afrikaner Circle in Johannesburg, he argued not only that the development of the reserves had to take place quicker, but that the Europeans in South Africa had to help the Native to become free: 'Africa is going to become free and if we do not help it will become free against us and we will be ploughed under. . . . Thus far we have been very half-hearted toward this. We want nationalism for ourselves but do not accord it to others. . . . Our conscience is guilty. We ourselves are oppressors of the non-White races. . . . We should say to them that we will divide South Africa. This is the only solution which can clear our consciences. . . . If South Africa really wants to be honest with the non-Whites we must go to the limit.' Du Plessis, 'Separate University Education', p. 5.
238. Eiselen, 'Harmonious Multi-Community Development', p. 14.
239. Ibid.
240. Posel, *The Making of Apartheid*, p. 235.
241. Ibid., p 230.
242. H.F. Verwoerd, 'Speech in the House of Assembly, 23 January 1962', in A.N. Pelzer (ed.), *Verwoerd Speaks*, Johannesburg 1966, p. 664.
243. B.J. Vorster, 'Extract from Speech at Heilbron on 16 August 1968', in O. Geyser (ed.), *B.J. Vorster. Select Speeches*, Cape Town 1977, p. 93.
244. Lazar, 'Conformity and Conflict', p. 231. See also the discussion of Marais's work by J.H. Coetzee in *Koers*. Coetzee offers a very even-handed review of the text. He points out that serious questions concerning the justification of apartheid are raised by Marais's critique of its biblical justification. See J.H. Coetzee, 'Die Kleurkrisis en die Weste', *Koers*, vol. XX, no. 4, pp. 145–9.
245. Oglethorpe argues that much of the 'new thinking' in the church could be

attributed to pressure from SABRA. See J. Oglethorpe, 'The Crisis in the Dutch Reformed Churches', *Africa South*, vol. 5, no. 3, pp. 44–8.

246. Quoted in S.R. Ritner, 'The Dutch Reformed Church and Apartheid', *Contemporary History*, vol. 2, no. 4, 1985, p. 34.

247. Ibid., p. 21.

248. Ibid., p. 36.

249. M. Horrel (compiler), *A Survey of Race Relations in South Africa, 1959–60*, Johannesburg 1961, p. 69.

250. HAD, 1960, col. 4302.

251. It is remarkable that during the crisis period from 1960 to 1963 not a single article in the SABRA mouthpiece, *Journal for Racial Affairs*, appeared on the crisis.

252. HAD, 1959, col. 6312.

253. For a discussion of the 'hinge-like' character of the hymen, see Derrida, *Dissemination*, pp. 175–226.

254. V. Descombes, *Modern French Philosophy*, Cambridge 1980, p. 140.

4 The Roots of an Expanding Imaginary

1. For a fuller discussion of this notion of an identitary logic, see A.J. Norval, 'Social Ambiguity and the Crisis of Apartheid', in E. Laclau (ed.), *The Making of Political Identities*, London 1994, pp. 118–21. The full implications of a need to take account of this dimension of the logic of apartheid are the subject of discussion in the concluding chapters of this book.

2. Gramsci, *Prison Notebooks*, p. 210.

3. S. Žižek, *For They Know Not What They Do. Enjoyment as a Political Factor*, London 1991, p. 189.

4. For a discussion of the contradictions and stresses to which the South African polity was subject during this decade, see G. Bloch, 'Sounds in the Silence. Painting a Picture of the 1960s', *Africa Perspective*, no. 25, 1984, pp. 3–23.

5. The average annual increase in the gross domestic product was 4.8 per cent in the 1950s, 5.6 per cent in the 1960s and fell to 3.4 per cent during the 1970s. For a discussion of the role of the growth of manufacturing industry during this period, see R.M. Price, *The Apartheid State in Crisis. Political Transformation in South Africa 1975–1990*, Oxford 1991, pp. 29–35.

6. Stultz points out that African membership at the UN grew from nine states in 1960 to thirty-two in October 1962. South Africa, after the declaration of the Republic, was increasingly threatened with diplomatic and economic isolation, which was coupled with the declared resistance by the newly created Organization of African Unity to all unrepresentative regimes in Southern Africa. See N.M. Stultz, 'The Politics of Security: South Africa under Verwoerd, 1961–6', *The Journal of Modern African Studies*, vol. 7, no. 1, 1969, p. 4.

7. This took place in Angola in 1961, in Mozambique in 1964, and in Zimbabwe and Namibia in 1966.

8. During the early 1960s, the regime was faced with continued resistance in the form of political strikes, stay-aways, and the prospects of a campaign of underground resistance by *Umkhonto we Sizwe* (MK), the newly formed armed wing of the ANC. A campaign of sabotage was conducted by MK, Poqo and the African Resistance Movement, and it produced 203 serious cases of sabotage between December 1961 and March 1964.

9. The extent of the use of these measures are shown in figures such as the following: nearly 10,000 people had been detained or arrested for political offences between 1960 and 1966; 366 persons had been placed under house arrest; and 1,095 persons had been detained under the ninety-day clause. Stultz, 'The Politics of Security', pp. 5–6.

10. Stultz points out that while no reference was made to communism in the annual addresses at the state opening of Parliament during the period from 1958–60, from 1961 onwards there was a marked increase in the time spent dealing with the alleged threat of communism. Ibid., p. 12.

11. 'The Safety of the State is Priority No.1. The Anti-Sabotage Act and what it Means', Pretoria 1962, pp. 1–2 (emphasis added) [INEG P11.7].

12. P.F.D. Weiss, 'The Communist Programme in Africa with Special Reference to South Africa', published by the *Volkskongres*, Pretoria *c*.1964, pp. 18–19 [INEG P20.57].

13. Stultz points out that one fifth of the people attending the conference were in fact English-speaking South Africans, reflecting the shift to the construction of a *white nation* threatened by communism. Stultz, 'The Politics of Security', p. 12.

14. See, for example, the contributions by Weiss, 'The Communist Programme in Africa', and by G. Kuypers, of the Free University of Amsterdam: 'Communism as a Method of World Revolution and Domination' [INEG P20.57].

15. Lenin, quoted in Weiss, 'The Communist Programme', p. 5.

16. A survey of Afrikaans newspapers during the 1960s reveals that these themes were repeated and disseminated in the press on an ongoing basis.

17. 'Tirannie 90', '90-Dag' Proteskomitee, Cape Town 1964, p. 1 [INEG P11.4].

18. B.J. Vorster, 'Openingsrede tydens die amptelike opening van die ASB-kongres op 28 Junie 1971', in Afrikaanse Studentebond (ed.), *Die Kleurlinge in Suid-Afrika*. Papers delivered to the twenty-third Congress of the ASB, Johannesburg 1971 [INEG P13.49] (emphasis added). This statement, of course, reflects the NPs authoritarian concern with protection of the *volkseie*.

19. S. Ratcliffe, 'The Shifting Dominance. The Foundations of the Armaments Industry during the 1960s', *Africa Perspective*, no. 25, 1984, p. 29.

20. In 1963 and 1964, the Security Council of the UN called for a voluntary embargo on sales of arms to South Africa. In 1964, the UK decided to end arms sales to South Africa, and in 1967 a formal arms embargo against South Africa was instituted by the UN.

21. The division between *verligtes* and *verkramptes* in the NP will be discussed shortly.

22. Ratcliffe, 'The Shifting Dominance', p. 31. In the 1969 budget, the Military Intelligence proportion of the defence budget was reduced from R830,000 to R39,000, while the budget for secret services under police command increased from R1,012,000 to R1,218,000, and BOSS was allocated R4 million.

23. Ibid., p. 32.

24. Ibid., pp. 33–4. In 1971, as a result of the expansion of resistance struggles, the SADF again took over the task of containing armed resistance.

25. A. Seegers, 'Apartheid's Military: Its Origins and Development', in W.G. James (ed.), *The State of Apartheid*, Boulder, Colo. 1987, pp. 143–72. The detail and implications of this strategy will be discussed in a forthcoming section of this chapter. The SSC remerged in the 1980s as a primary decision-making body. Chaired by P.W. Botha, the SSC stood at the head of the National Security Management System (NSMS), which co-ordinated over two thousand committees which monitored and managed all aspects of life. The secretariat of the SSC was dominated by high-ranking military personnel, and it supervised a network of Joint Management Centres (JMCs). The geographical division of the JMCs coincided with the areas of command of the Defence Force, and their task was to implement the 'total strategy'. For a further discussion of the NSMS, see D. Geldenhuys and H. Kotze, 'Aspects of Political Decision-Making in South Africa', *Politikon*, vol.10, no. 1, 1983, pp. 33–45.

26. Stultz, 'The Politics of Security', p. 7.

27. B.J. Vorster, 'Extract from a Speech Made at Koffiefontein on 11 August 1967', in O. Geyser (ed.), *B.J. Vorster. Select Speeches*, Cape Town 1977, pp. 80–88 (emphasis added).

28. H.F. Verwoerd, 'Speech at Meyerton, Transvaal, 26 March 1960', in A.N. Pelzer (ed.), *Verwoerd Speaks*, Johannesburg 1966, pp. 381–2.

29. D.C. Dalcanton, 'The Afrikaners of South Africa. A Case Study of Identity Formation and Change', PhD thesis, University of Pittsburgh 1973, p. 208.

30. J.W. Patten, 'Background and Analysis', *Journal for Racial Affairs*, vol. 13, no. 1, 1961, pp. 11–18; W. van Heerden, 'Agtergrond en Ontleding van die Huidige Situasie', *Journal for Racial Affairs*, vol. 13, no. 1, 1961, pp. 19–28; C.F.G. Gunter, 'Samewerking op Kultureel-Opvoedkundige Gebied', *Journal for Racial Affairs*, vol. 13, no.1, 1961, pp. 54–62.

31. B.J. Vorster, 'Extract from a Speech at the Opening of the National Party Congress of the Orange Free State at Bloemfontein on 18 September 1973', in Geyser, *B.J. Vorster*, p. 191 (emphasis added).

32. Moodie, *The Rise of Afrikanerdom*, p. 292.

33. B.J. Vorster, 'Extract from a Speech at Heilbron on 16 August 1968', in Geyser, *B.J. Vorster*, pp. 102–3 (emphasis added).

34. H.F. Verwoerd, HAD, 1962, col. 3923.

35. M. Horrel (compiler), *A Survey of Race Relations in South Africa, 1974*, Johannesburg 1975, p. 2; B.J. Vorster, 'Opening Speech at the Seventh Session of the CPRC, 8.4.74', in P. Hugo (ed.), *Quislings or Realists? A Documentary Study of 'Coloured' Politics in South Africa*, Johannesburg 1978, p. 93.

36. B.J. Vorster, HAD, 1975, col. 383–6.

37. J.A. du Pisani, *John Vorster en die Verlig/Verkramp Stryd. 'n Studie van die politieke verdeeldheid in Afrikanergeledere, 1966–1970*, Bloemfontein 1988, p. 49.

38. B.J. Vorster, 'Speech at Upington, 6 July 1968', in Geyser, *B.J. Vorster*, pp. 100–2.

39. B.J. Vorster, 'Extract from a Speech Made during a Political Meeting on 17 June 1971 at Naboomspruit in the Waterberg Constituency', in ibid., p. 148 (emphasis added).

40. The rift was evident also in what became known as the *Akademiestryd* (Academy Struggle), and in the *Broederbond* during 1967–69. It was also being fought out in the press between the more *verligte* newspapers of *Nasionale Pers – Die Burger* and *Die Beeld* – and the *verkrampte Afrikaanse Pers* newspaper, *Die Vaderland*.

41. W.J. de Klerk, 'The Concepts "Verkramp" and "Verlig"', in N.J. Rhoodie (ed.), *South African Dialogue*, Johannesburg 1972, pp. 519–31.

42. E. Malan called the *verkramptes* such as Albert Hertzog, Jaap Marais and Fanie Botha 'super deluxe Afrikaners' with prejudices against 'TV, the Beatles, *Die Burger*, the American Field Service and the South African Press Association'. Quoted in Du Pisani, *John Vorster*, p. 30.

43. Vorster, 'Extract from a Speech at Heilbron', p. 94.

44. Quoted in R. Balinger and G. Olivier, *Detente in South Africa. Two Views*, Braamfontein 1976, p. 8 (emphasis added).

45. Breyten Breytenbach 1976, free translation by Rykie van Reenen.

46. See in this regard, M.D. Arendse, 'The Formation of the Labour Party, June 1968', in Hugo, *Quislings or Realists?*, pp. 119–21.

47. I. Goldin, *Making Race. The Politics and Economics of Coloured Identity in South Africa*, Cape Town 1987, p. 108.

48. After a long and unconstitutional struggle, the Separate Representation of Voters Act of 1951 was declared effective retrospectively in 1956. Coloured men who had the vote in the Cape Province were placed on a separate voters' roll and would henceforth only be able to vote for four white representatives in the House of Assembly and two white representatives in the Cape Provincial Council. In 1959 an interim, partially elected Union Council for Coloured Affairs was established as advisory body to the government. In addition, in 1958 the Division of Coloured Affairs, which was instituted in the Department of the Interior in 1951, was converted into a full-scale Department of Coloured Affairs. It did not start to function until 1969. In 1968, the highly controversial Prohibition of Political Interference Act prohibited, ostensibly, the 'interference' of whites in the political affairs of the coloured community.

49. *The Educational Journal*, April–May 1968, p. 2. Similarly, the Transvaal

Congress of Representatives of the Coloured Community stated that it wished to put on record its 'emphatic opposition to the recent policies pursued by the Government' and argued that no peace would come to South Africa 'until the rights of all Non-white people to full and free participation in the political, economic and social life of the country' were realized. Horrel (compiler), *A Survey of Race Relations in South Africa, 1959–60*. For a systematic discussion of resistance during this period, see Goldin, *Making Race*.

50. *The Star*, 24/12/1960.
51. HAD, 1960, cols 4191–4.
52. M. Horrel (compiler), *A Survey of Race Relations in South Africa, 1961*, Johannesburg 1962, p. 11.
53. F. Snitcher, 'The Eiselen Scheme', *Africa South*, vol. 1, no. 3, 1957, p. 40.
54. W.W.M. Eiselen, 'The Coloured People and the Natives', *Journal for Racial Affairs*, vol. 6, no. 3, 1955, p. 1.
55. Ibid., p. 17.
56. Goldin, *Making Race*, p. 123.
57. Snitcher, 'The Eiselen Scheme', p. 42.
58. Du Pisani, *John Vorster*, p. 81.
59. Ibid., p. 88.
60. See G. van N. Viljoen, 'Die Politieke Toekoms van die Kleurlinge', in Afrikaanse Studentebond, *Die Kleurlinge in Suid-Afrika*, pp. 65–80 [INEG P13.49].
61. I.D. du Plessis, 'Die Kleurlinge in die Raamwerk van ons Rasseverhoudinge', *Journal for Racial Affairs*, vol. 8, no. 3, 1957, p. 112.
62. *Die Rapport*, 11/7/1971.
63. *Die Burger*, 23/7/1971.
64. *Die Burger*, 10/8/1971.
65. *Die Hoofstad*, 31/7/1971.
66. O'Meara in *Volkskapitalisme* and Du Pisanie in *John Vorster* both argue for this point.
67. *Die Burger*, 10/8/1971.
68. *Die Burger*, 26/8/1971.
69. Ibid.
70. Republic of South Africa, *Verslag van die Kommissie van Ondersoek na aangeleenthede rakende die Kleurlingbevolkingsgroep* (RP 38/1976), Pretoria (hereafter: Theron Commission).
71. Ibid., pp. 433–513.
72. Republic of South Africa, *Summary of the Chapters of the Report of the Commission of Inquiry into Matters Relating to the Coloured Population Group*, 1976, clause 2.52.
73. Republic of South Africa, White Paper. Provisional Comments by the Government on the Recommendations of the Commission of Inquiry into Matters Relating to the Coloured Population Group (WP S-1976).
74. *The Sunday Times*, 17/4/1977
75. *The Sunday Tribune*, 20/6/1976.
76. *The Sunday Tribune*, 20/6/1976.
77. The report was tabled on 18 June 1976.
78. See, for example, D.M. Curry, 'Black Consciousness – Point of View', pp. 199–204, and A.A. Boesak, 'Black Consciouness, Black Power and "Coloured Politics"', pp. 259–68, in Hugo, *Quislings or Realists*?
79. For a full discussion of the rise and force of Black Consciousness ideology in South Africa, see D.R. Howarth, 'Black Consciousness in South Africa. Resistance and Identity Formation under Apartheid Domination', PhD thesis, University of Essex 1994. See also G.M. Gerhart, *Black Power in South Africa. The Evolution of an Ideology*, Berkeley 1979.
80. Horrel, *A Survey of Race Relations in South Africa, 1974*, p. 8. This was enshrined in law by the *Tweede Wysigingswet op Swart Wetgewing*, No. 2 of 1978.

81. Theron Commission, p. 513.

82. Nasionale Party van Suid-Afrika, 'Toekomstige Staatsbestel vir Wit, Bruin en Indier' (n.p.) 1977 [INEG P24.400].

83. Swartz also points out that this made it more difficult to suppress resistance by entrenchment. D.I. Swartz, 'The Theory and Politics of State Economic Intervention in South Africa, with Specific Reference to Industrial Policy between 1979 and 1990. A Strategic Relation Approach', PhD thesis, University of Essex 1994, pp. 190–91.

84. D. Posel, 'Language, Legitimation and Control. The South African State after 1978', *Social Dynamics*, vol. 10, no. 1, 1984, p. 5.

85. R.H. Davies and D. O'Meara, 'The State of Analysis of the Southern African Region. Issues Raised by South African Strategy', *Review of African Political Economy*, no. 29, 1984, p. 67.

86. *Sake van die Dag*, 30/5/1977, 29/7/1977. The South African Broadcasting Corporation's early morning radio news commentaries, *Sake van die Dag*, played an important part in agenda-setting and in the formation of opinions.

87. For a brief discussion of Vorster's thinking on foreign policy, see D. Geldenhuys, 'The Head of Government and South Africa's Foreign Relations', in R. Schrire (ed.), *Leadership in the Apartheid State. From Malan to De Klerk*, Cape Town 1994, pp. 268–76.

88. *Sake van die Dag*, 29/7/1977.

89. It has been argued that the Nkomati Accord was not reconcilable with the ideology of the total strategy to the extent that Mozambique could no longer be portrayed as an enemy. In contrast to that, one may argue that the signing of the Accord precisely affirmed that enemies existed, and the Accord would then fit perfectly well with the strategy.

90. D. Geldenhuys, *Some Foreign Policy Implications of South Africa's 'Total National Strategy' with Particular Reference to the '12-Point Plan'*, Braamfontein 1981, p. 1.

91. Quoted in M. Hough (ed.), *Psychological Strategies*, Ad Hoc Publication No. 21, Pretoria 1985, pp. 4–5.

92. *Sake van die Dag*, 20/10/1977.

93. Republic of South Africa, *Report of the Commission of Inquiry into the Riots at Soweto and Elsewhere from the 16th of June 1976 to the 28th of February 1977*, Pretoria (RP 55/1980) (Chair: Cillie), pp. 75 and 122.

94. Defence White Paper 1977, pp. 4–5.

95. A. Beaufre, *An Introduction to Strategy*, London 1965.

96. Defence White Paper, p. 7 (emphasis added).

97. Vlok, cited in M. Hough and M. van der Merwe, *Selected Official South African Strategic Perspectives 1976–1987*, University of Pretoria, Institute for Strategic Studies Ad Hoc Publication No. 25, May 1988, p. 11.

98. See Posel, 'Language, Legitimation and Control', pp. 1–16.

99. The Federal Council of the National Party of South Africa, 'Women Our Silent Soldiers', August 1978/79, p. 6.

100. Ibid.

101. Ibid., p. 8 (emphasis added).

102. Ibid., p. 24.

103. Ibid., p. 22.

104. Ibid., p. 12.

105. 'Sound relations', ironically, was argued to form a top priority of the government, and women were warned to avoid inconsiderateness, rudeness and insulting language.

106. G. Malan, 'The Crisis in Our Country. A Conversation between the Housewife and Her Domestic Help', Johannesburg 1986 [INEG P16].

107. Ibid., p. 10 (emphasis in the original).

108. Ibid., p. 13 (emphasis in the original).

109. For a discussion of Afrikaans 'border' novels, see H.E. Koornhof, 'Works of

Friction. Current South African War Literature', in J. Cock and L. Nathan (eds), *War and Society. The militarisation of South Africa*, Cape Town 1989, pp. 275-82.

110. For a full discussion of the militarization of white education, see G. Evans, 'Classrooms of War: The Militarisation of White South African Schooling', in Cock and Nathan, *War and Society*, pp. 283–97.

111. Ibid., p. 284.

112. In Geldenhuys, 'Some Foreign Policy Implications', p. 12.

113. The first point revolved around the 'recognition and acceptance of the existence of multi-nationalism and of minorities' in South Africa; the second revolved around the acceptance of 'vertical differentiation' with a built-in principle of self-determination at as many levels as possible; the third addressed the question of the establishment of constitutional structures for African self-government in 'Black States'; the fourth addressed the question of the 'division of powers' between South African whites, South African coloureds and South African Indians, with a 'system of consultation and co-responsibility so far as common interests are concerned'; the fifth addressed the principle that where at all possible each population group should have its own schools and live in its own community; the sixth concerned the removal of 'hurtful and unnecessary discriminatory measures'; the seventh spelled out the recognition of economic interdependence; the eighth put forward the idea of a constellation of Southern African states; the ninth and tenth concerned foreign policy; the eleventh concerned the 'maintenance of effective decision-making by the State', and the need for clean government as well as strong security forces; the twelfth concerned the maintenance of free enterprise as the basis of economic and financial policy.

114. The 1977 proposals were presented to the NP caucus for approval. Not surprisingly, a storm of protest arose as a result. The proposals were condemned for being the work of a small white closed grouping. (The members of this group were: P.W. Botha, H.H. Smit, C.P. Mulder, J.P. van der Spuy, O.P.F. Horwood, M.C. Botha and S.J.M. Steyn.) No consultation with other members of Parliament, or with other 'population groups', took place at any stage. As a result, it was announced at the end of 1977 that the introduction of the proposals would be delayed so that further 'consultation' could take place. In April 1979 a complete constitutional bill of some sixty pages was published by the NP. Instead of introducing the Bill into Parliament, it was referred to a joint Parliamentary select committee, chaired by Alwyn Schlebush, who, in turn, created the President's Council, consisting of sixty nominated members from the white, coloured, Chinese and Indian populations. Africans had no representation.

115. In the 1977 proposals, three separate Parliaments were envisaged. In the later model, this was changed to a single tri-cameral Parliament. Under both systems the legislative process remained virtually the same. The initial plans were set out for public consumption in the following document: Nasionale Party van Suid-Afrika, 'Toekomstige Staatsbestel vir Wit, Bruin en Indier', (n.p.)1977 [INEG P24.400].

116. Much discussion took place around the 'dictatorial' powers ascribed to the State President. See, for example, N.M. Stultz, 'Interpreting Constitutional Change in South Africa', *Journal of Modern African Studies*, vol. 22, no. 3, pp. 353–79. The NP was aware of these criticisms, and tried to counter it. See National Party of South Africa, 'Questions and Replies on Constitutional Plan', Cape Town n.d. [INEG P24.397].

117. These themes were produced through an extensive survey of materials, including party pamphlets, booklets, information sheets, news briefings, commentaries, debates in the House of Assembly, newspaper advertising and articles, and daily news commentaries of the SABC.

118. At the 1980 Transvaal NP Congress, P.W. Botha expressed it in this way: 'Self-determination. The NP held on to this ideal . . . and we will continue to hold on to the concept of self-determination [applause] because it is the core, the core of our struggle. But, as a freedom-loving people, a people [*volk*] who have struggled for their right to self-determination in this country, and who threw off the colonial yoke . . . we

ought to give to others what we demand for ourselves.' P.W. Botha, 'Toespraak gelewer tydens die Nasionale Party Kongres van Transvaal op 1 September 1980', pp. 6–7 [INEG].

119. National Party of South Africa, 'Vote with Confidence. Vote National', Johannesburg, n.d. [INEG P24.604].

120. Ibid. (emphasis added).

121. Vorster, 'Extract from a Speech at the Opening of the National Party Congress of the Orange Free State at Bloemfontein on 18 September 1973', p. 191. This was repeated on numerous occasions. See, *inter alia*, B.J. Vorster, 'Toespraak by die Nasionale Party Kongres van die Transvaal op 14 September 1976.' Inligtingstuk van die Federale Raad van die Nasionale Party [INEG P24.630].

122. P.W. Botha, 'Toespraak gelewer tydens 'n Nasionale Party vergadering te Groblersdal op 1 Oktober 1977' [INEG].

123. P.W. Botha, 'Toespraak gelewer by die Universiteit van Pretoria op 30 Julie 1980', pp. 8–9 [INEG].

124. National Party of South Africa, 'NP Policy: The Facts!', Bloemfontein n.d. [INEG P24.609] (emphasis added).

125. HAD, 1984, col. 1258 (emphasis added).

126. Ibid., col. 1262.

127. Ibid., col. 1356.

128. See C. Charney, 'The National Party, 1982–1985. A Class Alliance in Crisis', in James, *The State of Apartheid*, pp. 5–36.

129. H. Smit, 'Grondwetplan gee Groot Momentum aan Staatkundige Aanpassing', *Pro-Nat*, September 1978, pp. 7–8.

130. HAD, 1984, cols 1260–61.

131. Ibid., col. 1262.

132. C. Heymans, 'Devolution in South Africa: Rhetoric or Reality? An Analysis of the Restructuring of Political Institutions on Different Levels of Government', paper presented at the Research Colloquium of the Political Science Association of South Africa, at the Rand Afrikaans University, Johannesburg, 8 October 1986, p. 10.

133. Botha, 'Toespraak gelewer tydens 'n Nasionale Party vergadering te Groblersdal', p. 14.

134. National Party of South Africa, 'Questions and Replies on Constitutional Plan'.

135. Ibid.

136. *Die Vaderland*, 24/2/1982.

137. S. van der Merwe, 'NP Position Paper No.1: Power-Sharing (and Related Concepts), Cape Town 1986, p. 2 (emphasis in the original).

138. Lijphart argues that it would be a mistake to view South African politics in black/white terms. Rather, both groups are each 'deeply divided' into a number of ethnic groups, and political arrangements such as majoritarianism would not lead to a democratic outcome. Instead, it is advisable that political institutions should be based upon 'power-sharing' between elites of all the representative groups. A. Lijphart, 'Power-Sharing in South Africa', *Policy Studies in International Affairs*, no. 24, University of California, Berkeley 1985, p. 36.

139. A. Lijphart, 'Majority Rule vs Democracy in Deeply Divided Societies', *Politikon*, vol. 4, no. 2, 1977, pp. 113–23. For a discussion and critique of the use of Lijphardt's ideas during the 1980s, see M. Macdonald, 'The Siren's Song: The Political Logic of Power-Sharing in South Africa', *Journal of Southern African Studies*, vol. 18, no. 4, 1992, pp. 709–25; A.J. Norval, 'Minoritarian Politics and the Pluralisation of Democracy', *Acta Philosophica*, vol. XIV, no. 2, 1993, pp. 121–40; for a defence of the plural society thesis, see L. Schlemmer, 'Theories of the Plural Society and Change in South Africa', *Social Dynamics*, vol. 3, no. 1, 1977, pp. 3–16.

140. By 1982, it was the NP's opinion that it did not serve its cause to hold strictly to any one constitutional model. It did not regard it as necessary to subscribe 'to the principle of consociational democracy because it would serve no useful purpose, or

may even cause confusion, if one were to commit oneself to a specific academic model.' Department of Foreign Affairs and Information, 'Constitutional Guidelines for Whites, Coloureds and Indians', Doornfontein 1982, p. 2. Similarly in 1986, readily available models such as federalism, confederalism and consociationalism were rejected. It was argued that the specific situation in South Africa required designing 'our own particular system . . . a system which no doubt would have some features of one or all of those systems, but which would not answer to the description of any particular one of them'. Van der Merwe, 'NP Position Paper No. 1', p. 4.

141. Van der Merwe, 'NP Position Paper No. 1', pp. 3–4.

142. W.P. Esterhuyse, *Apartheid Must Die*, Cape Town 1981, p. ii.

143. Ibid., p. 16.

144. For a much more thorough questioning of nationalist reformist politics and its implications for Afrikaner intellectuals, see A. du Toit, *Die Sondes van die Vaders*, Cape Town 1983. A shorter version of the argument was published: 'Facing Up to the Future: Reflections on the Predicament of Afrikaner Intellectuals in the Legitimation Crisis of Afrikaner Nationalism and the Apartheid State', *Social Dynamics*, vol. 7, 1981, pp. 1–24.

145. Botha, 'Toespraak gelewer by die Universiteit van Pretoria op 30 Julie 1980', p. 5 [INEG].

146. HAD, 1977, cols 5643–4.

147. Van der Merwe, 'NP Position Paper No 1', p. 9.

148. Ibid., p. 10.

149. P.W. Botha, 'Toespraak gelewer tydens 'n openbare vergadering in the D.F. Malansentrum te Stellenbosch soos gereël deur die Nasionale Party Jeugtak te Stellenbosch op 10 April 1980', p. 18 [INEG]; and P.W. Botha, 'Toespraak gelewer tydens 'n openbare vergadering te Kuruman op 10 Mei 1980', p. 19 [INEG].

5 A Crisis of Hegemony

1. Gramsci, *Prison Notebooks*, p. 177.

2. Ibid., p. 178 (emphasis added).

3. This caused some observers to argue that a decisive shift in the class basis of the NP had taken place, an interpretation with which I take issue here. See C. Charney, 'The National Party, 1982–1985' and Wolpe, *Race, Class and the Apartheid State*.

4. P.W. Botha, 'Toespraak gelewer tydens die Opening van die 35e Jaarkongres van die Afrikaanse Handelsinstituut te Port Elizabeth op 7 Mei 1980', p. 6 [INEG]. See also P.W. Botha, 'Toespraak gelewer tydens 'n Banket van die Kaapstadse Kamer van Nywerhede met hul 75e herdenking te Kaapstad op 22 Mei 1979', pp. 1–7 [INEG].

5. P.W. Botha, 'Toespraak gelewer tydens die Amptelike Opening van die Randse Skou op 11 April 1981', p. 4 [INEG].

6. L. Pretorius, 'The Head of Government and Organised Business', in R. Schrire (ed.), *Leadership in the Apartheid State. From Malan to De Klerk*, Cape Town 1994, pp. 224–5.

7. B.J. Vorster, 'Toespraak gelewer tydens die 74ste Jaarlikese ASSOCOM Kongres te Port Elizabeth op 18 Oktober 1976, p. 7 [INEG].

8. The irony being that the later Riekert Commission would play an overtly political role. For a discussion of the changing role and function of the EAC, see Pretorius, 'The Head of Government', pp. 222 and 238–9.

9. For a discussion of the Muldergate affair, see O'Meara, *Volkskapitalisme*, pp. 248–56.

10. Botha reduced the number of Cabinet committees from forty to five. These had to deal with finance, social affairs, constitutional and economic affairs, and security concerns, respectively.

11. See J.S. Saul and S. Gelb, *The Crisis in South Africa*, [London] 1986.

12. As Swartz points out, this position was not representative of the majority of the Afrikaner business community, who remained cautious in speaking out against the party and government. Swartz, 'The Theory and Politics of State Economic Intervention', p. 192.

13. J.A. Lombard, 'Free Market Banquet. Address by Prof. Jan Lombard', *Free Market*, no. 4, 1981, p. 4 (emphasis added).

14. Swartz, 'The Theory and Politics of State Economic Intervention', p. 201.

15. J.A. Lombard, *Freedom, Welfare and Order. Thoughts on the Principles of Political Co-operation in the Economy of Southern Africa*, Pretoria 1978, p. 28 (emphasis added).

16. Ibid., pp. 19–20.

17. For a discussion of the differences between Lombard's view on the correct strategy for promoting industrial growth and that of the monetarist Governor of the Reserve Bank, Gerhard de Kock, see Swartz, 'The Theory and Politics of State Economic Intervention', pp. 216–21.

18. Ibid., p. 226.

19. For a discussion of Rupert's philosophy of 'partnership', see W.P. Esterhuyse, *Anton Rupert. Advocate of Hope*, Cape Town 1986.

20. Rupert argued against what he considered to be two extremes: against those who saw the only function of business enterprise as the extraction of maximum profit without regard to factors outside the business sphere; and against those radicals who blamed all shortcomings in society on the business world. He stated, by contrast, that one should work within the free enterprise system to expand it, and that 'the contract between the business world and the community should be extended so that social responsibility becomes an additional function of the business world'. Quoted in ibid., p. 56.

21. The SBDC board of directors was multi-racial. It aimed to stimulate entrepreneurial talent through limited financing, training and advice; to identify entrepreneurial potential in all population groups; and to support small manufacturing concerns. The establishment of the SBDC helped to legalize the informal business sector in Soweto.

22. In this Rupert clashed with Verwoerd, who argued that property rights would give blacks a feeling of permanence which was contrary to the official policy of the day.

23. Quoted in Esterhuyse, *Anton Rupert*, p. 69. These themes continued to inform his writings. See, *inter alia*, A. Rupert, *Priorities for Coexistence*, Cape Town 1981.

24. P.W. Botha, 'Toespraak gelewer tydens die Beraad tussen die Eerste Minister en Sakeleiers, Carltonsentrum, Johannesburg op 22 November 1979', p. 9 [INEG].

25. Ibid., pp. 14–15.

26. Ibid., pp. 26–8.

27. Ibid., p. 33.

28. R.S. Jaster, *The Defence of White Power*, London 1988, p. 84.

29. HAD, 1959, col. 6526.

30. Botha, 'Toespraak gelewer tydens die Beraad', pp. 43–9.

31. Ibid., p. 45.

32. G.C. Olivier, 'Co-operation or National Security? Choices and Options for White and Black', *International Affairs Bulletin*, vol. 4, no. 3, 1980, p. 27.

33. Vorster argued that '[w]hen it comes to the exercise of political rights by urban blacks, those rights will have to be exercised in their own black states, and those rights are not illusory, because they have the right to vote. . . . Political rights – they have to be sought in the homelands, but when it comes to better facilities, when it comes to having a say in their own affairs in local authorities, when it comes to chances and opportunities in their own areas, when it comes to industrial rights, my door is open for negotiation. . . .' B.J. Vorster, 'SATV Onderhoud met C. Renken op 12 September 1976'. Information Document of the Federal Council of the National Party [INEG P24.630]

34. Swartz argues that these conditions resulted from a growth in the sheer physical

size of townships combined with a deliberate limiting of the provision of services by the state. Swartz, 'The Theory and Politics of State Economic Intervention', p. 189.

35. N.E. Wiehahn, *Die Volledige Wiehahn Verslag. Met aantekeninge deur prof. N.E. Wiehahn*, Pretoria 1982, article 1.17.

36. Ibid., article 1.19.1.

37. Minister of Labour, *Die Vaderland*, 25/2/1978.

38. The *de facto* existence of African trade unions can be ascribed both to international pressure for recognition of African unions and to the fact that the previous 'committee system' for African workers proved to be a dismal failure. P. Bonner and E. Webster, 'Background to the Wiehahn Report', *South African Labour Bulletin*, vol. 5, no. 2, 1979, pp. 3–11.

39. Wiehahn, *Die Volledige Wiehahn Verslag*, article 3.9.1.

40. Ibid., article 3.9.

41. White Paper: WPS-1979, para. 6.5.

42. *Die Vaderland*, 25/2/1979.

43. For a discussion of the development of trade unionism in South Africa since the 1970s, see M. Murray, *South Africa: Time of Agony*, London 1978 (esp. pp. 129–94), and J. Maree, 'The Emergence, Struggles and Achievements of Black Trade Unions in South Africa from 1973 to 1984', *Labour and Capital and Society*, Special Issue, vol. 18, no. 2, 1985.

44. *The Star*, 19/5/1979.

45. S. Duncan, 'Riekert: a Recipe for Disaster', *The Star*, 19/5/1979.

46. *Financial Mail*, 11/5/1979.

47. *Sake van die Dag*, 30/5/1977.

48. *Sake van die Dag*, 30/5/1977.

49. *Sake van die Dag*, 15/12/1978.

50. Posel, 'Language, Legitimation and Control', p. 16.

51. C. Heunis, Minister of Economic Affairs, *Citizen*, 9/5/1979; *Argus*, 21/6/1979.

52. 'Riekert in a Nutshell', *Financial Mail*, 11/5/1979.

53. National Party of South Africa, *Nat 80's*, n.d., p. 8.

54. *Rand Daily Mail*, 16/10/1979 (emphasis added). Well before this, it was already argued that home-ownership, a central component of a 'stable community', had made good progress, and that in some areas more than a third of the houses were owner-occupied. *Sake van die Dag*, 29/7/1977.

55. K. Tomaselli, G. Hayman, A. Jack, N. Nxumalo, R. Tomaselli and N. Ngcobo, 'Square Vision in Colour. How TV2/3 Negotiates Consent', in R. Tomaselli, K. Tomaselli and J. Muller (eds), *Broadcasting in South Africa*, London 1989, p. 155.

56. Ibid., pp. 158–74.

57. A. Rupert, 'Toespraak gelewer tydens die Beraad tussen die Eerste Minister en Sakeleiers, Carltonsentrum, Johannesburg op 22 November 1979', pp. 1–4 [INEG], and P.W. Botha, 'Speech Delivered at a Luncheon Following the Inaugural Meeting of the Proposed Small Business Development Corporation in Johannesburg on 27 November 1980', p. 1–6 [INEG]. The establishment of the national SBDC did not go smoothly. The government dragged its heels, and as a result, Rupert withdrew the offer he made at the Carlton Conference. It was only once De Kock and Lombard were appointed to give attention to the practical implementation of the idea that it finally got off the ground in February 1981.

58. Botha, 'Speech Delivered at a Luncheon', p. 6.

59. Republic of South Africa, *President's Council Report of the Committee for Economic Affairs on a Strategy for Small Business Development and for Deregulation*, Pretoria, 1985, p. 95.

60. F. de Clercq, 'Some Recent Trends in Bophuthatswana: Commuters and Restructuring in Education', in G. Moss and I. Oberey (eds), *South African Review II*, Johannesburg 1984, p. 271.

61. W. Cobbett, D. Glaser, D. Hindson and M. Swilling, 'A Critical Analysis of the South African State's Reform Strategies in the 1980s', in P. Frankel, N. Pines and

M. Swilling (eds), *State, Resistance and Change in South Africa. The Burden of the Present*, London 1988, p. 22; and D. Hindson, 'Orderly Urbanisation and Influx Control. From Territorial Apartheid to Regional Spatial Ordering in South Africa', in R. Tomlinson and M. Addleson (eds), *Regional Restructuring under Apartheid. Urban and Regional Policies in Contemporary South Africa*, Johannesburg 1987, p. 104.

62. S.S. Brand, 'Die Wisselwerking tussen Ekonomiese en Konstitusionele Hervormings in Suid-Afrika.' Paper delivered to the Annual Conference of the Political Science Association of South Africa, Rand Afrikaans University, 1981, p. 6 (emphasis added).

63. Ibid., p. 15. P.W. Botha further argued that cross-border co-operation was not simply an alternative to land consolidation in the 'homelands'. Land consolidation was high on Botha's rhetorical agenda in the early 1980s. However, it seems that the new 'soft borders' approach to regional economic development practically implied an abandonment of any futher consolidation: 'It is, of course, true that where land consolidation becomes not only financially astronomical but also economically ineffective, alternative income-creating economic assets will have to be shared with Black states in other ways. Participation in cooperation is one effective way in which the situation could be handled.' Botha 'Toespraak gelewer tydens die Amptelike Opening van die Randse Skou', p. 8.

64. Brand, 'Die Wisselwerking', p. 13.

65. Ibid., p. 15.

66. Ibid., p. 17.

67. Ibid., pp. 11–12.

68. Hindson, 'Orderly Urbanisation', p. 86.

69. With reference to the struggles at Crossroads and Kayalitsha, Hindson concluded that these struggles finally forced the state to concede the failure of the insider–outsider strategy, the impossibility of total territorial apartheid and the inevitability of African urbanization outside the homelands. Ibid., p. 87.

70. J. Grest, 'The Crisis of Local Government in South Africa', in Frankel, Pines and Swilling, *State, Resistance and Change*, pp. 87–116.

71. D.R. Howarth and A.J. Norval, 'Subjectivity and Strategy in South African Resistance Politics: Prospects for a New Imaginary', *Essex Papers in Government and Politics*, No. 85, 1992, p. 3.

72. Murray, *South Africa: Time of Agony*, pp. 165–94.

73. A.J. Norval, 'Letter to Ernesto', in Laclau, *Reflections*, pp. 148–53, and Howarth and Norval, 'Subjectivity and Strategy'. See also H. Barrell, 'The United Democratic Front and National Forum. Their Emergence, Composition and Trends', in South African Research Services (eds), *South African Review* 2, Johannesburg 1984, pp. 6–20; and J.-A. Collinge, 'The United Democratic Front', in South African Research Services (eds), *South African Review* 3, Johannesburg 1986, pp. 248–66.

74. UDF Publicity Department, 'Declaration of the United Democratic Front', n.d. See also P. Molefe, 'Resisting the Constitution', *Financial Mail*, 25/11/1983.

75. For a discussion of the crisis of black local government, see Grest, 'The Crisis of Local Government'. For a discussion of the practical operation of the Community Councils, see Murray, *South Africa: Time of Agony*, pp. 118–24.

76. Murray, *South Africa: Time of Agony*, p. 123.

77. The BLAs were to be self-financing and their financial resources were no more extensive than licensing fees and house rentals and service charges levied on the sub-economic townships. N. Haysom, *Apartheid's Private Army. The Rise of Right-Wing vigilantes in South Africa*, London 1986, p. 14.

78. United Democratic Front (Transvaal Region), 'Don't Vote for APARTHEID', n.d.

79. Ad-Hoc Anti PC Committee, 'No to PC – Forward to a Democratic South Africa', May 1983, p. 1.

80. Ibid., p. 2.

81. Patrick Lekota, 'Putting the UDF into its True Perspective', *Rand Daily Mail*, 29/6/1984.

82. Ibid. (emphasis added).

83. Department of Co-operation and Development, 'Local Authority Elections Wednesday 7 December 1983', p. 2.

84. For a discussion of differences in strategy during the 1980s, see Howarth and Norval, 'Subjectivity and Strategy'.

85. D. Niddrie, 'It's Testing Time for Cosatu', *Work in Progress*, no. 54, 1988, p. 8.

86. During 1986, 614 labour leaders, about 80 per cent of them with COSATU links, were arrested under the State of Emergency regulations, and more than two thousand rank-and-file members suffered the same fate. A. Fine, 'Trends and Developments in Organised Labour', in South African Research Services (eds), *South African Review 4*, Johannesburg 1987, p. 220.

87. Quoted in R. Lambert, 'Trade Unions, Nationalism and the Socialist Project in South Africa', in ibid., p. 247.

88. Sarakinsky points out that within the securocrats there were divisions between those generals emphasizing socio-economic factors in unrest and those favouring a more traditional counter-insurgency (COIN) strategy. General Charles Lloyd's accession to SSC secretary was indicative of the victory for the former grouping, including SADF Chief J. Geldenhuys and Air Force Head General J.P. van Loggerenberg. The COIN faction included General K. van der Waal, commander of special forces, General A.J.M. Joubert of the reconnaisance commandos and General C.J. van Tonder, the new head of Military Intelligence. I. Sarakinsky, 'A Web of National Manipulation', *Work in Progress*, no. 54, 1988, p. 41.

89. M. Swilling and M. Phillips, 'State Power in the 1980s. From "Total Strategy" to "Counter-Revolutionary Warfare"', in J. Cock and L. Nathan (eds), *War and Society. The Militarisation of South Africa*, Cape Town 1989, p. 137.

90. *Sake van die Dag*, 24/4/1986.

91. *The Citizen*, 24/4/1986.

92. Hindson, 'Orderly Urbanisation', p. 89.

93. Ibid.

94. The RSCs were funded by taxation on business turnovers, wages and salaries. This, it was hoped, would act as a disincentive for the employment of more Africans in the metropolitan areas, directing African employment to the deconcentration areas where the standards for acceptable housing were lowered, and the requirements in terms of health and safety provisions waivered.

95. S. van der Merwe, 'And What About the Black People?', *South Africa International*, 1985, pp. 8–23.

96. Ibid., p. 15.

97. Ibid., p. 19.

98. Ibid., p. 20.

99. Ibid., p. 21.

100. National Party of South Africa, 'Programme of Principles', Bloemfontein n.d., p. 6.

101. A. Seegers, 'South Africa's National Management System, 1972–90', *Journal of Modern African Studies*, vol. 29, no. 2, 1991, pp. 258–9.

102. Swilling and Phillips, 'State Power in the 1980s', p. 143.

103. Ibid.

104. The following activists were amongst the most well known of those killed during this period: Griffith Mxenge (1985); Matthew Goniwe, Font Calata, Sparrow Mlohato and Sicelo Mhlawuli (1985); Fabian Ribeiro and his wife (1986); Eric Mntonga (1987) and Sicelo Dhlomo (1988).

105. Hayson, *Apartheid's Private Army*, p. 7.

106. Ibid., p. 1.

107. Ibid., pp. 104–8.

108. Sarakinsky, 'A Web of National Manipulation', p. 41.

109. HAD, 1982, col. 8111.

110. HAD, 1984, cols 2669–70.
111. HAD, 1987, col. 5910.
112. Ibid.
113. Ibid., cols 5907–11.
114. Ibid., col. 5911.
115. A. Boraine, 'The Militarisation of Urban Controls. The Security Management System in Mamelodi, 1986–1988', in Cock and Nathan, *War and Society*, p. 173.
116. W. Ebersohn, 'The Headmen', *Leadership South Africa*, vol. 7, no. 5, 1988, p. 18.
117. W. Ebersohn, 'Interview with Leon Wessels, Deputy Minister of Law and Order', *Leadership South Africa*, vol. 7, no. 5, 1988, p. 22.
118. Goverment disinformation document, n.d. (Gail Gerhart collection; emphasis in the original).
119. National Party of South Africa, 'Programme of Principles', p. 4 (emphasis added).
120. D. Posel, '"A Battlefield of Perceptions": State Discourses on Political Violence, 1985–1988', in Cock and Nathan, *War and Society*, p. 262.
121. Ibid., p. 273.
122. *Sake van die Dag*, 10/10/1984.
123. *Sake van die Dag*, 7/11/1984; 24/12/1984; 10/4/1985; 25/4/1985; 14/6/1985; 25/6/1985; 28/6/1985; 22/7/1985; 23/7/1985, and so forth. A specific act against 'intimidation' was introduced by Parliament during May 1982.
124. RSA, White Paper on Defence and Armaments Supply 1986, pp. 13–14.
125. Statement by Nel, 28/3/1985.
126. Cobbett, Glaser, Hindson and Swilling, 'A Critical Analysis of the South African State's Reform', p. 20.
127. *Die Vaderland*, 3/5/1979.
128. *The Citizen*, 18/5/1979.
129. *The Citizen*, 3/5/1979 (emphasis added).
130. For example, minimum wages for artisans fell by 26 per cent in real terms between 1974 and 1984, while the income of farmers fell by 42 per cent during the same period. Charney, 'The National Party, 1982–1985', pp. 5–36.
131. L. Human and H. Pringle, 'The Attitude of White Workers to the Vertical Occupational Mobility of Blacks. An Introductory Study', *South African Journal of Labour Relations*, vol. 10, nos 3–4 1986, p. 33.
132. For a full discussion of these factors, see Price, *The Apartheid State in Crisis*, pp. 220–33.
133. J. van Rooyen, *Hard Right. The New White Power in South Africa*, London 1994, p. 127.
134. In the 1988 municipal elections, the KP actually took control of 53 of the local authorities in the Transvaal, by comparison to the NP's 38.
135. Price, *The Apartheid State in Crisis*, pp. 239–41.
136. Tony Bloom, quoted in 'A Moment in History', *Leadership South Africa*, vol. 4, no. 3, 1985, p. 30.
137. Price, *The Apartheid State in Crisis*, p. 239.
138. *Weekly Mail*, 4–11 March 1988.
139. C. Nel, 'Group Therapy', *Leadership South Africa*, vol. 7, no. 4, 1988, p. 35.
140. The Kairos Theologians, *The Kairos Document. Challenge to the Church*, Springs 1985.
141. M. Schneider, 'Johan Heyns and the NGK's Change of Heart', *Leadership South Africa*, vol. 5, no. 5, 1986.
142. J.N. Lazerson, *Against the Tide. Whites in the Struggle against Apartheid*, Boulder, Colo. 1994, p. 255.
143. Ibid., p. 256.
144. Ibid.
145. JODAC, 'Winning White Support for Democracy', *Work in Progress*, no. 53, 1988, p. 29.

146. Ibid., p. 30.
147. Ibid., p. 32.
148. Ibid., p. 32.
149. Ibid., p. 33.
150. Lazerson, *Against the Tide*, p. 257.
151. Ibid., p. 258.
152. In 1982, Maseru was raided and 42 persons were killed; the 1983 raids included one on a Maputu suburb, in which 64 persons were killed; 1984 and 1985 saw raids into Gaborone, Zambia and Zimbabwe, in addition to the ongoing wars in Angola and Namibia.
153. G. Cawthra, G. Kraak and G. O'Sullivan 'Introduction', in G. Cawthra, G. Kraak and G. O'Sullivan (eds), *War and Resistance. Southern African Reports*, London 1994, p. 8.
154. L. Nathan, 'Resistance to Militarisation. Three Years of the End Conscription Campaign', in South African Research Services, *South African Review* 4, p. 107.
155. Ibid., p. 8.
156. Divisions did exit within the NUSAS. Some argued that the main duty of anti-apartheid activists was to remain inside the country and to contribute to internal resistance, even if this meant serving in non-combatant roles, while others argued that there could be no justification for serving in any capacity whatsoever. As Cawthra et al. point out, this was indicative of a wider split within the the ranks of white anti-apartheid activists. The former group believed that taking a strong line on military service would diminish their chances of building a non-racial movement in which whites could take part, while the latter wanted to build a mass-based draft resisters movement along the line of the US experience. Cawthra, Kraak and O'Sullivan, 'Introduction', pp. 17–18.
157. Different sources place the date of the formation of the ECC in either 1983 or 1984.
158. By 1985, over thirty-five thousand SADF troops were deployed in the townships.
159. G. Evans, 'Battle is Over. ECC Packs Up Its Kitbag', *Weekly Mail*, 19/8/1994.
160. Cawthra, Kraak and O'Sullivan, *War and Resistance*, p. 19.
161. Nathan, 'Resistance to Militarisation', p. 111.
162. Ibid.
163. *Weekly Mail*, 5–11 August 1988, p. 3.
164. Evans, 'Battle is Over'.
165. G. Malan, ' The Dangerous Game (of the ECC/END to End Conscription). A Conversation with Our Women and Our Young People', Roosevelt Park n.d., pp. 4–5.
166. Ibid., pp. 6–7.
167. Veterans for Victory, 'The Rape of Peace', Houghton *c.*1988, p. 3 [INEG P16.89].
168. The document ends with the following quotation: 'You have never lived until you have almost died, and to those who fight for it, life has a flavour the protected will never know.'
169. Bureau of Information, 'Talking with the ANC . . . ', Johannesburg 1986.
170. Ibid., pp. 27–8.
171. Ibid., p. 33.
172. There were eighteen of these radical reformers in the caucus and at least four in the Cabinet.
173. The National Statutory Council, envisaged for the first time in January 1985, was created by law in 1988, and, according to the NP, it created an opportunity for participation by all South Africans in the making of a new constitutional dispensation for the country. P.W. Botha, ''n Nuwe Era Kry Beslag', *RSA Policy Review*, vol. 1, no. 2, 1988, p. 53.
174. W. de Klerk, 'Behind Closed Doors', *Leadership South Africa*, vol. 6, no. 6, 1987, p. 88.

175. J.-A. Collinge, 'Defiance: A Measure of Resistance', *Work in Progress*, no. 61, 1989, p. 6.

176. Z. Bauman, 'Modernity and Ambivalence', *Theory, Culture & Society*, vol. 7, nos 2–3, p. 163.

6 Competing Myths

1. G. van N. Viljoen, HAD, 1990, col. 62.

2. The NP, not surprisingly, provided contradictory justifications for its stance on the necessity of negotiation with the ANC, and gave contradictory accounts of the processes which led to it. The demise of the Soviet Union was unequivocally held up to have been a condition for the unbanning of the ANC and the SACP. The NP, however, was much more ambiguous on the role of internal resistance and external pressure in the form of sanctions. During the 1980s, it consistently denied that those factors played any role at all. By the early 1990s, however, this position had changed. Minister of Justice Kobie Coetzee, for example, claimed that 'the country had been bled white by sanctions'. De Klerk, himself, equivocated on this, arguing both that 'purely economic forces' had led to the change in their position, and that the country would have been plunged into chaos if the NP had not taken the calculated risk of unbanning the ANC. For a fuller discussion, see H. Giliomee, 'The National Party's Campaign for a Liberation Election', in A. Reynolds (ed.), *Election '94 South Africa. The Campaigns, Results and Future Prospects*, Johannesburg 1994, pp. 43–71. This equivocation could be argued to have been a necessary element of a strategy in which the NP had to be portrayed as both the instigator of change and the saviour of the nation against radical forces.

3. See chapter 4, where I discuss the NP position paper 'Power-Sharing (and Related Concepts)', drawn up by Stoffel van der Merwe, which argued that '[a]ll South African citizens (including Whites, Blacks, Coloureds and Indians) must participate fully in the governmental process up to the highest level.' Van der Merwe and Chris Heunis were amongst the most vocal proponents of the idea that the status of 'groups' had to be redefined.

4. No author, 'Realisme oor Groepe', *RSA Beleidsoorsig*, vol. 2, no. 4, 1989, p. 28.

5. Ibid.

6. For a period, after 1987, the NP toyed with the idea of an open or grey 'non-group' group which would be linked to free settlement areas. In March 1989, legal provision for such areas came into effect. The law on Free Settlement Areas did not replace the Group Areas Act, but made supplementary provision for (non-) regulation of settlement patterns, in close association with the strategy of orderly urbanization. The extent to which the discourse of the 'free market' penetrated NP thinking is also visible here. Roelf Meyer argued that the legal recognition of provision of free settlement areas was based upon the imperatives of 'supply and demand'. 'Oop Woongebiede sal Leer', *RSA Beleidsoorsig*, vol. 2, 1989, p. 4. To facilitate the participation of an 'open group' in the process of reform, the Unlawful Interference Act, which made 'multi-racial' membership of political parties illegal, was repealed. The Group Areas Act was finally repealed on 12 March 1991.

7. C. Heunis, 'Toekomsvisie vir Suid-Afrika', *RSA Beleidsoorsig*, vol. 2, no. 6, 1989, p. 71.

8. The NP was forced by the Independent Electoral Committee to withdraw the publication in question.

9. M. Kronberg interview with F.W de Klerk, 'Unity of Purpose is Challenge of '94', *RSA Beleidsoorsig*, vol. 6, 1993, p. 6.

10. F.W. de Klerk, 'Die Wording van 'n Nasie', *RSA Beleidsoorsig*, vol. 3, 1991, p. 58.

11. The NP's position on its constitutional attainment shifted over time. While De Klerk initially insisted upon a process of negotiation by unelected representatives of parties with proven support, in 1991 he accepted that the process would have to be undertaken by an elected constituent assembly.

12. C.J. van der Merwe, HAD, 1990, cols 82–3. This continued to be the position of the NP. Viljoen argued along similar lines that democracy 'has many different meanings. . . . The ANC's present point of view is that democracy only concerns the will of the majority. However, the standpoint that "the people must decide", is a total misrepresentation. There is no democracy in which the "people" . . . really make decisions.' See, G. van N. Viljoen, 'Towards an Effective Democracy', *RSA Beleidsoorsig*, vol. 3, 1992, p. 5.

13. Both the NP and the ANC were accused of 'elite pacting' during the process of negotiation. The very conception of negotation as a process through which elites establish a new order was clearly derived from the consociational model which had exercised such influence in NP circles during the 1980s.

14. HAD, 1990, col. 186. This portrayal continued to be prevalent during the transition period. On 8 May 1993, F.W. de Klerk devoted a whole media statement to the question, arguing that 'neither of these extremes can assist in the creation of the new South Africa. . . . Measured against these two extreme options, there can be no question but that the Government's vision of power-sharing within a Government of National Unity leading to a new, stable and prosperous South Africa is the only viable option for this nation. It is the Government's intention to bring this vision to reality through the process of negotiation and to withstand, at all costs, the irrational and dangerous pressures being brought to bear upon it from the left and the right. The Government will not allow itself to be prescribed to, whether it be by threats of strikes and mass action or by rumblings from the left or right. It will not concede its vision of the future, nor will it permit a slide into surrender of the moderate constituency it represents. . . . What we are currently experiencing is the last desperate attempt of the left and the right to disrupt the good progress which is being made with negotiations. . . . The implications of conceding to the demands and threats of extremists on the left and on the right are profound. South Africa would be dragged back into the past. International isolation would return, sanctions and economic collapse would follow, violence would increase and a bloody Bosnia-like civil war could ensue.' F.W. de Klerk, 'Appeal for Calm and Responsibility', *RSA Beleidsoorsig*, vol. 6, no. 5, 1993, pp. 82–6.

15. G. van N. Viljoen, Minister of Constitutional Development, HAD, 1990, col. 67. While Viljoen used this argument to refer to the ANC, it, of course, applied equally if not more so to the NP's decision to engage in negotiations.

16. The Minister of Law and Order, Adrian Vlok, described the alternative to the NP's reasoned response, in those terms. HAD, 1990, col. 186.

17. De Klerk argued in his New Year's message that '[t]he dangers of radicalism and the existing threats to the value system of all believing, moderate and peace-loving South Africans demand of us all to act constructively. A complaining, protesting, despondent and dissatisfied nation is a nation heading for disaster and will play into the hands of radicals.' F.W. de Klerk, 'Versoening die Uitdaging vir 1993', *RSA Beleidsoorsig*, vol. 6, no. 1, 1993, p. 88.

18. F.W. de Klerk, 'Op Weg na 'n Nuwe Suid-Afrika', *RSA Beleidsoorsig*, vol. 2, no. 9, 1989, p. 49.

19. Similarly, an NP poster claimed: 'South Africa is changing. We have done it.' Quoted in Giliomee, 'The National Party's Campaign', pp. 55 and 57.

20. In November 1992, the Goldstone Commission provided evidence of the links between the 'third force' and the highest echelons of the Directorate of Military Intelligence. Violent deaths in Natal rose from an estimated 800 in 1989 to a high of 2,009 in 1993. On the Witwatersrand, there were 1,000 deaths in 1990, and more than 2,000 in 1993. For a discussion of attempts to deal with violence during the period of transition, see M. Shaw, 'The Bloody Backdrop. Negotiating Violence', in S. Friedmand and D. Atkinson (eds), *South African Review* 7, Johannesburg 1994, pp. 182–203.

21. F.W. de Klerk, ''n Nuwe Benadering vir 'n Nuwe Bedeling', *RSA Beleidsoorsig*, vol. 10, 1992, p. 89.

22. The reasons for the violence were ascribed, *inter alia*, to the instability arising from reforms; socio-economic problems; hate and mistrust between ethnic groups; the fact that so many blacks grew up in conditions of unrest, and so forth. This apparent neutrality served to cover over the question as to why those conditions arose in the first place. These reasons were advanced in 1991, and the position of the government on this issue remained constant over the period of transition. No author, 'Gesprek oor Geweld', *RSA Beleidsoorsig*, vol. 7, 1991, p. 55. Similar reasons were advanced by Johan van der Merwe, the Commissioner of Police. See J. van der Merwe, 'Die SAP en Geweld', *RSA Beleidsoorsig*, vol. 4, 1992, p. 16.

23. Viljoen made this quite explicit in response to a question as to the viability of democracy in Africa, arguing that certain features of South African life had 'encouraging characteristics', which included the fact that the 'First-World element in South Africa' was larger than in the rest of Africa'. Viljoen, 'Towards an Effective Democracy', p. 11.

24. While not denying that people had a 'right to convene politically', government spokespersons proclaimed that 'in the present volatile climate of violence and intolerance, the right to demonstrate publicly should be weighed up against the right of innocent people to a peaceful existence.' G. Myburgh, 'Suspension of Violence a Priority', *RSA Beleidsoorsig*, vol. 6, no. 7, 1993, pp. 7–8.

25. F.W. de Klerk, 'Onderhandeling die Enigste Uitweg', *RSA Beleidsoorsig*, vol. 2, 1990, p. 63. In response to the question as to whether mobilization 'on the streets' was acceptable, Viljoen argued that it was a 'real possibility' but one which would be contrary to the spirit of negotiations. See Viljoen, 'Towards an Effective Democracy', p. 3.

26. Viljoen, 'Towards an Effective Democracy', pp. 9–10.

27. F.W. de Klerk, 'Hervorming Open Deure', *RSA Beleidsoorsig*, vol. 3, no. 3, 1990, p. 8.

28. M. Walden, 'Talk of War', *Leadership South Africa*, vol. 9, no. 4, 1990, p. 78.

29. These include the *Afrikaner Vryheidstigting* (Afrikaner Freedom Foundation), the *Boerestaat Party* (Boer State Party), the *Boere Weerstandsbeweging* (Boer Resistance Movement), the World Apartheid Movement, the *Wit Wolve* (White Wolves), the *Orde van die Dood* (Order of Death), the *Orde Boerevolk* (Order of the Boer *volk*), the *Pretoria Boere Kommando Groep* (Pretoria Boer Commando Group), the *Afrikaner Volksfront* (Afrikaner People's Front) and the *Vryheidsfront* (Freedom Front), to name but a few. This period also saw the formation of a number of religious organizations – such as the *Afrikaanse Protestantse Kerke* (Afrikaans Protestant Church) – splitting away from the traditional Afrikaans churches, as well as right-wing groupings – such as the *NG Bond* (DRC League) – operating with the confines of the DRC.

30. Van Rooyen, *Hard Right*, p. 1. While I am in agreement with Van Rooyen's assessment of the continuing presence of the white right, I disagree quite strongly with his interpretation of the white right as in essential continuity with the 'tradition' of Afrikaner nationalism.

31. This is not to say that there is any singularity or full agreement on the constitutive elements of this myth across the various far right movements. As I have argued with respect to apartheid, no such singularity is needed for the articulation of a mythical principle of reading.

32. I will not analyse all of the far right discourses here, but will concentrate on the strategies of primarily two of the groupings which have become particularly prominent in recent South African politics: the *Afrikaner Volksfront* (AVF, Afrikaner People's Front) and the *Vryheidsfront* (VF, Freedom Front). For a more detailed analysis of interpretations of the contemporary right, see A.J. Norval, 'Questions of Race and Identity. Understanding the White Right in Contemporary South Africa',

paper delivered to the British Political Studies Association Conference, York, April 1995 (mimeo).

33. This is clear, for example, in its proposal that a white homeland should take up two-thirds of the territory of contemporary South Africa.

34. Even before the creation of the AVF, there was a proliferation of different proposals around the broad idea of a *volkstaat*. These ranged from the KP proposals referred to earlier, to that of the *Oranjewerkers Unie* (Orange Workers' Union), which demanded a much smaller territory on the banks of the Orange River. Differences in strategy on how to attain a *volkstaat* in practice also varied greatly. One of the perceived difficulties within the ranks of those favouring a *volkstaat* is precisely their inability to agree on issues such as these.

35. The roots of this organization can be found some two years earlier in the activities of a small group of ideologues who organized a right-wing think-tank, the *Instituut vir Strategiese Studies* (INSA, Institute for Strategic Studies). INSA was founded under the leadership of Tienie Groenewald, a military general who took early retirement in 1990. While INSA did not initially make inroads into the general activities of the right, this situation changed with the creation, first, of a *Volkseenheidkomitee* (Vekom, *Volk*'s Unity Committee) and later of the AVF.

36. Some estimates put the number of generals involved in the *volkstaat* activities as high as fifty.

37. For a fuller account of the negotiations between these two groupings, see J. van Rooyen, 'The White Right', in Reynolds, *Election '94*, pp. 90–97.

38. 'ANC/AVF Onderhandelings: Die Inside Story', *Die Suid Afrikaan*, no. 47, 1994, p. 15.

39. Viljoen initially registered the VF for the elections while continuing to be a member of the AVF. Two events were decisive in his break with that organization: the rejection of his decision to participate by the *Volksraad* – the AVF's executive council – and the failure of the military intervention in Bophuthatswana in March 1994 as a result of the unwelcome intrusion by AWB 'troops'. As a result, the other generals followed suit, and the AVF was left severely weakened.

40. I draw here on a personal interview with P. Aucamp, spokesperson for the AVF. Pieter Aucamp, 'Personal Interview', Pretoria, May 1994.

41. Aucamp suggested that the issue of membership of the *volk* may be easily decided by applying the '*d/jakkals* test'. Should a person pronounce the Afrikaans word *jakkals* on its 'standard' pronunciation, then s/he is clearly a member of the *volk*. Should it be pronounced *djakkals* instead, such a person is excluded from membership. This racist test is clearly designed to exclude coloured Afrikaners from the *volk*, and is reminiscent of the various tests employed in the early apartheid years to establish a person's 'race'. Ibid.

42. This, he argues, is also evident on the rest of the African continent: having left the *uhuru* phase behind, Africa is now in a 'democratizing' phase.

43. For Mulder, the constitutional expert of the VF, it is important to remember in this context that emerging demands for ethnically based democracies cannot be separated from the increasing globalization of the world economy. Economic interdependence is coupled everywhere with demands for territorial separatism. In this manner, a distancing effect is created from the tradition of Afrikaner separatism as it was found, for example, in the early SABRA demands, for whom 'total apartheid' meant apartheid in both the political and economic spheres.

44. Corné Mulder argues in this respect that South Africa's problems are not unique. As in the rest of Africa, they are intimately related to the drawing of colonial boundaries which created 'artificial entities'; in the case of South Africa, non-existent 'South Africans'.

45. Vryheidsfront, 'Beginsel 34 en die Volkstaatraad', election pamphlet, 1994. The 34th (34.1) constitutional principle entails that the 'right of the South African people as a whole to self-determination shall not be construed as precluding, within the framework of said right, constitutional provision for a notion of the right to self-

determination by any community sharing a common cultural and language heritage, whether in a territorial entity within the Republic or in any other recognized way.'

46. Article 34 further states that self-determination may be established should there be substantial support from within the particular community for such a form of self-determination. This was used as the basis of the election campaign. The outcome of the elections, Viljoen argued, would give evidence of the amount of support there is for a *volkstaat*. The VF won 2.2 per cent of the total vote, placing it fourth after the ANC, the NP and the IFP. At regional level the VF was the third strongest party in six out of nine provinces.

47. C. Mulder, 'Personal Interview', Pretoria, 19 May 1994.

48. J. Taljaard, 'Alive and Sick and Living in Belgium', *Weekly Mail*, 7/10/1994.

49. It is, of course, clear that the real issue here concerns the position of Afrikaans-speaking coloureds. The VF, in attempting to distance itself from the racism of apartheid, has great difficulty in dealing with this question, therefore the strategy of not making pronouncements on the 'race' issue, leaving it to members of the *volk* to decide.

50. In NP discourse the idea of the *volkseie* was combined with a discourse of white supremacy which is somewhat weakened in the discourse of the *volkstaat*, especially to the extent that they have given up the idea of a white South Africa dominated by white interests.

51. That the position of the VF is not one that is regarded as entirely illegitimate is clear from the fact that Mandela continues to negotiate with it on the issue of a *volkstaat*.

52. Buthelezi speech, 29 June 1985, quoted in G. Maré and G. Hamilton, *An Appetite for Power. Buthelezi's Inkatha and South Africa*, Johannesburg 1987, p. 195.

53. Bell argues that until peace is secured in the KwaZulu/Natal region, the contagious spread of civil violence to the rest of the country will continue to undercut progress towards a national political settlement. P. Bell, 'The Heart of Darkness', *Leadership South Africa*, vol. 12, no. 2, 1993, p. 78. Similarly, Maré and Hamilton argued in 1987 that 'Buthelezi's appetite for power will not be satisfied in a subordinate context. The drive for power will be one of disruption and reaction, of division and of attempts to protect what has no place in a democratic future.' Maré and Hamilton, *An Appetite for Power*, p. 225. This argument still holds today. See also H. Adam and K. Moodley, *The Negotiated Revolution. Society and Politics in Post-Apartheid South Africa*, Johannesburg 1993, pp. 147–8; and M. Murray, *The Revolution Deferred. The Painful Birth of Post-Apartheid South Africa*, London 1994.

54. Both Adam and Moodley and Murray point out that this portrayal is problematic, especially insofar as it seeks to exonerate the ANC, and its campaign for 'ungovernability' waged in the townships in the mid-1980s. It also has to be noted that the issue of the Shell House massacre – which took place shortly before the elections – has not yet been resolved, and there seems to be little intention on the part of the ANC to address it.

55. See Adam and Moodley, *The Negotiated Revolution*, pp. 121–48; Murray, *The Revolution Deferred*, pp. 93–116; and R. Taylor, 'The Myth of Ethnic Division: Township Conflict on the Reef', *Race and Class*, vol. 33, no. 2, pp. 1–14.

56. A genealogy of these elements falls beyond the scope of this discussion. For further detail consult, *inter alia*, Maré and Hamilton, *An Appetite for Power*, which situates and contextualizes the emergence of Inkatha as a populist movement.

57. For an in-depth treatment of the reconstruction of 'tradition', see ibid., pp. 45–60, as well as P. Harries, 'Imagery, Symbolism and Tradition in a South African Bantustan: Mangosuthu Buthelezi, Inkatha, and Zulu History', *History and Theory*, vol. 32, no. 4, 1993, pp. 105–25. For a more general discussion of the conditions under which 'ethnicity' is mobilized, see J. Nederveen Pieterse, 'The Varieties of Ethnic Politics and Ethnicity Discourse', paper delivered to the Conference on Ethnicity, Identity and Nationalism in South Africa: Comparative Perspectives, Rhodes University, Grahamstown, 24–9 April 1993.

58. Accounts differ in the emphasis which they give to each of these factors in the explanation of the violence. According to Woods (of the Inkatha Institute), the violence is first and foremost the result of socio-economic processes, rooted in the fact that black unemployment rates in the KwaZulu/Natal region are estimated at 40 per cent for the population as a whole, and as much as 70 per cent for the economically active youth. Cited in M. Kentridge, 'War and Peace in Natal', in D. Innes, M. Kentridge and H. Perold (eds), *Power and Profit. Politics, Labour, and Business in South Africa*, Cape Town 1992, p. 47. In addition to unemployment – which is the second highest of all South Africa's regions – other socio-economic factors have to be taken into account here: the dependency ratio in the region (the relation between the number of economically active persons in employment and those not in employment) is the highest in the country; it has a low level of urbanization, 52 per cent compared to the national average of 66 per cent; and while its people constitute 23 per cent of the South African population, the region generates only 14.7 per cent of its GDP. P. Bell, 'The Heart of Darkness', p. 80. By contrast, others have argued that the rural–urban divide – which overlaps with a division between generations – is crucial. See C.B. Collins, 'Multiculturalism: The New Name for Apartheid', *Journal of Intercultural Studies*, vol. 13, no. 7, 1992, in this regard. Adam and Moodley – while not focusing on these factors to the exclusion of others – present the most cogent argument in this respect, showing that what is important is not simply the sociological presence of those divisions, but the manner in which they are experienced, especially by migrant workers in single-men's hostels. In this respect, Inkatha's appeal can be ascribed to the fact that it succeeded in giving symbolic representation to feelings of powerlessness and despair. Adam and Moodley, *The Negotiated Revolution*, p. 139.

59. Adam and Moodley, *The Negotiated Revolution*, p. 139. Harries offers a similar diagnosis: 'The invocation of a rich past of firm values and standards recreates a life in which people who have been uprooted, disoriented, and shaken by capitalism and apartheid are able to find an emotional security.' Harries, 'Imagery, Symbolism and Tradition', p. 124.

60. It is quite often pointed out that many of those involved in the violence in Natal have tended to be unaware of political differences between the ANC and Inkatha. The issue here, however, is not whether participants in the violence are able clearly to articulate the grounds upon which they engage in warring, but whether their battles are legitimated and facilitated by wider political struggles. While a specific struggle, for example around resource allocation in rural areas, may be argued to be encapsulated and particularistic, the activities of war lords and local power-brokers cannot be accounted for without consideration of the institutional support they either receive or lack. The current tendency to downplay the importance of political divisions could perhaps be ascribed to the fact that most accounts of the position of Inkatha at present tend to be constructed with the aim of accounting specifically for the violence, rather than investigating the broader question of the myth structuring and informing a range of activities, one crucial element of which is the violence.

61. Throughout the transition period Buthelezi threatened that giving in to the ANC's demands would precipitate 'nothing less than civil war'. *The Guardian*, 9/4/1991.

62. Already in 1982 the Buthelezi Commission concluded that federal dispensation 'appears to be most suited to all the conflicting conditions bearing upon the situation in the region'. *The Buthelezi Commission. The Requirements for Stability and Development in KwaZulu and Natal*, vol. II, Durban 1982, p. 111.

63. In November 1986, according to the KwaNatal Indaba proposals, it was argued that Natal should have a special autonomous status relative to the rest of the country, and that it should be a building block of a federal state.

64. Adam and Moodley make the claim that one of the great surprises of 1990 was the sudden emergence of the tribal factor: hitherto, 'it had been taboo for the disenfranchised to talk publicly about Zulu and Xhosa forces. Only apartheid's ideologues used such labels.' Adam and Moodley, *The Negotiated Revolution*, p. 134.

65. Maré and Hamilton, *An Appetite for Power*, p. 57.

66. For a discussion of the construction of 'womanhood' in the discourse of Inkatha, see S. Hassim, 'Family, Motherhood and Zulu Nationalism: The Politics of the Inkatha's Women's Brigade', *Feminist Review*, no. 43, Spring 1993, pp. 1–25.

67. Buthelezi speech, 6 April 1987, quoted in P. Harries, 'Imagery, Symbolism and Tradition', p. 122. Harries also points out that the offical name for Inkatha was changed in 1980 from *Inkatha YaKwaZulu* to *Inkatha Yenkululeku Yesiswe*. This change signified an effort to deny ethnocentrism, and to portray itself as a national cultural liberation movement.

68. This claim to non-violence sits uneasily alongside Inkatha's frequent rehearsal of 'warrior values'.

69. G. Maré, 'History and Dimension of the Violence in Natal: Inkatha's Role in Negotiating Political Peace', *Social Justice*, vol. 18, nos 1–2, 1991, p. 195.

70. Ibid., p. 199.

71. Buthelezi consistently referred to mass action in derogatory terms. Unrest, school boycotts and work stayaways were presented variously as 'unplanned', attributable to 'agitators', 'intimidators' and 'youth gone mad'. See C. McCaul, 'The Wild Card: Inkatha and Contemporary Black Politics', in P. Frankel, N. Pines and M. Swilling (eds), *State, Resistance and Change in South Africa. The Burden of the Present*, London 1988, p. 158.

72. Ibid., p. 153.

73. See Maré and Hamilton, *An Appetite for Power*, pp. 101–16.

74. Inkatha did not take part in CODESA (Convention for a Democratic South Africa) II. Buthelezi's refusal was 'justified' by the fact that King Goodwill Zwelethini was not allowed to represent the 'Zulu nation' as a full member at the talks. It is important, as Hamilton and Maré point out, when examining Inkatha's refusal to participate, that neither Buthelezi nor the IFP ever really left negotiations. Instead, they continued to demand concessions, and to enter into bilateral talks at the last moment. For a discussion of Inkatha's participation in the negotiation process, see Hamilton and Maré, 'The Inkatha Freedom Party', in Reynolds, *Election '94*, pp. 73–87.

75. Adam and Moodley, *The Negotiated Revolution*, p. 149.

76. Hamilton and Maré, 'Inkatha Freedom Party', p. 81.

77. This general statement has to be tempered with reference to differences between different homelands. See A. Sparks, *Tomorrow is Another Country. The Inside Story of South Africa's Negotiated Revolution*, Sandton 1994, pp. 197–225.

78. The Congress of Traditional Leaders of South Africa (CONTRALESA), an organization intitially formed in 1987 and opposed to homeland 'independence', came out in favour of the ANC after initial meetings with it in Lusaka in 1989. The ANC also recognized the importance of traditional leaders and chiefs in performing ceremonial and other functions allocated to them by law.

79. Recently there have been reports of a possible alliance between Winnie Mandela and 'traditional leaders'.

80. A. Sachs, 'The Constitutional Position of White South Africans in a Democratic South Africa', *Social Justice*, vol. 18, nos 1–2, p. 33 (emphasis added).

81. Throughout the 1980s debates raged within the 'left' on the nature of the relation between democracy (understood as national liberation) and socialism. With the events of 1989, this debate was opened up considerably. Joe Slovo's 1990 paper 'Has Socialism Failed?' contributed to that process. (Extract published with commentary in G. Moss, 'Debating Socialism', *Work in Progress*, no. 64, January 1990, pp. 18–22.) Much of this debate took place in the journal *Work in Progress*, a site in which activists and academics thrashed out their ideas. Some of the most interesting contributions to this debate are found in the work of D. Glaser. See, for example, 'Democracy, Socialism and the Future', *Work in Progress*, nos 56–7, November 1988, pp. 28–30; and 'Taking the Third Road', *Work in Progress*, no. 67, June 1990, pp. 35–8.

82. See also A.J. Norval, 'Decolonization, Demonization and Difference: The

Difficult Constitution of a Nation', *Philosophy and Social Criticism*, vol. 21, no. 3, 1995, pp. 31–51.

83. The question concerns democracy here not as a system of voting and protection of rights, but as a *regime*, an ordering principle of the social order.

84. Here, as in the previous sections, my concern is not so much with the precise detail of the negotiation process and the ANC's position in that process, as with the non-racial frame within which those interventions took place. For a discussion of the negotiation process, see, *inter alia*, Sparks, *Tomorrow is Another Country*; J. Rantete and H. Giliomee, 'Transition to Democracy through Transaction? Bilateral Negotiations between the ANC and NP in South Africa', *African Affairs*, vol. 91, 1992, pp. 515–42.

85. The Truth Commission was conceived in order to address this problem, and as a clear alternative to 'war crime tribunals'.

86. N. Mandela, 'A Time for Healing the Wounds', *The Star*, 11/5/1994.

87. As Sachs notes, from a 'purely moral point of view, it is not easy to accept that the fears of the white minority in South Africa should merit special attention. It is they who made the bed in which they are now so unwilling to lie. . . . Nevertheless, if we are to build a new nation on the ruins of apartheid, we have to address ourselves seriously to all the preoccupations of all the people, whatever their past roles might have been.' Sachs, 'The Constitutional Position of White South Africans', p. 20.

88. Ibid., p. 14.

89. Ibid.

90. Ibid., p. 30.

91. In 1990 Slovo published his rethinking of socialism, 'Has Socialism Failed?' Slovo argued later that 'socialism has failed in the sense that those who ran the existing socialist states perverted its objectives. In one sense, its most terrible failure was the separation between socialism and democracy, which infected every level of the socio-economic formation'. He also argued with reference to events in Eastern Europe that 'it would be naive to imagine that socialism hasn't taken a knock in the general sense, . . . I have no doubt that, as far as the people of South Africa are concerned – the workers, the youth – they will judge the party in South Africa on the basis of its record here, and not on some perverted, tyrannical groups in other parts of the world.' Quoted in P. van Niekerk, 'Chips off the Old Block', *Leadership South Africa*, vol. 9, no. 1, 1990, pp. 33–4. For a discussion of the position of the SACP during the period of transition, see T. Lodge, 'Post-Modern Bolsheviks – SA Communists in Transition', *South Africa International*, April 1992, pp. 172–9. Adam argues that a much more profound recognition of the failure of 'really existing socialism' has to come forth from the SACP, since they identified with Soviet strategy as politically desirable and ethically justifiable: 'They glorified and romanticised the Soviet Union against all criticism and thereby also discredited the anti-apartheid cause that was their first priority.' See H. Adam, 'Eastern Europe and South African Socialism – Engaging Joe Slovo', *South Africa International*, vol. 21, no. 1, 1990, p. 29.

92. For a discussion of the relation between 'the people' and democracy, see, *inter alia*, M. Morobe, 'Towards a People's Democracy', *South Africa International*, vol. 18, no. 1, 1987, pp. 30–38, as well as R. Suttner, 'The Freedom Charter – The People's Charter in the Nineteen-Eighties', *South Africa International*, vol. 15, no. 4, 1985, pp. 233–52.

93. It was not only the NP which was guilty of gross exploitation of the coloured community during the elections. The ANC did not shrink from using religion in their campaign 'to strike the fear of God into the very religious coloured communities', *Weekly Mail and Guardian*, 8–14 April 1994. Its leaders warned coloured voters that voting for the NP would be sinful: 'Your vote is secret, but not before God. Don't vote NP' warned one poster.

94. A series of errors of judgement in the run-up to the election were also made by the ANC. The appointment of Alan Boesak as Western Cape ANC leader was one of them, for Boesak's position within the coloured community had long been a

contentious one. By 1992 ANC figures admitted that they could not expect much support from the coloured community, since their fear of the future under a black government exceeded their anger at the treatment meted out by white racist governments of the past.

95. *The Star*, 11/5/1994. This belittling was most evident in the use of the prefix 'so-called' when referring to the coloured community. Since the elections, the very use of the appellation 'coloured' has been the subject of continuing debate.

96. The ANC's position in this respect has to be contrasted to that of the internal resistance movement, especially of that of the UDF. The fact that its leadership was initially sidelined in favour of the exiled old-guard increased the problem, for the internal movement was more in touch with conditions on the ground, and thus more sensitive – and some would argue more democratic – than the returned exiles. It is also notable that election outcomes in the Western Cape differed markedly from those in the Northern Cape region, where coloured voters were also in a majority, and which was won by the ANC with a 50 per cent share of the vote compared to the NP's 41 per cent. The differences between these two regions have to be ascribed to a variety of factors, of which one of the most important is the specificity of the history of the Western Cape, especially with regard to the 'Coloured Labour Preference Policy' in force from 1949 to 1984. This is more than likely to have had a significant impact on the shaping of divisions between coloureds and Africans. The historical 'protection' of 'coloured labour' made coloured workers in the Western Cape more vulnerable to the effects of affirmative action, and thus less likely to support an ANC regional government.

97. It is important to note that one dimension of affirmative action, as outlined in the Reconstruction and Development Programme, concerns the restructuring of the public sector in order to make it reflective of the society as a whole. ANC, *Reconstruction and Development Programme*, 1994, article 5.10.3. It is clearly crucial that the public bureaucracy is reformed, and if the experience of the NP after 1948 and also during the reformist period is taken into account, this is likely to take considerable time. The difficulties of transforming the public sector could be exacerbated by the fact that the NP, as a concession from the ANC during the negotiation process, had gained a guarantee of security of tenure for all civil servants.

98. Sachs, 'The Constitutional Position of White South Africans', p. 30. Sachs also argues that the negative experience of the USA would not be repeated in South Africa, since the persons implementing affirmative action would be in the majority. This, however, precisely avoids the difficult question of differences within 'the majority'.

99. A. Sachs, 'Watch Out – There's a Constitution About', *South Africa International*, vol. 22, no. 4, 1992, pp. 187–8.

100. The claims of 'socialism' are increasingly being addressed in the more limited terms of the institution of a social democratic order.

101. These principles were taken up in the *Reconstruction and Development Programme*, article 4.8.

102. H. Robertson, 'Radicals Left out in the Cold', *The Star*, 4/5/1994.

103. *The Star*, 27/4/1994. In this, one has to consider the difficulties facing the government of national unity in the implementation of redistribution, as well as the fact that there inevitably has to be a transition from a mass-based opposition movement to government.

104. It is important to note in this respect that COSATU, the largest trade union organization in South Africa, has resolved to keep its autonomy from the new government, and to continue to foreground the interests of workers. This distancing between the ANC and the organized trade union movement could be argued to be a prerequisite for the retention of a strong and independent labour movement. The fact of possible tension should thus not necessarily be regarded in a negative light.

105. Lodge is of the opinion that 'by maintaining its position as the party of labour and the advocate of the poor, the South African Communist Party may serve a wider social purpose as the most effective guarator of parliamentary democracy in South Africa'. Lodge, 'Post-Modern Bolsheviks', p. 177.

106. Swartz points out that the growth model favoured by the ANC, which relies on a tri-partite compact between the major corporations, trade unions and the government, does not adequately address the manner in which the socially marginalized and rural poor will gain access to economic power. Swartz, 'The Theory and Politics of State Economic Intervention', p. 287.

107. In this respect it is important to point out that, if compared by region, income differentials between blacks are in some cases already higher than between whites and blacks. The average black income in Gauteng (R9,375) is two and a half times higher than the national black average and six times higher than that of the Northern Transvaal. M. Chester, 'Mountain to Climb for Parity', *The Star*, 17/5/1994.

Conclusion

1. H.F. Pitkin, *Wittgenstein and Justice. On the Significance of Ludwig Wittgenstein for Social and Political Thought*, Berkeley 1972, p. 339.

2. This confirms Foucault's intuition that one ought to be aware of the effects of new discursive configurations on the community from which they emerged, and not only of their later extensions.

3. For example, one can think here, *inter alia*, of the music of *Johannes Kerkorrel en die Gereformeerde Blues Band* and the writings of Koos Prinsloo which were recognized to be part of a movement to distance Afrikanerhood from the political form it took under apartheid hegemony. This is not to say that a questioning of the tenets of the exclusivist conception of Afrikaner nationalism was absent earlier. One can think here of literary movements such as the *Sestigers* which did not accept those narrow limits. The point is that in popular culture that questioning only became more widespread during the 1980s.

4. Laclau, *New Reflections*, p. 67.

5. The very idea of a 'total refoundation' of society is one which, I would argue, is possible to conceive of only in principle.

6. Connolly, *Identity\Difference*, p. 8.

7. The friend/foe distinction, drawn from the work of Carl Schmitt, is premissed upon a logic of homogeneity which runs counter to any attempt to foster space for plural, non-homogeneous forms of identification. For a discussion of the problems of relating a radical conception of democracy to a conception of politics based upon that distinction, see W.E. Connolly, 'Review Essay: Twilight of the Idols', *Philosophy and Social Criticism*, vol. 21, no. 3, 1995, pp. 127–37.

8. Connolly, *Identity\Difference*, p. 9.

9. R.J. Bernstein and the Editors, 'Postmodernism, Dialogue, and Democracy: Questions to Richard J. Bernstein', in J.P. Jones II, W. Natter, T.R. Schatzki (eds), *Postmodern Contentions. Epochs, Politics, Space*, New York 1993, p. 106.

10. Connolly argues, in a similar fashion to Lefort, that democracy, more than any other social forms, accentuates 'exposure to contingency and increases the likelihood that the affirmation of difference in identity will find expression in public life'. Connolly, *Identity\Difference*, p. 193.

11. Ibid., p. 14.

12. Ibid., p. 90.

13. It is true that the ANC's discourse has recognized the fact that 'the oppressed may turn into a new oppressor'. However, it would probably be prudent to suspend judgement on the concrete realization of that recognition in the new South Africa.

14. F.R. Dallmayr, 'Democracy and Post-Modernism', *Human Studies*, vol. 10, no. 1, 1986, p. 163.

15. Connolly, *Identity\Difference*, p. 211.

16. M. Doornbos, 'Linking the Future to the Past: Ethnicity and Pluralism', *Review of African Political Economy*, no. 52, 1991, p. 62.

17. This has been evident in the 'culture of consultation' which has become a regular feature of South African political life.
18. Laclau and Mouffe define radical democracy precisely in these terms: in the extension of the field of democratic struggles to the whole of civil society and the state. Laclau and Mouffe, *Hegemony and Socialist Strategy*, p. 176.
19. Wittgenstein, *Philosophical Investigations*, p. 46e, remark 107.

Chronology*

1652–1795:	Dutch colonial rule.
1795–1802 and 1806:	British colonial rule.
1836–54:	Great Trek.
1838:	Battle of Blood River.
1840–99:	Boer Republics are established in the Transvaal, Orange Free State and in Natal.
1899–1902:	Anglo-Boer War/First War of Liberation. Boer Republics defeated by Britain.
1903–5:	South African Native Affairs Commission recommends 'blueprint' for segregation.
1906:	Bambatha (Zulu) rebellion defeated.
1910:	Union of South Africa formed from the former Boer Republics and the British colonies.
1911:	Mines and Works Act imposes colour bar in mines.
1912:	Formation of the South African Native National Congress, later to become known as the African National Congress.
1913:	Native Land Act establishes reserves; prohibits any purchase of land by Africans outside reserves (13 per cent of South African territory).
1913–14:	White strikes on Rand.

*In constructing this chronology, I have drawn heavily on R. Mkhondo, *Reporting South Africa*, London 1993, pp. 178–89.

1914:	South Africa enters First World War.
1919:	Formation of the Industrial and Commercial Workers' Union.
1920:	Native Affairs Act establishes the Native Affairs Commission and extends the Transkei Council system to other reserves.
1921:	Formation of the South African Communist Party. Massacre of 'Israelites' at Bulhoek.
1922:	Rand Revolt of white mine workers.
1923:	Natives (Urban Areas Act) provides for urban segregation and African influx control.
1924:	Coalition of Labour and National Parties wins election; Pact government under Hertzog; Afrikaans given official recognition. Industrial Conciliation Act excludes migrant workers from trade union representation.
1927:	Native Adminstration Act 'retribalizes' African government and law.
1930–32:	Native Economic Commission.
1930–33:	Great Depression.
1932:	Report of the Carnegie Commission on the 'poor white question'.
1934:	South African Party (under Smuts) and National Party (under Hertzog) unite in the United Party (UP) to form coalition 'Fusion' government. *Gesuiwerde Nasionale Party* (GNP) breaks away from UP under leadership of Malan.
1935:	Formation of the All African Convention.
1936:	Native Land and Trust Act consolidates reserves; Representation of Natives Act removes Africans from Cape common franchise.
1937:	Native Laws Amendment Act intensifies urban pass laws.

1938:	Great Trek Centenary celebrations. Formation of the *Ossewabrandwag* (OB).
1939:	Hertzog joins GNP, which then becomes known as the *Herenigde Nasionale Party* (HNP).
1943:	Formation of ANC Youth League.
1946:	African mine workers' strike.
1946–48:	Native Laws Commission (Fagan).
1948:	*Report of the Colour Commission of the HNP* published (Sauer report). HNP forms government with Afrikaner Party (AP).
1949:	The Mixed Marriages Act. The ANC adopts its Programme of Action.
1950:	Population Registration Act; Group Areas Act; Suppression of Communism Act; Immorality Amendment Act.
1951:	Bantu Authorities Act.
1952:	Launch of the defiance campaign. Term 'Bantu' replaces 'Native' in government discourse.
1953:	Reservation of Separate Amenities Act; the Bantu Education Act; Criminal Law Amendment Act; Native Labour (Settlement of Disputes) Act; Public Safety Act.
1953–54:	Resistance to destruction of Sophiatown.
1955:	*Report of the Commission for the Socio-Economic Development of the Bantu Areas within the Union of South Africa* Tomlinson report) published. Formation of the Coloured People's Organization. Formation of the South African Congress of Trade Unions. The Congress of People held at Kliptown, adopting the Freedom Charter. Native (Urban Areas) Amendment Act extends urban influx control.

1956:	Coloureds removed from the common voters' roll. One hundred and fifty-six leaders of the ANC and other organizations, including Nelson Mandela, are arrested; treason trial.
1958:	Sekhukuneland revolt against the imposition of 'puppet' authorities in the Eastern Transvaal. Upheavals against pass laws in Natal.
1959:	Formation of Pan-Africanist Congress (PAC). Promotion of Bantu Self-Government Act sets up ethnic 'homelands'.
1960:	21 March, Sharpeville massacre: sixty-nine blacks killed in pass law protest. Unlawful Organizations Act: ANC, Communist Party and PAC banned, Pondoland revolt.
1961:	South Africa becomes a republic. Twelve-day detention law passed. Formation of ANC military wing: *Umkhonto we Sizwe*.
1962:	Mandela rearrested. Banning of the Congress of Democrats, a small white anti-apartheid organization allied to the ANC.
1963:	Security Council of the UN calls for voluntary arms embargo on South Africa. Ninety-day detention law passed.
1964:	Beginning of Rivonia trial. Life sentences imposed on Nelson Mandela, Walter Sisulu, Govan Mbeki, Dennis Goldberg, Ahmed Kathrada, Andrew Mlangeni, Raymond Mhlaba and Elias Motsoaledi.
1966:	H.F. Verwoerd assassinated in Parliament by Stavendas, reputedly mentally ill. B.J. Vorster elected Prime Minister.
1968:	The Prohibition of Political Interference Act prevents different 'race' groups from belonging to the same political party.

1969:	*Herstigte Nasionale Party* breaks away from NP. Formation of South African Students' Organization under Biko.
1971:	Formation of Black People's Convention.
1973:	Natal strikes lead to black unionization across country.
1974:	Term 'Black' replaces 'Bantu' in NP discourse.
1975:	Formation of Inkatha under Buthelezi.
1976:	Publication of the *Report of the Commission of Inquiry into Matters Relating to the Coloured Population Group* (Theron Commission). Soweto uprisings. Over six hundred people killed in the following six months.
1976–81:	Nominal independence of 'homelands': Transkei (1976), Bophuthatswana (1977), Venda (1979), Ciskei (1981).
1977:	Steve Biko, Black Consciousness leader, dies in detention after torture. Banning of two newspapers and eighteen mainly Black Consciousness anti-apartheid organizations.
1978:	Vorster retires after 'Muldergate' scandal. P.W. Botha becomes Prime Minister. Botha introduces Total Strategy.
1979:	Carlton Conference meeting of government and business leaders. Publication of the *Report of the Commission of Inquiry into Legislation Affecting the Utilisation of Manpower* (Riekert). Easing of job colour bar. Publication of the *Report of the Commission of Inquiry into Labour Legislation* (Wiehahn). Black trade unions legalized.
1982:	Formation of *Konservatiewe Party* (KP) under the leadership of Andries Treurnicht. Formation of Black Local Authorities.

1983: Formation of the United Democratic Front.
Formation of Johannesburg Democratic Action Committee.
Formation of the End Conscription Campaign.

1984: Formation of tri-cameral Parliament, for whites, coloureds and Indians.
Violence erupts in the Vaal triangle, south of Johannesburg, and spreads throughout the Vaal triangle townships.
5–6 November: Largest stay-away in thirty-five years in the Transvaal.
Bishop Desmond Tutu wins Nobel Prize for peace.

1985: Mandela meets government delegates while in hospital.
Twenty protestors killed on the occasion of the twenty-fifth anniversary of the Sharpeville massacre.
Twenty-two UDF leaders charged with high treason.
SADF raid on Gabarone.
Declaration of partial state of Emergency.
Congress of South African Students banned.
First delegation of whites meet ANC at its Lusaka headquarters.
Formation of the Congress of South African Trade Unions.
International bank loans to South Africa called in and drive for sanctions intensified.

1986: Full property rights extended to blacks.
SADF raids Botswana, Zambia and Zimbabwe.
UDF launches 'Call to Whites' campaign.
Nationwide State of Emergency declared.
Over twenty thousand anti-apartheid activists detained within three months.
Repeal of pass laws.

1986–89: Widespread conflict between Inkatha and UDF in Natal.

1987:	Release of Govan Mbeki, ANC leader given life sentence in 1964.
1988:	ANC Lusaka headquarters bombed by government. ANC publishes its 'Constitutional Guidelines'.
1989:	P.W. Botha suffers stroke. Replaced by F.W. de Klerk. Botha meets Mandela. Formation of Mass Democratic Movement (consisting of many former UDF affiliates), and launch of defiance campaign against apartheid. De Klerk allows mass demonstrations against apartheid rule. Free Settlement Areas created. Mandela meets De Klerk.
1990:	De Klerk unbans ANC, SACP, PAC. Mandela released from jail. Namibia obtains independence. Political violence intensifies, especially in Natal. Police shoot eleven protesters in Sebokeng. First meeting between government and the ANC. Signing of the 'Groote Schuur Minute'. State of Emergency lifted. Inkatha becomes a political party, the Inkatha Freedom Party (IFP). Fighting between Inkatha and ANC supporters spreads to the Transvaal. At least one thousand, two hundred people killed between July and December. NP becomes multi-racial party. Public relaunch of SACP. Second ANC–government summit. Signing of the 'Pretoria Minute'. ANC suspends armed struggle. Repeal of Separate Amenities Act. ANC President Oliver Tambo returns to South Africa.

1991:	Repeal of Group Areas, Land and Population Registration Acts. Convention for a Democratic South Africa (CODESA) formed to negotiate democratic constitution. Signing of 'National Peace Accord' aimed at curbing township violence.
1992:	White referendum supports CODESA negotiations; breakdown of negotiations. Boipatong massacre, killing of forty-nine people. Twenty-eight ANC supporters killed after marching on Bisho, capital of Ciskei.
1993:	Multi-party negotiations resumed. SACP general secretary, Chris Hani, assassinated. Oliver Tambo dies. Launch of *Afrikaner Volksfront* (AVF).
1994:	Shell House massacre; thirty-eight Inkatha supporters killed after a march on the ANC's headquarters in Johannesburg. Formation of *Vryheidsfront* (VF). First non-racial national elections. ANC-led Government of National Unity formed.

Glossary

aksie fronte	action fronts
arbeiderstand	working 'class'
arbeidslaer	labour circle
armblankevraagstuk	poor white question
baasskap	mastership, supremacy
Boeredogters	Boer daughters
boerestand	farming 'class'
Boerevolk	Afrikaners
broedertwis	arguments between brothers
dogters	young women
Eeufees	Centenary (of the Great Trek)
eie	the own
gelykstelling	equalization
grensliteratuur	border literature
hereniging	reunion
Kappiekommandos	'Bonnet' commandos
kultuurstrewe	cultural striving
leenfronte	'borrowing' fronts
meisies	young Afrikaner women
nasie	nation
ontworteld	uprooted
Ossewagees	Oxwagon spirit
Ossewatrek	Oxwagon Trek
platteland	countryside, rural areas
rasvermenging	racial mixing, miscegenation
samesmelting	fusion
smelters	fusionists
soewereiniteit in eie kring	sovereignty in own/each sphere
stadsbegrip	conception of the city
studielaer	study circle

verbastering	bastardization
verlig	enlightened
verkramp	narrow-minded, bigoted
vervlegdheid	intertwinedness
volk	organic, ethnic unity of the 'people' or 'nation'
volkekunde	anthropology
volksaard	character of the *volk*
volksbeweging	movement of the *volk*
volkseenheid	unity of the *volk*
volkseie	that which is the 'own' of the *volk*
volksgedagte	idea of the *volk*
volksgemeenskap	*volk*'s community
Volkskongres	Congress of the *volk*
volksleier	leader of the *volk*
volkslewe	life of the *volk*
volksnasionalisme	nationalism of the *volk*
volkstrewe	striving of the *volk*
volksverband	bonds of the *volk*
volksverskeuring	diremption of the *volk*
volksvreemde	that which is foreign to the *volk*
Voortrekker	pioneer
welstand/welsyn	welfare

Index

www.ingramcontent.com/pod-product-compliance
Lightning Source LLC
Chambersburg PA
CBHW030856270326
41929CB00008B/448
* 9 7 8 1 8 5 9 8 4 1 2 5 9 *